Cyberpsychology

Cyberpsychology

Edited by

Alison Attrill

UNIVERSITY PRESS

Great Clarendon Street, Oxford OX2 6DP
United Kingdom

Oxford University Press is a department of the University of Oxford.
It furthers the University's objective of excellence in research, scholarship,
and education by publishing worldwide. Oxford is a registered trade mark of
Oxford University Press in the UK and in certain other countries

Impression: 6

Published in the United States of America by Oxford University Press
198 Madison Avenue, New York, NY 10016, United States of America

British Library Cataloguing in Publication Data
Data available

Library of Congress Control Number: 2014950241

ISBN 978-0-19-871258-9

Printed in Great Britain by
Ashford Colour Press Ltd, Gosport, Hampshire

Dedicated to Paul Smith, thank you!

Alison Attrill

Contents

Chapter 15:   Cognitive Factors in Online Behaviour   249

Lee Hadlington, De Montfort University, England

Introduction

ALISON ATTRILL

1.1 Introduction

Welcome to this text on *Cyberpsychology*, which emerged from a number of conversations on the need for a book that would be accessible for students on the rapidly emerging modules and courses on the topic. This is a very exciting time for psychology—rarely in our lifetimes will we see the emergence of a new sub-discipline within psychology that grows as quickly and has as much impact as this area has over the last twenty or so years. The only other sub-discipline I can personally think of to have had such an impact is Sport Psychology. Unlike that area, however, **cyberpsychology** affects nearly all of us in one way or another. We are living in an ever increasingly connected world. Technology is all around us. Where once we used just telephones and the written word to communicate offline, nowadays our communication choices are endless. We can stay in touch with family, friends, lovers, and people we have never met offline through an array of online media. We can make and break friendships and romances online, via the Internet, mobile phones, tablets, games consoles, and recently even via glasses (Google Glass) and watches. We use many different applications to do so.

There is a big commercial industry involved in us all staying in touch globally, an industry that requires trust and awareness about privacy, an industry that can bring crime directly into our homes via fraud and online scams, not to mention identity theft and other acts of criminality that attack both individuals (e.g., stalking and harassment) and groups (e.g., hate speech, the spread and perpetuation of xenophobia, or political influence). Otherwise law-abiding people who download material without paying are not always aware that they are committing a criminal act. That is not to say that there are no positive advantages of Internet use. There are many. We can now manage our finances and shop from the comfort of our own homes. We can organize holidays, excursions, and social gatherings. People who once thought that the end of a twenty-year marriage meant that they would be on their own for the rest of their life can now find a new life partner online. We can link up with like-minded others, no matter how obscure our interests. People who, for whatever reason, feel that they have little social capital offline can create and maintain a social existence online. Alone, these few examples of online interaction raise more questions than can be answered in a single textbook. We have therefore hand-picked some of the topics that appear to be receiving a lot of research and study interest in this area. Prior to outlining these, however, we first need to define the sub-discipline that has become known as cyberpsychology.

1.2 What is cyberpsychology and why study the topic?

Often, if you ask a psychologist what they believe cyberpsychology to be, they will give you a definition that is more in line with **human computer interaction** studies. Whilst the two topics might be very similar, there is a difference between the two. Whereas the latter considers the actual interaction between humans and technology, cyberpsychology considers the psychological processes, motivations, intentions, behavioural outcomes, and effects on both our online and offline worlds, associated with any form of technology. This ranges from Internet use to mobile phone and gaming console use, from how we use word processors and statistics packages to how we engage in online banking. That is, it focuses on the study of mind and behaviour in relation to how we use and communicate via technological devices. Throughout this text, it is hoped that you will come to see these devices as tools that either facilitate or hinder human communication and interaction. Focus is given mainly to how and why humans use the Internet as individuals and groups. It is important to note that the work in this text relates to use of the world wide interconnected web, the **Internet**, unless otherwise stated. This differs from an **internet**, which is a localized and often restricted network accessed by a set number of people.

Given the emergence of this area over the last 25 years or so, and the rapidly developing applications and uses of the technology, it is useful to bear in mind whilst reading that cyberpsychology is an ever-evolving and developing area that is trying to constantly catch up. We have been trying to explain how and why relationships are formed offline, for instance, for centuries. It should not be taken for granted that any offline theories and explanations formed over that time can simply be applied to understanding the same or similar behaviours online. Coming up with new relevant theories and explanations is time-consuming. Research might often be referred to that is somewhat older. Sometimes this research is included because it is the most appropriate for a given discussion, but other times it may be included because there is no more recent research that better addresses a discussion. In addition to this, research takes time. It takes time to carry out and have published. This is a particular difficulty in the area of cyberpsychology, where the technology is constantly changing and evolving. Readers over the age of 30 can probably remember a time without the Internet. Those under the age of 30 might, however, have 'grown up digitally', knowing nothing other than the Internet as a tool involved in most daily and/or routine activities. But what does it mean to have 'grown up digitally'? Does this mean that younger people are differently wired? Wired in a way that makes them more able to use the Internet more competently than their grandparents, or even their parents? These are some of the questions tackled in this book.

One of the overriding themes to emerge from pulling these chapters together is that of the Internet as a communication and interaction tool. Tool use for communication is not new to humankind. Before the Internet we had telephones. We even had a very rudimentary form of text messaging, albeit far more clumsy, time consuming, and expensive, in the form of the telegraph. Indeed, for those who wish to know more about the bygone era of telegraph communications, Standage (2014) offers a great overview in his text entitled *The Victorian Internet: The Remarkable Story of the Telegraph and the Nineteenth Century's On-Line Pioneers*. In this book he demonstrates how modern social activities that are carried out on the Internet were once carried out on these more rudimentary technological devices. The tools used for communication may have changed throughout the decades, but Standage hones in on the notion that humans will use and adapt any tool they can to fit their communications needs, desires, wants, and purposes, just as we are now doing with the Internet.

The ways in which we interact on the Internet are also constantly changing. Where once we may have used very basic asynchronous chat rooms, messenger applications, and early social networking sites like MySpace, we now have the advantages (or disadvantages?) of synchronous tools such as videoconferencing via Skype that enable us instant access to people the world over. These technological advances change the use of the Internet. It is no longer just about social and personality processes online. E-commerce, business, and government activities such as policing and counter-terrorism are increasingly more prevalent online. Developing tools that might prevent cognitive decay in old age, interactive tools to enhance children's education, or help prevent young people being vulnerable to predators—the list of evolving Internet applications is endless. All of these activities can benefit from some form of psychological input, as do their resulting interpretations, behaviours, and responses. These processes reach beyond the early interests of cyberpsychology on the social and personality aspects of online behaviour. That said, social networking sites, especially Facebook, and associated social processes relating to the self will feature heavily throughout this book. This is in part due to the early focus of cyberpsychology research on the impact of the Internet on the self and one's social existence. It is also partly to make the work more tangible and relevant to students' everyday online behaviours and interactions.

What has become apparent over the last decade, with an ever evolving Internet, is that online behaviour is simply not the same as offline behaviour. Motivations, needs, desires, wants, and abilities might drive online behaviour in a completely different way to which they drive offline behaviour. There are factors that initially appear absent in the online world. Take for example social cues; at first the way in which people talk, their vocal intonations, eye movements, and body language appear completely absent online. However, being the adaptors that they are, humans very quickly produced emoticons (or smileys) to convey these limited social cues. With evolved technology and applications like Snapchat and Skype, the social cues once believed to be absent are now becoming ever more present in online communications. Online interactions also offer some advantages over offline interactions. Factors that might facilitate human interactions, such as the time to think about the content of a correspondence, are more advantageous to online than offline behaviour. Although, an immediate negative of these considered communications in the absence of social cues could be a misunderstanding of an intended message. The reader is urged to consider their own online behaviours, activities, and interactions whilst reading this book. Think about how these differ to offline interactions, and whether behaviours are more or less cue-dependent online than offline. It is also worth considering the motivations and intentions that underlie offline and online behaviours and interactions. Are some more or less inhibited than others, and what role does anonymity play in those behaviours? Where once the Internet was awash with applications that people believed made them anonymous and completely unidentifiable, we now live in a world of the 'selfie', the self-broadcasting and often self-promotion of oneself via self-taken photos. Many will now understand the role of the IP address in being less anonymous to the Internet world than was previously assumed. We are no longer purely anonymous, but we now have a right to be forgotten on the Internet (see e.g., www .theguardian.com/commentisfree/2014/jul/02/eu-right-to-be-forgotten-guardian-google).

How does this drive online behaviour differently to interactions within an offline social network? What are the offline effects of this over-sharing of one's personal life online? Some of these questions will be addressed throughout this book. To conclude the definition of the subject area, it is important to briefly note that cyberpsychology considers psychological processing and behaviour beyond the Internet. Amongst other aspects of computer technology, it considers the psychological processes of artificial intelligence, cyberbots, and virtual reality. It attempts to do so by forming theoretical standpoints with testable hypotheses.

In 1949 the book *Nineteen Eighty-Four* by George Orwell was published, in which technology monitored a Great Britain that had become Airstrip One. Big Brother was not a TV programme that capitalized on human desires for fame and notoriety, but a party leader who oppressively ruled Airstrip One. Andy Warhol once famously said that 'in the future, everyone will be world-famous for 15 minutes.' The worldwide mass media and Internet culture makes both of these notions our every-day reality. The way in which videos 'go viral' via YouTube, or calls to raise funds for a given charity soon progress from the Internet to the national and international news, one wonders what other figments of scientific imagination from years past might evolve into reality. Are we all contributing to this reality through our Internet use? Are we creating a society, or a world even, in which we garner expectations of approval and adulation via the Internet? Think of your own use of social networking sites: If you post a status update, how do you feel if no one 'likes' it, or if it does not receive any comments? Looking at Internet use on a more societal level, what role does the Internet play in creating super-powers, facilitating uprisings such as the Egyptian Revolution of 2011, or the riots that swept through Great Britain, and London in particular, in 2011? The topic of cyberpsychology tries to tackle all of these questions and more, often by making use of interdisciplinary approaches that stretch beyond the involvement of different academic disciplines (e.g., sociology, physiology, biology, engineering, technology, cybersecurity, and mathematics) to working with industry providers and government bodies. This text book will focus largely on the academic applications of the theories and findings that arise from these integrative approaches to understanding online behaviour.

1.3 This book

This book brings together a number of leading and emerging authorities on the topic of cyberpsychology. We are very lucky to have been able to pull together chapters that span a number of Internet uses from diverse perspectives.

The first section of this book considers human relationships online. In order to do this, the first few chapters consider how people represent themselves online and the role that individual characteristics play in those representations. The text then moves on to considering whether a digital generation exists, a generation that is both characterized and characterizes Internet behaviour. At this point, the consideration of the Internet as a tool for goal-directed, needs, and motivation-related behaviours is given thorough examination prior to the interactions and behaviours of groups online being considered. One of the areas of research that has over the past two decades received a considerable amount of academic attention is that of online romantic relationships. Chapter 4 therefore explores the notion of people meeting their need for human **belongingness** in a goal-directed manner by using different types of online relationships: platonic, romantic and **familial relationships**. This chapter hopefully helps drive research attention beyond a focus on romantic relationships. This **self-presentation**, *personality*, and *human relationship* part of the book (Part I) subsequently considers individual and group behaviours in a chapter that focuses on human interactions in social media and networking behaviours. Moving forward with the theme of individuals representing themselves online, Chapter 7 explores how people use gaming and virtual reality worlds to interact with others online by focusing on the self in otherworldly lives.

The second section of this book focuses more on the *psychological processes* and *consequences* associated with positive and negative aspects of online behaviour. The first chapter of this section gives a brief overview of online criminal activities and deviance online. This is a particularly important consideration given that the mass media would have us believe that the Internet is corrupting people, taking them away from offline activities and causing a whole range of psychological, social, and financial problems. A chapter is therefore subsequently dedicated to focusing on a frequently reported negative behaviour by the mass media: cyberbullying and associated derogatory behaviours. Unfortunately, these are the negative activities that are increasingly becoming the focus of reports, to the detriment of positive applications and uses of the Internet. In light of this, what follows is a chapter that focuses on how people use the Internet in a positive manner, with a focus on health psychology online. That said, this chapter also touches upon the darker side of the web, to consider negative health-related behaviours such as pro-bulimia websites. Becoming members of online groups that promote any sort of behaviour, whether those are negatively or positively related to our offline activities, can have compulsive actions attached to them. The actions are sometimes considered to be addictions to online behaviours. We therefore subsequently turn our attention to the psychology of online addictive behaviours. Ironically, one of the places that individuals might seek support for these Internet-related behaviours could be online. People seek online support for a number of reasons, from bereavement to marital guidance, from information about running to a support group for a certain illness or disablement. Focus is therefore given in a chapter to support-seeking behaviour in times of illness. Another area of support and health related online behaviour is that of therapies and counselling. Chapter 13 offers an excellent overview of this emerging area of online activity.

Whilst reading this overview, you might question the privacy and trust concerns associated with all of these online behaviours. Of course, they carry a number of risks through the amount of information shared online as well as other factors. In light of this, the issue of sharing self-information online (self-disclosure) re-emerges throughout the text. The book also concludes with a look at the privacy and security risks associated with using the Internet to consider these factors in more detail. Consideration is also given to the cognitive processes that are associated with online behaviour and interaction. This is a rapidly expanding area of research that is receiving a lot of attention, especially since research around perception, interpretation, and memory in cyberspace is of applied interest. It also signifies a move away from focusing on Internet behaviour using social, personality, and developmental theories, to provide a more integrated overview of online behaviour. It was therefore considered appropriate to close the text with this chapter.

This whistle-stop overview of the chapters has hopefully whetted your appetite for reading this book, by the end of which you will hopefully have an insight into some of the main areas of work in cyberpsychology. Each chapter includes references for further reading that will help intensify knowledge around any particular topic. There are also a number of good resources online that provide reading lists around the topics covered in this book (see e.g., http://construct.haifa.ac.il/~azy/azy.htm). Discussion questions are provided at the end of each chapter for readers to test their understanding of the material presented.

Finally, if you would like to find out more about the contributing authors, most of them have their own web presence, with associated publications, usually via the university at which they are currently employed.

 ## References

Orwell, G. (1969/2013). *Nineteen Eighty-Four*. Penguin Classics.

Standage, T. (2014). *The Victorian Internet: The Remarkable Story of the Telegraph and the Nineteenth Century's On-Line Pioneers*. New York: Bloomsbury Publishing.

Warhol, A. (1968/2005). Cited from Guinn, J. & Perry, D. (2005). *The Sixteenth Minute: Life in the Aftermath of Fame*. New York: Jeremy F. Tarcher/ Penguin.

Part 1

Self-presentation, Personality, and Human Relationships Online

2 The Role of Personality in Online Self-presentation

CHRIS FULLWOOD

Learning objectives

After reading this chapter, it is anticipated that learners will be able to:

- Give an account of the different sorts of benefits that are associated with managing others' impressions of us.
- Identify a number of different types of impression management tactics that can be used to get others to behave in desired ways.
- Clarify why impression motivation and impression construction should be seen as two discrete processes.
- Explain why it is important to consider impression management in the online world.
- Describe at least five unique features that affect how we communicate and present ourselves online differently to face-to-face.
- Elucidate on the different ways in which our personalities may affect how we present ourselves to others in cyberspace.
- Explain how the context in which we present ourselves online will have an important influence on the manner in which we manage impressions.

2.1 Introduction

'You never get a second chance to make a first impression'.

Imagine that you're getting ready for a first date. Let us assume that you have high hopes for this date and that you are extremely motivated to impress the object of your desires. How much thought would you put into choosing what to wear? Would you try on a variety of different outfits before making your final decision or simply choose the first garment that comes to hand? Would you find choosing the 'right' outfit a straightforward task or a difficult one that requires immense deliberation (and perhaps a little advice from your friends)? You probably wouldn't be surprised to hear that not everybody would respond to these questions in the same way. Although most of us can appreciate that there are genuine repercussions associated with making a good impression (e.g. whether your date would want to see you again), people vary in how much they believe that aspects of their presentation of self will influence what other people think of them. There are, therefore, **individual differences** in the importance that people place on **self-presentation** and consequently the extent to which they attempt to manage and monitor the impressions that others form of them. Most of us understand that the communication context will also have a major influence on the extent and manner of **impression management** tactics used. The way we might present ourselves in one situation may not necessarily be appropriate or arresting in another one. Indeed, there are social norms that govern appropriate conduct in various formal and informal contexts. You would probably receive a few disapproving looks for example if you turned up to a wedding reception wearing a tracksuit. Similarly, your friends would also find it a little peculiar if you decided to wear a morning suit on a night out down the pub! Finally, we are not just limited to our choice of attire when it comes to making a favourable impression. We can make an impression on others with aspects of our appearance (e.g., a flattering hairstyle), non-verbal communication (e.g., a firm handshake or maintaining good eye contact), through the things that we say (e.g., with our knowledge or sense of humour), or even how we say them (e.g., paralinguistic features of speech like tone or intonation).

With the proliferation of the Internet, we are witnessing a dramatic transformation in the communication landscape. The Internet is ubiquitous and is playing an ever more prevalent role in our day-to-day lives. It provides us with increased opportunities for social interaction, for example we can support and sustain existing friendships or extend our social networks by making new contacts. We know that online dating is now the third most common way for heterosexual couples to meet in America for example (Rosenfeld, 2010) and that social networking sites like Facebook are attracting huge numbers of members (over one billion of them according to recent estimates) (Facebook Newsroom, 2013). While it would be difficult to deny the global impact that the Internet has had on the way in which we meet, communicate and relate to one another, it is also evident that the ways in which we present ourselves via the Internet can be very different to how we present ourselves face-to-face. For example, many theorists argue that we have a greater degree of flexibility in online self-presentation, because of the increased potential for **anonymity** (i.e., conditions in which our personal identity is unknown to others) and because we can more carefully edit and control aspects of our presentation of self. On Facebook, for example, we can choose to upload specific photos (e.g., 'selfies') to display us in the best possible light (although clearly they don't always have the desired impact!). In constructing an online dating profile, we can choose to promote our more positive attributes whilst underplaying or omitting our more undesirable ones. Individuals can therefore strategically edit elements of their online profiles to influence what other people think of them (Rosenberg & Egbert, 2011). Although we may also adopt similar strategies offline, we undoubtedly have much more freedom in how we manage impressions online. Indeed, we could pretend to be someone completely different if we wished to.

In this chapter we will evaluate the extent to which our personalities influence the different types of self-presentation tactics that we use online. Synthesizing this literature will be of specific interest to students and academics who want to better understand how advancements in Information and Communications Technology are shaping social dynamics. Although there are a number of different approaches to understanding personality, particular attention will be given to **trait theories** of personality. The chapter will begin with a consideration of the reasons why, and different ways in which, we manage impressions in more traditional communication contexts. It will then move on to discuss the importance of studying impression management in online environments, through deliberating how online interaction is distinct from face-to-face communication. We will then move on to examine specific personality traits and how they affect self-presentation strategies in cyberspace. Finally, we will consider how context is an important factor in shaping self-presentation strategies online and conclude by making a number of suggestions for further research in the area.

2.2 Characteristics of impression management

All the world's a stage and all the men and women merely players.

William Shakespeare, *As You Like It*, Act II, Scene VII

Before we consider the manner in which people manage impressions online, it is first important to understand the background and literature on self-presentation in a face-to-face context. In everyday life, we commonly encounter situations in which we desire to influence how others perceive us. In some cases these situations are formal and follow fairly standard conventions, for example, a job interview. In others, they are more informal and loosely structured, for example, a first date. In both cases there are real consequences associated with the type of impression that others form of us. We all know that leaving someone with a good impression can help us get on in life and have a wide variety of implications, leading to positive social, personal, occupational, and material outcomes (Leary & Allen, 2011). For instance, a successful job interview may lead to a better salary and increased job satisfaction from attaining a more desirable role. Because self-presentation leads to positive outcomes, we normally expend a great deal of reflection and time into evaluating how others perceive us. As a consequence we often try to behave in a fashion that will lead to others treating us in desired ways (Leary & Allen, 2011). We also know that there are individual differences in the value that we place on self-presentation. Some of us stick firmly to the mantra 'what you see is what you get', whereas on the other side of the spectrum there are others for whom the decisions they make about self-presentation may be a constant struggle and a source of anguish. Moreover, people who place value on how others view them will be more highly motivated to manage and monitor impressions in a larger number of situations (Leary & Allen, 2011).

The terms 'impression management' and 'self-presentation' are often used interchangeably by academics (Leary & Kowalski, 1990, Rosenberg & Egbert, 2011) and therefore, in this chapter I will do the same. Simply put, they refer to the different ways in which people convey to others during direct interactions information about, and images of, the self (Arkin, 1981, Baumeister, 1998). Impression management can be defined as 'the process of controlling the impressions that other people form' (Chester & Bretherton, 2007, p. 223) and should be seen as distinct from **impression formation**, which relates to how others actually perceive us. We can manage others' impressions about a variety of different things, for example objects, ideas, and even other people. However, the term impression management is normally used to describe the manner in which we influence the impressions of others about *ourselves* and this is why it is often synonymous with self-presentation. Even if we are not directly concerned with making a good impression, only under exceptional circumstances do we deliberately behave in a fashion that is likely to lead to unfavourable impressions (Leary, 1995). Impression management concerns therefore play a pivotal role in shaping our daily behaviour (Chester & Bretherton, 2007). Indeed, one has to simply consider how much money is spent on cosmetics, diet products, and fitness merchandise as a case in point. Most of these industries would surely suffer if we had no desire to make ourselves appear more attractive to others.

One of the first scholars to discuss impression management was Erving Goffman and therefore it would be remiss not to consider his seminal work *The Presentation of Self in Everyday Life* at this stage. Goffman (1959) drew a parallel between the impression management process and the theatre to illustrate the ways in which people manage how others perceive them. In his dramaturgical analogy self-presentation is viewed as a strategy to 'convey an impression to others which it is in his interests to convey' (p. 4). Goffman's (1959) theory helps us to understand how the manner in which we view ourselves within the social context influences our 'performance' and ultimately the ways in which other individuals may respond to us. One of the primary aims of social 'actors' is to impart positive impressions and therefore individuals tend to accentuate (e.g., positive attributes) and suppress (e.g., negative attributes) specific elements of the self. Moreover, individuals adjust their performance to the specific environment they are in and audience with whom they are communicating. In the presence of others, we will emphasize aspects of the self that align with the ideals and norms of the group we belong to or desire to belong to (Siibak, 2009). In many instances, individuals present an 'idealized' image of the self as 'a performer engenders in his audience the belief that he is related to them in a more ideal way than is always the case' (Goffman, 1959, p. 56). In an attempt to uphold favourable impressions, individuals may hide or play down specific aspects of the self that are contrary to the image of the idealized self (Wang & Stefanone, 2013).

All conscious attempts to manage how others perceive us necessitate a level of self-awareness and the ability to see ourselves through the minds and eyes of other individuals (Leary & Allen, 2011). There is therefore an important distinction here between **public self-consciousness** (i.e., the degree to which we consider how the observable aspects of the self are reacted to by other people), and **private self-consciousness** (i.e., the extent to which we may consider the inner, subjective aspects of who we are, which are not directly observable by others) (Leary & Allen, 2011). Drawing this distinction also gives rise to the notion that a conflict may exist between how we want others to perceive us and the limitations that are placed upon our ability to express ourselves. Indeed, Higgins' (1987) self-discrepancy theory suggests that we all have three types of self-domains: (1) the **actual self**—refers to our basic **self-concept**, in other words the attributes and abilities (e.g., intelligence, social competence, attractiveness, etc.) that we (and others) believe that we actually possess; (2) the **ideal self**—refers to the attributes and abilities that we would like to possess or that others would like us to have (e.g., our hopes, dreams, wishes, and aspirations); (3) the **ought self**—refers the attributes and abilities that we feel (or others feel) that we ought to possess (e.g., obligations, duties, responsibilities). A conflict may exist within us if there is a sizeable gulf between two of these self-representations. For example, if our sense of duty prevents us from having the freedom to be the type of person that we really want to be, then this is likely to lead to some degree of emotional turmoil.

According to Leary and Kowalski (1990) impression management entails two distinct processes; **impression motivation** and **impression construction**. They argue that it is important to consider these as two discrete processes, because although some individuals may be highly motivated to garner positive impressions, this does not always translate into 'overt impression-relevant actions' (p. 35). Impression motivation is concerned with one's desire to create specific impressions on other people and this is context specific. For example, the situation that one finds oneself in, as well as one's disposition to compare oneself to others will interact to predict the level of impression motivation that someone will have. For example, we would be much more likely to be concerned about what others think of us when taking part in a public presentation (a situation that fills most people with apprehension, even experienced lecturers!). Moreover, this concern would surely be amplified if we were being graded or assessed on this presentation or if we felt that our public speaking skills were somewhat lacking. Classic studies on deindividuation (e.g. Zimbardo's Stanford Prison Experiment) also demonstrate how we can lose self-awareness in groups and therefore are less likely to evaluate how our behaviour might be viewed by others. Impression construction relates to the behaviours that people may adopt in order to acquire particular impressions. It is concerned with the type of impression that the person wishes to convey (e.g., intelligent, self-assured, charismatic) as well the manner in which they might go about conveying it (e.g., through the way they dress or the things that they say). In this sense, Leary and Kowalski's (1990) model accounts for the reasons why people might be concerned about what other people think of them, but also why certain individuals might opt for one type of impression management tactic over another.

It seems fairly obvious to suggest that there are a myriad of different possibilities when it comes to influencing how other people perceive us. In other words, we may employ a variety of different types of self-presentation tactics to garner desired impressions. Moreover, as implied by Leary and Kowalski's (1990) two component model of impression management, we would expect there to be individual differences not only in impression motivation but also impression construction. A variety of different personality characteristics may relate to impression management concerns, particularly those that entail a preoccupation with the different ways in which we relate to other people. For example, Leary and Allen (2011) suggest that agreeable individuals would be particularly concerned with self-presentation. Those who are agreeable have a tendency towards compassion and cooperation, and are therefore accommodating of others. Because of these tendencies, one might therefore expect them to attempt to foster favourable impressions in others, for example they may want to be perceived as kind, pleasant, or friendly.

Although research linking personality with self-presentation tactics is somewhat limited, a few studies suggest that our personalities may influence how we present ourselves to others. For example, Lee, Quigley, Nesler, Corbett, and Tedeschi (1999) studied a variety of self-presentation tactics, including **defensive self-presentation** and **assertive self-presentation** tactics. Assertive tactics are characterized by the user's inclination to be proactive in how they yield desired impressions from others. Examples include: ingratiation (i.e., getting others to like you so you can gain an advantage), intimidation (i.e., inducing fear in others to get them to do what you want them to do), and supplication (i.e., making yourself appear weak so others will help you). Defensive tactics are characterized by the user's inclination to repair or restore a damaged impression. Examples include: excuses (i.e., denying responsibility for negative events that have occurred), apologies (i.e., an expression of guilt with an acceptance of responsibility for negative events), and justifications (i.e., offering overriding explanations but accepting responsibility for negative events). Clearly, self-presentation shouldn't always necessarily be viewed as positive. We can get people to treat us in a desired way but at the same time receive an unfavourable judgement. Although someone is unlikely to warm to us if we try to intimidate them for instance, we may still achieve our goal of getting them to behave in a desired way. A key finding from Lee et al.'s (1999) research was that specific personality traits correlated with one's intention to engage in self-presentation tactics. For example, socially anxious individuals and those with an external locus of control (i.e., the belief that external factors outside of our control are influential in shaping our lives) were more likely to engage in defensive self-presentation tactics. A further study by Sadler, Hunger, and Miller (2010) also demonstrated that individuals with high levels of negative emotionality reported using more self-presentation tactics. Taken together these findings suggest that anxious, less socially-skilled individuals may have more concern for how they are perceived by others and are therefore more wary of self-presentational failure. This could be one reason why they take proactive steps to develop a positive impression (e.g., via assertive tactics) or steps to repair their 'spoiled' identity (i.e., via defensive tactics). What these studies also show is that individual differences in personality are likely to predispose us differently towards self-presentation motivation and construction.

2.3 Why study impression management online? What's different about the Internet?

For those individuals who have never known a world without the Internet, it would be exceptionally difficult for them to conceive how they could ever live without it. For most of us the Internet makes many aspects of daily life simpler, safer, more convenient, and fun. Imagine life as a university student if the Internet ceased to exist. As a student there a variety of different tasks that can be accomplished far more easily with Internet access. You can send questions to your lecturers from a distance via email, search online databases for immediate access to research papers, and download copies of lecture slides and other educational materials from Virtual Learning Environments like Moodle. The Internet also makes education a far more realistic proposition for individuals with families and full-time jobs as they can structure their studies around their busy schedules. As well as providing a host of benefits for students, we are also all too aware of the many educational drawbacks that come with Internet access. For example, in his recent book *The Shallows: How the Internet is Changing the Way We Read, Think and Remember*, Nicholas Carr (2010) argues for the notion that the Internet is 're-wiring' our brains and promoting learning and understanding on a very superficial level. The Internet may encourage students to gather materials from unsuitable sources (e.g., web pages as opposed to peer-reviewed journal articles) and the ease with which information can be copied and pasted may lead to increased instances of plagiarism.

As with the example cited here, people often hold conflicting views on the Internet; on the one hand seeing the value that it has to offer them, but on the other acknowledging the many dangers and pitfalls of cyberspace. The way in which we connect with other individuals is another prime example of this bifurcation in attitudes. The Internet is regularly berated in the press for the ease with which bullies can gain access to and torment their victims. However, at the other end of the scale we are also aware of the many benefits bestowed by online support groups for those who live with stigmatized conditions (Fullwood & Wootton, 2009). Although many of the problems that occur online are certainly not unique to cyberspace (e.g., bullying happens in more 'traditional' contexts also), there are undoubtedly many idiosyncratic features that distinguish the online world from the offline world. Although the online world shouldn't necessarily be viewed as a homogenous entity (i.e., there is huge diversity and richness in cyberspace), McKenna, Green, and Gleeson (2002) suggest at least four factors that set many online spaces apart from the offline world: (1) a greater propensity for anonymous interaction, (2) a reduction in the importance of physical appearance, (3) a larger degree of control over time and pace of interactions, and (4) the ease with which we can find others who are similar to ourselves. However, one could also argue for an additional factor: (5) the potential to have complete control over the content that is generated. All of these features produce an environment in which we are given more freedom and flexibility in how we present ourselves to others. Moreover, these distinctive features make the study of impression management in the online world particularly important, and imply that what we know about how self-presentation operates in the offline world, may not always automatically apply to cyberspace.

2.3.1 **Anonymity**

In cyberspace, anonymity is best described as existing on a continuum. At one end of the scale, one can be completely identifiable. A good example of this would be one's profile on a social networking site like Facebook. As online social networking sites (OSNs) are used in an anchored way (i.e., they are tied to peoples' offline networks) (Zhao, Grasmuck, & Martin, 2008), profile owners tend to be highly identifiable with the inclusion of their real name and photographs of themselves. At the other end of the scale, there is the potential to be completely undetectable online. Although there may be an expectation that people reveal themselves on Facebook, this isn't necessarily true of all online spaces. For instance, one can lurk on a discussion board without anyone (except perhaps the site administrators) even knowing that you are there (Chester & Bretherton, 2007). On blog sites and chat rooms it is also more common not to reveal one's identity and interactions take place more regularly with complete strangers (Fullwood, Thelwall, & O'Neill, 2011, 2013). Even when identifying information is revealed, users are still afforded some degree of protection, because interactions will often take place with individuals who are geographically dispersed, so the chances of actually meeting them offline are quite slim (Fullwood, Melrose, Morris, & Floyd, 2013). So, although it may be context specific, there is at least some potential for individuals to hide aspects of their identity from others. A consequence of anonymity is that it may generate conditions in which people feel more comfortable disclosing certain aspects of the self, partly because the ramifications for one's real life are reduced (McKenna & Bargh, 2000, Valkenburg, Schouten, & Peter, 2005). Indeed, Suler (2004) described the 'online disinhibition' effect in more detail and considered 'dissociative anonymity' to be a key factor in predicting disinhibited conduct online (including 'benign disinhibition' or the tendency to self-disclose more personal information). Because many people often view the online world as being a distinct space from the offline world, it is easy for them to detach themselves from their online activity. The way we might behave on the Internet does not necessarily need to be consistent with how we conduct ourselves offline. Anonymity therefore gives us much more freedom in how we present ourselves to others—we don't have to adhere to the persona that everyone associates with us in the offline world.

2.3.2 **Reduced emphasis on physical appearance**

Because we cannot always see and hear the people we interact with (i.e., many forms of online communication are primarily text-based), individuals can mask or alter certain aspects of their physical appearance (McKenna et al., 2002). Attractive people have an advantage in the offline world because they are normally judged more favourably on other social attributes (e.g., they are seen as more likeable and intelligent) (Cialdini, 1984, Amichai-Hamburger, 2007). The Internet may therefore be considered a level playing field for those who are less physically attractive. For example, on an online dating site we can make claims about being taller, thinner, and so on. However, one would imagine that there is only so far one can go when making these claims, particularly if we don't want to get caught out at a first meeting. Indeed, Ellison, Heino, and Gibbs (2006) suggest that online daters have to walk a thin line between presenting an accurate presentation (i.e., in case they do actually meet up) and a desirable one (i.e., so they can attract potential mates). Although online daters may not blatantly lie about who they are, they may stretch the truth a little so they are perceived as more attractive. For example, they may suggest that they like to engage in various socially desirable activities (e.g., ones that demonstrate athleticism, such as hiking, surfing, and skiing) even if they rarely participate in them (Ellison et al., 2006). We may also make use of photo-editing software or take photos from strategic angles to show us in the most attractive light possible. In addition, because many online spaces do not require users to reveal themselves, those of us who feel constrained by our physical appearance will be able to interact with others with less concern about being judged on our looks (Amichai-Hamburger, 2007).

2.3.3 Increased control over time and pace of interactions

Communication online can be both synchronous and asynchronous. Synchronous communication takes place in real time and therefore responses are received with minimal delay. Asynchronous communication takes place outside of real time, and therefore there will be a delay between sending a message and receiving a reply. With email for example, although it is possible to receive a response within minutes, it could also potentially take hours, days, even weeks before we receive a reply. With synchronous modes of communication (e.g., chat rooms), although we may expect to receive a reply relatively quickly, because we do not have access to the message while it is being produced (i.e., we only receive it in full when the sender hits 'send') there is still going to be some form of time lag. In this sense, perhaps the only truly synchronous mode of communication online is one that provides Voice over Internet Protocol methodology (e.g., Skype). Because the majority of communications online are asynchronous (or only partially synchronous) in nature, this means that we have more time to think about what we say. For example, when sending an email, we can read it through again carefully and edit the message before sending it off. This, among other facets, has the potential to lead to an optimal presentation of the self, linking to Walther's 'hyperpersonal' theory of communication (Walther, 1996, Walther & Parks, 2002). Although early perspectives on technology-mediated communication tended to emphasize the notion that individuals would find it harder to connect with and relate to others due to a reduction in social and relational cues (e.g., social presence theory; Short, Williams, & Christie, 1976), Walther suggests that online communication can actually *exceed* face-to-face communication. Unlike face-to-face communication, where once we have made a remark it cannot be retracted, in the online world we have the space and time to carefully consider how we want to come across in our messages. Ultimately, this may mean that others have more positive perceptions of us.

2.3.4 **Ease with which we can find similar others**

The ease with which we can connect with similar others may be particularly salient to those individuals who have very specialized interests. For example, imagine that you're a collector of *Star Wars* memorabilia. Although this is undoubtedly an extremely cool hobby and definitely would not give your friends an excuse to poke fun at you, how easy would it be to find other like-minded individuals in your local community? While I am sure it's entirely possible to devise a formula for calculating the average number of *Star Wars* memorabilia collectors per square mile, one would imagine that these types of individuals are not necessarily hugely representative in society. The web offers abundant opportunities for individuals with specialized interests to connect with others, for example, via forums or blog rings. Therefore, it should be much easier to find others who share our interests online. In some instances, this might lead to particular individuals feeling more comfortable about disclosing certain aspects of their self to others. For instance, if mainstream society viewed your interest as socially undesirable, one would expect that it would be far easier to share your passions with others who share your interests than those who do not (McKenna et al., 2002).

2.3.5 **Increased control over content generated**

Finally, with the emergence of Web 2.0, the Internet can now be viewed as a space in which all of us can actively shape content, as opposed to being passive viewers of information. Even novice computer users can set up an online profile (e.g., via an OSN or blog platform) with relative ease and limited technical expertise. One of the key features of social media is that users have a great deal of control over the content that they generate. In the offline world we are constrained by a number of factors that place limitations on how we may present ourselves to others. For example, if we are shy or socially anxious, it may be more difficult to portray ourselves as confident and self-assured. We are constrained in this case by our own personality. Society may also, however, place constraints on us. For example, social norms may preclude us from behaving in ways that we desire. In contrast to this, in the online world we have more freedom of expression, because we are not limited by the same constraints and because we have a greater degree of control over the content that we generate (Mehdizadeh, 2010, Wang & Stefanone, 2013).

2.4 **Personality and identity management online**

Personality can be defined as 'a dynamic and organized set of characteristics possessed by a person that uniquely influences his or her cognitions, motivations, and behaviours in various situations' (Ryckman, 2000, p. 5). In the online world people leave traces of their personality through the way they present themselves and the manner in which they interact with others. For example we can make **identity claims** through explicitly disclosing our hobbies and interests or via the pictures that we choose to upload. Personality may also be expressed online in a more indirect fashion through **behavioural residue**. For example, inadvertent cues such as language choice may give us hints about the type of person that someone is (Gosling, Ko, Mannarelli, & Morris, 2002). Whether others pick up on these cues consciously or unconsciously is in a sense immaterial. Ultimately, it is the impact that they have on us that is important. Because our personality has a powerful influence on how we see the world and also our motivations for engaging in particular types of behaviours (e.g., extraverts will have a preference for activities that involve other people), it would not be unreasonable to expect that individual differences will also influence our motivations for engaging in particular online activities (Fullwood, Nicholls, & Makichi, in press). A significant body of literature has already established links between online user preferences and different personality types (for a review, see Orchard & Fullwood, 2010), however, there has been far less consideration of the impact of personality on online self-presentation.

Although there are numerous approaches to understanding personality, we will focus specifically on trait theories, principally because it is possible to observe and record how various personality traits impact upon different impression management strategies online. Briefly, traits can be defined as 'dimensions of individual differences in tendencies to show consistent patterns of thoughts, feelings and actions' (McCrae & Costa, 1990, p. 23). Traits are different to *states*, which describe temporary behaviours or feelings that change over time and in different contexts (e.g., our mood). Although there is a great deal of debate in the academic literature, many theorists argue that our personalities are relatively stable over time and across various social contexts. So for example, if I am an introvert now, I'm likely to be the same in ten or twenty years' time. Moreover, I'm likely to display behaviours and characteristics associated with introversion (e.g., shyness) in most environments that I'm likely to find myself in. We will now consider a number of specific traits and how these influence the manner in which people manage impressions in various online environments.

2.4.1 **Self-esteem**

Self-esteem is a term that describes an individual's overall evaluation of their own self-worth or personal value. Self-esteem incorporates both the beliefs that we have about ourselves (e.g., 'I am a valuable member of society') as well as a variety of emotions that link to feelings of self-worth, for example, pride and shame (Hewitt, 2009). Self-esteem has a complex nexus with **social comparison**, because the manner in which we evaluate ourselves is often tied up with how we see ourselves in comparison to others around us (Festinger, 1954). Indeed, if we evaluate ourselves as being worse than others (**upward social comparison**) this can lead to negative self-regard (Tesser, Millar, & Moore, 1988), whereas if we evaluate ourselves as being better than others (**downward social comparison**), this can lead to positive self-regard (Gibbons, 1986). Self-esteem involves the appraisal of a variety of different characteristics of the individual, including social competence, appearance, and capabilities (e.g., intelligence). Many psychologists consider self-esteem to be a personality trait, because it tends to be an enduring characteristic in humans. Indeed, there are a variety of scales that measure the trait self-esteem, including the Rosenberg Self-Esteem Scale (1965), which includes 10 items that respondents have to rate their level of agreement with on a four-point scale (e.g., 'on the whole I am satisfied with myself').

One would expect self-esteem to be a particularly important trait in shaping self-presentation strategies in the online world. The online world has the potential to support both **social enhancement** (rich get richer hypothesis) and **social compensation** (poor get richer hypothesis) (Zywica & Danowski, 2008). In other words, both individuals who are already thriving offline as well as those who are in some way lacking (e.g., in terms of their social competencies) can make use of the Internet to increase **social capital** (i.e., the resources and benefits that can be derived from others). For example, those with low self-esteem may be able to improve feelings of self-worth through receiving favourable comments from others or through receiving 'likes' or positive feedback on photos and status updates. Individuals with high self-esteem may sustain or enhance positive self-regard via the same processes. There is also the potential for increased social comparison in many online spaces. For example, via social media we are increasingly exposed to both the positive aspects of peoples' lives (e.g., their accomplishments, successes, and achievements) that may lead to upward social comparison, as well as negative aspects (e.g., failures and disappointments) that may lead to downward social comparison. Indeed, Haferkamp and Kramer (2011) noted how viewing attractive photos of users led to negative body image and that males who viewed the profiles of successful men evaluated their own careers less favourably. It would appear that social comparison is rife in the online world, perhaps because sites like Facebook place social relationships under the microscope. However, less is known about how this may interact with personality, in particular how individuals evaluate social comparison information. For example, it is understood that humans have a 'need for self-esteem' and therefore if the self is threatened, we engage in activities that may raise or maintain our sense of self-worth (Schlenker, 1985, Steele, 1988). Therefore, might we expect those with lower self-esteem to adopt more defensive tactics (e.g., deleting comments or un-tagging themselves from unattractive pictures) when they are exposed to information that threatens their self-worth?

In terms of the manner in which self-esteem may affect self-presentation, there appears to be evidence for both social compensation and social enhancement. Joinson (2004) noted how low self-esteem individuals had a preference for email over face-to-face communication, specifically when there was a perceived risk in the communication context (e.g., asking for a pay raise or a date). The author suggests that this may be because email offers many benefits to self-presentation for low self-esteem individuals. For example, they have more control over the pace of the interaction and the transmission of negative social cues such as nervousness. Mehdizadeh (2010) noted that lower scorers in self-esteem spent more time on Facebook and engaged in more self-promotional activities in terms of their main photo selection. In other words, they were more selective over the photos they chose to upload and were more likely to use photo-editing software. It is suggested that this was a form of strategic self-presentation that helped those with low self-esteem to present an idealized image of the self to others. Zywica and Danowski (2008) demonstrated that low self-esteem Facebook users engaged in a variety of self-presentation strategies. For example, they were more likely to share aspects of themselves with their online friends than their offline friends, express more facets of their selves in the online world, reveal more information online, exaggerate, or fabricate information about themselves, and engage in activities specifically to make themselves appear more popular. The authors suggest that these behaviours are indicative of attempts to enhance self-image, supporting the social compensation hypothesis. Finally, Banczyk, Kramer, and Senokozlieva (2008) showed that MySpace users with high self-esteem use more words in describing themselves than users with low self-esteem. Furthermore they integrated more pictures and animations of celebrities into their profile. This perhaps suggests that people with high self-esteem engage in more elaborate and confident self-presentation tactics, supporting social enhancement.

2.4.2 The Big Five markers of personality

One of the most common trait taxonomies for measuring personality in Psychology is the five-factor model, or **Big Five** (Goldberg, 1981, 1992, McCrae & Costa, 1987, De Raad & Perugini 2002). The model proposes five mutually independent dimensions of personality: openness, conscientiousness, extraversion, agreeableness, and neuroticism (easily memorized with the acronym 'OCEAN'). Those who score highly in openness are characterized as being imaginative, insightful, intellectually curious, and with a broad range of interests. Conscientious individuals tend to be meticulous, organized, thoughtful, and good at controlling their impulses. Extraverts are sociable, energetic, talkative, assertive, and emotionally expressive. Agreeable individuals are characterized by their concern for others, and therefore tend to be compassionate, altruistic, approachable, and friendly. Highly neurotic individuals are personified by a lack of emotional stability and are therefore prone to feelings of anxiety, moodiness, and sadness. It is worth noting that on each of these five factors individuals can score anywhere on a range between two extremes. For instance, with regard to extraversion, individuals can score anywhere from extreme extraversion to extreme introversion (i.e., quiet, solitary, and reserved); however, most of us do not exhibit characteristics at the extreme polar ends of each trait.

Considering the different characteristics that are associated with each of the Big Five markers of personality, and in particular how they uniquely relate to concerns about others and the self, one would expect distinctive patterns of online impression management behaviour for each trait. The majority of studies that have investigated Big Five traits and self-presentation tactics have focused on OSNs. One problem with investigating self-presentation strategies in the context of OSNs, however, is that they tend to be heavily tied to our offline networks (Zhao et al., 2008). Individuals therefore tend to present themselves *nonymously* (i.e., they are highly identifiable). An upshot of nonymous interaction is that individuals are more likely to present accurate representations of themselves. Indeed, individuals who are familiar with us would probably find it a little unusual if we presented a version of ourselves online that was very different from our offline self. We know that the Internet has the potential to support social enhancement. For example, less socially skilled individuals can compensate for many of the factors that might constrain them in the offline world. Focusing almost exclusively on nonymous and anchored online communication environments may therefore not provide contexts in which individuals can more freely control aspects of their self-presentation.

Unsurprisingly, much of the research on personality and self-presentation via OSNs suggests that individuals generally present themselves as an accurate reflection of their offline personality types (Back et al., 2010, Gosling, Augustine, Vazire, Holtzman, & Gaddis, 2011). Indeed, as Gosling et al. (2011) argue 'rather than being an escape from reality OSNs exist as a microcosm of people's larger social worlds' (p. 486). However, some research suggests that introverts in particular can benefit in the online world by some of the features discussed earlier, perhaps even in the context of OSNs. For example, Amichai-Hamburger and Vinitzky (2010) noted how introverts tend to have more detailed Facebook profiles, even if they do not have more friends than extraverts. They argued that this may be because they are compensating for a lack of social skills in the offline world and are perhaps working harder to promote themselves online. This finding is supported by previous research that suggests that introverts are more able to find their 'real me' in the online world (i.e., they are more able to express their 'true self' online)

(Bargh, McKenna, & Fitzsimmons, 2002, Marriott & Buchanan, 2014). Introverts may be constrained in the offline world by their own personality. Because they are shy, they may find it harder to promote themselves and make friends. However, the online world is a great leveller, because their personality will not constrain them in the same way. For example, shy individuals may be concerned about how they come across to others during social interactions. However, as people are essentially 'invisible' online (i.e., in most online communication contexts others cannot see us), this concern will be nullified. Further research suggests that introverted adolescents are more likely to engage in identity experiments online, in other words they may try out different types of identities (e.g., more flirtatious, older) (Valkenburg et al., 2005). Although this may seem deceitful, these findings combined support the social enhancement hypothesis. In other words, introverts can compensate for their inability to expresses themselves in ways that they desire to in the offline world while online.

If online users are somewhat limited by anchored relationships in terms of self-presentation in OSNs, the same may not necessarily be true of other areas of cyberspace. In the blogosphere, Fullwood et al. (in press) noted that agreeable bloggers were more likely to be motivated to blog for 'selective disclosure'. In other words, they were attracted to blogging precisely because it allowed them to choose which parts of their identity they wanted to reveal. Moreover, they argue that this may be more unique to blogging than OSNs because bloggers have more freedom to communicate anonymously. Because they want to be liked by others, agreeable people therefore may be selectively disclosing information (e.g., accomplishments and achievements) to show themselves off in the best possible light, supporting social enhancement. In other words, they are strategically shaping others' impressions of them, by presenting themselves in favourable ways. Guadagno, Okdie, and Eno (2007) also note that openness is a trait particularly characteristic of bloggers. This may be because they are given freedom to express themselves via blogs. Indeed, Fullwood et al. (in press) note that open bloggers are motivated by a need for self-expression. In addition to providing an outlet for self-expression, blogs may also allow open individuals to show off about how intelligent, witty, and creative they are, therefore shaping the impressions that others form of them.

In the online dating arena, agreeableness, conscientiousness, and openness have been related to misrepresentation of the self (Hall, Park, Song, & Cody, 2010). The fact that extraverts did not misrepresent themselves may suggest that they are happy with who they are, or that they expect others to be attracted to their personality. Less conscientious individuals were more likely to misrepresent and this may be because they are less likely to worry about the future ramifications of their current behaviours. More agreeable individuals were less likely to misrepresent and this may be because agreeable people are generally very well liked and are concerned for the welfare of others, therefore it would make sense that they would not want to mislead or deceive. Finally, less open people were more likely to misrepresent and this may be a form of social compensation—in other words they may have been strategically presenting a more attractive image of themselves to potential daters, for example representing themselves as more intelligent, adventurous, or interesting (Hall et al., 2010).

2.4.3 Narcissism

The term *narcissism* takes its origins from Greek mythology and the character Narcissus, who according to legend, fell in love with his own reflection in a pool of water. Unsurprisingly then, a narcissistic personality trait is characterized by a preoccupation with the self. Narcissists display persistent patterns of grandiosity (i.e., viewing themselves as superior to others), a need for admiration, and an inflated sense of self-importance (Oltmanns, Emery, & Taylor, 2006, Foster & Campbell, 2007). Because of their need for admiration, narcissists are also prone to boasting and arrogance (Carlson, Vazire, & Oltmanns, 2011). Fundamental to the majority of theoretical models of narcissism is the notion that narcissists attempt to regulate their self-esteem via their relationships with others (Campbell, 1999, Buffardi & Campbell, 2008). However, their relationships are also characterized as being superficial and lacking in intimacy. Rather than seeking meaningful and long-lasting commitments, they use their relationships with others for self-enhancement, for example to position themselves as attractive, successful, and of high status (e.g., via a 'trophy' partner or the number of friends they have) (Campbell, 1999, Mehdizadeh, 2010).

Studying the online self-presentation strategies of narcissists should reveal some interesting patterns of behaviour. For instance, one may expect narcissists to hold very positive attitudes about social media for a number of reasons. First, social media will give them ample opportunity to publicly boast about their achievements and accomplishments. Second, as narcissists seek out superficial relationships, social media sites like Facebook and Twitter should serve them very well—for example, they would not necessarily need to engage with others on a deeper level and social status can be achieved via the number of 'friends' or 'followers' that they have accrued. Third, narcissists can fulfil their need for admiration in a number of ways, for example via the number of 'likes' they receive on posed photographs or status updates demonstrating their successes. The fact that these 'likes' are displayed publicly is also a bonus to the narcissist as it may help them to use their relationships with others for self-enhancement.

Research findings do indeed suggest that narcissists not only favour social media sites, but they also engage in very explicit self-presentation strategies whilst using them. Mehdizadeh (2010) noted that narcissistic individuals spend longer periods of time on Facebook and engage in more self-promotional activities, for instance they pose for more photos or use photo-editing software to enhance their presentation of self. Ong, Ang, Ho, Lim, Goh, Lee, and Chua (2011) noted that narcissists make more regular status updates and tend to upload more attractive profile pictures. Buffardi and Campbell (2008) found narcissists to differ on a number of objective and subjective features of self-presentation via Facebook. In terms of objective features, it was noted that narcissists had on average more friends and made more wall posts. However, narcissists did not write more about themselves in their 'about me' sections—perhaps because this section is seen as redundant by many Facebook users. In terms of subjective measures, independent coders rated narcissistic profiles as including more self-promoting information and quotes, and more attractive and sexier photographs. This does not imply that narcissists are more attractive, however—indeed research suggests that they are not (Gabriel, Critelli, & Ee, 1994), rather Buffardi and Campbell (2008) propose that they may be intentionally uploading pictures that show them in the most attractive light.

Overall then it would appear that narcissists favour the use of social media, and this could be because it allows them to strategically edit their presentation of self (e.g., for self-enhancement) and because it satisfies their need for attention. However, although they may have more control over self-presentation, this does not necessarily imply that others will always have positive perceptions of them. Indeed, Buffardi and Campbell (2008) found that although the profiles of highly narcissistic individuals were rated highly in terms of agentic impression (i.e., more confident, higher status, more enthusiastic), they were rated low in terms of communal impression (i.e., they were seen as less cooperative, friendly, kind, and likeable). Interestingly, Buffardi and Campbell (2008) also speculate on the wider impact of narcissistic self-promotion via social media sites. Because narcissists are very active users, the average Facebook user is likely to have a distorted exposure to narcissistic individuals. Will this mean that the norms of expression via social media will be 'pulled in the direction of greater self-promotion' (p. 1311)? A more recent study by Bergman, Fearrington, Davenport, and Begman (2011) suggests that perhaps it might. Although **millennial** (i.e., younger individuals from the 'net' generation) narcissists were characterized by specific motivations for using OSNs (e.g., they like to have many friends), this did not translate into overt behaviours via these sites. For example, non-narcissists made as many status updates, uploaded as many photos and had as many friends as narcissists. Perhaps this suggests that as time goes by, narcissistic self-promotion will become the norm on OSNs.

2.5 Conclusions and future directions

In cyberspace, we all have more control over how we present ourselves to others. For example, we can strategically manipulate elements of our online profiles to put ourselves across in the most favourable light. We know that some individuals are deeply concerned with how they are perceived by other people. For these people, the Internet may be regarded as a particularly valuable impression management tool. The research that has been reviewed in this chapter points to the notion that less socially skilled individuals in particular gain distinct advantages in how they present themselves to others online, supporting the social compensation hypothesis. For example, introverts and low self-esteem individuals can make use of a variety of online spaces to promote a more positive self-image to others (e.g., by being more selective over the photos that they upload). However, research findings also support the social enhancement hypothesis. So, individuals who already have ample opportunity to promote themselves offline are provided with further outlets to show off and express their positive qualities to other online users. For example, narcissists enjoy the use of OSNs as a supplementary tool to promote their relationships with others for self-enhancement. Research has, however, tended to focus much more on impression construction than it has on impression motivation. So, although the overt self-presentation tactics of online users have been explored in some depth, we know comparatively less about what motivates people to engage in these specific behaviours and how this may vary with different personality types.

Most research in this area has also focused on self-presentation tactics in OSNs. However, as previously discussed, this may not allow for a full range of self-presentation activities to be explored because OSNs are so closely tied to pre-existing offline networks. In other words, individuals are constrained in terms of the identity claims that they can make. Therefore, further research should aim to investigate impression management in more anonymous online environments, for example, blog sites or chat rooms, where such constraints may not apply. Research has also generally considered individual online spaces in isolation. We know that the online world is incredibly diverse and rich and should therefore not be considered as a homogenous entity. For example, in chat rooms users will be much more likely to interact with strangers or individuals who they have never communicated with before. Although we know that different personality types favour specific online environments (Orchard & Fullwood, 2010), it is also conceivable that people with different personalities will display distinctive self-presentation tactics via different online spaces. For example, although an introvert may be able to explore brand new identities in a chat room (because they are communicating with strangers), they can use OSNs to increase social capital in their existing social networks with more subtle forms of self-presentation. OSNs may provide an ideal environment to express the 'possible-self' for instance (Markus & Nurius, 1986) because this represents what we would like to become, rather than a misrepresentation of who we currently think we are (Mehdizadeh, 2010). It could therefore be argued that communication context is all important in determining how different personality types engage in self-presentation. Further research should therefore investigate motivational differences between various personality types in multiple online environments simultaneously.

Finally, further consideration should be given to the outcomes of engaging in various impression management behaviours for different personalities. There have been some tantalizing hints in the research literature regarding the benefits that less socially skilled individuals accrue from engaging in the online world. For instance, Steinfield, Ellison, and Lampe (2008) report how low self-esteem individuals gain more from Facebook than high self-esteem individuals in terms of bridging social capital (i.e., improving links with more distant ties, for example workmates). However, we know comparatively little about the outcomes of different self-presentation tactics online in terms of how this impacts on the impressions that others form of us and the ensuing psychological connotations (e.g., in terms of subjective well-being).

2.6 Chapter summary

- Impression management concerns play a pivotal role in shaping everyday behaviour.
- Influencing how others perceive us is likely to lead to a variety of positive outcomes (e.g., material, social, and occupational).
- Impression management entails two discrete processes: impression motivation and impression construction.
- Individuals may employ a variety of impression management strategies to influence how others perceive them, including defensive and assertive presentation tactics.
- There are individual differences in the importance that we place on self-presentation.
- There are number of features associated with the online world that influence how we communicate and present ourselves to others (e.g., increased anonymity).
- We have more control over the manner in which we edit our presentation of the self in the online world.
- Our personality affects how we perceive the world and our motivations for engaging in various behaviours.
- Individual personality traits influence the different ways in which we present ourselves to others in cyberspace.

- The Internet supports social enhancement and social compensation in the self-presentation behaviours of online users.
- Context is a crucial factor in determining how personality shapes different self-presentation behaviours.

References

Amichai-Hamburger, Y. (2007). Personality, individual differences and internet use. In Joinson, A., McKenna, K., Postmes, T. & Reips, U. (Eds), *The Oxford Handbook of Internet Psychology* (pp. 187-204), Oxford: Oxford University Press.

Amichai-Hamburger, Y., & Vinitzky, G. (2010). Social network use and personality. *Computers in Human Behavior*, 26, 1289-1295.

Arkin, R.M. (1981). Self-presentational styles. In Tedeschi, J.T. (Ed.), *Impression Management Theory and Social Psychological Research* (pp. 311-333). New York: Academic Press.

Back, M.D., Stopfer, J.M., Vazire, S., Gaddis, S., Schmukle, S.C., Egloff, B., & Gosling, S.D. (2010). Facebook profiles reflect actual personality, not self-idealisation. *Psychological Science*, 21 (3), 372-374.

Banczyk, B., Kramer, N., & Senokozlieva, M. (2008). 'The wurst' meets 'fatless' in MySpace. The relationship between self-esteem, personality and self-presentation in an online community. *Paper Presented at the Conference of the International Communication Association*, Montreal, Quebec, Canada.

Bargh, J.A., McKenna, K.Y.A., & Fitzsimmons, G.M. (2002). Can you see the Real Me? Activation and expression of the 'True Self' on the Internet. *Journal of Social Issues*, 58 (1), 33-48.

Baumeister, R.F. (1998). The self. In Gilbert, D., Fiske, S., & Lindzey, G. (Eds), *The Handbook of Social Psychology* (pp. 680-740). New York: Random House.

Bergman, S.M., Fearrington, M.E., Davenport, S.W., & Begman, J.Z. (2011). Millennials, narcissism, and social networking: What narcissists do on social networking sites and why. *Personality and Individual Differences*, 50, 706-711.

Buffardi, L.E. & Campbell, W.K. (2008). Narcissism and social networking web sites. *Personality and Social Psychology Bulletin*, 34, 1303-1314.

Campbell, W.K. (1999). Narcissism and romantic attraction. *Journal of Personality and Social Psychology*, 77, 1254-70.

Carlson, E.N., Vazire, S., & Oltmanns, T.F. (2011). You probably think this paper's about you: Narcissists' perceptions of their personality and reputation. *Journal of Personality and Social Psychology*, 101, 185.

Carr, N. (2010). *The Shallows: How the Internet is Changing the Way We Read, Think and Remember*. London: Atlantic Books.

Chester, A. & Bretherton, D. (2007). Impression management and identity online. In A. Joinson, K., McKenna, T. Postmes, & Reips, U. (Eds), *The Oxford Handbook of Internet Psychology* (pp. 223-236). Oxford: Oxford University Press.

Cialdini, R. (1984). *Influence: The New Psychology of Modern Persuasion*. New York: Quill Publishing.

De Raad, B. & Perugini, M. (2002). *Big Five Assessment*. Hogrefe and Huber Publishers.

Ellison, N., Heino, R., & Gibbs, J. (2006). Managing impressions online: Self-presentation processes in the online dating environment. *Journal of Computer-Mediated Communication*, 11, 415-441.

Facebook Newsroom (2013). *Retrieved* January 3rd, 2014 at http://newsroom.fb.com/Key-Facts (accessed 1st September, 2014).

Festinger, L. (1954). A theory of social comparison processes. *Human Relations*, 7 (2), 117-140.

Foster, J.D. & Campbell, W.K. (2007). Are there such things as 'narcissists' in social psychology? A taxometric analysis of the narcissistic personality inventory. *Personality and Individual Differences*, 43, 1321-1332.

Fullwood, C. & Wootton, N. (2009). Comforting communication in an online epilepsy forum. *Journal of Cybertherapy and Rehabilitation*, 2 (2), 159-164.

Fullwood, C., Thelwall, M., & O'Neill, S. (2011). Clandestine chatters: Self-disclosure in UK chat room profiles. *First Monday*, 16 (5) (Available at http://firstmonday.org/ojs/index.php/fm/article/view/3231/2954, accessed 15th September, 2014).

Fullwood, C., Melrose, K., Morris, N., & Floyd, S. (2013). Sex, blogs and baring your soul: Factors influencing UK blogging strategies. *Journal of the American Society for Information Science and Technology*, 64 (2), 345–355.

Fullwood, C., Nicholls, W., & Makichi, R. (in press). We've got something for everyone: How individual differences predict different blogging motivations. *New Media and Society*.

Gabriel, M.T., Critelli, J.W., & Ee, J.S. (1994). Narcissistic illusions in self-evaluations of intelligence and attractiveness. *Journal of Personality*, 62, 143–155.

Gibbons, F.X. (1986). Social comparison and depression: Company's effect on misery. *Journal of Personality and Social Psychology*, 51 (1), 140–148.

Goffman, E. (1959). *The Presentation of Self in Everyday Life*. New York: Garden City.

Goldberg, L.R. (1981). Language and individual differences: the search for universals in personality lexicons. *Review of Personality and Social Psychology*, 2 (1), 141–165.

Goldberg, L.R. (1992). The development of markers for the Big-Five factor structure. *Psychological Assessment*, 4, 26–42.

Gosling, S.D., Ko, S.J., Mannarelli, T., & Morris, M.E. (2002). A room with a cue: Personality judgments based on offices and bedrooms. *Journal of Personality and Social Psychology*, 83 (3), 379–398.

Gosling, S.D., Augustine, A.A., Vazire, S., Holtzman, N., & Gaddis, S. (2011). Manifestations of personality in online social networks: self-reported Facebook-related behaviors and observable profile information. *Cyberpsychology, Behavior and Social Networking*, 14 (9), 483–488.

Guadagno, R.E., Okdie, B.M., & Eno, C.A. (2007). Who blogs? Personality predictors of blogging. *Computers in Human Behavior*, 24 (5), 1993–2004.

Haferkamp, N. & Kramer, N.C. (2011). Social comparison 2.0: Examining the effects of online profiles on social networking sites. *Cyberpsychology, Behavior and Social Networking*, 14 (5), 309–314.

Hall, J.A., Park, N., Song, H., & Cody, M.J. (2010). Strategic misrepresentation in online dating: The effects of gender, self-monitoring and personality traits. *Journal of Social and Personal Relationships*, 27 (1), 117–135.

Hewitt, J.P. (2009). *Oxford Handbook of Positive Psychology*. Oxford University Press.

Higgins, E. T. (1987). Self-discrepancy: A theory relating self and affect. *Psychological Review*, 94, 319–340.

Joinson, A.N. (2004). Self-esteem, interpersonal risk, and preference for email to face-to-face communication. *Cyberpsychology, Behavior and Social Networking*, 7 (4), 472–478.

Leary, M.R. (1995). *Self-Presentation, Impression Management and Interpersonal Behaviour*. Madison, Wisconsin: Brown and Benchmark.

Leary, M.R. & Allen, A.B. (2011). Personality and persona: Personality processes in self-presentation. *Journal of Personality*, 79 (6), 889–916.

Leary, M.R. & Kowalski, R.M. (1990). Impression management: A literature review and two component model. *Psychological Bulletin*, 107 (1), 34–47.

Lee, S., Quigley, B.M., Nesler, M.S., Corbett, A.B., & Tedeschi, J.T. (1999). Development of a self-presentation tactics scale. *Personality and Individual Differences*, 26, 701–722.

Markus, H. & Nurius, P. (1986). Possible selves. *American Psychologist*, 41 (9), 954–956.

Marriott, T.C. & Buchanan, T. (2014). The true self online: Personality correlates of preference for self-expression online, and observer ratings of personality online and offline. *Computers in Human Behavior*, 32, 171–177.

McCrae, R.R. & Costa, Jr., P.T. (1987). Validation of the five-factor model of personality across instruments and observers. *Journal of Personality and Social Psychology*, 52 (1), 81–90.

McCrae, R.R. & Costa, Jr., P.T. (1990). *Personality in Adulthood: A Five-Factor Theory Perspective*. New York: Guilford Press.

McKenna, K.Y.A. & Bargh, J.A. (2000). Plan 9 from cyberspace: the implications of the Internet for personality and social psychology. *Personality and Social Psychology Review*, 4 (1), 57–75.

McKenna, K.Y.A., Green, A.S., & Gleeson, M.J. (2002). Relationship formation on the Internet: What's the big attraction? *Journal of Social Issues*, 58, 9–32.

Mehdizadeh, S. (2010). Self-presentation 2.0: Narcissism and self-esteem on Facebook. *Cyberpsychology, Behavior and Social Networking*, 13, 357–364.

Oltmanns, F.T., Emery, E.R., & Taylor, S. (2006). *Abnormal Psychology*. Toronto: Pearson Education Canada.

Ong, E.Y.L., Ang, R.P., Ho, J., Lim, J.C.Y., Goh, D.H., Lee, C.S., & Chua, A.Y.K. (2011). Narcissism, extraversion and adolescents' self-presentation on Facebook. *Personality and Individual Differences*, 50, 180–185.

Orchard, L.J. & Fullwood, C. (2010). Current perspectives on personality and Internet use. *Social Science Computer Review*, 28 (2), 155–169.

Rosenberg, J. & Egbert, N. (2011). Online impression management: Personality traits and concerns for secondary goals as predictors of self-presentation tactics on Facebook. *Journal of Computer-Mediated Communication*, 17, 1–18.

Rosenberg, M. (1965). *Society and the Adolescent Self-Image*. Princeton, NJ: Princeton University Press.

Rosenfeld, M.J. (2010). Meeting online: The rise of the internet as a social intermediary. *Paper presented at the annual meeting of the American Sociological Association Annual Meeting.* Retrieved from www.allacademic.com/meta/p409508_index.html

Ryckman, R. (2000). *Theories of Personality (7th Edition)*. Stamford, CT: Thomson/Wadsworth.

Sadler, M.E., Hunger, J.M., & Miller, C.J. (2010). Personality and impression management: Mapping the Multidimensional Personality Questionnaire onto 12 self-presentation tactics. *Personality and Individual Differences*, 48 (5), 623–628.

Schlenker, B.R. (1985). Identity and self-identification. In Schlenker, B.R. (Ed.), *The Self and Social Life* (pp. 65–99). New York: McGraw-Hill Book Company

Short, J., Williams, E., & Christie, B. (1976). *The Social Psychology of Telecommunications*. Toronto, ON: Wiley.

Siibak, A. (2009). Constructing the self through the photo selection: Visual impression management on social networking sites. *Journal of Psychosocial Research on Cyberspace*, 3 (1), article 1.

Steele, C.M. (1988). The psychology of self-affirmation: Sustaining the integrity of the self. In Berkowitz, L. (Ed.), *Advances in Experimental Social Psychology*, 21 (pp. 261–302). San Diego: Academic Press.

Steinfield, C., Ellison, N.B., & Lampe, C. (2008). Social capital, self-esteem, and use of online social network sites: A longitudinal analysis. *Journal of Applied Developmental Psychology*, 29, 434–445.

Suler, J. (2004). The online disinhibition effect. *Cyberpsychology, Social Networking and Behavior*, 7 (3), 321–326.

Tesser, A., Millar, M., & Moore, J. (1988). Some affective consequences of social comparison and reflection processes: The pain and pleasure of being close. *Journal of Personality and Social Psychology*, 54 (1), 49–61.

Valkenburg, P.I., Schouten, A.P., & Peter, J. (2005). Adolescents' identity experiments on the internet. *New Media and Society*, 7(3), 383–402.

Walther, J.B. (1996). Computer-mediated communication: impersonal, interpersonal, and hyperpersonal interaction. *Communication Research*, 23, 3–43.

Walther, J.B. & Parks, M. (2002). Cues filtered out, cues filtered in. In Knapp, M.L. and Daly, J.A. (Eds), *Handbook of Interpersonal Communication*, (pp. 529–563). Thousand Oaks, CA: Sage.

Wang, S.S. & Stefanone, M.A. (2013). Showing off? Human mobility and the interplay of traits, self-disclosure and Facebook check-ins. *Social Science Computer Review*, 31 (4), 437–457.

Zhao, S., Grasmuck S., & Martin, J. (2008). Identity construction on Facebook: digital empowerment in anchored relationships. *Computers in Human Behavior*, 24, 1816–1836.

Zywica, J. & Danowski, J. (2008). The faces of Facebookers: Investigating social enhancement and social compensation hypotheses; predicting Facebook and offline popularity from sociability and self-esteem, and mapping the meanings of popularity with semantic networks. *Journal of Computer Mediated Communication*, 14 (1), 1–34.

 Further reading

Amichai-Hamburger's (2007) book chapter 'Personality, individual differences and internet use' discusses many of the leading theories on personality and considers how aspects of these theories may relate to the different ways in which people use the Internet and interact with others in cyberspace.

Goffman's (1959) *The Presentation of Self in Everyday Life* presents a theory of social interaction that draws on an analogy with the theatre to elucidate on how we may conceal and reveal aspects of the self to garner more positive impressions from others.

Leary and Allen's (2011) research paper 'personality and persona: personality processes in self-presentation' discusses the role that our personalities play in shaping the different ways that individuals manage the impressions that others form of them.

Orchard and Fullwood's (2010) 'Current perspectives on personality and Internet use' reviews the extant literature outlining the manner in which personality shapes online user preferences and communication strategies. The review draws on Eysenck's three-factor model as a framework for understanding why different personality types may favour certain online environments over others.

 ## Discussion questions

1. Why is it in our best interests to leave others with favourable impressions of us?
2. Describe the difference between impression motivation and impression construction.
3. In what ways does the Internet alter the manner in which we can present ourselves to others? What advantages does this offer to those individuals who may have poorer social skills?
4. What pattern of self-presentation do narcissists display online? Is this consistent with their offline impression management behaviours?
5. Why might it be important to consider the communication context in considering the self-presentation strategies of different personalities in the online world?

3

Age versus Goal-directed Internet Use

ALISON ATTRILL

Learning objectives

After reading this chapter, we hope that you will be able to:

- Identify the key differences in explaining online behaviour according to a digital age divide and to a goal-directed, needs, and motivation approach.
- Outline a number of key theories that can be used to explain online behaviour from a goal-directed, needs, and motivation perspective.
- Explain why it is important to evaluate individual differences when considering online behaviour.
- Consider the Internet as a heterogeneous landscape that requires more than one theory to explain diverse individual behaviours.
- Explain why the Internet should be considered as a tool rather than an instrument of human behaviour.

3.1 Introduction

Nowadays almost every household in western society is connected to the Internet. Whether via personal computer, laptop, games console, or mobile phone, it is becoming increasingly rare to encounter individuals who do not engage in at least some form of Internet activity. Yet, since the inception of the Internet, research has tried to convince us that it is only the young who are technologically engaged and able, with older people often being made to feel technologically inferior and unknowledgeable. That Ivy Bean, aged 102 years, hit the headlines as the oldest member of the social networking site (**SNS**) Facebook, and became a Twitterer aged 104 years belies this notion of the Internet being a playground reserved for the young (Wikipedia, 2014). Increasing numbers of grandparents are using modern technology to stay in touch with their loved ones around the world, from Skype to email and instant messaging, from sending videos and photographs via the Internet to e-cards, older people may not have grown up with the World Wide Web, but many are trying to keep up with the digital times. Nonetheless, research remains focused on demonstrating age as one of the most influential factors impacting upon Internet use (Hills & Argyle, 2003, Koyuncu & Lien, 2003, Akman, Yazici, Mishra, & Arifoglu, 2005, Zhang, 2005). This chapter will seek to lay this notion to rest by putting a different spin on Internet use, namely one of goal-directed, need-driven, and motivated behaviour use. In doing so, it also aims to shatter the perception of the Internet as a homogenous arena, where people behave the same regardless of what they are doing on diverse and varied types of Internet website. From shopping to banking, social networking or dating to gaming, seeking health-related information to engaging in online counselling sessions, the Internet is awash with different types of activities. There has been a tendency for research to treat psychological aspects of online behaviour as similar across all of these varied activities. Consider for a moment your own offline and online behaviours. Different human needs, wants, motivations and psychological processes would be considered to underlie such diverse offline behaviours. Why, then, should we assume that all online behaviour can be explained with a singular model, or the same generalized processes? Moreover, given that individuals adapt and change their behaviour to suit social roles and environmental factors offline, we need to consider whether similar adaptations take place online. These questions will be explored from a human needs perspective. It will be suggested that humans use the Internet to meet needs in much the same way as they engage in diverse behaviours offline to satisfy needs. The digital age debate is a good place to begin this journey, by considering whether age should remain a dominant factor in trying to understand who uses the Internet how, or whether the focus should switch to considering why different age groups adopt varied approaches to Internet use.

3.2 The digital age divide

The term '**generation gap**' is widely used in western societies to refer ' . . . to differences between people of a younger generation and their elders . . . particularly with respect to such matters as musical tastes, fashion, culture and politics' (Wikipedia, 2014). In other words, age differences appear in a number of activities engaged in online. Popular culture, the mass media, and researchers alike have attempted to categorise, define and label individuals according to age groups reflecting the technological advances made during their lifetime. One influential definition is that of a '**Net-Generation**' (Net-Gen, N-Gen), which Tapscott (1998) defined as individuals born between 1977 and 1996. They are 'the first cohort to grow up fully wired and technologically fluent' (Hempel & Lehman, 2005, p. 88). Tapscott later suggested that those born after 1997 are a '**Generation Next**', a generation who have not known anything but a technological existence. Other authors give slightly different definitions to individuals born post-1980 ('Digital Natives'; Prensky, 2001a, 2001b) and to those born between 1982-1991 ('Millenials'; Oblinger & Oblinger, 2005), with the consensus being that there is a generation of individuals born around the late 1970s/early 1980s who are often perceived to have grown up more technologically savvy than their older counterparts. Categorizing and labelling different age groups has led both the mass media and research alike to propose the Internet to be a place of social interaction for those who have grown up with the rapid technological advances seen over the last 2-3 decades. Whilst some research supports this notion, research to the contrary is emerging. A study by Attrill and Jalil (2011) found, for instance, no significant differences between similar-aged student and non-student participants in their online disclosures, suggesting that this digital age divide may not be as prominent as often suggested.

Upon considering the limited available literature that offers a balanced overview of this material, it becomes apparent that research has mainly focused on singular Internet activities, without exploring behaviours related to those activities in greater depth. Ample research is now emerging, for instance, to consider who uses social networking sites (SNSs), or who shops online, but finding literary examples of the actual behaviours of different age groups on varied sites is difficult to say the least. Moreover, there is a dearth of research that focuses on how older individuals engage with different *types* of Internet websites. It is important to consider how older individuals engage in online communities and social networks to build social capital, for example, since elderly people are amongst those most likely to have a dwindling offline social network (Cumming & Henry, 1961). As Jaeger and Xie (2009) point out, it is somewhat surprising that not more research has considered activities of older individuals online, especially since age-related differences in actual Internet use between the young and old are rapidly closing. The age-gap of Internet use is closing around the world! In the USA a quarter of Internet users are believed to be aged 55+ years, with home Internet access in this age group doubling over a three-year period from 2005–2008 (Jones & Fox, 2009). It would thus seem somewhat unrealistic to continue to promote a generation gap in terms of Internet use, but to consider which activities people carry out on different types of website. After all, in your offline world, if you want to engage in online banking you do not visit a speed dating event! Why should it be the case then that online your intentions, motivations, and behaviours would be exactly the same regardless of whether you are visiting an online banking or online dating site? There may of course be feasible explanations for age differences in some activities, such as online shopping; an older person may, for example, be more cautious of providing their bank details online because they have not been used to doing so and may thus be more concerned or worried about revealing personal and financial information via the Internet. The Internet can, however, be conceived of as a tool for many facets of human interaction, including education, business and entertainment (Weiser, 2000). As such it offers individuals various arenas in which they can fulfil their own goals (Nithya & Julius, 2007). Individual goals may not only differ according to personality, situational, economic, and functional factors, to name but a few, but could also vary according to age-specific goals and demands (Potosky, 2007). It may thus not be the case that different age groups do or do not use the Internet, but that they use it differently, in a more goal-directed, task-related, or age-suited manner. The remainder of this chapter therefore explores the notion that it is not necessarily age that differentiates online activities, but goals, needs, and motivations. In order to do so, a brief overview is now provided of age- and goal-directed differences in selected Internet activities, namely non-specified Internet use, social networking, and communication.

3.3 Non-specified Internet use

Several studies suggest the existence of a generational divide in general information and communication technology usage such as email and Internet search activities (Cothey, 2002, Hargittai, 2004, Kiel, 2005). According to The Pew Internet and American Life Project (2001), participants aged 20–30 years were the most frequent Internet users at that time. The social demographics of Internet use have considerably changed since 2001. A number of factors have been considered in terms of who uses the Internet, where, why, and for which activities (see e.g., http://www.pewresearch.org/ or http://www.internetworldstats.com/ for the most current statistics on Internet usage around the world). The purpose of this chapter is to illustrate how the notion of the Internet as a playground for a specific age group (the digital generation) is based on older research, research that often offers conflicting results. This in turn implies the need for a different approach to understanding Internet usage, not least since we are only a few decades away from a population of everyone having grown up digitally. Some examples of the conflicting research in this area will now be discussed.

Actual Internet use has also been shown to decline with age, with Livingstone, Van Couvering, and Thumim (2005) showing that 52% of participants aged 55–64 years of age use the Internet compared to only 15% of those 65 years or over. Further evidence for a digital age divide in Internet use and access comes from Kaare, Brandtzaeg, Endestad, and Heim (2007) who found that, in Austria and Norway, Internet non-users are most likely to be over the age of 45 years. Similarly, 48% of 55–64 year olds questioned in a study in Belgium reported not using the Internet, as did 76% of over 65 year olds. Weiser (2000) also demonstrated that individuals over the age of 65 were less likely to go online than any other age group. At face value, these data appear to suggest the digital divide to be a universal phenomenon amongst westernized cultures. There is, however, some evidence to suggest that not only is Internet use most rapidly increasing amongst individuals over the age of 55 years (Carpenter & Buday, 2007), but that those aged 60+ are also increasing their Internet uptake (Martin & Robinson, 2007). Moreover, older people have been shown to use the Internet more at home than at work (Klobas & Clyde, 2000), and to go online more generally for email, hobby-related information and news (Fox et al., 2001). This pattern of results suggests that it may not be the case that a digital age divide exists, but that the different age groups use the Internet for different, possibly goal-related activities. It is also worth considering at this point, the dates of much of the research outlined in this and other sections. The Internet is one of the fastest, most rapidly changing technological advances ever known to humankind. Over the past five years or so, Internet usage has become a lot less clumsy and more logical. The flow through websites via a number of web links is becoming easier, as is understanding what might have once appeared to be an alien computer-related jargon. In other words, Internet usage has become far more accessible since a lot of this research was reported. Research is, however, taking its time in catching up with these advances and statistical reports of different types of Internet use. Nonetheless, we now turn to considering some of the research that has considered goal-directed Internet use.

3.4 Computer-mediated communication

Computer-mediated communication (**CMC**) occurs when two or more people interact via electronic devices. The focus of CMC in this chapter is on exchanges that take place via the Internet, such as email, instant messaging, chat rooms, and so on. In terms of how individuals engage in CMC, the pattern appears to be somewhat complex. Most work seems to have compared preferences for online to offline behaviour. Thayer and Ray (2006), for instance, found that young adults not only preferred online communication with friends and strangers alike, compared to middle and older aged adults, but that they were also more likely to build relationships online with unknown others. This is in line with the observation that 20–30 year olds are more likely to use the Internet for communication than are middle-aged or older adults (The Pew Internet and American Life Project, 2001; http://www.pewinternet.org). Young adults have also been shown to engage more frequently in instant messaging and chat sites than older individuals (Hughes, 2006). That is not to say that individuals aged 30+ years do not participate in CMC. To the contrary, it appears to be more a case of older participants using different forms of CMC. A study by Seniors Online (2004) found that when older people do go online, they mainly spend their time emailing others. Older Internet users (aged 50-64 years) have also been shown to be more likely to use the Internet as a tool for maintaining familial contact via email, and for work-related activities. They simply do so to a lesser degree than their younger counterparts (Howard, Raine, & Jones, 2001).

3.5 Social networking

As recently as a dozen years ago, the concept of social networking sites (**SNSs**) was an alien concept to most individuals. Some of us might have been dabbling with the likes of MySpace or Bebo, but Facebook was yet to explode as an online socializing tool for the masses. Nowadays, those individuals who do not use Facebook have become the exception rather than the rule, regardless of their age. Whereas most early research focused on MySpace, research around the use of Facebook as the mainly adopted SNS has now more or less become the norm. The nature of the initial roll out of SNSs across university students and its gain in popularity over the last few years have both largely contributed to the somewhat blind assumption that SNSs are more popular amongst younger than older Internet users. Pfeil, Arjan, and Panayiotis Zaphiris (2009) sum up this assumption of age-related SNS use by stating that:

> ... it is widely accepted that young people use social software like blogs, SNS and online communities more often than older people, leading to an intergenerational 'digital divide'. Like it is the case with many other Information and Communication Technologies (ICT), SNS are often targeted and more widely used by young people.

> (Pfeil et al., 2009, p. 643)

This assumption is not wholly unfounded with recent research showing that across three studies in three different countries, 55+ year olds were unlikely to use Facebook (Karahasanovic et al., 2009). Pfeil et al. (2009) do, however, also point out that there are SNSs specifically aimed at older individuals (see e.g., www.overfiftiesfriends.co.uk). This suggests that it may not be the case that people of a certain age are more or less prone to using SNSs, but that individuals may specifically seek out a SNS that is relevant or useful to them. Some interesting statistics from Facebook itself dated 2006 show no clear digital age divide amongst Facebook users in the USA, as measured by unique visitors to the site during August of that year. These consisted mainly of 35-54 year olds (33.5%) and 18-24 year olds (34%), followed by 12-17 year olds (14%). Only 8.6% of 25-34 year olds and 7.6% of those aged over 55 years signed up to Facebook during this time. Putting this research into perspective, it could be somewhat misleading as to the non-existence of a digital generation. Whilst it does show that almost as many 35-54 as 18-24 year olds signed up to Facebook during this one month, it was very soon after Facebook opened its digital doors to the masses, having previously been an exclusive SNS for college and university students. Furthermore, in the last few years, it has almost become the norm to have a Facebook account regardless of age or any other demographic background, at least in westernized cultures. Even if we look at other cultures, where Facebook use might not be as prevalent, there are also culture-specific SNSs that appear more popular. For example, in China the most rapidly growing SNS, with 623.3 million users, is Qzone (www.qzone.qq.com), and the most visited SNS in India and Brazil is Orkut (www.orkut.com) rather than Facebook. This highlights that there are many more factors other than age that appear to affect whether people partake in SNS activities, with the digital generation debate in relation to SNS painting a very sketchy picture. That said, rather than focusing on age groups who do/do not use SNSs, it could be more informative to consider possible age-related differences in the types of behaviours carried out on SNSs. Is it, for instance, the case that different age groups are more or less likely to post status updates than engage in instant messaging, or do younger people post more pictures and videos to SNSs than do older people, and who is most likely to use a SNS to make, break, or maintain friendships or romantic liaisons? Unfortunately, the limited available research in this area has mainly focused on friends and acquaintances of SNS users and various modes of interaction with those individuals. Young adults have been shown to be more likely to build online relationships with both existing offline friends and unknown others, than are middle-aged and older adults (Thayer & Ray, 2006). Younger participants in Thayer and Ray's study also spent more time communicating online than did two older groups. Some work has suggested that individuals use SNSs to strengthen established weak and close offline contacts rather than for seeking new acquaintances (Ellison, Steinfeld, & Lampe, 2007) suggesting possible age-related differences in who people will add as friends on SNSs.

A further consideration in relation to SNSs can be given to the type of interactions that individuals have with those they have already befriended on these sites. SNSs generally have a function that enables users to make status updates about their current thoughts, activities and feelings. They can share photos and videos, and can engage in instant chat with people they have befriended. Recent research has shown that teenagers are more likely than older people to comment on social interaction sites (Boyd, 2008). A finding echoed by Pfeil et al.'s (2009) observation that teenagers received ten times as many SNS comments than did older participants. This suggests that younger people are more likely to exchange their thoughts and post comments on SNSs than are older individuals. Whilst these findings imply that there do appear to be some differences in how different age groups use SNSs, we need to remember the statistics that also indicate a closing gap in the numbers of young and older people who sign up to social networking sites. It might therefore be the case that young and old alike tend to use SNSs, but (a) they choose a site that suits their own behavioural goals or needs, and (b) that there may be individual differences in the use of various functions such as instant messaging, digital media sharing, and status updates. Some people might be more or less passive or active in their SNS use, a tendency that likely has little to do with their age, but more to do with their psychological make-up and behavioural goals or needs.

3.6 What causes a digital divide if not age?

A number of possible explanations for differences in Internet behaviours will now be considered, including individuals operating within their comfort zones. Schofield-Clark (2009) offers the interesting notion that a digital divide observed by early Internet research could be due to a knowledge gap between the young digitally able and older digitally inexperienced. Accordingly, it is a difference in technological understanding that leads older individuals to only use the Internet within their self-defined comfort zones (Kvasny, 2006) rather than exploring digital activities that require the learning of new skills and abilities. It is exactly this type of activity within one's comfort zone that could reflect goal- or need-related behaviour rather than a digital age divide. If this is the case, it would apply not only to older digitally less able individuals but also to younger digitally able people. Whilst one individual might log on to an Internet site with the specific aim of buying a certain product, for instance, someone else might spend more time browsing various sites for a more competitive price on the same item. Both individuals are behaving in a goal-related manner (to purchase the item), but the latter might be more willing to step outside of their comfort zone. This difference in behaviour would thus be unrelated to the age of the two different Internet users.

That Internet access and use is goal-related across different age groups is supported by Akman and Mishra's (2010) observation that within a professional organization, employees aged 40+ years reported a higher average daily use of the Internet than did those aged 40 years and under. This age-related difference likely reflects older employees using the Internet in a work-related capacity. This brings us to another key factor to consider when assessing the research on age differences in online behaviour, namely the observation that much of the work focuses on select samples. Zhang (2005) points out that research demonstrating more positive attitudes towards general Internet use amongst younger than older samples is largely based on samples of only students or only employees from a given corporation or minority profession. Like many other studies, Akman and Mishra's (2010) demonstration of goal-related Internet use considered employees of only one corporation. Nonetheless, we need to consider the diverse findings outlined thus far from a theoretical standpoint, regardless of the samples used. In order to do so, there now follows a brief exploration of a number of existing theoretical perspectives and models that may be useful in understanding differences in online behaviours and activities.

3.7 Theoretical models and perspectives

Bargh and McKenna (2004) provide a useful outline of some of the guiding models of Internet behaviour in their consideration of the Internet and social life. They describe the uses and gratifications theory proposed by Blumler and Katz (1974), which has been used to explain online behaviour. From this perspective, a person uses the Internet with a purpose in mind, with the aim of gratifying that purpose through the use of the Internet. This is not dissimilar to Spears, Postmes, Lea, and Wolbert's (2002) proposal that individual goals and needs determine how individuals use the Internet. According to a third perspective outlined by Bargh and McKenna (2004), the social context of different types of Internet website affects the quality of an online interaction, with needs and goals playing a role in how different online social contexts are used for gratification. These three approaches are all similar in that they suggest that online activity is more than a random act without thought or goal direction. That goal direction may not always be externally driven; if you are currently reading an online version of this text as required for your studies, for instance, then you might be fulfilling an extrinsically driven goal (i.e., your tutor told you to read the book!) rather than an intrinsically motivated behavioural goal (i.e., you are reading the text because you are personally curious as to why people behave how they do on the Internet). Both types of behavioural goal are driven by a need. One might be the need to complete coursework (external), whilst the internally driven goal might be to satisfy your curiosity. Human beings have a range of both internal and external needs that are driven by a whole host of psychological processes. Let us now consider some aspects of human needs in more detail, in particular how people might meet different types of human needs through their online interactions.

3.8 Human needs and belonging

According to Baumeister and Leary (1995) human beings have a fundamental need to feel like they belong. That is, they feel the need to develop long lasting significant relationships with other human beings. Two features of interaction that foster the satisfaction of this need are (1) frequent positive interactions with other people, and (2) that these interactions produce a sense of stability and continued interaction that promotes a sense of caring. Baumeister and Leary call this a sense of *belongingness*, a human need that they suggest to be almost as powerful as the need for food and other physiological determinants of survival. The motivation to seek belongingness is driven by a number of factors, including the sense that there will be direct affective, cognitive, and behavioural consequences of an interaction that provides a sense of belonging (for a fuller overview see Baumeister & Leary, 1995). These suggestions are not entirely new or novel, with both Maslow (1968) considering the role of *love and belongingness* needs in his motivational hierarchy, and Bowlby (1969, 1973) suggesting a need for humans to form and maintain social bonds and relationships. However, all of these conceptualizations have one thing in common—they propose that an absence of belongingness can lead to negative affective, cognitive, and behavioural consequences, including stress, anxiety, and psychological pathology (Baumeister & Leary, 1995). Baumeister and Leary suggest that individuals engage in increased goal-directed activity to form relationships in order to avoid such consequences. Building such lasting bonds and relationships used to be a time-consuming activity (Sternberg, 1986). Nowadays, however, the Internet provides a never-before seen interconnectivity with people literally clicking their way to new acquaintances, friendships, enemies, and even long-lasting love! Moreover, some people might use the Internet to forge this sense of belongingness when it does not exist in their offline world.

In order to explore this notion further let's consider people who might feel ostracized from their offline world due to a self-perceived stigmatized social identity. Such stigmas come in all shapes and sizes and include sexual orientations, political, and racial beliefs, as well as illnesses and disabilities, to mention just a few. Someone who has a particular illness, for example, might be struggling to come to terms with that aspect of their identity. They might isolate themselves socially in their offline world, but seek out online interactions to maintain some sense of social belonging. The age of people using the Internet in this way would be irrelevant in such instances, with some features of the Internet such as perceived anonymity possibly outweighing other factors such as comfort zones and individual ability when seeking approval from like-minded others online. If people use the Internet in this way, then they are not only using it as a tool in a goal-directed manner (i.e., to find social acceptance and satisfy the humanistic need of belonging), but are also engaged in helping shape the environment of the Internet to meet their needs (Fischer, 1992, Hughes & Hans, 2001). This brings us to the idea of the Internet as a two-way reciprocal tool: People use it to meet their needs, but it needs people to provide input to keep it functioning! That said, if a sense of belonging is forged over a period of time as suggested by Baumeister and Leary, with mutual interactions that are based on shared experiences and intimacies, then the Internet may not meet this sense of belonging for many individuals. Whilst the Internet provides a multitude of opportunity for making friends, it may not be conducive to forging long-lasting platonic or romantic relationships, especially if they exist purely online. Consider Facebook as an example, which has a cap of 5,000 on the number of 'friends' any one person can have. In our offline worlds, maintaining sensible and meaningful social ties to more than around 20 individuals would prove difficult. This raises the question as to how many online 'friendships' can be maintained in a way that ensures a human's need to belong. Baumeister and Leary do suggest that social bonds and acquaintances can be readily formed for a multitude of reasons. However, they also state that for a full sense of belongingness to emerge, regular contact needs to be upheld. Are our Facebook friends real friends? Are they social bonds that provide a sense of belonging? Or do we need to reconsider how humans achieve belongingness in a time of computer-mediated communication? Regardless of how we answer these questions, one conclusion that might be evident from this brief exploration of human belongingness is that different people may use different features of the Internet in different ways, ways that may be conducive to providing a sense of social belonging, or ways that may help individuals meet completely different goals.

3.9 Social motivations

Chiang, Chiang, and Lin (2013) suggest that some online activities may serve social motivations. In particular they focus on blogging behaviours that serve to meet social, entertainment, and goal orientations. In its early forms blogging was most often associated with an individual providing an online commentary, almost like an online diary in relation to any topic of their choice. This would appear to be very much a one-way information flow, an arena for an individual to almost vent or release information, possibly in a cathartic manner. As the World Wide Web has developed and progressed, blogging now often allows for the provision of feedback in response to an online post. It is this feedback that might enhance an individual's sense of acceptance or belongingness. This type of feedback can, however, also have dire consequences. It might be the case that one's expressions on a certain topic attract a lot of negative feedback. Feedback of any kind might serve the goal of shaping and/or reinforcing one's sense of self-identity, sense of belonging, or lack thereof. Consider, for example, a severely depressed individual who seeks reinforcement of their negative qualities to maintain their depressed mood. The Internet offers an ideal, if also dangerous, arena in which to seek such reinforcement through blogging or any other form of CMC. This, again, has nothing to do with age-related behaviours, but could be seen as individuals using the Internet to meet their current psychological needs. This proposal is in line with Leung's (2007) observation that individuals use the Internet as a mood management tool, as well as to provide social compensation in a manner that offsets the negative psychological impact of offline stressful life events. Specifically, Leung found that amongst a surveyed sample of 8–18 year olds, in particular online entertainment and relationship maintenance temporarily reduced levels of stress experienced offline. Leung notes that this type of Internet use is similar to Zillman's (1982) proposal that some people watch television to escape a current social reality or to alleviate feelings of negative affect or stress. Zillman and Bryant (1985) noted that the type of programme that people choose to watch is related to the level and cause of their stress. If this is the case, and mood, motivation, stress, and social factors play a role in determining how different people choose to watch different types of television programme or film, it stands to reason that Internet behaviour may be equally individually dependent upon such factors. Indeed, using Zillman's notion of mood management to understand underlying motivations for Internet use all but eliminates a continued need for thinking of the World Wide Web in terms of age-specific domains. Rather, the Internet offers an array of different activities that can be individually tailored to meet diverse individual needs and requirements. Let us once again return to the notion of stigmatized illnesses to consider this proposal. There is evidence to suggest that people suffering from depression who received support via frequent interactions with an online support group showed better improvement of their depressive symptoms than counterparts who less frequently engaged with such an online group (Houston, Cooper, & Ford, 2002). If we consider this in relation to SNS use, it might also be the case that some people post status updates on sites such as Facebook with the intention of receiving positive feedback, or positive reinforcement in the name of mood management. Someone who feels down after a relationship breakdown might, for example, seek comfort from their online Facebook friends to enhance their negative affect. Evidence for such a selective use of the Internet comes from Leung's (2007) study of adolescents. Although only representative of the sampled age group (8–18 year olds), Leung did observe that different explanations for feelings of stress led to different types of Internet use. For instance, stress resulting from experiences of illness or family separation resulted in behaviours related to entertainment, social recognition, and relationship maintenance, whereas stress resulting from school related problems led to behaviours associated with relaxation, positive acceptance, and reinforcement such as receiving encouragement from others via the Internet. This is in line with Yu and Chou's (2009) proposal that people use the Internet to foster happiness. They proposed that the Internet serves daily functions that help create and maintain happiness such as staying in touch with friends. Although it should be noted that the notion of mood management is one of enhancing a positive mood rather than seeking to maintain or enhance negative affect (Knobloch, 2003), there are instances where the Internet serves nothing other than to maintain an individual's negative or damaging behaviours. Whilst activities such as seeking reinforcement via Facebook status updates might serve to enhance the positive aspects of one person's identity, similar activities might also create a negative impact upon another person of a different psychological make-up. An example of such behaviours might be excessive gambling or gaming online that has detrimental effects on a person's offline existence, effects that could vary in nature from a financial to a social impact. What is emerging from the literature is a pattern of individually determined Internet behaviour rather than a pattern influenced by the decade in which people are born. In line with this proposal, we now consider whether there are individual factors that may or may not influence how people behave online.

3.10 Individual factors

To date, very little work has specifically pitched different individual factors against one another in experimental designs that foster an understanding of the individual factors that determine general Internet behaviour. Where work has been carried out, it has usually linked individual factors and characteristics to the use of specific types of website. There is, for instance, a paper by Gangadharbatla (2008) that provides a useful overview of four overarching factors believed to influence people's use of social networking sites: *Internet self-efficacy, need for cognition, need to belong,* and *collective self-esteem*. We will use these four factors to explore further the notion of Internet behaviour as a whole being individually goal-directed rather than age-specific.

Internet self-efficacy: Eastin and LaRose (2000) defined Internet self-efficacy as 'the belief in one's capabilities to organize and execute courses of Internet actions required to produce given attainments, . . . a potentially important factor in efforts to close the digital divide that separates experienced Internet users from novices'. This is similar to Schofield-Clark's (2009) notion of one's technological comfort zone. Accordingly, people need to feel that they can use the Internet confidently and competently to achieve their desired outcomes. If a person feels able to do something on the Internet, they will be more likely to do it. An individual's **need for cognition** is their desire to both employ cognitive effort and to enjoy the rewards of that effort. It influences a number of online behaviours, including information seeking (Carenini, 2001) and attitude formation (Zhang, 1996). A person's need for cognition will influence how they use the Internet. Gangadharbatla (2008) suggests that analytical individuals will evaluate Internet sites from a more cognitive perspective than those who prefer a more visual representation. These individuals would, for example, be more likely to focus on the design of a website than its content. Such processing preferences will in turn influence an individual's attitude towards any given website. Gangadharbatla's (2008) use of individuals' **need to belong** is based on Baumeister and Leary's (1995) notion of humans having a 'fundamental human motivation that is something all humans possess . . . to form and maintain at least a minimum quantity of lasting, positive, and significant interpersonal relationships' (p. 497). As previously mentioned, the level or intensity of this need fluctuates from individual to individual and could play a role in the level and frequency of communication sought on the Internet. Gangadharbatla suggests that it may be an underlying principle of how people interact via SNSs, given that sites such as Facebook offer users the opportunity to meet this fundamental human need. Of importance for the current chapter is the notion that user activity on SNSs would thus, at least in part, be guided by this need to belong, rather than being driven by age-appropriate, or inappropriate, behaviours. Not only do people need to feel that they belong on an individual level, but they also need to experience **collective self-esteem**. This is an aspect of an individual's self-identity that stems from their sense of belonging to one or more social groups. Other than stemming from a sense of group-belongingness, collective self-esteem operates in a similar manner to personal self-esteem (Tajfel & Turner, 1986, Kim & Omizo, 2005). This is thus a factor that not only fluctuates from individual to individual, but is gained through one's interactions with others, such as those carried out online via SNSs, gaming, dating, email, instant messaging, and many more. Gangadharbatla (2008) demonstrated in a questionnaire study that these four factors (Internet self-efficacy, need for cognition, need to belong, and collective self-esteem) positively influenced individuals' tendencies for SNS membership. If the factors fluctuate at the individual level and can be used as predictors of whether people engage in a certain activity online, then once again it begs the question as to whether these factors would outweigh age-determinants of online behaviours. Of course, it could be the case that these findings are an artefact of the sample used. A 65-item questionnaire was given to 237 students ranging in age from 18–30 years. One might assume that these individuals are more *au fait* with online activities and therefore more likely existing members of SNSs than a sample aged, say, 40–60 years of age, especially if the latter are not employed in a sector that requires them to frequently use the Internet. Whilst future work will no doubt consider these sample effects, of relevance for the current debate is the notion that age alone does not appear to determine how people behave on the Internet. Gangadhar-batla's outline of these four factors demonstrates that there are a range of other factors that are possibly more important than age in influencing online activity. Another individual factor that strengthens this suggestion is a person's experience of 'flow'.

3.10.1 **Flow theory**

Flow is a concept that has been applied to many behaviours. It represents the idea of achieving a psychologically optimal experience that occurs when people become totally immersed in a current activity, an immersion that sees a person as completely absorbed by what to them is a positive experience characterized by a clear objective, feedback, concentration, a sense of control, and loss of self-consciousness, amongst other factors (Csikszentmihalyi, 1975). Flow theory has been applied to a number of online behaviours including that of online gaming addiction. The sense of optimal flow may be easily achieved in the early stages of a person's online gaming. However, the more they game, the harder it may become to create that psychological state. This could result in increased amounts of time being spent gaming online to the detriment of one's offline existence. There is, however, little evidence to support this proposal, with Wan and Chiou (2006) observing no positive relationship between individuals' addictive tendencies towards online gaming and their flow states.

Other researchers have distinguished between **goal-directed** and **experiential flow**. Adopting Csikszentmihalyi's (1975, 1990) initial concept of flow, Hoffman and Novak (1997) suggested that flow in online behaviour occurs when a person navigates the Internet seamlessly, derives enjoyment from doing so, becomes unconscious of the self and finds reinforcement of the self in the activity. This can only be achieved if the individual feels that they are able to complete the desired online activity, but at the same time feel sufficiently challenged. Novak, Hoffman, and Duhachek (2003) found that whilst evident for both types of activity, flow was more likely to occur for goal-directed than experiential activities. Hoffman and Novak (1997) provide an overview of the differences between experiential and goal-directed flow:

Goal-directed	Experiential
extrinsic motivation	intrinsic motivation
instrumental orientation	ritualized orientation
situational involvement	enduring involvement
utilitarian benefits/value	hedonic benefits/value
directed (prepurchase) search	nondirected (ongoing) search; browsing
goal-directed choice	navigational choice
cognitive	affective
work	fun
planned purchases; repurchasing	compulsive shopping; impulsive buys

According to Tapscott's digital generation notion, it might be the case that younger people are more inclined to engage in experiential flow whereas older individuals might be inclined to adopt a more goal-directed flow experience. More recently, Rai and Attrill (2014) carried out research that involved both self-report and behavioural measures to assess what types of Internet activity people are most likely to engage in at work and in the home environment. Some of their findings indicated that individual levels of impression management (self-promotion, intimidation, and supplication) related to what people did during their work time on the Internet, whilst age was negatively correlated with type of Internet use in the home. This fits with Hoffman and Novak's (1997) distinction of flow, whereby the work environment provides a focused goal-directed approach towards Internet use, whilst experiential flow is achieved through private Internet use. This distinction could also be used to underline a couple of Gangadharbatla's (2008) four factors of Internet use outlined previously. Of particular interest is the inclusion of a need for cognition labelled as *cognitive* in Hoffman and Novak's goal-directed category. Experiential flow, on the other hand, is driven by affect. Another interesting aspect of this distinction is the notion that goal-directed flow and experiential flow are guided by different motivations. Whereas the former is influenced extrinsically, experiential flow is driven by an intrinsic motivation, one that would seemingly appear to be pleasure based. This would suggest that people tend to use the Internet based on the outcome they are aiming to achieve. Even if their behaviour is of an experiential nature, there is some type of goal or outcome associated with it. If it is of an affective nature, it might be to enhance positive mood. This would be in line with Yu and Chou's (2009) suggestion that Internet use can foster happiness and provide a general mood management tool (Knobloch, 2003). Deci and Ryan (2000) propose a model whereby such goal-directed behaviours, regardless of their task- or experiential-oriented nature, are driven by the needs that are gratified through a behavioural outcome.

3.10.2 **Self-determination theory**

According to self-determination theory (**SDT**), human beings have needs that are satisfied through goal-directed behaviour (Deci & Ryan, 2000). The literature around offline goal-directed behaviour dates back almost a century, with most early theories revolving around the notion that people behave in a goal-directed manner in order to achieve desired behavioural outcomes (Tolman, 1932, Lewin, 1936). No distinction was initially made between types of goals achieved in terms of their psychological properties, other than that they might be differently valued. Half a century later, it was recognized that different types of goals may have psychological consequences, such as creating positive or negative affect. This led to numerous distinctions, for example, between behaviours that lead to the development of an ability (*ability-development goals*) and those which demonstrate ability (*ability-demonstration goals*) (Nicholls, 1984, Dweck, 1986). Self-determination theory is different to both of these approaches because it considers both the content of behavioural outcomes (goals) and the regulatory processes that drive the behaviours to achieve these goals. Thus, according to this theory, Internet behaviour might be driven by the pursuit of goal attainment (a behavioural outcome) that satisfies a basic human psychological need. An example hereof would be that people who suffer social anxiety still have the basic human need to feel connected to other people. As they avoid offline social experiences, they might seek to satisfy their sense of belonging by actively seeking out online interactions and relationships. According to Deci and Ryan (2000), there are three basic innate psychological human needs that drive goal attainment, psychological growth, and well-being: *competence*, *relatedness*, and *autonomy*.

- **Competence**: This refers to the need to feel able and capable to carry out activities.
- **Relatedness**: In line with Baumeister and Leary's (1995) definition of belongingness, relatedness refers to the need for a reciprocated feeling of love, being wanted, and cared for.
- **Autonomy**: A sense of autonomy is gained through the experience of simultaneously feeling free and integrated in line with one's own sense of self and control over one's own actions and behaviours.

All three of these needs require satisfaction in order to maintain positive psychological well-being. Individual fluctuation comes into play in SDT through the extent to which individuals seek to satisfy their needs with these three needs providing the link between the opportunities offered by a social world and individual tendencies to further develop, maintain, and protect psychological well-being and sense of self. In particular, Deci and Ryan (2000) identify three social contexts that support these three basic human needs (for a fuller outline, see Deci & Ryan, 2000):

- The maintenance or enhancement of intrinsic motivation.
- The facilitation, internalization, and integration of extrinsic motivation to provide a more autonomous motivated and regulated orientation of behaviour.
- The promotion or strengthening of aspirations or life goals that continuously provide satisfaction of the basic human needs.

Accordingly, the notions of extrinsic and intrinsic motivation also play a role in how people attain behavioural outcomes. Motivation that comes from within the individual (*intrinsic motivation*) is more likely to afford positive behavioural outcomes and affective experiences, along with a more positive mental health, whereas extrinsically motivated activities are more likely to evoke frustration, less of a positive experience and diminished psychological well-being. Deci and Ryan's *organismic-dialectical principle* suggests that overt behaviour is a result of the optimization of motivations, and both internal and external resources to attain a desired goal to meet the individual's needs, a principle that fits with our theme of this chapter of people using the Internet to meet their own desires and needs in a goal-directed manner. From this perspective, the notion of the Internet as an external resource that people can use in any way, shape or form that they need to in order to attain a desired behavioural goal offers an ideal formulation that opposes the notion of the Internet being an age-related playground. Indeed, it is this notion of the Internet as a *tool* that provides the final argument of this chapter against the existence of a digital generation.

3.11 The Internet 'tool'

There has been a long-standing debate in almost all areas of psychology as to whether human behaviour is a product of nature or nurture. The viewpoint that humans are a product of their environment is the premise of a number of social psychological theories, most notably *social learning theory* (**SLT**) (Bandura, Ross, & Ross, 1961, Bandura, 1977). According to SLT, people mimic and model behaviours through either direct or indirect learning. This theory came into being shortly after some classic research by Berkowitz and LePage (1967) created a turning point in social psychology. Berkowitz and LePage carried out a series of studies that demonstrated that individual behaviour is very much influenced by social cues, by items, objects, and events happening in the social environment or situation in which a person finds him or herself. Their participants expressed higher levels of feeling aggressive when completing a task in the presence of a gun compared to the presence of some sports equipment. These findings along with SLT very much suggest that individuals not only learn how to behave from their surroundings, but that their actions are likely a product of that learning and interactions with the available social cues, items, objects, and people around them. To illustrate, let's take the example of an individual who wants to buy a new television. If that person lives within a sensible distance of a shop that sells electrical goods, s/he may simply go to the shop and purchase said television. The shop in this instance acts as the environment, the *tool* if you like, that facilitates and makes the purchase possible. If, however, the person has no urgent need for the television, and wants to get the best financial deal possible, s/he might spend some time browsing the Internet to find the best price for the television. In this instance, the Internet is the tool that facilitates the purchase. Neither the shop nor the Internet *makes* the person buy any given television. They both serve as tools in this example. When carrying out any act online, the Internet might thus be considered to be the tool (or one of a number of tools) used to complete a desired behavioural goal, especially if we consider the notions of SDT and SLT in conjunction with one another. According to SDT, competence, relatedness, and autonomy are the human needs that guide behaviour. These are either intrinsically or extrinsically motivated. Social learning theory would suggest that how either intrinsic or extrinsic motivation is acted upon is a socially learned behaviour. If a person has learned to act more in line with their intrinsic motivations to meet their psychological needs, then they might be more likely to achieve a fulfilled and positive behavioural goal. These proposals are also linked to a further social psychological phenomenon, namely of an individual's basic self-concept consisting of their *actual*, *ideal*, and *ought* selves (see Chapter 2). If a person is happy and content with their actual self, they will experience less psychological discomfort than when there is a cleft between their actual and ideal, or between their actual and ought selves. If they are acting mainly upon extrinsic motivation, it could be the case that they are not behaving in line with their actual self at all, but performing entirely as an ought self. This ought-self behaviour could be the result of a lengthy social learning process that has led the individual to present themselves in this manner. It is highly unlikely, then, that this behaviour would be an artefact of the age of the actor, but rather would be a product of their learned behavioural patterns and the desired behavioural outcomes.

3.12 Age-related or goal-directed behaviours?

Exploring the whys and wherefores as to why a person behaves as they do on the Internet is dealt with in many of the other chapters of this text. For the purpose of drawing the thoughts of the current chapter together, let us now take a closer look at a couple of human behaviours in relation to these considerations. First, consider SDT's notion of relatedness and Baumeister and Leary's notion of belongingness. If all humans have a need to feel connected to others in a manner that creates a sense of belonging, then it stands to reason that people actively seek out a partner with whom to create that special bond. That is, their *actual self* might be one of a single person, but their *ideal self* would be romantically connected to another individual. There would thus be a discrepancy between their actual and ideal selves. The desire to reduce this discrepancy and meet their relatedness need might primarily be driven by their intrinsic motivations to reduce a psychological sense of loneliness. It might, however, also be driven by an extrinsic motivation to feel less stigmatized as a single lonely person, and to gain social acceptance and approval. In order to do so, SLT would have us believe that they will adopt learned behaviours to meet a desired other. Whether they instigate this partner-seeking behaviour in their online or offline world (or both) could then be a product of their socially learned behavioural repertoire. If they attend lots of social events, are constantly surrounded by potential romantic partners, or if they simply have ample opportunity to meet someone offline, then this is how they will most likely go about finding a new romantic partner. This might well be the case, for example, for university students. However, what if such opportunities do not present themselves to someone, or if they have had no success trying to find a new partner offline? Such individuals might think it more advantageous to take their search online. These behaviours might be less likely driven by the age of the romance seeker, but more by their learned behaviours, motivations, needs, and behavioural goals!

3.13 **Chapter summary**

- This chapter has explored two main notions, one of a digital generation that is the primary user of the Internet and the second of the Internet as being equally used by people of all ages in a goal-directed, needs, and/or motivated manner.

- Two main theories, uses and gratification theory, and flow theory have been outlined to ascertain whether people of all ages use the Internet differently according to the environment in which Internet use takes place.

- The Internet has been presented as a heterogeneous tool, with people using different types of website for different activities. The conclusion from this notion is that we should not be looking for one theory that can account for *all* types of online behaviour. Rather, we need specific theories for specific types of online activity, just as different theories are used to understand different aspects and types of offline human behaviours.

- Extrinsic and intrinsic motivations have been explored from both a social learning theory and self-determination theory perspective to highlight the Internet as nothing other than a tool that people use to meet their own desires, wants, and needs.

- The over-riding theme of this chapter has been to present a debate that falls on the side of the Internet being used by individuals of all ages in a way that meets their own motivations and needs. This would suggest that there no longer exists a digital generation per se, but that older people may be more reluctant to use the Internet outside of the digitally able comfort zone.

- The conclusion of this chapter is therefore that young and old alike use the Internet according to current goals, needs, and motivations.

 **References**

Akman, I. & Mishra, A. (2010). Gender, age and income differences in internet usage among employees in organizations. *Computers in Human Behavior*, 26, 482–490.

Akman, I., Yazici, A., Arifoglu A., & Mishra, A. (2005). e-Gov: A Global Perspective and an empirical assessment of citizens' attributes. *Government Information Quarterly*, 22 (2), 239–257.

Attrill, A. & Jalil, R. (2011). Revealing only the superficial me: Exploring categorical self-disclosure online. *Computers in Human Behavior*, 27, 1634–1642.

Bandura, A. (1977). *Social Learning Theory*. Englewood Cliffs, NJ: Prentice Hall.

Bandura, A., Ross, R., & Ross, S. (1961). Transmission of aggression through imitation of aggressive models. *Journal of Abnormal and Social Psychology*, 63, 575–582.

Bargh, J.A. & McKenna, K.Y.A. (2004). The Internet and social life. *Annual Review of Psychology*, 55, 573–590.

Baumeister, R.F. & Leary, M.R. (1995). The need to belong: desire for interpersonal attachments as a fundamental human motivation. *Psychological Bulletin*, 117(3), 497–529.

Berkowitz, L. & LePage, A. (1967). Weapons as aggression-eliciting stimuli. *Journal of Personality and Social Psychology*, 7, 202–207.

Blumler, J.G. & Katz, E. (1974). *The Uses of Mass Communication*. Thousand Oaks, CA: Sage.

Bowlby, J. (1969). *Attachment and Loss: Vol. 1. Attachment*. New York: Basic Books.

Bowlby, J. (1973). *Attachment and Loss: Vol. 2. Separation Anxiety and Anger*. New York: Basic Books.

Boyd, D. (2008). Why youth (heart) social network sites: The role of networked publics in teenage social life. In Buckingham, D. (Ed.), *Youth, Identity, and Digital Media*. Cambridge, MA: The MIT Press.

Carenini, G. (2001). An analysis of the influence of need for cognition on dynamic queries usage. *Ext. Abstracts CHI2001, Seattle*: ACM Press, 383–384.

Carpenter, B.D. & Buday, S. (2007). Computer use among older adults in a naturally occurring retirement community. *Computers in Human Behavior*, 23, 3012–3024.

Chiang, I-P., Chiang, Y-H., & Lin, Y-C.L. (2013). The antecedents and consequences of blogging behaviour. *Social Behavior and Personality*, 41(2), 311–318.

Cothey, V. (2002). A longitudinal study of world wide web users' information-searching behaviour. *Journal of the American Society for Information Science and Technology*, 3(2), 67–78.

Csikszentmihalyi, M. (1975). *Beyond Boredom and Anxiety*. San Francisco: Jossey-Bass.

Csikszentmihalyi, M. (1990). *Flow: The Psychology of Optimal Experience*. New York: Harper & Row.

Cumming, E. & Henry, W.E. (1961). *Growing Old, the Process of Disengagement*. New York: Basic Books.

Deci, E.L. & Ryan, R.M. (2000). The 'what' and 'why' of goal pursuits: Human needs and the self-determination of behaviour. *Psychological Inquiry*, 11(4), 227–268.

Dweck, C.S. (1986). Motivational processes affecting learning. *American Psychologist*, 41, 1040–1048.

Eastin, M.S. & LaRose, R. (2000). Internet self-efficacy and the psychology of the digital divide. *Journal of Computer Mediated Communication*, 6l (1), Available at http://onlinelibrary.wiley.com/doi/10.1111/j.1083-6101.2000.tb00110.x/full. (accessed 15th September, 2014).

Ellison, N., Steinfeld, C., & Lampe, C. (2007). The benefits of Facebook 'friends': Exploring the relationship between college students' use of online social networks and social capital. *Journal of Computer-Mediated Communication*, 12(4), 1143–1168.

Fischer, C. (1992). *America Calling: A Social History of the Telephone to 1940*. Berkeley: University California Press.

Fox, S., Rainie, L., Larsen, E., Horrigan, J., Lenhart, A., Spooner, T., et al. (2001). Wired Seniors: A fervent few, inspired by family ties. A report from Pew Internet and American Life Project. Retrieved 20 May 2008, available from http://www.pewinternet.org/2001/09/09/wired-seniors/ (accessed 5th September 2014).

Gangadharbatla, H. (2008). Facebook Me: Collective self-esteem, need to belong, and Internet self-efficacy as predictors of the iGeneration's attitudes toward social networking sites. *Journal of Interactive Advertising*, 8(2), 5–15.

Hargittai, E. (2004). Internet access and use in context. *New Media and Society*, 6(1), 137–143.

Hempel, J. & Lehman, P. (2005). The MySpace generation, *BusinessWeek* (12 December), at http://www.businessweek.com/ (accessed 12th July 2011).

Hills, P. & Argyle, M. (2003). Uses of the Internet and their relationships with individual differences in personality. *Computers in Human Behavior*, 19, 59–70.

Hoffman, D. & Novak, P.T. (1997). A new marketing paradigm for electronic commerce. *Information Society; Special Issues on Electronic Commerce*, 13, 43–54.

Houston, T.K., Cooper, S., & Ford, D.E. (2002). Internet support groups for depression: a 1-year prospective cohort study. *American Journal of Psychiatry*, 159, 2062–2068.

Howard, P., Rainie, L., & Jones, S. (2001). Days and nights on the Internet: the impact of diffusing technology. *American Behavioral Scientist*, 45, 450–472.

Hughes, D.R. (2006). Recent statistics on internet dangers. Available from: http://www.protectkids.com/dangers/stats.htm. (accessed 15th September, 2014).

Hughes, R., Jr. & Hans, J.D. (2001). Computers, the internet, and families: a review of the role new technology plays in family life. *Journal of Family Issues*, 22, 778–792.

Jaeger, P. & Xie, B. (2009). Developing online community accessibility guidelines for persons with disabilities and older adults. *Journal of Disability Policy Studies*, 20 (1), 55–63.

Jones, S. & Fox, S. (2009). *Generations Online in 2009*. New York:Pew Internet & American Life Project.

Kaare, B.H., Brandtzaeg, P.B., Endestad, T., & Heim, J. (2007). In the borderland between family orientation and peer-culture: The use of communication technologies among Norwegian tweens. *New Media & Society*, 9(4), 603–624.

Karahasanovic, A., Brandtzaeg, J.H., Heim, J., Lüders, M., Vermeir, L., Pierson, J., Lievens, B., Vanattenhoven, J., & Jans, G. (2009). *Computers in Human Behavior*, 25(3), 655–678.

Kiel, J.M. (2005). The digital divide: Internet and e-mail use by the elderly. *Medical Informatics and the Internet in Medicine*, 30, 19–23.

Kim, B. & Omizo, M.M. (2005). Asian and European American cultural values, collective self-esteem, acculturative stress, cognitive flexibility, and general self-efficacy among Asian American college students. *Journal of Counseling Psychology*, 52(3), 412–419.

Klobas, J.E. & Clyde, L.A. (2000). Adults learning to use the Internet: a longitudinal study of attitudes and other factors associated with

Internet use. *Library and Information Science Research*, 22, 5–34.

Knobloch, S. (2003). Mood adjustment via mass communication. *Journal of Communication*, 53, 233–150.

Koyuncu, C. & Lien, D. (2003). E-commerce and consumer's purchasing behaviour. *Applied Economics*, 35(6), 721–726.

Kvasny, L. (2006). Social reproduction and its applicability for community informatics. In *Proceedings of Journal of Community Informatics, 2006*.

Leung, L. (2007). Stressful life events, motives for Internet use, and social support among digital kids. *Cyberpsychology & Behavior*, 10(2), 204–214.

Lewin, K. (1936). *Principles of Topological Psychology*. New York: McGraw-Hill.

Livingstone, S., Van Couvering, E. & Thumim, N. (2005). *Adult media literacy. A review of the research literature*. Available from http://www.ofcom.org.uk/ (accessed 5th September, 2014).

Martin, S.P. & Robinson, J.P. (2007). The income digital divide: Trends and predictions for levels of Internet use. *Social Problems*, 54(1), 1–22.

Maslow, A.H. (1968). *Toward a Psychology of Being*. New York: Van Nostrand.

Nicholls, J.G. (1984). Achievement motivation: Conceptions of ability, subjective experience, task choice, and performance. *Psychological Review*, 91, 328–346.

Nithya, H.M. & Julius, S. (2007). Extroversion, neuroticism and self-concept. Their impact on internet users in India. *Computers in Human Behavior*, 23, 1322–1328.

Novak, T.P., Hoffman, D.L., & Duhachek, A. (2003). The influence of goal-directed and experiential activities on online flow experiences. *Journal of Consumer Psychology*, 13(1 & 2), 3–16.

Oblinger, D.G. & Oblinger, J.L. (2005). Educating the net generation, an Educase-e-book publication. Available at http://www.educause.edu/ir/library/pdf/pub7101.pdf (accessed 1 September 2014).

Pfeil, U., Arjan, R., & Zaphiris, P. (2009). Age differences in online social networking—A study of user profiles and the social capital divide among teenagers and older users in MySpace. *Computers in Human Behavior*, 25, 643–654.

Potosky, D. (2007). The Internet knowledge (iKnow) measure. *Computers in Human Behavior*, 23, 2760–2777.

Prensky, M. (2001a). *Digital Natives, Digital Immigrants. On the Horizon.* NCB University Press, Vol. 9(5).

Prensky, M. (2001b). *Digital Natives, Digital Immigrants Part II: Do They Really Think Differently? On the Horizon.* NCB University Press, Vol. 9(6).

Rai, R. & Attrill, A. (2014). The effects of synchronous and asynchronous internet communication, personality, and representations of the self on the uptake of online video communication. *Poster presented at the 16th International Conference on Human Computer Interaction*, Crete, June 2014.

Schofield-Clark, L. (2009). Digital media and the generation gap. *Information, Communication & Society*, 12(3), 388–407.

Seniors Online (2004). *Seniors online increase* article. Available from Senior Citizens Online web site: http://www.seniorjournal.com (accessed 15th September, 2014).

Spears, R., Postmes, T., Lea, M., & Wolbert, A. (2002). When are net effects gross products? The power of influence and the influence of power in computer-mediated communication. *Journal of Social Issues*, 58(1), 91–107.

Sternberg, R.J. (1986). A triangular theory of love. *Psychological Review*, 93, 119–135.

Tajfel, H. & Turner, J.C. (1986). The social identity theory of intergroup behavior. In Worchel, S. & Austin, W. (Eds), *Psychology of Intergroup Relations* (pp. 7–24). Chicago: Nelson-Hall.

Tapscott, D. (1998). *Growing up Digital: The Rise of the Net Generation.* New York: McGraw-Hill.

Thayer, S.E. & Ray, S. (2006). Online communication preferences across age, gender and duration of Internet use. *Cyberpsychology & Behavior*, 9(4), 432–440.

Tolman, E.C. (1932). *Purposive Behavior in Animals and Men.* New York: Century.

Wan, C.-S. & Chiou, W.-B. (2006). Psychological motives and online games addiction: A test of flow theory and humanistic needs theory for Taiwanese adolescents. *Cyberpsychology & Behavior*, 9(3), 317–324.

Weiser, E. (2000). Gender differences in Internet use patterns and Internet application preferences: a two-sample comparison. *Cyberpsychology & Behavior*, 4, 167–178.

Wikipedia (2014). Available at: http://en.wikipedia.org/wiki/Ivy_Bean.

Yu, S.-C. & Chou, C. (2009). Does authentic happiness exist in cyberspace? Implications for understanding and guiding college students' Internet attitudes and behaviours. *British Journal of Educational Technology*, 40(6), 1135–1138.

Zhang, Y. (1996). Responses to humorous advertising: The moderating effect of need for cognition. *Journal of Advertising*, 25(1), 15–18.

Zhang, Y. (2005). Age, gender, and Internet attitudes among employees in the business world. *Computers in Human Behavior*, 21, 1–10.

Zillman, D. (1982). Television viewing and arousal. In Pearl, D., Bouthilet, L., & Lazar, J. (Eds), *Television and Behaviour: Ten Years of Scientific Progress and Implications for the Eighties*, Vol. 2, *Technical Reviews* (pp. 53–67). Washington, DC: Government Printing Office.

Zillman, D. & Bryant, J. (1985). Affect, mood, and emotion as determinants of selective media exposure. In Zillmann, D. & Bryant, J. (Eds), *Selective Exposure to Communication* (pp. 157–190). Hillsdale, NJ: Lawrence Erlbaum.

 Further reading

Tapscott, D. (2009). *Grown Up Digital*. McGraw Hill.
This book offers an overview of the digital generation debate up until 2009.

Buckingham, D. & Willett, R. (2006). *Digital Generations: Children, Young People, and the New Media*. Routledge.
A further book that offers an excellent debate around the existence of a digital generation and considers the influence of mass media on young people.

There are two core papers to understanding *Social Learning Theory*. Reading these, you might not initially make the link between social learning and Internet use. However, if you get to grips with social learning theory, it will help you understand how the Internet is used as a tool to shape our behaviour:
Bandura, A. (1977). *Social Learning Theory*. Englewood Cliffs, NJ: Prentice Hall.

Bandura, A., Ross, R., & Ross, S. (1961). Transmission of aggression through imitation of aggressive models. *Journal of Abnormal and Social Psychology*, 63, 575–582.

Another theory that is pivotal to understanding the proposals made by this chapter is that of *uses and gratification*. The original paper for this theory is:

Blumler, J.G. & Katz, E. (1974). *The Uses of Mass Communication*. Thousand Oaks, CA: Sage.

Finally, in order to enhance your understanding of how humans are *motivated* to meet their *humanistic goals*, read the following two papers:

Baumeister, R.F. & Leary, M.R. (1995). The need to belong: desire for interpersonal attachments as a fundamental human motivation. *Psychological Bulletin*, 117(3), 497–529.
Maslow, A.H. (1968). *Toward a Psychology of Being*. New York: Van Nostrand.

 ## Discussion questions

1. Critically consider whether online behaviour is age related.
2. Outline and assess possible differences in different types of online behaviours.
3. Why is it important to consider the Internet as an amalgamation of different types of goal directed behaviours?
4. Why is it important to consider social identity and self-determination theories in conjunction to explain online behaviours?
5. Outline and critically consider the theoretical standpoints made in this chapter.

4 Online Relationships

JOHANNA MYDDLETON & ALISON ATTRILL

 Learning objectives

After reading this chapter, we hope you will be able to:

- Identify the different types of online relationships, their characteristics, and how these might make different use of CMC.
- Outline a number of key theories that can be used to explain relationship formation online, including aspects that relate to initial attraction online.
- Consider the nature of friendships online and how they may or may not be considered less 'real' than offline friendships.
- Discuss the nature of propinquity and homophily and how these play a role in relationships online.
- Consider how online relationships may benefit or alternatively be detrimental to different individuals.

4.1 Introduction

The term 'relationship' can refer to many varied and diverse associations that individuals have with either single or multiple others. Consider for a moment your own relationships: you may have a wife, husband, partner, girlfriend, boyfriend, best friend, brother, sister, aunt, uncle, grandparents, work colleagues, sports club acquaintances, teachers, university friends, drinking buddies, gaming acquaintances . . . this list could go on and on! Not all of these ties or associations will be of equal strength, closeness, or value to you, but they all serve some purpose in your life. Prior to the advent of the Internet, relationships were less complicated! Or were they? People may have had a handful of friendships to maintain along with a direct and extended family. Nowadays, they have hundreds if not thousands of 'friends' on social networking sites, can use Internet dating sites like a catalogue to find a new romantic liaison, and even have relationships that are entirely formed and maintained online, with no intention of ever moving them to their offline worlds. This chapter will explore some of the prominent theories and research around the formation, maintenance and possible dissolution of different types of relationship in the online world. In doing so, it will need to explore some of the existing offline work that has led to formulations for understanding relationships online. When you hear the term 'online relationship' we suspect that you immediately think of online dating. This is not uncommon, and provides us with a sensible starting point for our foray into understanding current online relationship research.

4.1.1 **Early online dating research**

One of the main focuses of early online relationship research was on the notion of romantic connections online. Particularly, initial research focused on specific online dating sites and the ways in which people created both representations and misrepresentations of themselves online. Under this umbrella heading of 'online relationships', there was also a focus on the dangers of meeting potential partners online, including identity theft, relationship scams, in which vulnerable people are deceived and manipulated, often into sending money to people they believe to have formed an intimate relationship with, as well as grooming, stalking, harassment, and more sinister aspects of dating online. Whilst it can be tempting, even curious, to focus solely on the negative aspects of this area we must remember that these instances of deception and fraud are relatively low in comparison to the millions of adults worldwide who have turned to the Internet to seek relationships in all shapes and forms, often with relatively positive outcomes.

4.1.2 **Current online dating research**

Individuals may use online dating sites and applications to actively seek romantic partners with the instrumental goal of moving that relationship from online to offline in the near future. This process is becoming increasingly sociably acceptable and occurring more frequently in developed countries (Dutton et al., 2009). There has been some debate as to whether this is a more streamlined process that better fits modern, busy lifestyles or whether it is a risky arena in which people are often not what they seem. The media would have us believe the latter whilst research suggests that those using dating sites are conscious of the potential consequences of lying to partners online and the toll this could take on the impending offline meeting (Ellison, Heino, & Gibbs, 2006). Whilst this area is of great interest to psychologists and the general population alike, it must also be noted that only around a third of romantic relationships formed online develop from the use of dating sites (Baker, 2005). More friendships than romantic connections are formed online, with some being sustained entirely online, wholly without expectation of offline encounters between the communicating friends or lovers (Baker, 2008). As will be discussed later in this chapter, a multitude of online arenas and communication media vary greatly in many aspects and functions that could influence the way in which people behave in these arenas. As such it may seem obvious that the cyberspace in which people meet and interact may also shape the way their relationships develop both on and offline, which is why we now turn our attention to platonic relationships online.

4.2 Are all online relationships the same?

As well as romantic relationships it is important to consider the role of platonic relationships conducted via the Internet. Whilst in adulthood our romantic partner may be seen to most closely influence our attitudes and decisions, close friends also shape our identity and activities. Platonic relationships are thus defined as friendships or acquaintances with whom we have non-romantic relationships. In terms of computer-mediated communication (**CMC**) it might be intuitive to think that we have more communication with platonic friends than romantic partners online. It therefore becomes essential to consider the role that these friendships play, both online and offline, in peoples' lives. Considering non-romantic relationships is particularly important if we think about the amount of time we spend with friends online rather than with romantic partners. But why are friendships so important to human beings? And why do we seek out their creation and maintenance via the Internet? Friendships are well known to be a vital component contributing to child, adolescent, and adult well-being (Newcomb & Bagwell, 1995). Friends can make us feel good, share time and experiences with us, help us construct happy memories (and sometimes not so happy ones!), offer advice and support, and often keep us from feeling lonely. Being part of offline social groups helps shape our personal identity and can influence our attitudes, behaviours, and even the way in which we create an external identity. Moreover, friendships in childhood and adolescence are thought to pave the way through exploration for more intimate relationships entered into in adulthood (Bagwell, Schmidt, Newcomb, & Bukowski, 2001). If we ponder this outline for a second, it seems to describe mainly those types of 'friendships' that an older generation is used to experiencing in an offline world. Who are your online friends? Do they fulfil these criteria? Maybe they meet these criteria better than do your offline friends. However, with the advent of new technologies and the nature of online relationship formation and maintenance constantly changing without consideration of age, race, creed, social status, or gender, recent research has questioned the concept of friendship, and indeed the very meaning of the word 'friend' (Amichai-Hamburger, Kingsbury, & Schneider, 2013). Perceptions of online friendship currently seem to fall into one of three categories: those who believe online friendships simply cannot exist, those who believe online and offline friendships are equal and simply conducted via different media, and those who suggest online and offline friendships to be qualitatively different in some way. The remainder of this chapter will address various notions of the existence of online relationships, including relevant theories and research pertaining to romantic, friendship, and **familial relationships** as distinct from and an extension of offline relationships.

4.3 How real are online friends?

Friendship in the past has been defined as comprising three main components: mutual esteem or simply liking one another, a willingness to help one another, and participation in shared activities (Briggle, 2008). Cocking and Mathews (2000) suggested that given the absence of a shared physical space online, friendships conducted solely online cannot fulfil these set parameters for classification as true friendship. They further suggest that there are additional barriers to friendships conducted solely online that are too great to overcome. For instance, an essential part of friendship is the shaping of each member of the relationship through mutual interpretation and feedback. This process is supported by involuntary self-disclosures that do not occur online. Offline, involuntary self-disclosures are aspects of the self that are conveyed in non-direct language. These could include tone of voice or facial expressions that occur unconsciously and give clues as to our true feelings about the topic under discussion. Online, there are two types of involuntary self-disclosures, those that are similar to offline cues and those that represent individual or personal information required to complete an online interaction (see Attrill, 2012b for a fuller discussion). Of concern here are the former types of involuntary self-disclosures. Some researchers would have us believe that all self-disclosures online are carefully considered and that when constructing a version of the self online, we are more likely to present our *ideal* self rather than our **actual** or **ought selves** (for a fuller discussion of the different selves, see Chapter 2). Of importance here is that the ideal self is the person we would most like to be, our perfect self if you like; the person we would be most happy being. If you are a regular poster to a social networking site such as Facebook, consider how you make status updates. You might write a sentence, read it, edit it, think about it a little bit more, and then after some further editing post it. This would be a carefully crafted update to reflect your 'self' at that particular moment in time. Now consider interactions in your offline world. If you want to provide a carefully considered response to a question, you might take a moment to think of that response. However, whilst doing so, your body language, your facial expression, and the final intonation of your reply will convey more than just the actual words spoken. Some researchers believe that these involuntary self-disclosures, which are seen as vital in friendship formation, maintenance, and even dissolution, simply do not occur online. If this is the case, it would suggest that neither can truly intimate friendships. On the other hand, it could be for these very same reasons that the Internet may provide an arena for true and strong friendships.

In the offline world self-presentation occurs for a number of reasons. An abundance of social norms are linked to a desire to be liked. In turn, this desire can be a dictating force in how we choose to behave and the self-image we portray to others. The reaction to this portrayal is instant in our immediate offline interactions. Of course, there are instances where this feedback is not immediate. Imagine, for instance, a first date, after which you anxiously wait to see if the person rings, texts, Facebooks, instant messages, video calls (oh dear, the list is endless!) you back. Although this would count as delayed feedback, it would also be based on how you had carried yourself during the date, your movements, voice, facial expressions, and so on. You may also have had more inhibitions about the information that you revealed on the date because the person was in your direct physical space. If you were initially communicating with that person online, the distance afforded by CMC may have actually lowered these inhibitions due to a perceived lesser fear of social rejection. During CMC, we might often be prone to being more honest expressions of our *true* self. This in turn could lead to stronger, deeper, and more 'real' friendships than those offline, given that you would be exchanging more personal and intimate information with your online communications partner(s) (Briggle, 2008). Research to support this suggestion comes from Bargh, McKenna, and Fitzimons (2002) who found that people who felt better able to express their true selves online were not only more likely to form friendships online but were also more likely to successfully transfer these friendships offline, which in turn showed high levels of stability and durability over a two-year period. Further research has also indicated that people can relatively accurately assess others' characteristics and personality traits through written medium alone based on relatively low levels of direct self-disclosure. This suggests that involuntary self-disclosures do also occur online and that communication partners can interpret these in a way that mimics the offline interaction and feedback processes that have been proposed to be an essential component of shaping both offline and online friendships (Cocking & Mathews, 2000). Moreover, research has also indicated that **behavioural confirmation** can occur via communication tools such as the telephone, instant messaging systems, and online games (Snyder, Tanke, & Berscheid, 1977, Yee & Bailenson, 2007). Behavioural confirmation is the process through which one's interpretation or expectation of another person influences the way in which we interact with them. This, in turn, influences the respondent's behaviour and so a process of continual shaping of one another's actions and reactions occurs (Snyder et al., 1977). Behavioural confirmation has been demonstrated in CMC and has also been shown to influence the individual's own perception of themselves at a later date (Gonzales & Hancock, 2008). For instance, those who were asked to present themselves as extroverts in a public format online were seen to have increased extroversion scores at a later date. Equally, those who were asked to act more introverted in an online interaction with others rated themselves as more introverted at a following time, showing an identity shift. It would thus appear that not only are online friendships 'real friendships', but that these can also be pivotal in shaping both individual characteristics and self-concepts as well as offline friendships.

In addition, let's briefly consider the notion of shared activity online in shaping platonic online relationships. The Internet offers the opportunity for social interaction on a hitherto unseen scale, from collaborative online gaming, large scale discussions of mutual interests, one-on-one and multiple other video conversations, as well as the organization of offline activities, to name but a few, all occur in a shared online space. It would appear, then, that the Internet *can* provide a virtual space that although not enabling direct physical contact, can at least mimic our offline physical spaces. As such, it offers itself as a tool for conducting shared activity that overcomes boundaries of geographical distance. Boundaries that, prior to the Internet, would have hindered the formation and maintenance of many an offline or long distance friendship!

It would thus appear that although the space and conditions of creating online friendships might differ in some aspects, it might be timely to reconsider traditional definitions of the words 'friends' and 'friendships' to encompass bonds forged through exchanges via CMC. Communicating via the Internet offers more time to reflect, contemplate the self, and the relationship that is being communicated. It provides a positive arena for enhanced mutual revelations, bonding, sharing, and understanding. Consequently, CMC can be seen to support online-only friendships, as well as helping to maintain our offline ties, bonds, and friendships. This rosy picture we paint of making real friends online is, however, somewhat tainted by theorizing and research that has demonstrated a negative impact of online bonds on offline relationships. We will now turn to considering this in the form of the displacement and stimulation hypotheses.

4.4 The dark and light of online friendships

The *displacement hypothesis* speculates that online communications have a negative impact on current offline friendships, partly because the time previously spent socializing and interacting offline is now displaced and spent on online activities. This supposedly reduces the quality of offline friendships (Valkenburg & Peter, 2011). A number of side effects have been proposed to be linked to this communications displacement, including increased incidences of negative psychological effects such as loneliness and depression. Whilst early research did indeed suggest that frequent use of the Internet was related to heightened levels of loneliness (Kraut et al., 1998), more recent research does not seem to substantiate claims of a causal relationship between Internet use and loneliness. Not only did Kraut et al. (2002)

subsequently qualify their initial suggestions based on further exploration of their initial findings, but Mesch (2001) found loneliness to be a trait that caused individuals to more frequently and actively seek out online friendships over offline. Mesch found that adolescents who had fewer close ties and friends offline were more likely to be frequent Internet users. In addition to loneliness predicting increased online activity, individuals who display both social anxiety and loneliness have been shown to actually prefer communicating via CMC. Valkenburg and Peter (2011) carried out a study amongst adolescents, which demonstrated that text-messaging, instant messenger, and other forms of CMC were perceived to be less 'risky' due to improved levels of control, anonymity, and asynchronicity than immediate face-to-face communications. That is not to say that these individuals necessarily experience increased numbers of online friendships, a notion that in and of itself raises the question of how many friendships are 'enough friendships'? Considering the displacement hypothesis alone does not provide an answer to this question. Indeed, no currently published hypothesis provides an answer to this question as type, duration, intimacy, length, and time of communication, to name but a few factors affecting friendships, are all extremely subjective factors. We can, however, further explore evidence that appears to contradict the displacement hypothesis.

The **stimulation hypothesis** suggests that time spent communicating with friends through CMC can enhance the quality of those friendships and have a positive effect on well-being (Valkenburg & Peter, 2011). Valkenburg and Peter (2007) found support for the stimulation rather than the displacement hypothesis. Their study of over 1,200 Dutch teenagers found a mediating relationship between time spent with existing friends and quality of the relationships on the adolescents' well-being. There was, however, a mode of communication difference, with instant messaging programs increasing well-being whilst more public forums used for communicating with strangers failed to impact upon their well-being. The stimulation hypothesis can also be seen as theoretically linked to the '**rich get richer**' perspective on Internet communication, which suggests that those who are more socially adept and better skilled at forming and maintaining friendships will forge more and stronger bonds online than those who are socially 'poor' (Kraut et al., 2002). This notion was supported empirically by Kraut and colleagues who found that individuals who used the Internet more frequently also spent more time in face-to-face (FtF) interactions with family and friends and expanded both their local and distant social circles.

It has been suggested that time communicating online can actually strengthen existing offline bonds between friends, and subsequently lead to more telephone and face-to-face interactions (Kraut et al., 2002). Equally, those who are chronically shy or socially anxious may feel a reduced sense of anxiety and reduced inhibition whilst using CMC compared to FtF interactions, due to an increased sense of control and preparation. Could it be possible, however, that the deficit in social communication skills may be too great to overcome and may limit these individuals' ability to meet and forge new relationships even online? Research suggests that those who communicated more frequently with strangers than offline friends did not receive the same positive benefits and whilst those shy individuals with few friends found it easier to self-disclose intimate information online that strengthened their current friendships. In other words, they were not able to expand their social circle via CMC (Birnie & Horvarth, 2002). This seems to suggest that the deficit may not be completely overcome through use of CMC, however, the debate as to whether the 'rich get richer' online or whether individuals can compensate for offline deficits online, known as the **social compensation** hypothesis, is ongoing (see Lee, 2009 for an overview).

4.5 Social capital and social networks

It has also been suggested that particular online arenas such as social networking sites (**SNSs**) can actually offer unique opportunities to strengthen weak offline bonds and increase **social capital**. Social capital has been defined as the resources gained via any type of relationship existing between individuals (Coleman, 1988). These resources are not necessarily of a physical or monetary value, but can also be psychologically important. For instance, an individual rich in social capital will likely feel fulfilled and wanted in their social existence. They will feel that they 'belong' (Baumeister & Leary, 1995) and are valid members of their social communities. It is unsurprising then, that increased social capital has been shown to have a positive impact on behaviours such as community involvement (Kavanaugh, Carroll, Rosson, Zin, & Reese, 2005). Social capital can be gained via both offline and online resources. How the individual seeks out any particular resource will most likely depend on the form and function of the type of relationship(s) that are to be strengthened. Social capital has been linked to social cohesion, improved community involvement, and decreased social disorder (Kavanaugh et al., 2005). Higher levels of social capital between friends and neighbours have also been linked to psychological well-being, including higher self-esteem, and general satisfaction with life (Bargh & McKenna, 2004, Helliwell & Putnam, 2004). It may follow from this outline that we could expect those individuals who feel unable to seek out social capital offline, may use the Internet as a compensatory mechanism or tool for enhancing this component of their life. In order to further consider this proposition, we need to ascertain whether different types of social capital as defined by Granovetter (1982) fulfil different functions that can be met both online and offline:

- **Bridging social capital** occurs with loosely connected individuals. These are the weak ties or associations with others who may not be overly significant to our offline lives.
- **Bonding social capital** stems from the strong ties that we share with close, intimate others.

Bridging social capital might include gaining access to additional information or various viewpoints whereas bonding social capital would provide support that we would only request from those to whom we feel closely connected. Given that social capital greatly affects our ability to complete tasks and reach goals in everyday life, it is feasible to suggest that it plays a large role in our online relationships. Moreover, it is not unrealistic to suppose that offline behaviour may be influenced by social capital gained online. This proposition is indeed supported by research that found that those local communities that were supported by online networks showed an increase in community interaction, involvement, and levels of social capital (Kavanaugh et al., 2005). This could indicate that offline social capital can be enhanced by spending more time on the Internet than out in the physical local community (Ellison, Steinfield, & Lampe, 2007). But where do people go online to find this social capital? One type of online arena where individuals can interact to increase social capital is social networking sites.

Social networks such as Facebook can be seen as the ideal environment for strengthening weak ties and therefore increasing social capital as well as facilitating the ability to maintain a larger number of weak ties than could ever be possible offline. Some might argue that online relationships require fewer cognitive and time restricting resources than do offline relationships, though see Chapter 13 for a consideration of the cognitive processes involved in online behaviour. Nonetheless, consider for example the posting of a status update that reaches many contacts at once. How could the same effect be achieved offline? Online, one click of a button enables you to communicate with many friends and acquaintances at once, regardless of the time and location within which they exist. All of these people can be approached simultaneously with requests for resources in a fairly short period of time, especially when utilizing functions such as the 'share now' feature that allows messages to be shared instantaneously across different networks with relative ease. The question that arises is whether we should consider this to be bridging or bonding social capital. Social networks can help provide the individual with a wide range of diffuse resources. Whilst Facebook in particular is overwhelmingly used to maintain and intensify offline relationships, it does offer the opportunity to easily connect with 'friends of friends' or people with whom we only have a weak offline bond. To this end, it has been suggested that Facebook offers the opportunity to crystallize ephemeral ties and make potential bonds that would normally remain latent ties in order to increase social capital (Ellison et al., 2007). This may perhaps happen by identifying similar interests with weak connections that are easily visible on online profiles but that may not have been discussed offline. It is useful to consider this notion in conjunction with the rich get richer hypothesis. Individuals who are more able to forge connections offline may also be better at strengthening those relational bonds online and therefore increase their social capital (Kraut et al., 2002.) It has also been suggested that use of SNSs may be particularly useful in mitigating the loss of social capital. An example hereof might be when individuals move away from friends and family, for instance, when you leave home to go to university or move away to pursue career opportunities in a new location. Ellison et al. (2007) found, for example, that university students were most likely to use SNSs and other forms of CMC to maintain geographically distant relationships. It might thus be the case that diverse forms of online CMC are not used with the explicit aim of forging new relationships and thereby enhancing social capital, but that they are utilized in a way that sustains a readily available resource of social capital under circumstances of geographical distance that is rapidly increasing due to a never before seen enhanced social mobility, especially amongst western societies. Alas, we have once again returned to our rosy picture of the Internet in providing a useful tool for creating and maintaining social capital online. We should, however, point out that this is not as straightforward a process as may have been thus far implied. And why should it be? After all, making and maintaining offline friendships is not an effort-free process. We therefore now consider some of the barriers that might hamper our online relationship efforts.

4.6 Digital barriers

There are many barriers to forming and maintaining relationships, both in the online and offline world, with some being more obvious than others. For example, the physical distance between partners in a long distance relationship may be an offline hindrance, but could be overcome through online communication. Other barriers may not be immediately apparent, such as social norms, physical appearance, and stereotypes. Using CMC could help overcome many of these obstacles. We will now look at some of these in more detail.

4.6.1 Distance

The term 'distance' can be used to define different kinds of spaces between two or more people. Two of the commonly used terms in relation to relationships are **physical distance** and **emotional distance**. Whereas the former implies a geographical tangible space between two people, emotional distance refers to levels of intimacy, feeling connected, and emotional involvement between two people. Emotional distance is often considered typical of dysfunctional relationships and to be a contributor to relationship breakdowns. **Functional distance** is also considered to be a key contributor to relationship formation and maintenance and is often considered to be the space between locations in which people come together. Function and physical distances are thus not dissimilar. Clearly, the actual functional or physical space between two people communicating via the Internet can seldom be physically reduced. However, CMC can be used to bring two people closer together. In other words, it can be used to create an emotional closeness between people. In doing so, CMC can actually make people feel more connected, creating a kind of pseudo-physical closeness. It could therefore be argued that the advent of new communication technologies such as telephones and the Internet can reduce psychological and emotional distance, and help promote the formation and maintenance of relationships regardless of individuals' geographic location. Of course, there will be differences in the promotion of different types of closeness depending upon the type of CMC in which people engage. The point here is, however, that people can use CMC to feel connected, both emotionally and physically, depending upon the technology used, to another person. Together with the notions of self-disclosure outlined earlier in this chapter, it would seem that what may have once proved to be a significant barrier to forming a relationship (i.e., physical distance) may actually be less of a barrier in online communication.

Let us consider this notion in terms of online dating or online interactions via a SNS. In an initial flurry of email or IM exchanges with someone who you have met online, you might lose all inhibitions and splurge information about yourself that you would not so freely offer up in an offline interaction, especially if you do not yet know the person very well. This might initially create a notion of emotional closeness between you and your online friend. Now ponder for one minute that you have arranged to meet this person offline, this person to whom you have divulged much personal and intimate information. How would you feel? You might feel slightly embarrassed, or nervous, or even regretful that you have shared intimate and personal information about yourself. You might seek validation of your online relationship via different modes of communication prior to meeting up with the person offline. It might also be the case that meeting up offline is not feasible because of a physical distance between you. The point of this pondering? We return to our rosy picture: Yes, it may appear easy for two people to create a closeness online, but the transference of that relationship to the offline world may not be as straightforward as it seems. The other side to this is, of course, that if we create emotional closeness via the Internet, we become emotionally invested, especially if these relationships occupy a large proportion of our time. In other words, functional, psychological, or emotional distances may become a barrier to a relationship initially formed online at a later date. Baker (2005) highlights exactly this barrier in work that demonstrated that of those individuals who developed a romantic relationship through the use of chat rooms, discussion sites, or other online domains, the ones who lived furthest away generally took much longer to meet offline.

That is not to say that online relationships cannot be fulfilling. Long distance relationships that use CMC have been found to be superior in terms of duration and satisfaction, levels of love, and intimacy than relationships that are not maintained via CMC (Gunn & Gunn, 2000), possibly due to an increased reliance on verbal and written communication and an increased level of trust (Dainton & Aylor, 2000). It might also be the case that increased relationship maintenance via CMC enhances communication and relational skills at the cost of emotional distance (Ben-Ze'ev, 2005). Continuing in this vein of thought, relationships maintained online may be stronger over a two-year period (Bargh et al., 2002), because they are founded on investments of factors other than pure emotion. We might thus need to consider 'distance' as an offsetting factor for different types of relationships formed online, rather than as a hindrance to the formation of emotional distance and assistant to the breaking down of physical distance in online relationship formation per se.

4.6.2 Synchronicity

Computer-mediated communication comes in many shapes and forms these days. One main attribute that distinguishes some forms from others is synchronicity. Whereas **synchronous communication** is that which is considered to have no time delay between communicators (e.g., instant messaging, video communication), **asynchronous communication** offers a chosen time delay between receiving and responding to an exchange (e.g., email). Using different modes of communication could play a role in whether CMC is conducive to forming and maintaining online relationships. Synchronous communication may, for example, be beneficial to overcoming the boundary of different time zones if two people are in geographically opposing locations. It also allows people to take a break from a conversation without interrupting the flow. Emails may, for instance, be exchanged almost instantaneously if both parties are online at the same time but the conversation is unaffected if one party does not reply until their next break at work or until five days later when they return from a holiday. Even when using synchronous modes of communication such as instant messaging, people can take the time to create, edit, re-edit, and post their responses to a conversation. All that the other person sees is that they are writing. Asynchronous communication does enable the maintenance of communication on one's own terms. In fact, if we consider this, it would appear that it is not necessarily the type of communication engaged in, but how the communication is offered. Whilst I am typing this, I am thinking about the words I use, I am constructing sentences, editing paragraphs, and considering the flow of the text as a whole. If I was creating an online video, I would not be doing so. It would be more of a splurge of information. Therefore, rather than consider the synchronicity, it might be more conducive to consider the method of communication. Writing enables a more considered, mindful response, and could thus help overcome any barriers of time zones or schedules. It could, however, also enable the construction of a false sense of self, an ideal, or ought self. That said, when considering conceptualizations such as hyperpersonal communications theory (Walther, 1996), mindful, thought-through responses could be perceived to be a negative aspect of relationship maintenance, especially when online communication becomes the norm and preferred form of social interaction for an individual. This will be explored more in the following discussion on romantic relationships online.

4.7 Romantic relationships online

Social psychology suggests that one of the most fundamental human needs is that of belonging (Maslow, 1968, Bowlby, 1973, Baumeister & Leary, 1995). Fulfilment of this need leads to psychological well-being. An absence thereof as characterized by a lack of social acceptance has been thought to result in negative affect, anxiety, stress, and in some extremes, psychopathologies (Baumeister & Leary, 1995). This need to belong can be fulfilled by forming long lasting social bonds that promote a sense of caring and provide opportunities for frequent positive social interactions (Baumeister & Leary, 1995). In other words, friendships fulfil a basic need that is considered by some as equally important as physiological requirements vital to survival. These strong social bonds need to be developed and cultivated over time. This begs the question as to the role that CMC plays in this process. It appears that communication technology may now be an additional tool that people use to seek new contacts, form new close ties, and maintain fulfilling friendships, but how is this sense of belonging achieved via the Internet?

Many of the theories that attempt to explain how relationships are formed online are taken from models of offline behaviour. Whilst these may be a useful starting point they often conceptualize the Internet as a single space, do not account for the differences between communication technologies, and often ignore the users' underlying goals and motivations. We will now consider some of these theories, and as each one is discussed maybe you could consider its appropriateness for explaining online behaviours. Also, consider whether you can think of any ways in which adapting these theories might make them more suitable for explaining online relationship behaviours.

4.7.1 Propinquity

It has long been suggested that we form friendships with those to whom we are physically close, or come into regular physical contact with, a notion known as **propinquity** (Amichai-Hamburger et al., 2013). In its purest form, propinquity refers to physical distance as outlined earlier. More recently, the notion has, however, been expanded to suggest that a process of shared commonalities may underlie observed propinquity, rather than relationships being created based purely on physical distance. Nonetheless, offline friendships are far more likely to arise between individuals who share a physical space. An obvious example hereof is the individuals you might meet regularly through work. Returning again to social psychology, Zajonc's (2001) mere exposure effect demonstrates how people who become familiar with one another through **repeated exposure**, or interactions, demonstrated increased liking for one another. Liking has been suggested to be one of the building blocks of romantic relationships (Amichai-Hamburger et al., 2013). However, whilst liking might not always lead to a romantic relationship, it would appear to be an important element of most platonic relationships. Research to support occurrence of the mere exposure effect in online relationship formation comes from a study that demonstrated that people who responded more often and frequently in a CMC study were seen to be more attractive by their partners, partly due to their feeling that the partner was present in this scenario (Ghoshal & Holme, 2006).

Walther and Bazarova (2008) put forward the **electronic propinquity theory**, which outlines a number of factors linked to the creation of psychological closeness through CMC, including the idea that individuals need to possess enhanced communication skills in order to foster feelings of emotional closeness. They also suggest that when people experience this sense of closeness online they are more likely to be satisfied with their online communications. This is not dissimilar to some of the notions of the rich get richer theory (Lee, 2009), whereby individuals who demonstrate higher levels of communications skills are better able to develop and maintain relationships than those who are not best able to communicate.

In order for propinquity to be relevant to online relationship formation, an adaptation may be required to classical definitions of *closeness*. For instance, individuals may frequently visit the same tavern in the online game *World of Warcraft*, or repeatedly communicate with the same people in a specific discussion forum online. These 'repeated exposures' to the same people could resemble the shared physical space referred to in order to create closeness offline. Have you ever signed in to any Internet arena, game, discussion board, or group hoping to find a certain person online? Not only would this represent Zajonc's repeated exposure effect online, but may also suggest that you feel some level of 'connectedness' to that person. Of course, there are sensible times when it becomes important to consider offline physical distances when interacting with people online. One of those instances might be when looking for a new romantic partner online. Whilst we are all familiar with tales of love across the miles, most people would naturally limit their search for a new partner on a dating website to those within a certain travel time or distance, especially if they expect to transfer an online relationship offline in the future (Baker, 2008). On the other hand, those who meet opportunistically online and who progress to forming an offline relationship, or those who seek an online-only relationship, may be more concerned with finding a like-minded other rather than factoring geographical distance into their search. Moreover, these types of relationship may foster frequent online interaction as they can proceed with little inconvenience or the high time and monetary costs associated with travelling to meet offline (Cooper & Sportolari, 2007). That said, you are referred back to our discussion previously with regard to how 'real' online relationships are. When does an online romance become a real romance? Is it only when two people actually physically meet and enter into a romantic relationship? Hollywood movies would have us believe that all romantic relationships are built on eternal love, fluffy clouds, roses, and hearts! This may not always be the case. Romantic relationships come in many shapes and forms, and exist for a multitude of reasons. Often, people seek out a similar other to themselves. This is known as the **similarity attracts hypothesis** (Barnes, 2003) and may not be as uniquely distinct to propinquity in online arenas as first thought. If we meet a new partner in the offline world, for instance in the workplace, little effort may be required to repeatedly see them. Online, some effort is required to create a presence in an online space. This effort may be reflected in the way in which someone seeks out a certain arena associated with a shared interest (e.g., a music fan web page or discussion group). If this is the case, then maybe similarities to others outweigh propinquity in shaping and forming online relationships (Baker, 2008).

4.7.2 **Homophily**

The liking of those who are similar to us is known as **homophily** and is considered to be an important factor in the development of both platonic and romantic relationships (Amichai-Hamburger et al., 2013). People tend to show a preference for those similar to themselves in factors as diverse as culture, appearance, traits and characteristics, or interests. The Internet can be seen as a tool for promoting interactions with similar others. Firstly, it provides instant access to more people, expanding the likelihood that there is someone who shares factors that you value. Secondly, it offers the opportunity for quickly identifying like-minded others. Indeed on platforms such as SNSs or dating sites, individuals are specifically asked to disclose information about themselves, whether this be demographic information or hobbies and interests, therefore making it easier for individuals to spot like-minded others without the use of extensive time or energy. Research supports the notion of homophily in determining who we interact with online. Barnes (2003) found, for instance, that perceived similarity was quoted as a key factor when deciding whether or not to pursue an online relationship with a person. Further research has also found that use of the Internet is related to increased connections with people who hold the same political and/or religious beliefs (Amichai-Hamburger & Hayat, 2011). Mazur and Richards (2011) also found that on SNSs, 'friends' often shared race, were similarly aged, and resided in the same state. However, as previous research indicated that SNSs are most frequently populated with offline friends and utilized for maintaining offline connections rather than forming new relationships, this may not be the best place to look online for homophily in relationship formation! However, consider if you have an obscure hobby or interest. For instance, maybe you are an aspiring property developer and have a slightly awkward obsession with Kevin McCloud (for those of you not familiar with Kevin McCloud, use the Internet to Google him). Maybe you would not want your offline social circle to know about this obsession, but would quite like to indulge your need for information and discussion about him by speaking to like-minded others online. The Internet is particularly useful for those who have more obscure interests or hobbies for finding other people with similar interests (Ben-Ze'ev, 2005). If you are not a fan of Kevin McCloud, consider the classic example of the 'school geek' who is ostracized by his schoolmates for his obsession with a specific sci-fi classic (see Chapter 2), yet can join thousands of people online discussing an indefinite number of possible plot progressions with equally enthusiastic fans. Returning to our slightly more serious approach to understanding online behaviour, early selection of a potential mate or friend based on homophily could provide a tool for filtering out those with whom we have little in common (Amichai-Hamburger et al., 2013). McKenna, Green, and Gleeson (2002, p. 11) described this as 'getting a head start' by quickly establishing an understanding of basic shared interests and therefore allowing progression of the conversation by seeking other shared commonalities and developing the relationship at a faster than usual pace.

With regard to the development of romantic relationships online, Fiore, Taylor, Zhong, Mendelsohn, and Cheshire (2010) showed that people on online dating sites, particularly women, were more likely to connect with others of the same ethnicity. Whilst people often restrict their search for potential dates by age, similarity does not seem the key component here, with men seeking increasingly younger partners as they age and women's preferences becoming increasingly more diverse. Preferences for similarity of age seem to be less important than other factors such as education, physical attractiveness, and status (Skopek, Schmitz, & Blossfeld, 2011). Skopek et al. explain this finding in terms of evolutionary theory. They suggest that women traditionally seek men of higher quality, status, and ability to provide for themselves and potential offspring, whilst men seek women who demonstrate signs of fertility (Fiore et al., 2010). If this is the case, and homophily is not the key to creating lasting online bonds, then it is worth briefly considering whether the matchmaking tools often employed by online dating websites are useful.

'Scientific' methods for matching potential partners on dating websites seem to rely on the assumption that similarity attracts and as such automatically generate and suggest potential dates based on similar interests, location, ages, and personality traits. It is thought that people prefer those who are similar in attitudes, traits, and desires as this reinforces their notion of who they are, their self-concept. Drawing on the **social exchange theory** (Thibaut & Kelley, 1959) of relationship formation, this perceived reinforcement would act as a reward and therefore an enticement towards forming a relationship with that individual. Social exchange theory suggests that relationships are formed to fulfil human needs. Accordingly, relationships are like an exchange of resources, emotions, affection, and psychological reinforcement. It asserts that people develop relationships based on mutual interests, which in turn suggests that we are attracted to individuals who can reciprocate and reinforce our sense of self. In order to do this, relationships need to be equitable. This equity, it should be noted, does not refer only to materialistic and monetary equity. It can be equity based on appearances and individual characteristics. Accordingly, research has found that individuals who met on online dating websites that had filtered profiles and matched them on a number of equitable factors, compared to couples who had an unfettered choice of mate, had a significantly higher level of marital quality and had a notably higher probability of sustaining a relationship (Carter & Buckwalter, 2009). The authors of this study suggest that this improved functioning results from better matched partners, similar on personality, affect, and traits from the outset of the relationship, as selected by the online dating system. It would seem that the similarity attracts hypothesis carries over to relationships that are formed online! This brings us to the question of whether some factors are more important than others when matching for similarity.

4.7.3 **Physical attraction**

Physical attraction to a potential mate is considered essential in offline relationship formation (Cooper & Sportolari, 2007). Whilst the importance of physical attraction is thought to be diminished online, with erotic relationships stemming from emotional intimacy rather than desire triggered by physical attraction (Cooper & Sportolari, 2007), it nonetheless has a role to play, particularly in online romantic relationships. In instances where a relationship progresses to the point of meeting offline, it is not unusual for the relationship to be terminated after the initial meeting if a persons' appearance is drastically different to that presented online. If a photograph has not been provided, the imagined appearance conjured through interactions and often shaped by the individual's needs and desires rather than based on actual information conveyed may also lead to a premature relationship termination (Baker, 2005, 2008). But why are people so influenced by physical attractiveness? Surely, if you connect with a person online, especially if you feel that you have developed an emotional closeness with them, do looks really matter? If you are not yet familiar with the MTV programme *Catfish*, now might be the time to go watch a few episodes. This will give you plenty of fodder to fuel the debate of whether shared closeness or physical appearance triumphs in progressing with an online created relationship offline. If you fall down on the side of physical attractiveness being the stronger determinant, you might be falling foul of the **halo effect** (Asch, 1946). According to the halo effect, people who are physically attractive are often considered to possess a wealth of other good characteristics such as kindness and intelligence. It might surprise you to read that in the online world, the halo effect is often demonstrated for attributes other than obviously physical traits, such as wit and writing ability (Shtatfeld & Barak, 2009). An assumption is often made that people who are able to express themselves eloquently online are often considered to have an attractive personality. This, in turn, is often associated with an attractive personality of positive characteristics. This online attraction of writing style extends as far as the screen name used by people on dating websites. Whitty and Buchanan (2010) demonstrating that men were more attracted to, and also more likely to contact, women whose screen names indicated physical attractiveness (e.g., cutegirl, sexysusie), whereas women were more attracted to those whose screen names indicated intelligence (e.g., Wellread) or were neutral (e.g., Smith48). In this case it would seem that even written indicators of attractiveness may influence individuals' wish to initiate a relationship with others online. In order for a relationship to progress online, however, there needs to be some exchange of information. As soon as you reveal any aspect of yourself online, you are engaging in a process of self-disclosure. We therefore now turn our attention to considering the role of revealing self-information online in online relationships.

4.8 Self-disclosure

Sharing information about the self with an individual or groups is called self-disclosure (Cozby, 1973). Self-disclosures contain any type of information about the self that is shared either intentionally or non-intentionally. It is thus unsurprising that they can vary greatly in breadth and depth, from simple facts about the self such as age or gender to intimate and private details of one's personal life (Derlega & Berg, 1987). Self-disclosure has been shown both on and offline to be a reciprocal process. For example, if you meet someone for the first time, you tell them your name. They reciprocate by telling you their name. You then tell them your age, they tell you their age, and so on. This to-and-fro of information continues. It is a gradual and reciprocal process that is believed to underlie the formation of offline relationships, as conceptualized in the **social penetration theory** (Altman & Taylor, 1973). Indeed, Altman and Taylor suggest that this increasingly intimate exchange of self-information is what characterizes the formation and maintenance of all human relationships. Recent research has indicated that self-disclosures (voluntarily and involuntarily) also occur online and that a range of factors influence individuals' willingness to share self-information, including trust (Joinson, Reips, Buchanan, & Paine Schofield, 2010), personality traits (Kramer & Winter, 2008), and relationship type (Schwartz, Galliher, & Rodriguez, 2011).

Self-disclosures can be either personal—a straightforward revelation of information about the self—or relational. Relational disclosures reveal how the individual feels about their partner as well as offering an opportunity to gain insight into how their partner views the relationship (Baxter, 1987). This is, however, seen as a risky strategy for gathering feedback on the relationship as it is direct and may lead to rejection. An obvious example of relational self-disclosure online it the ominous Facebook relationship request that asks the romantic partner to confirm the nature of their relationship and announces this to other members of their social network. Relational disclosures have, however, been linked with higher levels of perceived intimacy and closeness in online relationships (Tidwell & Walther, 2002). Revelations of various types of self-information via CMC have been linked with increased intimacy, which in turn has been related to increased relationship satisfaction. There is, however, some research that suggests that the type of information shared may alter according to the media channel used to convey the information. For example, negative or embarrassing information is more likely to be shared via email or text than face-to-face, whereas positive information is shared when people can see receiver expression and gain praise (O'Sullivan, 2000). Attrill and Jalil (2011) also demonstrated that people are not prone to simply splurging any information about themselves online, but that they selectively share personal and intimate details, a sharing process that is partly dependent upon the mode of communication used (Attrill, 2012a). That is not to say that people only share self-information in a positive manner online. There is some research to suggest that people often deal with negative aspects of their relationships using CMC. For example, some people might find ending a relationship via email or telephone easier than doing so in person (Ben-Ze'ev, 2005) (for a fuller overview of self-disclosure online see Attrill, 2012b).

This very brief overview of self-disclosure would suggest that there might be individual differences in what people share about themselves and how they do so online. For example, people who are chronically shy have been shown to be able to better disclose online rather than face-to-face in a way that improves their current offline relationships. Although it should be noted that their online self-disclosures do not appear to be compensatory in terms of expanding their friendship circle to include more social contacts (Birnie & Horvath, 2002). A word of caution is, however, needed here. A lot of work that was initially carried out to assess this role compared online to offline disclosures. Moreover, as Attrill and Jalil (2011) point out, much of the work used diverse and varied methodologies. For instance, some studies used word-count rather than content analysis and therefore did not distinguish between the depth and breadth of information. One of the initial assumptions of a more prolific splurging of self-information online compared to offline has been shown to be a more selective process than initially implied (Attrill, 2012b). What does, however, emerge from the current literature is that research into the role played by self-disclosure in creating and maintaining relationships online provides a varied pattern of results, the commonality amongst which appears to be that some pattern or level of self-disclosure almost certainly plays a role in developing an online relationship. It appears essential to creating a long-lasting relationship, but what else might influence the successful transfer of online romances to offline relationships?

4.9 The ups and downs of online romances

Online dating seems to be gaining popularity, with one in ten Americans having used a dating site or app, and 38% of those looking for a partner doing so online (Pew Internet Report, 2013). Whilst unfortunately there is still a level of stigma towards online dating, those who believe only desperate people use online dating sites now seem to be in the minority and online daters themselves tend to agree that it is a good way to meet people (Pew Internet Report, 2013). One survey of daters showed that 66% have met up offline with someone they met online, and 23% met their spouse or long-term partner through a dating site, with 41% of college graduates knowing someone who met their spouse or long-term partner online (Pew Internet Report, 2013). Not only do people who use dating sites say they feel it gives them a better match, but empirical research also indicates that marriages between partners who met through a dating site show higher levels of satisfaction than in marriages where couples met in other ways (Carter & Buckwalter, 2009), suggesting that this method might not only be more convenient for daters but might actually be more successful than meeting partners offline. This is further substantiated by the observation that people who met via dating sites typically met offline within a fortnight of first contacting each other online (Baker, 2002), and that people who wait longer to meet offline are more likely to have a sustainable and more satisfying relationship that has a better chance of enduring offline than those who meet in the physical world much more quickly (Baker, 2008).

So it seems that the Internet might actually improve our chances of a good match, and it would certainly seem to save us a lot of time, money, embarrassing chat-up lines, and rejections at the pub! But what about the relationships whilst they are online? Anderson and Emmers-Sommer (2006) suggest that some romantic relationships may be conducted online without ever meeting offline. The satisfaction of those engaged in these online-only romantic relationships was found to be closely linked to intimacy, trust, and communication, with increased levels of each leading to increased satisfaction, which mimics patterns found in offline couples. What seemed different, however, was that openness seems to be much more important to these online-only relationships than to offline romantic relationships (Whitty & Gavin, 2001). However, this work also focused on transferring online relationships to the offline sphere, as well as those traditional components of offline relationships being important to online couples. Whitty and Gavin (2001) found that effective conflict management and increased time communicating seems to be key to successfully transferring online relationships offline (Baker, 2002). Transition of a relationship offline is also thought to be facilitated through a thorough exchange of information, thoughts, and feelings online, prior to meeting offline (Baker, 2002). Five key behaviours enacted by couples have been shown to aid maintenance and satisfaction in offline relationships (Strafford & Canary, 1991):

1. Positivity: being cheerful.
2. Openness: being direct, self-disclosing, and discussing the relationship.
3. Assurances: stressing commitment, love, and demonstrating faithfulness.
4. Sharing tasks: a level of equality in tackling the tasks facing the couple is required.
5. Networks: spending time with common friends/acquaintances.

We have already seen how self-disclosure can be enacted online and the positive effect it seems to have on intimacy and relationship satisfaction online, but it may be difficult to understand how sharing tasks and spending time with common friends may be completed online in order to successfully maintain an online-only romantic relationship. There seems to be a dearth of research and theory on online-only romantic relationships, stemming from what seems to be an assumption that the goal of romantic relationships is to progress offline, or that physical characteristics of romantic relationships (e.g., physical intimacy) cannot be conducted online.

It is therefore often assumed that online-only romantic relationships cannot be real. However, intimacy might be created by the couple spending more time communicating, which could constitute sharing tasks. Equally, spending time in open discussion groups, conference calling with multiple friends, playing online games or sharing photos, and swapping stories about times spent offline with friends may be deemed as sufficient to fulfil the networking aspect of relationship maintenance. As such it could be argued that online romantic relationships are able to fulfil the same behaviours for successful maintenance as offline relationships. That said, rather than trying to assess online relationships via offline methods or apply offline theories to understanding online relationships, it would perhaps be more appropriate to create a new theory of the ways in which online-only romantic relationships are maintained successfully and consider whether this may be enough to constitute a real and successful relationship. Or, is it the case that an online romantic relationship can only be deemed truly successful if it is transferred offline? On pondering this question, it seems clear to us that far more research needs to be carried out around the perceived 'realness' of online communications, especially of online romantic relationships. For now, our final attention in this chapter turns to another type of relationship that may exist online, familial relationships.

4.10 Familial relationships

Throughout this chapter we have frequently referred to the diverse nature of relationships. So far we have focused on platonic and romantic relationships. To illustrate the diversity of CMC as a relationship tool, the final section of this chapter will consider the role of the Internet in the ties and bonds that you have with your family members, your 'familial relationships'. As well as the Internet becoming a place to meet new people, form new connections and a place for romance to blossom, CMC tools also have a role to play in the maintenance of existing offline relationships. The Internet provides multiple communications tools for remaining in contact with family members near and far. Due to an ever increasing social mobilization, families are now often spread throughout a country, if not throughout the world. Whilst this is a positive aspect of online interaction, there is a more sinister side to spending increased amounts of time online. There has, for instance, been some speculation that time spent online takes away from relationships, family, and social connections in the offline world. An example of this is the media's supposition that time spent online is time neglecting the family and that using technology in the home is detracting from traditional family values and weakening familial bonds (Kraut et al., 1998). This negative impact could be increasing given the ever smaller devices with which we can now access and communicate via the World Wide Web. In actual fact, we no longer even need the World Wide Web to communicate digitally in a way that could damage familial relationships, with the availability of communications tools such as *WhatsApp* and *Skype*. Consider the last time you went out for a meal. It is more than likely that you saw occupants of at least one dining table using a mobile phone whilst someone at their table was still eating. Early mobile phone use research highlights that use of mobile phones tends to create higher distress within a family over a two-year period (Chesley, 2005). Even though this research is now almost a decade old, and mobile phone use has rapidly increased in this decade, the findings by Chesley (2005) indicate a spilling over of mobile phone use from people's work to home lives. Whilst not outlining exactly for what the participants were using their mobile phones, given the current connectivity of most devices to the Internet, including mobile phones, tablets, notebooks, and handheld PDAs, we might expect the rate of crossover or interference between work and private use to only increase in the next few years. Regardless of the device used to access the Internet, it would appear to be negatively associated with family time that was previously used to share activities that promote communication, interaction, and memory making, which help form a family identity (Nie, Hillygus, & Erbing, 2002), a notion supported by low Internet use having been associated with a better quality of family relationships (Mesch, 2001).

Despite this seemingly negative impact of the Internet on family relationships, Horst (2012) found that media use could actually be incorporated as a family activity and provide more opportunities for bonding. Parents who saw the benefits of this described the process as taking an interest in their adolescents' hobbies and shared time with their children creating and learning new media, watching TV, films, and online videos as valued time together. On a further positive note, mobile phones may be becoming invaluable for parents to support communication with their offspring (Mesch & Frankel, 2011) as well as other family members. Women in particular who consider themselves to be the social hub of the family and are more expressive in their communication style, seem to take greater advantage of telephone and email to keep in contact with relatives geographically distant from them (Boneva, Kraut, & Frohlich, 2001). There are also generational differences in connectivity via CMC with grandparents in particular reporting that they contacted their grandchildren more frequently via email than their grandchildren initiated contact via the same medium. The jury still appears to be out on the effects of CMC on familial relationships. Whilst some findings point to a positive effect, others indicate negative consequences of online interactions on familial relationships. Of course, this brief outline does not consider the types or content of the communications that have each of these effects. There is clearly scope for future research to assess these possible contributing factors to familial relationships.

4.11 Chapter summary

This chapter has explored a variety of online relationships, including romantic, platonic, and familial relationships. It has:

- Highlighted that relationships come in many shapes and forms, from platonic to romantic to familial, and a few different kinds in between!
- Outlined the different types of closeness found in diverse relationships and considered how these might be achieved via CMC. In particular, it focused on emotional and physical closeness and how these might be facilitated or inhibited via the Internet.
- Outlined definitions of relationships to emphasize the notion that not all relationships are the same. We considered Baumeister and Leary's notion of a sense of human **belongingness** to highlight the fact that different types of relationship are founded on diverse individual motivations and needs.
- Considered some factors that have been shown to influence the formation of offline relationships in the online context, with emphasis given to homophily and self-disclosure.

Whilst these operate online, they do so in a different manner to the formation of offline relationships.

- Self-disclosure was considered in relation to enhancing a sense of intimacy and satisfaction for relationships created and maintained online, as well as for those transferred from the online to offline world.

- Social compensation and social capital were outlined. The different forms of social capital were focused upon to highlight that capital comes in many shapes and forms, with the Internet playing a role in the number of acquaintances and ties that we now foster online.

- Social capital was also explored in relation to the mass media populated notion of the sacrifice of offline relationships in favour of spending time online, the demise of traditional family time, and the weakening of familial ties.

- Our overarching conclusion for this chapter would be that humans will always seek out relationships and will use whatever tools they have to do so. They will adapt their tool use to suit their needs and motivations, whether this is looking for love, support, friends, a brief liaison, or an enduring bond via the wires. The main point is that the Internet is nothing other than a new tool being used in new ways to create and maintain these ties.

 ## References

Altman, I. & Taylor, D. (1973). *Social Penetration Theory*. New York: Holt, Rinehart & Winston.

Amichai-Hamburger, Y. & Hayat, Z. (2011). The impact of the Internet on the social lives of users: A representative sample from 13 countries. *Computers in Human Behaviour*, 27, 585–589.

Amichai-Hamburger, Y., Kingsbury, M., & Schneider, B.H. (2013). Friendship: An old concept with a new meaning? *Computers in Human Behaviour*, 29, 33–39.

Anderson, T.L. & Emmers-Sommer, T.M. (2006). Predictors of relationship satisfaction in online romantic relationships. *Communication Studies*, 57 (2), 153–172.

Asch, S.E. (1946). Forming impressions of personality. *Journal of Abnormal and Social Psychology*, 41, 258–290.

Attrill, A. (2012a). Sharing only parts of me: Selective categorical self-disclosure across Internet arenas. *International Journal of Internet Science*, 7 (1), 55–77.

Attrill, A. (2012b). Self-disclosure online. In Zheng, Y. (Ed.), *Encyclopedia of Cyber Behavior* (pp. 855–872). New York: IGI Global.

Attrill, A. & Jalil, R. (2011). Revealing only the superficial me: Exploring categorical self-disclosure online. *Computers in Human Behavior*, 27, 1634–1642.

Bagwell, C.L., Schmidt, M.E., Newcomb, A.F., & Bukowski, W.M. (2001). Friendship and peer rejection of adult adjustment. In Nangle, D. W. & Erdley, C. A. (Eds), *The Role of Friendship in Psychological Adjustment* (pp. 25–49). San Francisco, CA: Jossey-Bass.

Baker, A. (2002). What makes an online relationship successful? Clues from couples who met in cyberspace. *CyberPsychology and Behaviour*, 5 (4), 363–375.

Baker, A. (2005). *Double Click: Romance and Commitment Among Online Couples*. Cresskill, NJ: Hampton Press.

Baker, A.J. (2008). Down the rabbit hole: The role of place in the initiation and development of online relationships. In Barak, A. (Ed.), *Psychological Aspects of Cyberspace: Theory, Research, Applications* (pp. 163–184). Cambridge: Cambridge University Press.

Bargh, J.A. & McKenna, K.Y.A. (2004). The Internet and social life. *Annual Review of Psychology*, 55 (1), 573–590.

Bargh, J.A., McKenna, K.Y.A., & Fitzsimons, G.M. (2002). Can you see the real me? Activation and expression of the 'true self' on the Internet. *Journal of Social Issues*, 58 (1), 33–48.

Barnes, S. (2003). *Computer-Mediated Communication: Human-to-Human Communication Across the Internet*. Boston: Allyn & Bacon.

Baumeister, R.F. & Leary, M.R. (1995). The need to belong: Desire for interpersonal attachments as a fundamental human motivation. *Psychological Bulletin*, 117 (3), 497–529.

Baxter, L. A. (1987). Self-disclosure and relationship disengagement. In Delega, V.J. & Berg, J.H. (Eds), *Self-Disclosure: Theory, Research, and Therapy* (pp. 155–174). New York: Plenum.

Ben-Ze'ev, A. (2005) 'Detachment': The unique nature of online romantic relationships. In Amichai-Hamburger, Y. (Ed.), *The Social Net: Human Behaviour in Cyberspace* (pp 116–138). New York: Oxford University Press.

Birnie, S. & Horvath, P. (2002). Psychological predictors of Internet social communication. *Journal of Computer-Mediated Communication*, 7 (4). Online http://jcmc.indiana.edu/vol7/issue4/horvath.htm (accessed 1st September, 2014).

Boneva, B., Kraut, R., & Frohlich, D. (2001). Using e-mail for personal relationships: The difference gender makes. *American Behavioural Scientist*, 45 (3), 530–549.

Bowlby, J. (1973). *Attachment and Loss: Vol. 2. Separation Anxiety and Anger*. New York: Basic Books.

Briggle, A. (2008). Real friends: How the Internet can foster friendship. *Ethics and Information Technology*, 10, 71–79.

Carter, S.R. & Buckwalter, J.G. (2009). Enhancing mate selection through the Internet: A comparison of relationship quality between marriages arising from an online matchmaking system and marriages arising from unfettered selection. *Interpersona: An International Journal on Personal Relationships*, 3, 105–125.

Chesley, N. (2005). Blurring boundaries? Linking technology use, spillover, individual distress, and family satisfaction. *Journal of Marriage and Family*, 67, 1237–1248.

Cocking, D. & Mathews, S. (2000). Unreal friends. *Ethics and Information Technology*, 2 (4), 223–231.

Coleman, J.S. (1988). Social capital in the creation of human capital. *American Journal of Sociology*, 94 (Supplement): S95–S120.

Cooper, A. & Sportolari, L. (2007). Romance in cyberspace: Understanding online attraction. *Journal of Sex Education and Therapy*, 22 (1), 7–14.

Cozby, P.C. (1973). Self-disclosure: A literature review. *Psychological Bulletin*, 79 (2), 73–91.

Dainton, M. & Aylor, B. (2000). Patterns of communication channel use in the maintenance of long-distance relationships. *Communication Research Reports*, 19, 118–129.

Derlega, V.J. & Berg, J.H. (Eds) (1987). *Self-Disclosure: Theory, Research, and Therapy*. New York: Plenum.

Dutton, W.H., Helsper, E.J., Whitty, M.T., Li, N., Buckwalter, J.G., & Lee, E. (2009). The role of the Internet in reconfiguring marriages: A cross-national study. *Interpersona : An International Journal on Personal Relationships*, 3 (2), 3–18.

Ellison, N.B., Heino, R.D., & Gibbs, J.L. (2006). Managing impressions online: Self-presentation processes in the online dating environment. *Communication Research*, 33 (2), 152–172.

Ellison, N.B., Steinfield, C., & Lampe, C. (2007). The benefits of Facebook 'friends': Social capital and college students' use of online social network sites. *Journal of Computer Mediated Communication*, 12 (4), 1143–1168.

Fiore, A.T., Taylor, L.S., Zhong, X., Medelsohn, G.A., & Cheshire, C. (2010). Who's right and who writes: People, profiles, contacts, and replies to online dating. *Presented at 43rd Hawaii International Conference on System Sciences*. Online http://www.computer.org/csdl/proceedings/hicss/2010/3869/00/03-06-05-abs.html (accessed 1st September, 2014).

Ghoshal, G. & Holme, P. (2006) Attractiveness and activity in Internet communities. *Physica A*, 364, 603–609.

Gonzales, A.L. & Hancock, J.T. (2008). Identity shift in computer-mediated environments. *Media Psychology*, 11 (2), 167–185.

Granovetter, M. (1982) The strength of weak ties: A network theory revisited. In Marsden, P. & Lin, N. (Eds), *Social Structure and Network Analysis*. Beverley Hills: Sage.

Gunn, D. O. & Gunn, C.W. (2000, September). The quality of electronically maintained relationships. Paper presented at the *Annual Conference of the Association of Internet Researchers*, Lawrence, KS.

Helliwell, J.F. & Putnam, R.D. (2004). The social context of well-being. *The Royal Society*, 359, 1435–1446.

Horst, H. (2012). New media technologies in everyday life. In Horst, H. A. & Miller, D. (Eds), *Digital Anthropology*. New York: Berg Publications.

Joinson, A.N., Reips, U-D., Buchanan, T., & Paine Schofield, C.B. (2010). Privacy, trust and self-disclosure online. *Human Computer Interaction*, 25 (1), 1–24.

Kavanaugh, A., Carroll, J.M., Rosson, M.B., Zin, T.T., & Reese, D.D. (2005). Community networks: Where offline communities meet online. *Journal of Computer-Mediated Communication*, 10 (4). Online http://onlinelibrary.wiley.com/doi/10.1111/j.1083-6101.2005.tb00266.x/full (accessed 1st September, 2014).

Kramer, N.C. & Winter, S. (2008). Impression management 2.0: The relationship of self-esteem, extraversion, self-efficacy, and self-presentation within social networking sites. *Journal of Media Psychology*, 20, 106–116.

Kraut, R.E., Patterson, M., Lundmark, V., Kiesler, S., Mukhopadhyay, T., & Scherlis, W. (1998). Internet paradox: A social technology that reduces social involvement and psychological well-being? *American Psychologist*, 53 (9), 1017–1032.

Kraut, R., Kiesler, S., Boneva, B., Cummings, J., Helgeson, V., & Crawford, A. (2002). Internet paradox revisited. *Journal of Social Issues*, 58 (1), 49–74.

Lee, S.J. (2009). Online communication and adolescent social ties: Who benefits from Internet use? *Journal of Computer-Mediated Communication*, 14, 509–531.

Maslow, A.H. (1968). *Toward a Psychology of Being.* New York: Van Nostrand.

Mazur, E. & Richards, L. (2011). Emerging adults' social networking online: Homophily or diversity? *Journal of Applied Developmental Psychology*, 32, 180–188.

McKenna, K.Y.A., Green, A.S., & Gleason, M.E.J. (2002). Relationship formation on the Internet: What's the big attraction? *Journal of Social Issues*, 58, 9–31.

Mesch, G.S. (2001). Social relationships and Internet use among adolescents in Israel. *Social Science Quarterly*, 82 (2), 329–339.

Mesch, G.S. & Frankel, M. (2011). Family and technology, from balance to imbalance. In Wright, K. & Webb, L. (Eds), *Computer Mediated Communication in Close Personal Relationships*. Cresskill, NJ: Hampton Press.

Newcomb, A.F. & Bagwell, C.L. (1995). Children's friendship relations: A meta-analytic review. *Psychological Bulletin*, 117, 306–347.

Nie, N.H., Hillygus, D.S., & Erbing, L. (2002). Internet use, interpersonal relationships, and sociability: A time diary study. In Wellman, B.

& Haythornthwaite, C. (Eds), *The Internet in Everyday Life* (pp. 215–244). Oxford: Blackwell.

O'Sullivan, P.B. (2000). What you don't know won't hurt me: Impression management functions of communication channels in relationships. *Human Communication Research*, 26, 403–431.

Pew Internet Report (2013). Report available online at http://www.pewinternet.org/2013/10/21/online-dating-relationships/ (Accessed 3rd September, 2014).

Schwartz, A.L., Galliher, R.V., & Rodriguez, M.M. (2011). Self-disclosure in Latino intercultural and intracultural friendships and acquaintanceships: Links with collectivism, ethnic identity, and acculturation. *Cultural Diversity and Ethnic Minority Psychology*, 17 (1), 116–121.

Shtatfeld, R. & Barak, A. (2009). Factors related to initiating interpersonal contacts on Internet dating sites: A view from the Social Exchange Theory. *Interpersona: An International Journal on Personal Relationships*, 3 (2), 19–37.

Skopek, J., Schmitz, A., & Blossfeld, H.-P. (2011). The gendered dynamics of age preferences—Empirical evidence from online dating. *Journal of Family Research*, 3, 267–290.

Snyder, M., Tanke, E.D., & Berscheid, E. (1977). Social perception and interpersonal behavior: On the self-fulfilling nature of social stereotypes. *Journal of Personality and Social Psychology*, 35, 656–666.

Strafford, L. & Canary, D.J. (1991). Maintenance strategies and romantic relationship type, gender and relational characteristics. *Journal of Social and Personal Relationships*, 8 (2), 217–242.

Thibaut, N. & Kelley, H. (1959). *The Social Psychology of Groups.* New York: Wiley.

Tidwell, L.C. & Walther, J.B. (2002). Computer-mediated communication effects on disclosure, impressions, and interpersonal evaluations: Getting to know one another a bit at a time. *Human Communication Research*, 28, 317–348.

Valkenburg, P.M. & Peter, J. (2007). Online communication and adolescent well-being: Testing the stimulation versus the displacement hypothesis. *Journal of Computer Mediated Communication*, 12 (4), 1169–1182.

Valkenburg, P.M. & Peter, J. (2011). Online communication among adolescents: An integrated model of its attraction, opportunities, and risks. *Journal of Adolescent Health*, 48 (2), 121–127.

Walther, J.B. (1996). Computer-mediated communication: Impersonal, interpersonal, and hyperpersonal interaction. *Communication Research*, 23, 3–43.

Walther, J.B. & Bazarova, N.N. (2008). Validation and application of electronic propinquity theory to computer-mediated communication in groups. *Communication Research*, 35, 622–645.

Whitty, M.T. & Buchanan, T. (2010). 'What's in a "screen name"?' Attractiveness of different types of screen names used by online daters. *International Journal of Internet Science*, 5 (1), 5–19.

Whitty, M. & Gavin, J. (2001). Age/Sex/Location: Uncovering the social cues in the development of online relationships. *CyberPsychology and Behaviour*, 4 (5), 623–630.

Yee, N. & Bailenson, J. (2007). The proteus effect: The effect of transformed self-representation on behaviour. *Human Communication Research*, 33, 271–290.

Zajonc, R.B. (2001). Mere exposure: A gateway to the subliminal. *Current Directions in Psychological Science*, 10 (6), 224–228.

Further reading

Two books are highly recommended for further reading around the notion of *romantic relationships online*:

Ben-Ze'ev, A. (2004). *Love Online: Emotions on the Internet*. Cambridge: Cambridge University Press.

Whitty, M. & Carr, A. (2006). *Cyberspace Romance: The Psychology of Online Relationships*. Basingstoke & New York: Palgrave MacMillan.

If you have not yet read them, the two Kraut et al. papers cited in this chapter are a must for understanding how research has explored the impact of the Internet on familial relationships:

Kraut, R., Kiesler, S., Boneva, B., Cummings, J., Helgeson, V., & Crawford, A. (2002). Internet paradox revisited. *Journal of Social Issues*, 58 (1), 49–74.

Kraut, R.E., Patterson, M., Lundmark, V., Kiesler, S., Mukhopadhyay, T., & Scherlis, W. (1998). Internet paradox: A social technology that reduces social involvement and psychological well-being? *American Psychologist*, 53 (9), 1017–1032.

Discussion questions

1. Critically consider the role played by social capital in promoting the formation and/or maintenance of online relationships.

2. Outline and evaluate different theories of online relationship formation.

3. What role might behaviour confirmation play in online relationships?

4. Discuss how computer mediated communication technologies can be seen to both create and overcome relationship barriers.

5. Discuss the notion of 'realness' in relation to different types of online relationships.

6. Critically consider whether the positives outweigh the negatives of making new friends and finding new lovers online.

5 Online Groups

CLIONA FLOOD, BRENDAN ROONEY,
& HANNAH BARTON

 Learning objectives

Upon finishing this chapter, you will hopefully be able to:

- Identify the main theme or trend in social psychology of self in online groups.
- Describe key terms in the social psychology of the self in online groups.
- Discuss the various types of online groups and the functions they serve to the member and society.
- Evaluate the positive and negative impact of online group membership for the individual and society.

5.1 Introduction

The more the Internet develops, the more people are using it to get together, communicate and interact with others in online groups. The online self is one that exists in the context of others. It is viewed by others, it develops, interacts, takes from, and works with other online users. These online groups shape many aspects of the individual member and society. Many robust social psychological theories remain consistently useful when applied to the online world, yet in other ways, online groups have developed various unique characteristics.

In this chapter we will address the question of why people join groups in online environments. What motivates people to join online groups and what functions does membership give? Membership can be motivated by a number of things, for example, learning, networking, and socializing. Online groups also facilitate social support and collaboration with experts on topics of mutual interest, the sharing of experiences, and creation of knowledge. We can collaboratively problem solve online and play interactive games. Most of all, this interaction with a diverse community of similar minded individuals brings people together in a space where they can share, get feedback, act as agents of change, and learn from each other. We will also look at how the individual can contribute to the social processes within the online group. The chapter begins by exploring the definition and problems with defining an online group. It will then discuss some similarities and differences in how online groups can affect a member's thoughts or behaviour. The rest of the chapter is divided into two parts: the first part will explore the functions of online groups for individual members and the various benefits for the individual. The second part will look at the outcomes of these online groups and the way they have served a function for society.

5.2 **The online self in the context of online others**

You might wonder why we would talk about groups in a book about **cyberpsychology**. Human survival relies on our ability to interact with others and this interaction involves identifying with others and distinguishing ourselves from others. According to Benson (2001) self is primarily a locative system designed by evolution and culture for negotiating our ways through the physical and psychological human world. Importantly, it acts to position the person in relation to others. Without the existence of others, there is no need for a self. In Aristotle's Politics, he describes humans as social animals. People live and interact in groups and they carry their society and culture with them when they are alone. So it is no surprise that, as the Internet grew in size and functionality, it would become a social place. For example, Gamers report that the social aspect of online gaming is one of the strongest motivators to engage in gaming (Jansz & Tanis, 2007).

The Internet can facilitate offline 'real-life' groups to stay connected by computer mediated communication (**CMC**) such as email and instant messaging. In addition, there are also countless groups that primarily form and exist online (e.g., a support group for a very rare medical condition). Often these groups have evolved from offline to online or *vice versa*. In some cases, it might be difficult to define the group as either offline or online; for example, consider a Facebook group set-up for your college class. Perhaps the class is considered 'the real group,' the offline group. But what if the online method is the most consistent aspect of the group communication, that even continues over the holidays or after graduation. Is this still an offline group?

5.3 **Defining an online group**

Arnold et al. (2010) defines a group as 'two or more people who are perceived by themselves and others as a social entity' (p. 621). This can apply to any face-to-face group situation, such as work, college, or social situations. The size of a group is limited by the function and the purpose of the group itself. But what about an online group? Howard and Magee (2013), (drawing on the work of McKenna & Green, 2002, Baker, 2008, McKenna, 2008) define an online group as three or more people who consider themselves a group and interact via the Internet. These might be text-based and include chat-rooms and forums, or some use video, voice, and avatars to interact. Social networking tools are particularly useful in the development of online groups; sites such as Facebook and MySpace will be familiar to many readers.

One of the most common ways to categorize online groups is by classifying them based on the primary function of the group, that is, the reason the majority of people joined (Bargh & McKenna, 2004). Following this method, a typology by Howard (2014) uses four categories. The first category is what Howard calls the **stigmatized identity groups**. Generally, these groups include members who have a shared characteristic, and that characteristic is/was traditionally socially objectionable. For example, groups that form around sexual orientation or extreme political views. The second classification is for the groups that offer support to members. These **support groups** typically comprise members who have medical, health, or social difficulties. These groups can be particularly helpful in cases where the members' experience is uncommon and thus support may be difficult to find. Howard also categorizes **shared interest groups**, where members have a particular pastime and/or pursuit (e.g., a forum for gamers or people planning a wedding). These groups are generally about sharing resources and experiences of the activity. Finally, Howard identifies **organizational groups**. These groups include members who are primarily interested in doing tasks for their work. For example, a committee may keep in touch and work in an online forum. While Howard's classification is helpful to consider the purpose of various groups, it is important to note that these categories may not be mutually exclusive. That is, many groups might be considered to fit in to more than one category. Consider a group that campaigns for equal rights for some socially marginalized group. While they have a shared interest (shared interest group?), they might also value the support offered (support group?) to those who feel stigmatized (stigmatized identity groups?).

5.4 The online group and the individual

For a long time social psychologists have known that being in a group can have a positive or negative influence on our thoughts, feelings, and behaviours. One of the most powerful ways in which groups can influence the self, is through the establishment of norms. **Norms** are shared standards of conduct and behaviour among group members and they can be either explicit (rules, like no talking in the library) or implicit (common practice like shaking hands). Once people have learned these norms (through a process we call *socialization*) they often conform and comply with requests of group members so as to fit in and obtain social approval (called **normative influence**) or perhaps because they accept what the group are doing is correct, or that the group members have more experience or knowledge than they do (**informational influence**).

Just like offline groups, online groups also have expected norms of behaviour. Sometimes members learned these by experience, or sometimes these are written down in rule form, or a members' charter, other times they are communicated by a moderator or a **Frequently Asked Questions (FAQ)** section. Just like offline groups, online groups can (explicitly or implicitly) reprimand violations of the stated norms, using warnings or expulsion from the group. The threat of being excluded from a group can be just as powerful in an online group as an offline group. For example, Williams, Cheug, and Choi (2000), using a virtual tossing game in an online experiment, found that cyber-ostracism led to participants experiencing a loss of control and having a more negative mood. For this reason, many group members feel the same social pressures to conform in online groups and try to present themselves in a socially cohesive manner online (but not always, as we will talk about later).

In addition to our choices and attitudes, groups can also influence our ability to perform tasks. For example, some of the earliest work in social psychology, identified the phenomenon of **social facilitation** (Triplett, 1898, Allport, 1924). Social facilitation occurs when our performance on a task improves due to the presence of others. This is often restricted to easy or well-rehearsed tasks. Typically, if the task is more complex and/or not well rehearsed then social inhibition can occur. This may be evident in online groups, when we look at the rise of social gaming. Despite the fact that gamers no longer need to be in the same location to play games together, for instance, Entertainment Software Association (ESA, 2011) reports that 65% of gamers surveyed do play in co-location with other gamers; that is, gamers are physically in the same location, while playing a game together online.

5.4.1 **Why be a member of an online group?**

It looks as though online groups are just like offline groups, right? Perhaps, in some ways, but in other ways, they can be very different. For example, groups in cyberspace offer individuals a place to interact in a different way than they would in a face-to-face environment. In many groups, things like time, culture, and social status may not be as important in the online world. Communication in online groups often involves just text, often with an absence of non-verbal cues (things like facial expression or posture are missing when we communicate through text alone). The 'cue-filtered' nature of these spaces can mean that online groups have some unique characteristics (positive and negative) when compared to traditional offline groups.

5.4.2 **To be any self**

In an online group a person might remain anonymous, or chose a pseudonym to conceal their identity. Indeed, a person could represent many aspects of their personality or identity (openness, intelligence, age, gender) to the group in a more 'managed' fashion. Thus online groups can be said to facilitate **impression management**. That is, members of online groups have an opportunity to present themselves to the group in a more desirable way. Perhaps they can try out a range of different personae, easily, on a whim, or they can work hard to construct a new identity over a long period of time. This malleability of self-representation can then lead to some different social rules or norms online. For example, Kim (2009) argues that when social cues are supplied they may be magnified by others as a particularly important aspect of the member's character. It can also be the case that, in the absence of many social cues, the sharing of demographic similarities may in fact become highlighted in cyberspace.

In addition to this increased ability to present oneself in a different way online, the lack of visual cues, cultural context or other social cues that often temper and modify communication offline, can enable a freedom of expression that is not available in the face-to-face world. For this reason, Nguyen, Bin, and Campbell (2012) argue that there is an impression that disclosure of personal information happens more often online than offline. However, this assumption had not been tested until they looked at the problem. From the findings of their research, the assumption is not so straightforward, as disclosure can depend on numerous factors such as relationships between group members, the mode of communication, and the context (Attrill, 2012).

One factor that may affect the freedom of communication is what Suler (2004) describes as an **online disinhibition effect**, where a person can feel less restricted by their traditional ways of behaving, because they feel distanced from the group. Suler argues that this interaction can either be benign or toxic. Benign interaction may offer people the opportunity to explore parts of themselves and interact in new ways with people and this can enable personal self-growth. Some people may benefit from engaging with openness and acceptance, share every aspect of their personal lives and they can be kind and generous to fellow members. **Toxic inhibition** can also offer opportunities to act in ways not practised in everyday life, yet it can be negative and destructive. Social interactions that are disinhibited can involve rudeness, unkind criticism, anger, flaming, trolling, cyberbullying, crime, and other violence.

5.4.3 To be part of the in-group

So far we talked about how group members can manage and change how they represent their identity to other group members. People can also shape and maintain their identity by merely selecting from and joining the myriad groups that exist online. The groups to which a person belongs forms what Henri Tajfel and John Turner in the 1970s referred to as their **social identity**. That is, the way they present and think about themselves in terms of the groups they belong to and identify with. This social identity is extremely important for what Rogers (1959) described as our **self-concept**, that is, the overall collection of ideas we have about ourselves and about how others think of us. **Social identity theory (SIT)** (Tajfel, 1974, Tajfel & Turner, 1979) argues that when we identify with a group, we will categorize and compare ourselves to others based on group membership. It states that individuals define themselves in terms of their group memberships and seek to maintain a positive identity through association with positively valued groups and through self-serving comparisons with other groups (Tajfel & Turner, 1979).

Membership of various groups can also shape our behaviour. Early studies in social psychology (Tajfel & Turner, 1979) have revealed that we feel more positive towards members of our group (**in-group**) and less positive to members of other groups (**out-group**). In order to maintain our **self-esteem** we can often focus on the strengths of the in-group and its members, while also making negative associations with members of another group, the out-group. This in-group favouritism and out-group derogation can lead to an increase in self-esteem, but can also fuel an 'us versus them' type of perception and behaviour. For example, Tynes, Reynolds, and Greenfield (2004) showed that for teenagers interacting online, ethnic identity is salient and often explicitly stated in online communications. This means that ethnicity often features as a defining characteristic of online identities and the belief that one's own ethnicity is superior (**ethnocentrism**) can be common in an online environment. It has been thought in the past, that ethnocentrism was activated through competition between groups, but Tajfel et al. (1971) report that merely being categorized as a group member is sufficient to create competitive intergroup behaviour. Amichai-Hamburger (2005) has shown that this paradigm also applies to behaviour in online groups and can spark hostility between members of different online groups.

5.4.4 For reciprocity and social capital

From the previous section 5.4.3 we can see that certain factors affect our identification with various groups. This identification is important and can determine our level of participation within the group and the strength of our bond to the group. In an effort to explain why people contribute to online groups and communities, Kollock (1999) recognizes the importance of anticipated reciprocity and recognition for the contribution. Reciprocity is an important motivator in social behaviour. It can be explained as *quid pro quo* behaviour. For example, trust and reciprocity have been described as the most significant factors that drive knowledge sharing (Davenport et al., 1998), and can be destroyed by non-reciprocation or non-disclo-sure of information. The returns on our contribution do not necessarily have to be large, but contributions must be acknowledged in order to enhance commitment to the group. For example, Facebook's 'like' feature is used effectively in group interactions to allow group members to efficiently acknowledge contributions and enhance reciprocity. The idea behind this is **social exchange theory**, (Homans, 1958), which states that we typically expect recip-rocal benefits such as praise, approval, and trust when we act in accordance with social norms. We act to maximize our rewards (positive emotions, self-esteem) and minimize our social costs such as time, effort, or even negative emotions. The more rewards we get from the group (praise and acknowledgement) the more our commitment to the group is enhanced.

We can refer to the rewards we get from being in a group as **social capital**. This is the col-lective benefit one gains from the social interactions and networking. According to Ellison, Steinfield, and Lampe (2006), social capital can be seen as the glue that holds together social collectives such as networks of personal relationships, communities, or even whole nations. **Bridging social capital** refers to benefits from weak social ties that people have when they feel inspired and informed by each other, while **bonding social capital** comes from the stronger social ties that come with emotional support and understanding. Gaming as well as social networking sites like Facebook have been shown to increase bridging social capital (Huvila, Holmberg, Ek, & Widén-Wulff, 2010) but the results are mixed in terms of how these online groups contribute to bonding social capital (Lee & Lee, 2010).

5.4.5 **To get information or individual gain**

People join online groups for many reasons. These include information seeking or individual gain. However, people also join online groups in order to further their education. Massive Open Online Courses (**MOOCs**) offer online participants the opportunity to gain knowledge and expertise in areas in which they are interested. Assessment is mainly carried out by peers and participation in the online discussion forums, with break-out groups providing an import-ant part of the learning process. However, not every learner is willing to, or is comfortable in contributing to the group process. Ringelman's concept of **social loafing** (cited in Latane, Williams, & Harkins, 1979) is a term commonly used when describing face-to-face group members who reduce their individual effort compared to the effort they would make when working alone. The term '**Free Riding**' is used to describe individuals who do not contribute their share to the group project, yet share the benefits of the group (Jones, 1984, Albanese & Van Fleet, 1985). Does social loafing occur in an online group? The virtual environment has its own 'personalities' when it comes to group participation and there is no doubt that people interact and contribute to online blogs, forums and online communities in different ways. For example, Bishop (2011) reports that 90% of people visiting websites are merely pas-sive consumers of information, rather than contributors to the group. The term '**lurker**' has been around since the 1990s (Beaudouin & Velkovska, 1999, King, 1994, Parks & Floyd, 1996). Lurking may be more acceptable online than offline and according to Preece, Nonnecke, and Andrews (2004) there can be many reasons for lurking. Some reasons for non-participation include browsing, having nothing to offer, not having time to contribute, the number of mes-sages already posted, or technical reasons. Some lurk to find out the way that a group inter-acts without participating, others to explore the expected behaviour. Sometimes lurking is due to personality reasons such as shyness, or even privacy concerns. Interestingly, Preece et al. (2004) did not find lurkers to be 'selfish free-riders' (p. 221), that is they are not people who take but do not give back (Kollock, 1999). Haythornthwaite (2009) has described lurking as a reaction to information overload and it can be thought of as a way of reacting to the chaos that is often found in online communities. Sebastian (2013), has identified many different types of contributors to online groups such as Ultras, Dippers, Deniers, Virgins, Peacocks, Ranters, Challengers, Ghosts, Informers, Quizzers, and Approval Seekers (see Giles, 2010, and *Ragan's PR Daily* (http://www.prdaily.com/Main/Home.aspx) for more details on these different types of group-contributors).

5.4.6 **For support**

The Internet provides a wealth of resources to those seeking information, help, and affirmation. For instance, individuals might seek support and information on a variety of life issues such as health, treatments, sexual issues, mental health advice, and child-rearing online. This support is usually non-professional and free of charge. People come together and share coping strategies and treatments for illness. They share their experiences, listen and accept others' experience, and in general provide a supportive and sympathetic social network. The management of self-help or peer-support groups is mainly carried out by volunteers who have personal experience in the topic.

Online groups differ to some extent to offline groups in that the online community can be large and more diverse than in a face-to-face situation. As mentioned earlier, such online groups can feature an online disinhibition effect (Suler, 2004) where some members self-disclose more than they would in a face-to-face situation. Members may also act more intensely than if they were in a non-virtual situation. Barak, Boniel-Nissim, and Suler (2008) report that online support groups have been in existence for quite a long time and argue that there are conflicting findings as to their effectiveness. They reviewed a number of studies and state that personal and interpersonal dynamics are increased by the online disinhibition effect. Factors such as the act of writing, expressing emotions, collecting information and knowledge, being part of a social network, enhanced decision-making skills, and changed behaviour all help participants' empowerment when in distress. They argue that such groups enhance well-being, self-confidence, independence, and a sense of control by participation in support groups. However, they also warn of the potential downside, such as the development of dependency on the support group, distancing from in-person contacts and the potential for unpleasant social engagement relating to cyberspace experiences.

However, there is strong evidence that the Internet has enabled people to develop better coping skills via computer-mediated communication, particularly in the area of health. Coulson (2005) examined the support network of sufferers of irritable bowel syndrome. From his research he suggested that of the 572 posted messages looked at, they fell into five categories of social support—that of *emotional, esteem, information, network,* and *tangible assistance.* His analysis suggested that the main function of this group was that of communication and information, particularly in the area of symptom interpretation, illness management and interactions with professional health carers. Van Uden-Kraan et al. (2008) explored the presumption that online support groups had an empowering impact for patients who participated. They confirmed that the participation in online support groups was in fact empowering to participants.

From the previous sections we can see that online groups offer people a range of benefits that might motivate them to engage in such Internet-based social interaction. But in addition to the benefits of online groups for the individual, the existence of online groups also has implications for the productivity and culture of the wider society.

5.5 The online group and society

When individuals collaborate or compete in online groups their behaviours and discussions produce what can be referred to as a **collective intelligence** (Russell, 1995, Levy, 1997). For example, in his book, *The Wisdom of Crowds*, Surowiecki (2004) writes about how the audience in the television game show *Who Wants to Be a Millionaire?* gave the correct answer 91% of the time, whereas the individual experts were only correct 65% of the time. Surowiecki (2004) reports that 'under the right circumstances, groups are remarkably intelligent, and are often smarter than the smartest people in them'. This form of group work builds on the idea that the whole is greater than the sum of its parts and so collective intelligence is seen as an accelerated form of human performance (Nguyen, 2008). Thus, the term collective intelligence focuses on the outputs of the group rather than the ability of any individual (Levy, 1997). Indeed some argue that the group can be conceptualized as an individual rational agent with a mind of its own (Russell, 1995).

Many enterprising organizations and individuals have successfully harnessed the strengths of collective intelligence to solve problems or to guide future individuals and organizations' action. This collective intelligence has been fostered and harnessed in a number of various and overlapping ways that we will consider next. One main distinction between the ways in which collective intelligence can emerge online is whether or not the individuals involved work as a group and interact or remain as sole contributors to a large collection of responses.

5.5.1 Online collaborative learning

When participants engage in discussion and collaboration for learning purposes collective intelligence can emerge. Importantly, engaging in such activities in an online environment may provide advantages over a face-to-face forum (Joiner, 2004). The open and democratic nature of CMC allows for online real-time and even simultaneous exchanges and contributions, while also allowing for deliberation and reflection on what has already been contributed. These qualities are ideal for allowing groups to work together and learn. There is also research to suggest that CMC features such as anonymity or the disinhibiting effects of an online forum create an environment where more equal participation occurs (Joiner, 2004). Comparatively, research suggest that in an offline environment people might concede and/or conform more to individuals or views that are perceived to be 'high status' (Bonito & Hollingshead, 1997). In other words, when you're face-to-face with people, the group often conform to the most senior, or the most qualified person there. In the online environment, contributors appear to be more equal.

However, CMC is not infallible when it comes to other forms of group work online. For example, Baltes, Dickenson, Sherman, Bauer, and LaGanke (2002) reviewed and analysed a number of studies comparing group work and decision making using CMC and face-to-face communication. They report that both types of decision making have advantages and disadvantages but the unique and novel nature of CMC meant that users needed to develop their skills for working effectively in an online group. For this reason, CMC was not superior to face-to-face. However, they do argue that it has the potential to be superior, if used appropriately. They argue that specific steps can be taken to enhance collaboration, constructive communication, and equality.

5.5.2 Crowd sourcing

As mentioned, collective intelligence can emerge from collaborative discussions and group work online, where individuals work together to solve problems or explore information. Nguyen (2008) points out that collective intelligence necessarily involves some variance in knowledge and even opposing views. In the process of collaborative learning, disagreements might be discussed and perspectives might be compromised. However, there is an alternative approach to harnessing collective intelligence. Rather than compromising or averaging responses and ideas, it is also possible to simply aggregate responses so as to illuminate the optimal course of action or the preferred product. For example, an individual or an organization might simply look to the most creative or popular solution from a large number of responses. Indeed, Surowiecki (2004) argues that the Internet and CMC provides a unique opportunity to facilitate such aggregation of high quantities of disparate contributions so as to produce solutions that are superior to those of individuals or collaborative groups. This sort of activity has been termed **crowdsourcing**.

Crowdsourcing was first described by Jeff Howe (2006) as the outsourcing of work previously done by employees to large groups or networks within the online community. According to Howe, crowdsourcing was operated by businesses in the form of an 'open call' for people to help solve a problem or contribute to a task or decision. By allowing large groups of people to contribute and decide on the best outcome, businesses could harness the collective intelligence and source truly excellent ideas. Popular ideas or responses are usually rewarded and the organization or individual who made the call can use the responses for their benefit (Brabham, 2008). Thus crowdsourcing is an inexpensive and effective process of problem solving in corporate research and development (Howe, 2006, Brabham, 2008, Brito, 2008, Haklay & Weber, 2008, Fritz et al., 2009).

While crowdsourcing is primarily driven by individual submissions, it can sometimes involve collaborative submissions; for example, when groups might collaborate to design projects that get discussed, pitched, and voted on by others. Nevertheless, crowdsourcing emphasizes the aggregation of crowd knowledge rather than collaboration, to identify the optimal course of action or choice (Nguyen, 2008). Within the various uses of collective intelligence there are some further distinctions (Parvanta, Roth, & Keller, 2013) for further details on various major types of crowdsourcing).

5.5.3 Types of crowdsourcing

The first way in which business can capitalize on the behaviour of online crowds is by having them do the work. This can be referred to as '**crowdlabour**' (Parvanta et al., 2013). This is where a business will set a task that requires a certain skill or ability and large groups of online users work. Sometimes these tasks might require specialized skills and other times they might simply require a large number of dedicated people. Parvanta et al. (2013) cite the example of using online crowds to monitor communications, maybe on a helpline or other similar system, where the organization can be notified when a message comes through. Some tasks benefit from crowdsourcing if they are labour intensive but cannot be performed (optimally) by software. For example, Graber and Graber (2012) cite the example of **Foldit**, an online puzzle game where participants will try to identify the structural configuration of proteins. The solutions that score highest are reviewed by experts for consideration. This way, people are playing games online while scientific research benefits from the collective wisdom. Graber and Graber point out that, because the only incentive that a player receives is a place on the leaderboard, Foldit is a very low cost way of recruiting labour.

Another common example of crowdlabour can be found in the area of translation studies and in the development of health promotion materials. For health promotion materials to be effective they must be designed carefully with feedback from individuals within the target audience, especially when the message originates in a language different to the one of the target audience. This can often be expensive and time consuming. Here, crowdsourcing offers an ideal opportunity to source large numbers of translators. For example, Turner, Kirchhoff, and Capurro (2012) report that it only took them 12 days and US $374 to recruit just under 400 participants. The authors report that in addition to the efficiency of such crowdsourcing, it also allows for accessing a more diverse population.

The second way in which crowdsourcing can be used places less emphasis on doing the work, because it involves a direct request for (typically small) financial contributions from large groups of people. This **crowdfunding** is quite commonly requested to seed fund creative projects. It is also used by some who might have more short term goals or aim to recoup some previous loss (Parvanta et al., 2013). Due to the dependence on individual investments, many crowdfunding projects depend largely on the organization's or individual's ability to convince their audience that their project is worth investing in.

Crowds can also be recruited in the name of more traditional data collection or information finding. **Crowd research** can gather input and feedback on all sorts of topics from large groups in an efficient manner. A simple example of crowd research comes in the form of text voting that can be seen on major reality television shows (Parvanta et al., 2013). While this system allows for opinions to be sourced from large groups very quickly, research demonstrates that even when this is managed well, social bias and herding effects can develop (Brabham, 2010). For this reason, Parvanta et al. (2013) consider crowd voting to be more of an awareness generating tool rather than a market research technique. Other forms of crowd research can produce much higher quality data and more authentic representations of the participants' knowledge, views, or experiences. For example, consider the use of online questionnaires and surveys that might be used in an undergraduate psychology research project. The questionnaire can be distributed to large diverse groups simultaneously to explore the variables in question. While research has demonstrated that online questionnaires are comparable to traditional offline questionnaires in various ways (Krantz & Dalal, 2000, Smither, Walker, & Yap, 2004, Cole, Bedesian, & Feild, 2006, Deutskens, de Ruyter, & Wetzels, 2006, Luce, Winzelberg, Das, Osborne, Bryson, & Taylor, 2007, Reips, 2008), online questionnaires can be particularly useful for avoiding certain 'traditional' problems with questionnaires such as reluctance to respond (Weisband & Kiesler, 1996, Tourangeau, 2004) or socially desirable responses (Frick, Bachtiger, & Reips, 2001). They can thus also be considered as a crowd or group research tool online.

5.5.4 **Motivations of the crowd**

As we can see, business and other organizations have much to gain from the employment of a crowdsourcing technique, but this doesn't explain what motivates the individuals within the crowd to engage in such behaviours. Why do people help, labour, respond, and produce goods or services for these tasks?

Brabham (2010) conducted a qualitative analysis of crowd members' responses to an exploratory interview. Emerging from this work and building on previous research (Brabham, 2008), various motivations for engaging in such processes were identified. While some people engage in crowdsource activities to acquire the included bounty or incentives (i.e., financial gains), many participated in response to a sense of community or the feeling of contributing to a bigger goal. Other findings indicated that many people are motivated by the love of the task itself. For example, it is quite common to see open source software produced for free (Hars & Ou, 2002, Hertel, Niedner, & Hermann, 2003, Bonaccorsi & Rossi, 2004). Specific contributor motivations will vary depending on the task and the organization. Some might, for instance, wish to refine their skills at a skill like photography and receive feedback from the crowd about their work, while others might see it as an opportunity to promote themselves or their work and acquire offline opportunities.

When exploring contributor motivations, Brabham (2010) reports that, for some individuals, their activities might represent a potentially problematic addiction, in a similar way that other problems have been identified such as gaming (Griffiths, 2008) or social networking addictions (Kuss & Griffiths, 2011). The issue is potentially problematic for ethical reasons and experts have argued that crowdsourcing activities have the potential to cause harm to those who engage in them (Graber & Graber, 2012). According to Graber and Graber (2012), the individuals in the crowd are particularly vulnerable when the organizers employ techniques so as to manipulate users into continued participation. In this regard, Graber and Graber (2012) consider the idea of a '**greme**', which is a game-research hybrid that may allow the organization to use members of the crowd as research participants. These greme-studies also offer members rewards and thus might be considered to have the same damaging effects as a slot machine. Intertwined in the issues stated here, Graber and Graber (2012) argue that some of the participants may be minors and might be particularly vulnerable to this harm. For this reason, they call for institutional Ethics Review Boards to employ specific scrutiny when evaluating proposals for crowdsourcing activities.

5.5.5 **Human flesh search**

So far we've looked at ways in which organizations or individuals can use online group behaviours to achieve various goals. But some group behaviours are not always so structured or strategic. Another controversial and ethically questionable way in which online crowd behaviour has been used (or in some cases, has naturally emerged) is in **human flesh search** (**HFS**). That is, online crowds are used as a search mechanism to locate or identify previously anonymous individuals. Typically, this sort of search occurs using an open call and by exposing personal details about the target, in response to something the individual is reported to have done (Chao & Tao, 2012). This is usually instigated to bring about a perceived 'justice', group harassment, public humiliation, or vigilantism. However, more recent research has identified other ways HFS has been used such as exposing scientific fraud or illegal acts like hit-and-run offences (Wang et al., 2010). Research exploring HFS has reported that they typically involve a more natural form of group self-organization than other types of crowdsourcing. For this reason, some of the major factors that influence its escalation are the number of users or community size, the ways in which information is shared, cultural and subcultural values, and user-computer skills (Chen & Sharma, 2011). They go on to point out that on one hand it can solicit civic engagement, fight illegal activities, and deter unethical behaviour; on the other hand the HFS can involve violations of privacy, sometimes violence, and unintended side effects.

5.6 Future directions

Concerns that the Internet is threatening social life are not unheard of today. There are many people who fear that the constant checking of mobile devices and staring at screens is changing human nature and creating a solitary animal. Meanwhile there are alternative arguments. People see new technologies as a facilitator for people to become more social, more human, and to do so more efficiently. While there are valid arguments on each side, these debates often focus on the online versus the offline, and it is likely that these sorts of discussions will soon become limited if not irrelevant. As technology develops, the distinction between online and offline is becoming more blurred. Technologies are allowing people to come together and maintain groups in a way that integrates the offline and online worlds. During this time, researchers are presented with a wonderful opportunity to explore human nature in a new and changing social context, but equally we have a responsibility to guide our society through these changes towards a positive world of social development.

5.7 Chapter summary

- The Internet can facilitate offline 'real-life' groups to stay connected via CMC. It can also enable virtual groups of people to form who would not have the opportunity to meet up in 'real-life'.
- Howard's (2014) four types of groups are a useful way to categorize the different types of online groups, that is, stigmatized groups, support groups, shared interest groups, and organizational groups.
- Online and offline groups share similarities. However, in online groups consideration must be given to the fact that people may behave differently due to the lack of visual social cues, 'cue-filtering', the disinhibition effect, impression management, and how an individual can construct their sense of self online.
- Online groups can be beneficial to users and support them in engaging with other like-minded people. They can share and support each other. Social engagement in the form of online gaming and problem solving is possible.
- Online groups are not without their challenges and problems. Not all group members contribute equally to the online group. Social loafing may be an issue. The online group

can have a powerful impact on society. Collective intelligence, collaborative learning, and crowdsourcing can push out the boundaries of knowledge and learning.

- Online groups can, and do, contribute to research.

 ## References

Albanese, R. & Van Fleet, D.D. (1985). Rational behavior in groups: The free-riding tendency. *Academy of Management Review*, 10, 244-255.

Allport, F.H (1924). *Social Psychology*. Boston: Houghton Mifflin.

Amichai-Hamburger, Y. (2005). Internet minimal group paradigm. *Cyberpsychology and Behaviour*, 8(2), 140-145.

Arnold, J., Randall, R., Patterson, F., Silvester, J., Robertson, I., Cooper, C., Burnes, B., Swailes, S., Harris, D., Axtell, C., & Hartog, D.D. (2010). *Work Psychology*. Harlow: Prentice Hall.

Attrill, A. (2012). Self-disclosure online. In Zheng, Y. (Ed.), *Encyclopedia of Cyber Behavior* (pp. 855-872). New York: IGI Global.

Baker, A.J. (2008). Down the rabbit hole: The role of place in the initiation and development of online relationships. In A. Barak (Ed.), *Psychological Aspects of Cyberspace*, (pp. 163-184). Cambridge: Cambridge University Press.

Baltes, B.B., Dickenson, M.W., Sherman, M.P., Bauer, C.C., & LaGanke, J.S. (2002). Computer-mediated communication and group decision making: a meta analysis. *Organisational Behaviour and Human Decision Processes*, 87, 156-179.

Barak, A., Boniel-Nissim, M., & Suler, J. (2008). Fostering empowerment in online support groups. *Computers in Human Behaviour*, 24, 1867-1883.

Bargh, J.A. & McKenna, K. (2004). The Internet and social life. *Annual Review of Psychology*, 55, 573-590.

Beaudouin, V. & Velkovska, J. (1999). The Cyberians: an empirical study of sociality in a virtual community. Paper presented at the *Ethnographic Studies in Real and Virtual Environments: Inhabited Information Spaces and Connected Communities Conference*, Edinburgh.

Benson, C. (2001). *The Cultural Psychology of Self: Place, Morality and Art in Human Worlds*. London: Routledge.

Bishop, J. (2011) Transforming lurkers into posters: The role of the participation continuum. In *Proceedings of the Fourth International Conference on Internet Technologies and Applications (ITA'11)*, Glyndwr University, Wrexham, September 2011.

Bonaccorsi, A. & Rossi, C. (2004). Altruistic individuals, selfish firms?: The structure of motivation in open source software, *First Monday*, 9(1). Online: http://firstmonday.org/ojs/index.php/fm/article/view/1113/1033 (accessed 1st September, 2014).

Bonito, J.A. & Hollingshead, A.B. (1997). Participation in small groups. *Communications Yearbook*, 20, 227-261.

Brabham, D.C. (2008) Crowdsourcing as a model for problem solving: an introduction and cases. *Convergence: The International Journal of Research into New Media Technologies*, 14(1), pp. 75-90.

Brabham, D.C. (2010). Moving the crowd at Threadless: Motivations for participation in a crowdsourcing application. *Information, Communication & Society*, 13(8), 1122-1145. doi: 10.1080/13691181003624090.

Brito, J. (2008). Hack, Mash, & Peer: crowdsourcing government transparency. *The Columbia Science and Technology Law Review*, 9, pp. 119-57.

Chao, C. & Tao, Y. (2012). Human flesh search: A supplemental review. *Cyberpsychology, Behavior and Social Networking*, 15(7), 350.

Chen, R. & Sharma, S.K. (2011). Human flesh search-Facts and issues. *Journal of Information Privacy and Security*, 7, 50-71.

Cole, M.S., Bedesian, A.G., & Feild, H.S. (2006). The measurement equivalence of web-based and paper-and-pencil measures of transformational leadership. *Organizational Research Methods*, 9, 339-363.

Coulson, N.S. (2005). Receiving social support online: An analysis of a computer-mediated support group for individuals living with irritable bowel syndrome. *Cyberpsychology & Behaviour*, 8(6), 580-584.

Davenport, T., Prusak, L., Wills, G., Alani, H., Ashri, R., Crowder, R., et al. (1998). *Working Knowledge*. Harvard Business School Press.

Deutskens, E., de Ruyter, K., & Wetzels, M. (2006). An assessment of equivalence between online and mail surveys in service research. *Journal of Service Research*, 8, 346-355.

Ellison, N., Steinfield, C., & Lampe, C. (2006). Spatially bounded online social networks and social capital: The role of Facebook. In *Proceedings of the Annual Conference of the International Communication Association*, June 19-23, Dresden, Germany.

Entertainment Software Association (2011). *Essential Facts About the Video Game Industry*. Washington, DC: Entertainment Software Association.

Frick, A., Bachtiger, M.T., & Reips, U.-D. (2001). Financial incentives, personal information and drop-out in online studies. In Reips, U.-D. & Bosnjak, M. (Eds), *Dimensions of Internet Science* (pp. 209-219). Lengerich: Pabst.

Fritz, S., McCallum, I., Schill, C., Perger, C., Grillmayer, R., Achard, F., Kraxner, F., & Obersteiner, M. (2009). Geo-Wiki.org: the use of crowdsourcing to improve global land cover. *Remote Sensing*, 1(3), 345-354.

Giles, D. (2010). *Psychology of the Media*. Basingstoke and New York: Palgrave Macmillan.

Graber, M.A. & Graber, A. (2012). Internet-based crowdsourcing and research ethics: the case for IRB review. *Journal of Medical Ethics*, 39, pp. 115-118. doi:10.1136/medethics- 2012-100798.

Griffiths, M.D. (2008). Videogame addiction: Further thoughts and observations. *International Journal of Mental Health Addiction*, 6, 182-185.

Haklay, M. & Weber, P. (2008). OpenStreetMap: user-generated street maps. *IEEE Pervasive Computing*, 7(4), pp. 12-18.

Hars, A. & Ou, S. (2002) Working for free?: Motivations for participating in open source projects. *International Journal of Electronic Commerce*, 6(3), pp. 25-39.

Haythornthwaite, C. (2009). Online knowledge crowds and communities. In *International Conference on Knowledge Communities*. Reno, USA: Center for Basque Studies, University of Nevada, Reno, pp. 1-16.

Hertel, G., Niedner, S., & Hermann, S. (2003). Motivation of software developers in the open source projects: an Internet-based survey of contributors to the Linux kernel. *Research Policy*, 32(7), 1159-1177.

Homans, G.C. (1958). Social behavior as exchange. *American Journal of Sociology*, 63(6), 597-606.

Howard, M. (2014). An epidemiological assessment of online groups and a test of a typology: What are the (dis)similarities of the online group types? *Computers in Human Behavior*, 31, 123-133.

Howard, M. & Magee, S. (2013). To boldly go where no group has gone before: An analysis off online group identity and validation of a measure. *Computers in Human Behaviour*, 20, 2058-2071.

Howe, J. (2006) The rise of crowdsourcing. *Wired*, 14(6). Available at: http://www.wired.com/wired/archive/14.06/crowds.html (accessed 1st September, 2014).

Huvila, I., Holmberg, K., Ek, S., & Widén-Wulff, W. (2010). Social capital in second life. *Online Information Review*, 34, 295-316.

Jansz, J. & Tanis, M. (2007). Appeal of playing online first person shooter games. *Cyberpsychology & Behavior*, 10, 133-136.

Joiner, R. (2004). Supporting collaboration in virtual learning environments. *Cyberpsychology & Behavior*, 7(2), 197-200.

Jones, G.R. (1984). Task visibility, free riding, and shirking: Explaining the effect of structure and technology on employee behavior. *Academy of Management Review*, 9, 684-695.

Kim, J. (2009). 'I want to be different from others in cyberspace.' The role of visual similarity in virtual group identity. *Computers in Human Behavior*, 25, 88-95.

King, S.A. (1994). Analysis of electronic support groups for recovering addicts. *Interpersonal Computing and Technology: An Electronic Journal for the 21st Century*, 2(3), 47-56.

Kollock, P. (1999). The economies of online cooperation: Gifts, and public goods in cyberspace. In Kollock, P. & Smith, M.A. (Eds), *Communities in Cyberspace* (pp. 220-239). New York: Routledge.

Krantz, J.H. & Dalal, R. (2000). Validity of Web-based psychological research. In Birnbaum, M.H. (Ed.), *Psychological Experiments on the Internet* (pp. 35-60). New York: Academic Press.

Kuss, D.J. & Griffiths, M.D. (2011). Online social networking and addiction—a review of the psychological literature. *International Journal of Environmental Research and Public Health*, 8, 3528-3552; doi:10.3390/ijerph8093528.

Latane, B., Williams, K., & Harkins, S. (1979). Many hands make light the work: The causes and consequences of social loafing. *Journal of Personality and Social Psychology*, 37, 822-832.

Lee, J. & Lee, H. (2010). The computer-mediated communication network: Exploring the linkage between the online community and social capital. *New Media & Society*, 12, 711-727.

Levy, P. (1997). *Collective Intelligence: Mankind's Emerging World in Cyberspace*. New York, NY: Perseus Books.

Luce, K.H., Winzelberg, A.J., Das, S., Osborne, M.I., Bryson, S.W., & Taylor, C.B. (2007). Reliability of self-report: Paper versus online administration. *Computers in Human Behavior*, 23, 1384–1389.

McKenna, K.Y.A. (2008). Influences on the nature and functioning of online groups. In Barak, A. (Ed.), *Psychological Aspects of Cyberspace: Theory, Research, Applications* (pp. 228–242). Cambridge: Cambridge University Press.

McKenna, K.Y.A. & Green, A.S. (2002). Virtual group dynamics. *Group Dynamics*, 6, 116–127.

Nguyen, M., Yu Sun Bin, Y.S., & Campbell, A. (2012). Comparing online and offline self-disclosure: A systematic review. *Cyberpsychology, Behaviour, and Social Networking*, 15(2), 103–111.

Nguyen, N.T. (2008). Inconsistency of knowledge and collective intelligence. *Cybernetics and Systems: An International Journal*, 39, 542–562. doi: 10.1080/01969720802188268.

Parks, R.M. & Floyd, K. (1996). Making friends in cyberspace. *Journal of Computer-Mediated Communication*, 1(4), 80 pages. Available from http://onemvweb.com/sources/sources/making_friends_cyberspace.pdf (accessed 1st September, 2014).

Parvanta, C., Roth, Y., & Keller, H. (2013). Crowdsourcing 101: A few basics to make you the leader of the pack. *Health Promotion Practice*, 14(2), 163–167.

Preece, J., Nonnecke, B., & Andrews, D. (2004). The top five reasons for lurking: improving community experiences for everyone. *Computers in Human Behavior*, 20, 201–233.

Reips, U.D. (2008). How Internet-mediated research changes science. In Barak A. (Ed.), *Psychological Aspects of Cyberspace: Theory, Research, Applications*, (pp. 268–294). Cambridge: Cambridge University Press.

Russell, P. (1995). *The Global Brain Awakens: Our Next Evolutionary Leap*. 2nd edn. USA: Global Brain, Inc.

Rogers, C. (1959). A theory of therapy, personality and interpersonal relationships as developed in the client-centered framework. In Koch, S. (Ed.), *Psychology: A Study of a Science. Vol. 3: Formulations of the Person and the Social Context*. New York: McGraw Hill.

Sebastian, M. (2013). 12 types of social media personalities. *Ragan's PR Daily*. Available at: http://www.prdaily.com/Main/Articles/12_types_of_social_media_personalities_14296.aspx# (accessed 1st September, 2014).

Smither, J.W., Walker, A.G., & Yap, M.K.T. (2004). An examination of the equivalence of web-based versus paper-and-pencil upward feedback ratings: Rater- and ratee-level analyses. *Educational and Psychological Measurement*, 64, 40.

Suler, J. (2004). The online disinhibition effect. *CyberPsychology & Behaviour*, 7(3), 321–326.

Surowiecki, J. (2004). *The Wisdom of Crowds: Why the Many are Smarter than the Few*. New York, NY: Abacus (a division of Random House Inc.).

Tajfel, H. (1974). Social identity and intergroup behaviour. *Social Science Information*, 13, 65–93.

Tajfel, H. & Turner, J.C. (1979). An integrative theory of intergroup conflict. In Austin, W.G. & Worchel, S. (Eds), *The Social Psychology of Intergroup Relations*, (pp. 94–109). Monterey, CA: Brooks-Cole.

Tajfel, H., Billig, M.G., Bundy, R.P., & Flament, C. (1971). Social categorization and intergroup behaviour. *European Journal of Social Psychology*, 1, 149–178.

Tourangeau, R. (2004). Survey research and societal change. *Annual Review of Psychology*, 55(1), 775–802.

Triplett, N. (1898). The dynamogenic factors in pacemaking and competition. *American Journal of Psychology*, 9, 507–533.

Turner, A.M., Kirchhoff, K., & Capurro, D. (2012). Using crowdsourcing technology for testing multilingual public health promotion materials. *Journal of Medical Internet Research*, 14(3), 240–248.

Tynes, B., Reynolds, L., & Greenfield, P.M. (2004). Adolescence, race and ethnicity on the Internet: A comparison of discourse in monitored vs. unmonitored chat rooms. *Journal of Applied Developmental Psychology*, 25, 667–684.

van Uden-Kraan, C.F., Drossaert, C.H.C., Taal, E., Shaw, B.R., Seydel, E.R., & van de Laar, M.A.F.J. (2008). Empowering processes and outcomes of participation in online support groups for patients with breast cancer, arthritis, or fibromyalgia. *Qualitative Health Research*, 18(3), 405–417.

Wang, F.Y., Zeng, D., Hendler, J.A., Zhang, Q., Feng, Z., Gao, Y., Wang, H., & Lai, G. (2010). A study of the human flesh search engine: crowd-powered expansion of online knowledge. *Computer (IEEE Computer Society)*, 43(8), 45–53. doi:10.1109/MC.2010.216. ISSN 0018-9162.

Weisband, S. & Kiesler, S. (1996). Self-disclosure on computer forms: Meta-analysis and implications. *Proceedings of C HI96*. Available from: http://www.sigchi.org/chi96/proceedings/ (accessed 18th September, 2014).

Williams, K.D., Cheung, C.K.T., & Choi, W. (2000). CyberOstracism: effects of being ignored over the Internet. *Journal of Personality & Social Psychology*, 79, 748–62.

Further reading

The authors in this chapter outline the issues of social influence, people in groups, intergroup relations and prejudice along with aggression and helping behaviour in:

Martin, G.N., Carlson, N.R., & Buskist, W. (2013) *Psychology.* **Pearson. Chapter 16.**

This article outlines how people share personal information online. It explores the six factors that interact to cause what Suler calls the 'Online Disinhibition Effect':

Suler, J. (2004). The online disinhibition effect. *CyberPsychology & Behaviour,* 7(3), 321–326.

 Discussion questions

1. How do the psychological theories of self contribute to our understanding of how people act in an online group?
2. Outline the benefits of online group participation.
3. Do you think online groups threaten or support self-discovery?
4. Why do people join online groups?
5. Does crowdsourcing do more good than harm?
6. Evaluate the differences between online and offline groups.
7. How can online group participation act as an agent of change in today's world?

6 Social Media and Networking Behaviour

BRENDAN ROONEY, IRENE CONNOLLY, OLIVIA HURLEY,
GRÁINNE KIRWAN, & ANDREW POWER

 Learning objectives

Upon finishing this chapter we hope that you will be able to:

- Identify the main theme or trend in theories of self and self-presentation.
- Describe key terms in the area of the self and online self-representation.
- Describe how the self is portrayed and managed online in different contexts and by different people such as politicians, athletes, young people, and victims of cybercrime.
- Describe how Social Networking Sites can make the self vulnerable to acts of aggression, bullying, and/or crime.
- Evaluate the positive and negative impact of Social Networking Sites on the self and on self-presentation.
- Provide specific examples from areas such as politics, sport, bullying, and cybercrime to illustrate where Social Networking Sites may impact on the self.

6.1 Introduction

Social media and social networking websites are a staple of daily online activity for many users. These websites often require that members use their real names, and frequently involve online interactions with individuals who users know in offline settings. This usage of real names and offline contacts demonstrates a significant change from previous mainstream online interactions, which commonly involved the use of pseudonyms and online-only contacts. Prior to the popularization of social media and social networking, many online researchers examined the way individuals in online contexts would portray a highly idealized or managed version of the self. The debut of social media and social networking websites brought with it new ways to present the self and form identities. Paradoxically, in many cases, it also seems to have brought with it a portrayal of a more genuine self in place of an idealized self. Nevertheless, in many cases, there still appears to be a tendency for the user to portray some aspects of an idealized self in their profiles, particularly in relation to traits such as sociability.

In this chapter we will outline various ways in which the advent of social networking has provided people with a new and powerful tool to form, reform, present, and represent the self. On the one hand technology allows us all the freedom to present ourselves in ways that liberate us from the usual things we do or say. We can present and reinterpret behaviours by sharing pictures and editing our blogs before they are circulated. Yet, on the other hand, in online environments, the things we do and say are more accessible, wide reaching, and long lasting than they ever were before. This is evident when we think of any viral video of a 'dance fail' or an alleged cruel act towards an animal, and how these events form or reform our impression of the person in the video. In this way, social networking sites (**SNS**s) can bring about damage to the self.

This chapter examines the portrayal of a genuine versus idealized self in social media and social networking, and the ways in which social networking can allow for both self-management and damage to the self. For illustrative purposes, the chapter considers these issues of self-management and self-damage by exploring social networking behaviour in four useful areas, namely political use of social networking, sport psychology, cyberbullying, and cybercrime.

6.2 Self: Now and beyond

In everyday life we may think of the self as the unchanging constant. My self is the bit of me that survives the ever-changing world I live in. It's the part of me that has been around the longest and it's the part that all my thoughts and emotions centre around. Yet the major theories of self that have been proposed throughout the history of psychology present a different model, a model of multiple, changing selves. Indeed, the idea of multiple selves is one of the major commonalities between the large numbers of differing theories of self. William James (1890), one of the earliest and most influential thinkers in psychology, presented one such model of self that distinguished between our physical bodily self and our social self. James writes that our social self is how we are known, what he calls our 'honor' (p. 293) or fame. This involves the stories we tell about ourselves or the way we behave in social situations. Later, theorists such as George Herbert Mead (1934) and Sigmund Freud (1948) also distinguished between different selves or aspects of self. They wrote of the distinction between the immediate instincts and impulses we have in a given situation and the self that behaves in a society, with expectations, social behaviours, and rules. Higgins (1987) used the concept of the **ought self** to describe the way we present ourselves in social situations when we must behave in a particular way, the way we ought to be. This might involve behaviours such as being polite to older strangers, or forming a queue while waiting for a bus.

Carl Rogers (1959), a pioneer of the humanistic psychology movement that rose in the 1950s and 1960s, saw the self as a phenomenological experience and emphasized the positive potential of every human. Yet he still presented a structured idea of 'self' that involved self-representations. These representations are ideas we form of our own thoughts and behaviour. According to Rogers (1959), this collection of ideas we have about ourselves and about how others think of us forms our **self-concept**. But importantly, Rogers (1959) distinguished self-concept from the **ideal self**, that is, the way we would like to be; the goals we have for ourselves. This ideal self, according to Rogers, is dynamic and forever adapting to the events in our lives and our updated self-concept. People constantly evaluate their current self-concept against their ideal self and these evaluations result in ideas of self-worth. For example, an athlete might aim to be a faster sprinter, and they might think they are lacking in this regard. According to Rogers, such inconsistency between our self-concept and our ideal self can lead to problems. With these ideas came the notion of **self-esteem** (Rosenberg, 1965). Related to self-concept, self-esteem is the result of self-evaluation. It is the overall worth we place on our thoughts, behaviours, and abilities.

Most authors accept the dichotomous distinction between the sense of self acting located in one time and environment, and a sense of a continuous self that persists over time. Damasio (1999) and Gallagher (2000) referred to this persisting self as the **narrative self** that links basic interactions and experiences. In this way, the narrative self can be thought of as 'the story of me'. According to Benson (2001) the narrative self offers coherence and continuity to our past, present, and future thoughts and behaviours. This narrative self is the basis for our **identity**, which is a constructed representation that integrates our experiences and goals. A person's identity is the way they think about and express their individuality or their affiliation with others. Identity or narrative self is constantly being transformed with new aspects being added or re-evaluated and other aspects being forgotten or dismissed. Thus, the presented self is a dynamic process. According to Benson (2001) another important feature of this dynamic narrative self is that, like all good stories, it is deeply rooted in a social, cultural, and historical context.

So, from previous theories and research in psychology, we can see that the self is two things. It is the way we respond in a specific situation, *and* it is a representation of many responses and many situations. It is a kind of story we build to represent our thoughts and behaviours. Thus the story we tell, and the image we present, is very important in shaping of the self. People can make a conscious or unconscious effort to present themselves in a good light and positively influence other peoples' perception of events. This behaviour is referred to as **impression management** (Schlenker, 1985)—it is the controlling of the impressions that other people form, in the same way you might try to look your best for an interview or a first date. In this way we are managing our self-presentation so that we present the self in a way that is ideal (ideal self) or the way we think we ought to be (ought self). In the rest of this chapter we will refer to this type of self as the **managed self** (ideal self or ought self). Some theories and theorists have referred to the other types of self as a 'real' or 'actual' self. Others have challenged the idea that anyone has any single true self. For this reason, in this chapter, we will use the term **genuine self** to refer to the self that is less idealized or less managed.

6.3 Self and anonymity online

In modern times people's selves are increasingly being represented online. Until the arrival of social networks, the Internet was used primarily as a means of finding information. Google was the leading search engine and number one Internet application since the late 1990s. As White and Le Cornu (2011) pointed out, a key distinction between information gathering and SNSs is that the latter invite people to project their personas online as an **online identity** via text, image, and video. And with ever growing technological advancements come new and more powerful ways to employ impression management. In online environments people can employ techniques of impression management in areas of their life that were previously outside of their control in face-to-face interactions (Chester & Bretherton, 2007). Online identity 'need in no way correspond to a person's real life identity; people can make and remake themselves, choosing their gender and the details of their online presentation'

(Mnookin, 1996, para. 5). When online we can control what we show to others, we might use more positive expressions, and we can even edit or Photoshop the pictures and videos that represent us.

The ability to manage identity also provides the possibility of anonymity. A person can attempt to hide their identity, choosing a pseudonym and not disclosing any personal information. This is the characteristic of the 'faceless hacker' often portrayed in the media. The perceived anonymity of the Internet can have a disinhibiting effect on a person's actions and remove a sense of responsibility. The potential to undermine an individual's inhibitions, combined with the ability to act anonymously, has the potential to lead to a breakdown in acceptable behaviour. In his book, *Future Minds*, Richard Watson (2010, p. 7) said, 'The anonymity of the web is eroding empathy, encouraging antisocial behaviour, and promoting virtual courage over real emotion.' Later in this chapter we will look at some examples of this in relation to cyberbullying and cybercrime online.

While the Internet might provide the opportunity to remain anonymous online, at the other extreme a person may reveal a large amount of personal information such as their name, date of birth, location, occupation, interests, and hobbies on social networking websites such as Facebook. However, most users fall somewhere between these two extremes, providing some personal information but choosing what details to provide depending on the circumstances. In contrast to gaming or blogging sites, where in-game identities or pseudonyms are common, a feature of social networks is a mixture of online and offline friends or contacts, and a resulting tendency of users to be open about their true identity.

Managing or concealing online identity is not as common as it has previously been. This may be because people now think about cyberspace as an aspect of everyday life, rather than a different and separate world (Wellman & Haythornthwaite, 2002). This change is recent and generational. In the past, Johnson and Post (1996) argued that cyberspace constituted a new and different space where different rules must apply. Their argument was that in the offline world there is generally a correspondence between borders drawn in physical space, between nation states, and borders in legal space. The idea of cyberspace as a place you can go to where new laws might apply is supported by the fact that you must make a decision to go there, normally by deciding to access a computer and enter a password. In this sense there is a boundary you cross to get 'there'.

Now the Internet has become just another part of life, rather than a place where different rules apply. For example, Chester (2004) found that online self-presentations were influenced more by participants' current perceptions of themselves than desirable future selves, and those aspects of identity that the participants considered central to their identity were more likely to be presented online than those rated as less important. Chester (2004) also found the intention to present a real version of self is quite strong, possibly due to participants' desires to connect with others online. With the current popularity of social networking websites, based on creating links between people who already know each other, there is no benefit in altering online identity, and people generally continue to express a less idealized version of self to those whom they initially met in person, whether the interaction takes place online or not (McKenna & Seidman, 2005).

Although it is common, not all Internet users depict themselves accurately. Both boyd (2004) and Jung, Hyunsook, and McClung (2007) described the use of false information on social networking websites. Chester (2004) also noted that while some individuals did engage in identity management, these were more likely to be people who were relatively inexperi-enced online—those who spent more time in online environments were more likely to be truthful. Participants also noted that it was difficult to maintain a dishonest online identity. The accuracy of many online representations has also been supported by researchers such as Gosling, Gaddis, and Vazire (2007) who compared impressions that people formed after viewing a Facebook profile with those formed by people who knew the profile owner from everyday life—the personality impressions showed some consensus for the two groups.

So what are the implications of such a cyber-world, where, to some extent, the user can create an identity as they wish, but are limited by the fact that their online community over-laps with their offline community? How does the blurring of the offline and online worlds impact on the self for different users? In the following sections we look at some areas of life that seem particularly illustrative of how the use of social networking can be particularly help-ful for self-management or particularly damaging to the self. For example, we identify some specific areas where impression management is often employed, such as politicians' use of social networking and athletes' engagement with reports of their own performance and with their fans. On the other hand, social networking has also been associated with more negative aspects of life, such as cyberbullying and online acts of crime.

6.4 Political use of social media

Managing identity and others' impressions of identity is particularly important for politicians, who need to be conversant with the concerns and communication preferences of those they represent. For this reason many politicians have started to take advantage of the way we can manage identity using SNS. Thus, social networking has grown in importance for working politicians in their capacity as public representatives. In the UK a number of studies (Jackson, 2006, Francoli & Ward, 2008, Jackson & Lilleker, 2011) have seen a 'jumping on the band-wagon' approach amongst some MPs by adopting e-newsletters, weblogs, and SNSs. Others have a strategic purpose and are using such technologies to enhance their ability to perform their representative roles.

The image of politicians can, in part, be created and managed through selective disclosures about their private lives (Stanyer & Wring, 2004). Politicians have used the Internet as a way of showing that they are likeable and may include providing details of their personal interests in music, sport, or films, thus showing a sense of humour or displaying any other of a myriad of personal traits they wish to disclose. Jackson and Lilleker (2011) found that for about half of MPs in the UK parliament who are on Twitter, this social network had become a regular part of their political life.

Politicians' preference seems to be for Twitter rather than Facebook. Part of the issue with using Facebook for political communication is the language of Facebook that forces users to become 'Followers' or to 'Like' a particular politician. This is likely to discourage all but those who already feel a strong allegiance to a particular politician or party. As mentioned earlier, sharing our likes and dislikes on SNS presents an image of our own self. Users of SNS need to manage these representations and may not want to show that they 'like' or are 'friends' with a particular politician. For this reason, some of those politicians using Twitter have attempted to address this by having a Facebook account that 'mirrors' their Twitter account. However, this often results in a less interactive or rich Facebook experience. Politicians who do use Facebook tend to use it, much like members of the public, to keep in touch with their friends, rather than as part of their representative role (Jackson & Lilleker, 2011). However, their use of Twitter seems more focused, where they present themselves as hard-working parliamentarians and constituency servants as well as individuals with a strong sense of personal and political identity. Jackson and Lilleker (2011, p. 101) argue that such 'tweets can break down the barriers between representative and the represented, can encourage greater trust and interest and build an impression of the MP that surpasses pejorative media narratives'. They also suggest that 'there may be democratic benefits if MPs and the public begin to listen to one another, correspond, and so adapt the micro-blog platform to incorporate a more participatory platform of engagement' (Jackson & Lilleker, 2011, p. 101).

Twitter is seen as having a considerably wider impact than the number of followers a politician's Twitter account would suggest. This is because their accounts are followed by journalists from the print media who follow the politician's tweets and pick up stories that interest them for publication in more traditional forms of media. Twitter is also seen as a more direct and immediate form of communication, less likely to suffer from being mediated or spun than traditional forms of communication between politicians and their public. Jackson and Lilleker (2011) showed that political journalists who use Twitter tend to follow all tweeting MPs, suggesting that there are benefits to those politicians in terms of gaining publicity across wider media.

Twitter appears to perform two functions for politicians, *self-promotion* and keeping in touch with constituents. A study of 300,000 Twitter users by Heil and Piskorski (2009) noted that 90% of posts were one-way, one-to-many broadcast communication, rather than two-way, many-to-many interactions. This supported the notion of Twitter as a tool of self-promotion and fits well with norms of political communication. However, Twitter also offers the potential for politicians to build communication networks. Bradley Joyce from Tweetcongress.org noted that tweeting helped politicians to quickly and clearly reach constituents (Harnden, 2009). Prior to the advent of SNS technologies most political activity online was one-way and took the form of content-heavy electronic brochures. Websites, newsletters, and blogs sought to promote their political work and thinking on current affairs, but it had limited interactivity. The move to SNS offers at least the opportunity to be more engaged with constituents. Jackson and Lilleker (2011) argued that politicians seek to attain a personal vote by being good constituency workers, and in order to demonstrate the activities they carry out as part of this role they must have an impression management strategy to publicize their achievements. Twitter, they argue, can support this objective. Lee and Shin (2012, p. 519) argued that 'people use Facebook primarily for *relationship maintenance*, while using Twitter for *information sharing*'. This would seem to fit with the use of Twitter by politicians.

Coleman and Blumler (2009, p. 181) described politicians adopting a new role as facilitators of public discussion rather than remote orators addressing an increasingly disengaged audience. They also point out that one of the most common mistakes made by top-down political leaders is that they imagine that online communication is a form of broadcasting based upon a model of a well-resourced centre and a more remote audience. In their view 'the Internet is more likely to engage users when it is conceived as a distributive space—a network of networks in which power is poly-centrically dispersed' (Coleman & Blumler, 2009, p. 180).

So the use of SNS may be an extremely beneficial way to manage impressions online, and especially in the political sphere where impression management is very important for a politician's career. But, needless to say, politicians are not the only users of SNS. Even people working in areas that seem less directly related to the online world are using SNS and directly or indirectly managing their identity, as we will see from the next section.

6.5 Athletes and social media

Campbell (2012, p. 1) stated that 'over 70 million people worldwide follow pro (professional) athletes and teams on Twitter, while another 400 million Facebook users have clicked the 'like' button on pages dedicated to sports stars and squads'. However, according to Sanderson and Kassing (2011), despite other social media platforms available, such as Facebook, Instagram, and LinkedIn, Twitter has dominated the usage figures among the sporting elite. Academics working in the world of sport psychology have, like their colleagues in disciplines such as **cyberpsychology** and politics, also become interested in this boom in social media use, specifically within their own sporting community. They have begun to examine the impact of such phenomena on their athletic clientele (Browning & Sanderson, 2012). Many athletes appear to have been drawn to Twitter as the social media of choice because it provides them, like the politicians discussed previously, with a mechanism to communicate and interact directly with their supporters and followers. Such interactions allow them to by-pass the 'middle man', who in the past was often a journalist. This benefit of social media appeals to many athletes who may have been misquoted by such journalists in interviews (Pegoraro, 2010, Hutchins, 2011). However, the communications posted by athletes on social media, such as Twitter, also allow researchers interested in how individuals present themselves online to examine a popular and performance driven group. Answers to questions such as, 'how do athletes manage their public, and indeed private, persona online?', and 'how can their interactions on social media be potentially damaging to the offline self?', have the potential to provide interesting and revealing insights into how the genuine self may be protected online, while the managed self is exposed in a way that may be potentially beneficial for the athlete.

Evidence of athletes embracing the new world of social media was clearly present during the London 2012 Olympics, which were referred to as the 'Twitterlympics' (Adebayo, 2013), the 'Social Media Olympics' (Androich, 2012), or the 'Socialympics' (Pfanner, 2012). But why do athletes join Twitter? Some general reasons for athletes tweeting have been proposed. The first reason is the instant contact and information about the world that Twitter provides (Browning & Sanderson, 2012). For fans and spectators of sport, Twitter communications can be seen to narrow the 'gap' between them and their sporting idols. It allows both groups to interact and converse directly with each other (Clavio & Kian, 2010). Therefore, tweeting can be seen to provide individuals with 'person' contact, that is not actually personal, and yet it may feel as though it is. A second reason athletes may use Twitter is that it can act as a source of entertainment, and even competition within teams, with many team-members competing to see who gains the most 'followers' on Twitter, or the most 'friends' on Facebook. Given that many elite sportspeople are often described as competitive by nature, using such social media for this purpose is perhaps unsurprising, and may give athletes a way to enhance, boost, or moderate their *athletic identity*. Athletic identity is a term used to describe how invested athletes are in their sport (Brewer, Van Raalte, & Linder, 1993). Typically, it is desirable for athletes to be highly invested in their sport, without being overly invested in it. Having interests and friends outside of the sporting environment should be encouraged in order to help maintain a balance in the athlete's life, and social media interactions may assist in this process. A third reason for tweeting is that it can provide athletes who are looking to safeguard their futures by setting up businesses during their competitive careers with a means to connect with their consumers. Indeed, all forms of social media allow athletes to promote their 'brand' and sell their business products (Atencio, 2010, Feil, 2012). Some teams have gone so far as to replace the names of their players on their jerseys with their Twitter handles for team promotion purposes (Knapp, 2011).

While the reasons athletes use social media is important to document, perhaps of even greater interest to researchers examining athletes' communications online is what athletes actually say on such social media, and how their communications provide an insight into their 'public' and 'private' selves, or their genuine and managed self. Pegoraro (2010), in a case study of athletes' use of Twitter, commented that athletes tended to use Twitter to share aspects of their daily lives with their fans, and to answer fans' queries about many areas of their sporting and non-sporting, or private, lives. Fans can read or see (via pictures posted on Twitter or Instagram, for example) images of events taking place in the daily lives of elite athletes. This may lead such supporters to develop a 'parasocial' relationship with the athletes. The term *parasocial relationship* is used to describe relationships where members of the public are very aware of the activities of celebrities, such as famous athletes in this scenario; however, the athletes do not have the same awareness of the members of the public, they are only their 'followers' on Twitter, or 'friends' on their Facebook pages (Baek, Bae, & Jang, 2013). Fans may read the daily tweets of elite athletes and feel 'Hey, they're just like me! They do normal, everyday things, like doing laundry or going for coffee'. However, such revelations by athletes online may only reveal their idealized self, the self they wish the public to see. This self may often be the self they might feel that the public wants to see. This self may, of course, be similar to their more genuine self. However, it is possible that it may also be quite different to the athlete's genuine self. Such departures from the genuine self may become apparent when athletes appear in person, in real life, for televised or streamed interviews perhaps. This may be the reason why it is often said, 'you should never meet your sporting idols', because there is a real danger the impressions of the athletes created in a person's mind do not match up to the actual experience of meeting such individuals. Such encounters could even be distressing for a member of the public if it results in the 'shattering of childhood dreams of idols' who may have greatly influenced a person's life in some way up to that point.

As stated earlier, many athletes use social media such as Twitter to make themselves heard (Browning & Sanderson, 2012). But is this statement really true? Are they really being heard, or, in some cases, are others talking on their behalf? For example, offensive tweets may be the result of hackers (O'Brien, Bechtel, & Beech, 2013), friends, or 'frenemies' (enemies posing as friends), secretly taking a team member's mobile phone and sending tweets posing as that person. Such behaviour is often referred to as 'fraping'. Fraping was coined to describe situations where people leave their Facebook profiles logged in and unattended, and others update their status, usually in comical or embarrassing ways. However, such behaviour has the potential to damage an athlete's self because it can leave the athlete vulnerable to ridicule and cyberbullying (discussed later). Social media, such as Twitter, can often provide 'frapists' with the cloak of anonymity (Oakland, 2013), as the victimized athletes in such cases are the actual targets of the negative comments made about these unintended posts (Browning & Sanderson, 2012, Trotter, 2012). The unsavoury comments posted by members of the public on social media was vividly illustrated during the London 2012 Olympic Games when Team Great Britain diver, Tom Daley, was the subject of some very unkind comments from an individual on Twitter, following his, and teammate Pete Waterfield's, performance in the paired diving event (BBC, 2012). Such behaviour actually resulted in the individual who posted the comments being arrested. This example of cyberbullying is perhaps a lesson for individuals considering engaging in such bullying behaviour of elite athletes, as it is a myth to think that most online activity cannot be traced (see next section). Nevertheless, the damage to an athlete's self from cyberbullying is only now being proposed as a worthy avenue of psychological research.

The negative consequences for athletes using social media prompted officials at London's 2012 Olympic Games to go to great lengths to advise athletes and volunteers before the Games started about their use of all social media during the Games (Jeffery, 2011, O'Connor, 2011, Horn, 2012, Zmuda, 2012). Interestingly, Browning and Sanderson (2012) reported that while athletes often face negative comments on social media such as Twitter, they persist with its use, and often check it very frequently to see what others are saying about them. The student athletes interviewed by Browning and Sanderson remarked that they were not bothered by the negative comments posted about them, implying their real self was not damaged by such posts. However, Browning and Sanderson reported that they were not convinced by such responses from the athletes they interviewed, given the athletes' frequent 'checking' behaviour for what their followers on Twitter were saying about them. Perhaps they cared more than they were willing to admit, or indeed, more than they themselves consciously thought.

While what others say about them may, in fact, impact on athletes' sense of self more than they might admit, what is also important to consider is how athletes specifically and purposely portray themselves on social media such as Twitter. A good example for this point is the case of Newcastle footballer, Joey Barton, who, despite his controversial tweets portraying a sometimes angry individual, also considers himself as quite philosophical in his comments online (Bernstein, 2011). This point illustrates the ability of social media to portray the many facets of an athlete's personality, perhaps providing a window into the home of the real self. Twitter, in allowing open communications, provides athletes with a means to display the many layers of their personality not often portrayed in interviews or in competitive situations in their sport (Johnston, 2009). However, athletes are also no different than non-athletes in their sometimes ill-advised and unconsidered comments posted on social media. Many examples of athletes sending controversial tweets are documented. Some posts have resulted in athletes facing serious consequences, such as fines and bans from their clubs and sporting organizations, which one could be justified in thinking is very damaging to the self of the athlete. Some athletes have even faced criminal charges for their social media posts (Poeter, 2012). These problems caused by some athletes using Twitter have resulted in their clubs, and sporting organizations, placing 'twitter-bans' on their players. For example, North Carolina University's football team, The Tar Heels, placed a ban on their players using Twitter after one of their American football players, Marvin Austin, sent what were regarded as revealing tweets about his spending habits. Such revelations cast a spotlight on such players receiving funds from unpermitted sources within their amateur sport. While Austin went on to secure a place on the New York Giants, The Tar Heels were punished in a number of ways, including being forced to pay $50,000 in fines and being removed from the 2008/9 college football season (Gregory, 2012). It could be argued that such outcomes could also damage their team's sense of identity.

With problems outlined here regarding how the self of an athlete might be damaged, it is no wonder that some schools have also started to monitor their student-athletes' social media sites (Dunning, 2011) and that many coaches have banned tweeting for certain periods of time, often agreed with the athletes, before and after games. Some sporting leaders have gone so far as to say Twitter is dangerous (including Newcastle boss Alan Pardew, and Manchester United's former manager, Sir Alex Ferguson). Sir Alex Ferguson said in 2011, 'I just don't get it!' in reference to Twitter (O'Connell, 2011). Indeed, Manchester United has been described as 'doing its best to ignore it [Twitter]' (Reynolds, 2012). However, in contrast, in a recent interview, Russell Stopford (Head of Digital at Manchester City) was quoted as saying, 'Manchester City is now a digital-first brand. Social media fits with the brand values of the club: transparency and giving the fans something unique' (Reynolds, 2012, p. 29). Stopford went on to say, 'We don't actively encourage players to be on Twitter: it is up to them. But if they want to be on social media, we support them with best practice' (Reynolds, 2012, p. 29). Such comments portray the attitude of clubs, such as Manchester City Football Club, regarding social media's ability to provide their players with the means to communicate their ideal selves in a way that could benefit the persona and public profile of their clubs.

Similarly, a recent survey by the football fan website fourfourtwo.com asked 100 professional players about a number of issues within their sport, including recreational drug use, fame and money. When asked specifically about whether the social media Twitter should be banned among players, 70% 'disagreed' that it should be banned (fourfourtwo.com, 2012). So while athletes do appear to acknowledge the negative side of social media use, they seem unprepared to remove themselves from such a world. It would appear that those involved in managing such sports stars must continue to allow them to use such media to portray themselves online to their public, while supporting and advising them on how best to use such media to portray the self that is most beneficial to them, and while minimizing the negative impact of the technology on the athletes as they go about their job of performing in their sport (Irish Rugby Union Players' Association, 2013).

6.6 Cyberbullying

The growing use of social media by professionals such as politicians and athletes to enhance their profile can expose these individuals to the risk of cyberbullying. However, in reality anyone who uses SNSs runs the risk of being cyberbullied. Cyberbullying has been defined as 'an aggressive, intentional act carried out by a group or individual, using electronic forms of contact, repeatedly and over time against a victim who cannot easily defend him or herself' (Smith et al., 2008, p. 376). Research suggests that cyberbullying is increasingly placing pressure on the psychological welfare of young people (Mason, 2008). However, for young people, online communication using SNSs plays a vital part in the development of their social world. Their self-esteem and self-concept can be affected by their online interaction with others. The literature regarding bullying and self-esteem consistently finds that victims of bullying tend to have lower self-esteem than non-victims (Salmivalli, Kaukiainen, Kaistaniemi, & Lagerspetz, 1999, Wild, Flisher, Bhana, & Carl, 2004, Patchin & Hinduja, 2010). It may be that the experience of being bullied decreases one's self-esteem, or that those who have low self-esteem are more likely to be targets of bullying. In addition, studies found that those who were bullied online experienced lower self-concept than those who were not (Kowalski, Limber, Zane, & Hassenfeldt, 2008, Katzer, Fetchenhauer, & Belschak, 2009, Patchin, Hinduja, & Denney, 2009). The significance of this is that individuals with low self-concept may often feel sad, depressed, anxious, guilty, ashamed, frustrated, and angry alongside having a generally negative overall opinion of themselves, judging themselves negatively, and placing a negative value on themselves as a person (Lim, Saulsman, & Nathan, 2005). Despite the potential harm of cyberbullying on self-esteem and self-concept young people continue to access SNSs regularly. A theoretical debate as to whether young people should or should not continue to use technology to socialize is ongoing.

Some professionals in favour of online interaction view this environment as having a positive effect, emphasizing that it provides a forum for developing and expressing one's own identity (Bargh, McKenna, & Fitzsimons, 2002, Livingstone, 2008). A study conducted by *The New York Times* Customer Insight Group (2011) revealed that 68% of the 2,500 surveyed users of online sharing sites used them to provide others with a more comprehensive sense of themselves and things of importance to them. The expression of identities on or through these sites can be affected by the actual structural design of SNSs (Hills, 2008, Mendelson & Papacharissi, 2011). When focusing on online behaviour connected to potential risk to a young person's self-identity, Livingstone (2008) reported two aspects, identity as display or connection. Some risks to young people can result in the self-display of intimate information to those viewing the SNS, not all of whom will be their real friends and family. Focusing on 'identity as connection' can pose risks also, where young people have confidence in their own ability to judge and trust others with whom they are close, as well as understanding those who potentially will neglect or exclude them (Livingstone, 2008). Exposing intimate information about themselves on SNSs, to people with whom they feel they can trust, may unwittingly make them more vulnerable to becoming the victims of cyberbullying.

Opposing groups view SNSs with negativity, emphasizing that they promote self-obsession and narcissism (Rosen, 2007, Buffardi & Campbell, 2008, Dalsgaard, 2008, Hills, 2008, Turkle, 2011). The group opposing SNS use appear to blame technology for the fraudulent way in which people socialize and hence view themselves (Sauter, 2013). Part of the blame may lie with the role of anonymity, where the belief that they cannot be identified seems to remove social inhibition and norms (Hinduja & Patchin, 2006) resulting in disinhibition (where young people say, and do, things online that they might never do face-to-face). For some the Internet is a hiding place, as Brown, Jackson, and Cassidy (2006) have revealed, where the anonymity associated with some SNSs allows young people to foster different identities and personalities when partaking in activities online that they might not be involved in offline. Cassidy, Jackson, and Brown (2009) found that pretence online was carried out, with 52% of adolescents pretending to be older online, 23% pretending to be another gender, 19% adopting another physical appearance and 15% acting contrary to how they would behave in the real world. In essence the anonymity of SNSs allows for this behaviour, and in some cases for cyberbullying to occur.

Both the pro- and anti-views of SNSs assume that a person's identity is a pre-existing reality, but where the pro-view group argue that identity can be enhanced using online communication, the anti-view group argue that it can be impaired by using SNSs. The use of technology is an integral aspect of young people's social interaction. Yet, the self-esteem and self-concept of those exposed to cyberbullying are at psychological risk. Therefore, steps need to be taken to ensure a positive and self-enhancing experience for all accessing SNSs. The removal of anonymity online would aid this to a certain extent; however, education, and an emphasis on pro-social online behaviour from both school and home, is the key to a solution. Furthermore, certain aspects of cyberbullying, such as cyberharassment or cyberstalking, could have legal ramifications for the perpetrators and may be pursued in a criminal manner.

6.7 Crime and social media

Cyberbullying is not the only harmful aspect of social media—**cybercrime** is also a prevalent element of such environments. It is hard to imagine a society where crime doesn't exist. Indeed, such a society could be considered more than unusual—it would probably be considered abnormal, despite its utopian potential. In a similar manner, crime has become a routine part of online society—as we bring more of our lives online, it is a natural progression that we are increasingly vulnerable to cybercriminals. These online criminals can take many forms—for example, there are cyberterrorists, sexual predators, fraudsters, identity thieves, malware developers, malicious hackers, and those involved in digital piracy.

As mentioned previously, individuals share significant amounts of personally identifying information on social networks. The availability of this information can result in several types of victimization, most notably **identity theft** and **fraud**, and so we will focus on these types of cybercrime here (although it should be noted that several other types of cybercrime can, and do, occur on social media platforms—see Kirwan and Power, 2013, for a review of these). How information about the self is managed online can have a vital role in the vulnerability of an individual to cybercrime—the more personally identifying information that is provided, the higher the risk that the individual will disclose details that may result in identity theft. We learn more about security and disclosure of personal information online in Chapter 14.

While fraud and identity theft are similar concepts, and can occur in the same crime, they are not synonyms. Fraud is more likely to involve trickery, while identity theft involves the use of someone else's documentation or information to impersonate them (Kirwan & Power, 2013). Victimization of either kind can impact on an individual's sense of self-identity, and we will now explore some of these types of victimization, their effects on the victim, and how they might be prevented.

There are several types of possible social networking site attacks (Bilge, Strufe, Balzarotti, & Kirda, 2009). Many of these rely on the user's willingness to share personal information, either with the social networking site itself, or with third parties, in the expectation of receiving goods or services in return (such as entry into a prize draw, or viewing of an interesting video). The presentation of large amounts of information online can leave users open to threat, with younger people and those seeking a relationship tending to disclose the largest amount of personal information (Nosko, Wood, & Molema, 2010).

Apart from a direct attempt to infiltrate a person's account, and thereby access their information, a potential fraudster or identity thief may attempt to provoke the user into clicking on specific links, visiting certain websites, playing certain videos, or installing specific applications. Such actions might give the fraudster access to some of the user's profile information or they might repost the link or message to the user's profile page without their knowledge. The infiltration might install malware onto the user's computer, which could be used for other types of cybercrime, or the user might be persuaded to complete an online form that may provide the cybercriminal with enough information to engage in identity theft.

Many of these attacks make use of **social engineering** techniques. These are where a fraudster or identity thief manipulates the human element in the security chain. Marshall and Stephens (2008) described such social engineering mechanisms as 'encompassing a number of related ideas, all emphasizing the importance of the human element ... particularly in relation to identity theft and fraud' (p. 184). For example, attacks are regularly linked to recent events (in October 2011, posts appeared on Facebook advertising free iPads in memory of Steve Jobs, within hours of his death). Social engineering tactics take advantage of human emotions such as fear, greed, guilt, and compassion. A common variety of these schemes involves an application, which indicates that, once installed it will provide victims with information about which of their friends views their profile the most often—thus manipulating human curiosity, and also possibly romantic attraction. These types of posts are generally propagated during the victimization process—when victims allow the scheme access to their profile, it often posts a copy of itself as an update to their profile. This suggests to other users that the victim has endorsed the application as being legitimate. The victim is often unaware of this update until they are informed of its presence by other users, and they may feel that their sense of self has been compromised, as they played an unwilling part in the dissemination of the scheme, or appeared to endorse or like content that they feel does not fit with their identity, or the identity that they wish to portray to others.

There has been little research examining the effects of such fraud on users of social media; however, there has been some examination of the impact of other types of fraud on victims. Yar (2006) suggested that victims of fraud may not report the crime due to embarrassment caused by the fact that they were deceived. Straude-Muller, Hansen, and Voss (2012) distinguished between types of online victimization, and discovered that the seriousness of the incident can have an impact on the levels of distress of the victim—notably they classified impersonation among the more serious incidents. Greater distress was particularly evident among those with higher levels of neuroticism, chronic stress, and prior experience of online victimization. Whitty and Buchanan (2012) examined online dating fraud, specifically attempting to examine the extent of such fraud in Great Britain. They indicate that victims need more support and advice when reporting their victimization.

In many cases the financial effects of identity theft are frustrating and inconveniencing, but relatively short-lived (Winterdyk & Thompson, 2008). This is because banks or credit organizations will often cover any losses. However, this cover is less frequently extended to cases of fraud. For some victims there may also be psychological effects. Ess (2009) considers the impact of identity theft on the victim. He suggested that it is more harmful to us personally than theft of other property, indicating that property can generally be replaced, but that

Table 6.1 Components of Protection Motivation Theory and their application to social media and cybercrime.

Component	Applied to Social Media	Sample Cognition
Perceived severity of the threatened event	Beliefs regarding the damage that may result should victimization occur	'A fraudster may gain access to all my personal information, and may use this to steal my identity'
Perceived probability of the threat	Person's belief that they are likely to be victimized	'Identity theft online is very rare, and it is unlikely to happen to me'
Perceived response efficacy of preventative measures	Person's belief that preventative measures will be effective	'Even if someone does get access to my account, the information they can see is limited, and is not enough to steal my identity'
Perceived self-efficacy in using preventative measures	Beliefs regarding ability to properly avoid victimization	'I know what the most common scams online are, so I'm unlikely to fall for them'
Potential rewards	Expectations of successfully avoiding victimization	'If I pay close attention to what I'm doing online, I won't fall victim to the scam, and so my friends won't tease me'
Potential costs	Sacrifices the person may have to make to prevent victimization	'Scams are relatively rare, and it takes a lot of effort to look out for them'

it is not possible to 'buy a replacement identity' (p. 58). He argued that it is harm against the person, not just their property. In this instance, it could be perceived that the victim's sense of self has been attacked, in addition to any financial or material damage.

Finally, the individual's sense of self might be an important aspect of the protection mechanisms that they utilize to avoid victimization. Lee, Larose, and Rifon (2008) applied Protection Motivation Theory (devised by Rogers, 1975, 1983) to use of anti-malware software, but it could equally be applied to avoiding victimization of other types of cybercrime on social media. Rogers' theory proposes that there are six main components that influence the intention to protect the self from a threat. Look at Table 6.1, which describes these six components, along with their application to victimization on social media, and sample cognitions that are representative of each component.

Consistent with this theory, Lee et al. (2008) found that a number of variables predicted intention to adopt virus protection behaviour in a sample of college students, including perceived self-efficacy in using virus protection measures. It is interesting that this aspect of the self—the extent of the belief that users have in themselves to protect themselves—is so important in taking action to protect the self, and it is possible that it holds similar importance for avoiding victimization on SNSs. Similarly, Ng and Rahim (2005), Ng, Kankanhalli, and Xu (2009), and Johnston and Warkentin (2010) also found that self-efficacy can partly predict online security behaviour. As such, users' perceptions of the self as a capable guardian of their information and accounts could be an important factor in predicting their efforts to protect those resources.

As can be seen earlier, many aspects of the self can impact on our vulnerability to cybercrime and our response to cybercrime victimization. Our perception of the self can influence the protective measures that we take, while our portrayal of the self can influence how much information we provide potential criminals with to carry out identity theft or fraud. Finally, the sometimes publicly visible outcomes of our victimization (via events on our social media profiles that are generated by the criminal act) can influence our ability to portray ourselves in the manner we desire.

6.8 Chapter summary

- Instead of a single unchanging self, psychological theory and research proposes that people have multiple selves in various different situations. People have a core self that exists and interacts in the here and now, and they have a narrative self or identity, which is how they represent their behaviours and thoughts over time.

- This idea of multiple selves allows for people to manage what they present so it is more favourable to their audience.

- SNSs allow people greater control over how they manipulate and present their identity. But it also allows other people to observe for themselves the unmanaged online interactions.

- SNSs also leave the self vulnerable to online aggression, crime, and fraud.

- The political image of politicians can, in part, be created, and managed through selective disclosures about their private lives.

- SNSs appear to perform two functions for politicians, self-promotion and keeping in touch with constituents.

- Athletes present themselves to their supporters online. Such presentations can have both positive and negative outcomes for the athletes. Athletes can manage the self online, by communicating directly with members of the public. However, such behaviour may expose them to cyberbullying and criticism by other individuals also engaged on social media.

- SNSs play an important role in young people's self-development. Both self-esteem and self-identity can be harmed or enhanced through the use of SNSs. Young people can flourish as a result of positive social experiences in the online world but can be badly affected by being the target of cyberbullying. This negative experience can result in high levels of anxiety or depression for the young person.

- Several types of cybercrime can make use of social media platforms as an element of their execution, including identity theft and fraud.

- The amount and type of information provided by a user can influence their risk of cybercrime victimization.

- Certain types of cybercrime victimization on social media can distort the user's portrayal of themselves online, making it appear that they endorse certain applications or media files. This perceived endorsement may be at odds with the user's desired portrayal of themselves.

- Users' perception of self-efficacy in avoiding cybercrime can be an important determinant of the protective measures they use.

- Providing education about appropriate online behaviour, uses of impression management, and mechanisms to deal with cyberbullying and cybercrime when they occur, has the potential to make the online world a more pleasurable experience for all.

 References

Adebayo, D. (2013). Eye on the stars: Twitter and the sporting hero. *Index on Censorship*, 42 (1), 62–65.

Androich, A. (2012). Demanding their share. *Marketing Magazine*, 117 (12), 8–10.

Atencio, J. (2010). New sponsored athletes can perform through social media. *Bicycle Retailer & Industry News*, 19 (13), 46.

Baek. Y.M., Bae, Y., & Jang, H. (2013). Social and parasocial relationships on social network sites and their differential relationships with users' psychological well-being. *Cyberpsychology, Behaviour & Social Networking*, 16 (7), 512–517.

Bargh, J.A., McKenna, K.Y.A., & Fitzsimons, G.M. (2002). Can you see the real me? Activation and expression of the 'True Self' on the Internet. *Journal of Social Issues*, 58 (1), 33–48.

BBC (2012). *Tom Daley Twitter abuse: Boy arrested in Weymouth*. Retrieved from http://www.bbc.co.uk/news/uk-england-19059127 (accessed 1st September, 2014).

Benson, C. (2001). *The Cultural Psychology of Self: Place, Morality and Art in Human Worlds*. London: Routledge.

Bernstein, J. (2011, August 22). The Fan: Joey Barton, the philosopher footballer. Back Pages: *New Statesman*, 140, p. 57.

Bilge, L., Strufe, T., Balzarotti, D., & Kirda, E. (2009). All your contacts belong to us: Automated identity theft attacks on social networks. Paper presented at the *International World Wide Web Conference 2009*, Madrid, April 20–24.

boyd, d.m. (2004, April). Friendster and publicly articulated social networking. Paper presented at the *Conference on Human Factors in Computing Systems*, Vienna, Austria.

Brewer, B., Van Raalte, J.L., & Linder, D.E. (1993). Athletic identity: Hercules' muscles or Achilles heel? *International Journal of Sport Psychology*, 24, 237–254.

Brown, K., Jackson, M., & Cassidy, W. (2006). Cyber-bullying: Developing a policy to direct responses that are equitable and effective in addressing this special form of bullying. *Canadian Journal of Educational Administration and Policy*, 57. Retrieved from http://umanitoba.ca/publications/cjeap/articles/brown_jackson_cassidy.html (accessed 1st September, 2014).

Browning, B. & Sanderson, J. (2012). The positives and negatives of twitter: exploring how student-athletes use Twitter and respond to critical tweets. *International Journal of Sport Communication*, 5, 503–521.

Buffardi, L.E. & Campbell, W.K. (2008). Narcissism and social networking web sites. *Personality and Social Psychology Bulletin*. Retrieved from http://psp.sagepub.com/cgi/content/abstract/34/10/1303 (accessed 1st September, 2014).

Campbell, M. (May, 2012). Niche networks getting into the social media game. *Toronto Star*.

Cassidy, W., Jackson, M., & Brown, K.N. (2009). Sticks and stones can break my bones, but how can pixels hurt me? *School Psychology International*, 30 (4), 383–402. doi: 10.1177/0143034309106948.

Chester, A. (2004). Presenting the self in cyberspace: Identity play online. Unpublished doctoral dissertation, University of Melbourne.

Chester, A. & Bretherton, D. (2007). Impression management and identity online. In Joinson, A., McKenna, K., Postmes, T., & Reips, U. (Eds), *The Oxford Handbook of Internet Psychology* (pp. 223–236). New York: Oxford University Press.

Clavio, G. & Kian, T.M. (2010). Uses and gratifications of a retired female athlete's Twitter followers. *International Journal of Sports Communication*, 3 (4), 485–500.

Coleman, S. & Blumler, J.G. (2009). *The Internet and Democratic Citizenship: Theory, Practice and Policy*. Cambridge: Cambridge University Press.

Dalsgaard, S. (2008). Facework on Facebook: The presentation of self in virtual life and its role in the US elections. *Anthropology Today*, 24 (6), 8–12.

Damasio, A.R. (1999). *The Feeling of What Happens: Body and Emotion in the Making of Consciousness*. New York: Harcourt Brace.

Dunning, M. (2011). Social media has schools on defense. *Business Insurance*, 45 (29), 4–10.

Ess, C. (2009). *Digital Media Ethics*. Cambridge: Polity Press.

Feil, S. (2012). The social side of sponsorship. *Adweek*, 53 (4), S1–S4.

Fourfourtwo.com (February, 2012). *The Players' Poll*, 46–57.

Francoli, M. & Ward, S. (2008). 21st Century Soapboxes? MPs and their blogs. *Information Polity*, 13 (1/2), 21–39.

Freud, S. (1948). *Group Psychology and the Analysis of the Ego*. London: Hogarth.

Gallagher, I.I. (2000). Philosophical conceptions of the self: implications for cognitive science. *Trends in Cognitive Science*, 4 (1), 14–21.

Gosling, S.D., Gaddis, S., & Vazire, S. (2007, March). Personality impressions based on Facebook profiles. *Paper presented at the ICWSM*, Boulder, Colorado.

Gregory, S. (October, 2012). Jock Police. *Time*, 180 (17), 56–57.

Harnden, T. (2009). Twitter craze brings U.S. politicians closer to constituents. *Daily Telegraph*. Retrieved from http://www.telegraph.co.uk/technology/twitter/4573155/Twitter-craze-brings-US-politicians-closer-to-constituents.html (accessed 1st September, 2014).

Heil, B. & Piskorski, M. (2009) New Twitter research: men follow men and nobody tweets, *Harvard Business Review Blog Network*, June 1, 2009 available at: http://blogs.hbr.org/2009/06/new-twitter-research-men-follo/ (accessed 1st September, 2014).

Higgins, E.T. (1987). Self-discrepancy: A theory relating self and affect. *Psychological Review*, 94, 319–340.

Hills, M. (2008). Case study: social networking and self-identity. In Creeber, G. & Martin, R. (Eds). *Digital Cultures: Understanding Media* (pp. 117–121). Maidenhead: Open University Press.

Hinduja, S. & Patchin, J. W. (2006). Bullies move beyond the schoolyard: A preliminary look at cyberbullying. *Youth Violence and Juvenile Justice*, 4 (2), 148–169.

Horn, L. (2012). London Olympics volunteers warned about social media use. *PC Magazine*.

Hutchins, B. (2011). The acceleration of media sport culture: Twitter, telepresence and online messaging. *Information, Communication & Society*, 14 (2), 237–257.

Irish Rugby Union Players' Association (IRFU, 2013). Social media and social networking. *In Touch*, 21, 32–33.

Jackson, N. (2006). An MP's Role in the Internet Era—the impact of e-newsletters. *Journal of Legislative Studies*, 12 (2), 223–242.

Jackson, N. & Lilleker, D. (2011). Microblogging, constituency service and impression management: UK MPs and the use of Twitter. *The Journal of Legislative Studies*, 17 (1), 86–105.

James, W. (1890). *The Principles of Psychology*, Vol. 2. New York: Holt.

Jeffery, N. (June, 2011). Games athletes must keep tweets sweet. *The Australian*, 39.

Johnson, D. & Post, D. (1996). Law and borders—The rise of law in Cyberspace. *The Stanford Law Review*, 48 (5), 1367–1402.

Johnston, A.C. & Warkentin, M. (2010). Fear appeals and information security behaviours: An empirical study. *MIS Quarterly*, 34 (3), 549–566.

Johnston, S. (2009, June 5). How Twitter will change the way we live. *Time*. Retrieved from http://www.time.com/time/business/article/0,8599,1902604,00.html (accessed 1st September, 2014).

Jung, T., Hyunsook, Y., & McClung, S. (2007). Motivations and self-presentation strategies on Korean-based 'Cyworld' weblog format personal homepages. *Cyberpsychology and Behaviour*, 10 (1), 24–31.

Katzer, C., Fetchenhauer, D., & Belschak, F. (2009). Cyberbullying: Who are the victims? A comparison of victimisation in Internet chatrooms and victimisation in school. *Journal of Media Psychology: Theories, Methods, and Applications*, 21 (1), 25–36.

Kirwan, G. & Power, A. (2013). *Cybercrime: The Psychology of Online Offenders*. Cambridge: Cambridge University Press.

Knapp, A. (December, 2011). *Pro lacrosse team replaces names with Twitter handles on jerseys*. Retrieved from: www.forbes.com.

Kowalski, R., Limber, S., Zane, K., & Hassenfedt, T. (2008). Cyber Bullying: Bullying in the Digital Age. Paper presented at the *Annual Meeting at the Southeastern Psychological Association*, Charlotte, NC.

Lee, D., Larose, R., & Rifon, N. (2008). Keeping our network safe: A model of online protection behaviour. *Behaviour & Information Technology*, 27, 445–454.

Lee, E.J. & Shin, S.Y. (2012) Are they talking to me? Cognitive and affective effects of interactivity in politicians' Twitter communication. *Cyberpsychology, Behaviour and Social Networking*, 15 (10), 515–520.

Lim, L., Saulsman, L., & Nathan, P. (2005). *Improving Self-Concept*. Perth, Western Australia: Centre for Clinical Interventions.

Livingstone, S. (2008). Taking risky opportunities in youthful content creation: teenagers' use of social networking sites for intimacy, privacy and self-expression. *New Media and Society*, 10 (3), 393–411.

Marshall, A. & Stephens, P. (2008). Identity and identity theft. In Bryant, R. (Ed.), *Investigating Digital Crime* (pp. 179–193). Chichester: John Wiley & Sons, Ltd.

Mason, K.L. (2008). Cyberbullying: A preliminary assessment for school personnel. *Psychology in Schools*, 45 (4), 323–348.

McKenna, K. & Seidman, G. (2005). You, me, and we: Interpersonal processes in electronic groups. In Amichai-Hamburger, Y. (Ed.), *The Social Net: Human Behaviour in Cyberspace* (pp. 191–217). Oxford: Oxford University Press.

Mead, G.M. (1934). *Mind, Self & Society from the Standpoint of a Social Behaviorist*. In Morris, C.W. (Ed.). Chicago: University of Chicago Press.

Mendelson, A. & Papacharissi, Z. (2011). Look at us: collective narcissism in college student Facebook photo galleries. In Papacharissi, Z. (Ed.), *A Networked Self–Identity, Community, and Culture on Social Network Sites* (pp. 251–273). New York: Routledge.

Mnookin, J. (1996) Virtual(ly) law: The emergence of law in LambdaMOO. *Journal of Computer-Mediated Communication*, 2 (1). doi: 10.1111/j.1083-6101.1996.tb00185.x.

Ng, B.Y. & Rahim, M.A. (2005). A socio-behavioral study of home computer users' intention to practice security. *The Ninth Pacific Asia Conference on Information Systems*, 7–10 July, Bangkok, Thailand.

Ng, B.Y., Kankanhalli, A., & Xu, Y.C. (2009). Studying users' computer security behaviour: A health belief perspective. *Decision Support Systems*, 46, 815–825.

Nosko, A., Wood, E., & Molema, S. (2010). All about me: Disclosure in online social networking profiles: The case of Facebook. *Computers in Human Behaviour*, 26, 406–418.

Oakland, R. (February, 2013). Getting inside an athlete's brain. *The Toronto Star*.

O'Brien, R., Bechtel, M., & Beech, M. (2013). A ridiculously short history of ... hacked athletes. *Sports Illustrated*, 119 (4), 18.

O'Connell, H. (2011). Alex Ferguson on 'waste of time' Twitter: 'Go to the library and read a book instead'. Retrieved from: http://www.thescore.ie/alex-ferguson-on-waste-of-time-twitter-go-to-the-library-and-read-a-book-140759-May2011/ (accessed 1st September, 2014).

O'Connor. A. (July, 2011). Athletes urged to 'think first, tweet later.' *The Times*.

Patchin, J.W. & Hinduja, S. (2010). Cyberbullying and self-esteem. *Journal of School Health*, 80 (12), 614–621.

Patchin, J.W., Hinduja, S., & Denney, T.W. (2009, March 14). What's the big deal, it's only text: An Analysis of the Emotional Effects of Cyberbullying. Presented at the *Annual Meetings of the Academy of Criminal Justice Sciences*, Boston, MA.

Pegoraro, A. (2010). Look who's talking: athletes on Twitter: A case study. *International Journal of Sport Communication*, 3, 501–514.

Pfanner, E. (July, 2012). Social media's role in London games grows with surge in users. *New York Times*.

Poeter, D. (April, 2012). Infographics: athletes tweeting up a storm. *PC Magazine*.

Reynolds, J. (2012). Russell Stopford: Manchester City. The marketing interview. *Marketing*, 29–31. Retrieved from: marketingmagazine.co.uk.

Rogers, C. (1959). A theory of therapy, personality and interpersonal relationships as developed in the client-centered framework. In Koch, S. (Ed.), *Psychology: A Study of a Science. Vol. 3: Formulations of the Person and the Social Context*. New York: McGraw Hill.

Rogers, R.W. (1975). A protection motivation theory of fear appeals and attitude change. *The Journal of Psychology*, 91, 93–114.

Rogers, R.W. (1983). Cognitive and physiological processes in fear appeals and attitude change: a revised theory of protection motivation. In Cacioppo, J. & Petty, R. (Eds) *Social Psychophysiology* (pp. 153–176). New York: Guildford Press.

Rosen, C. (2007). Virtual friendship and the new narcissism. *The New Atlantis: A Journal of Technology and Society*, Summer, pp. 15–31.

Rosenberg, M. (1965). *Society and the Adolescent Self-Image*. Princeton, NJ: Princeton University Press.

Salmivalli, C., Kaukiainen, A., Kaistaniemi, L., & Lagerspetz, K.M. (1999). Self-evaluated self-esteem, peer-evaluated self-esteem, and defensive egotism as predictors of adolescents' participation in bullying situations. Personality and Social Psychology Bulletin, 25, 1268–1278.

Sanderson. J. & Kassing, J.W. (2011). Tweets and blogs: Transformative, adversarial, and integrative developments in sports media. In Billings, A.C. (Ed.), *Sports Media: Transformation, Integration, Consumption* (pp. 114–127). New York: Routledge.

Sauter, T. (2013). 'What's on your mind?' Writing on Facebook as a tool for self-formation. *New Media & Society*. Retrieved from http://nms.sagepub.com/content/early/2013/07/05/1461444813495160 (accessed 1st September, 2014).

Schlenker, B.R. (1985). Introduction: Foundations of the self in social life. In Schlenker, B.R. (Ed.), *The Self and Social Life* (pp. 1–28). New York: McGraw-Hill.

Smith, P.K., Mahdavi, J., Carvalho, M., Fisher, S., Russell, S., & Tippett, N. (2008). Cyberbullying: its nature and impact in secondary school pupils. *Journal of Child Psychology and Psychiatry*, 49 (4), 376–385.

Stanyer, J. & Wring, D. (2004) Public Images, Private Lives: An Introduction. *Parliamentary Affairs*, 57 (1), 1–8.

Straude-Muller, F., Hanson, B., & Voss, M. (2012). How stressful is online victimization? Effects of victim's personality and properties of the incident. *European Journal of Developmental Psychology*, 9, 260–274.

The New York Times Customer Insight Group (2011). The psychology of sharing. Retrieved from http://nytmarketing.whsites.net/mediakit/pos/ (accessed 1st September, 2014).

Trotter, J. (2012, January 30). Facebook, Twitter taking over: Social media for better or worse is changing the way recruiting game is played.

Retrieved from: http://espn.go.com/college-sports/recruiting/story/_/id7510010/social-media-makes-mark-recruiting (accessed 1st September, 2014).

Turkle, S. (2011). *Alone Together: Why We Expect More from Technology and Less from Each Other*. New York: Basic Books.

Watson, R. (2010). *Future Minds*. London: Nicholas Brealey Publishing.

Wellman, B. & Haythornthwaite, C. (2002). *The Internet in Everyday Life*. Oxford: Blackwell.

White, D. & Le Cornu, A. (2011). Visitors and Residents: A new typology for online engagement. *First Monday*, 16 (9). Available: http://firstmonday.org/htbin/cgiwrap/bin/ojs/index.php/fm/article/view/3171/3049 [accessed 1st September, 2014].

Whitty, M.T. & Buchanan, T. (2012). The online romance scam: A serious cybercrime. *Cyberpsychology, Behavior and Social Networking*, 15, 181–183.

Wild, L.G., Flisher, A.J., Bhana, A., & Carl, L. (2004). Associations among adolescent risk behaviours and self-esteem in six domains. *Journal of Child Psychology and Psychiatry*, 45, 1454–1467.

Winterdyk, J. & Thompson, N. (2008). Student and non-student perceptions and awareness of identity theft. *Canadian Journal of Criminology and Criminal Justice*, 50, 153–186.

Yar, M. (2006). *Cybercrime and Society*. London: Sage.

Zmuda. N. (2012). The social-media strategy for Olympic athletes: Better safe than sorry. *Advertising Age*, 83 (28), 2–3.

 ## Further reading

Browning, B. & Sanderson, J. (2012). The positives and negatives of Twitter: exploring how student-athletes use Twitter and respond to critical tweets. *International Journal of Sport Communication*, 5, 503–521.
This paper describes, in detail, the responses of athletes from various sports who were interviewed about the impact of social media on their lives, both inside and outside of their sport.

Corcoran, L., Connolly, I., & O'Moore, M. (2012). Cyberbullying: A new dimension to an old problem. *Irish Journal of Psychology*, 33 (4), 153–165.
This research paper explores the prevalence of cyberbullying in Irish second level schools and examines the relationships between these cyberbullying experiences, personality and self-concept.

Kirwan, G. & Power, A. (2013). *Cybercrime: The Psychology of Online Offenders*. Cambridge: Cambridge University Press.
This book describes the main types of cybercrime and examines how psychology can help us to understand both offenders and victims.

Lilleker, D. & Jackson, N. (2011). *Political Campaigning, Elections and the Internet: Comparing the US, UK, France and Germany*. London, England: Routledge.

This book explores how the political candidates and political parties of three election campaigns in Europe and the US used SNS and Web 2.0 technologies to manage their campaigns.

Scullion, R., Gerodimos, R., Jackson, D., & Lilleker, D. (2013). *The Media, Political Participation and Empowerment*. London: Routledge.

This book explores the ways and means by which media and the Internet can empower and dis-empower citizens and audiences

Patchin, J.W. & Hinduja, S. (2010). Cyberbullying and self-esteem. *Journal of School Health*, 80 (12), 614-621.

This article explores the association between students' self-esteem and their experiences of bullying or being bullied.

Straude-Muller, F., Hanson, B., & Voss, M. (2012). How stressful is online victimisation? Effects of victim's personality and properties of the incident. *European Journal of Developmental Psychology*, 9, 260-274.

This paper describes a large scale victimization study, examining the emotional distress caused by online victimization in terms of properties of the incident and characteristics of the victim.

Subrahmanyam, K. & Greenfield, P. (2008). Online communication and adolescent relationships. *The Future of Children*, 18 (1), 119-146.

The authors of this paper explore the way in which adolescents use Internet technologies and media to relate to family, romantic partners, friends, and strangers.

Discussion questions

1. How is online impression management different to offline impression management?
2. Does social media enhance or undermine democratic debate?
3. Why should sporting organizations consider athletes' use of social media as a positive tool to enable them to communicate the ethos of their sporting environment?
4. Evaluate how the role of disinhibition and anonymity contribute to the role of cyberbullying on SNSs.
5. How can users of social media be encouraged to protect themselves against cybercrime?

7 The Presentation of Self in Otherworldly Life

MARK COULSON & JANE BARNETT

 Learning outcomes

At the end of this chapter, we hope that you will have an understanding of:

- The online self in relation to the offline self, motivation, behaviour, and emotions.
- Theories that outline the way in which the self is defined, created, and experienced online.
- The way in which the self is experienced through representation in online virtual and gaming environments.
- The model of offline and online selves that describes the way in which online and offline selves present, change, and influence one another.

7.1 Introduction

When we think about our self, our experience is of a single entity, with a set of beliefs and abilities that may change over time but somehow remain part of a consistent whole. Just as we have one body, defined in physical space, so it feels natural to think of a single indivisible self, defined by our sense of identity, anchored by our past, and projecting into our future. While we may acknowledge that the 'me' of today is not the same as the 'me' of ten years ago, nor will the me of ten years ago hence be the same as me today, we nonetheless maintain the belief that there is something, some sense of self, which remains constant.

Like many questions that touch upon existence, mind, and psychology, the self turns out to be rather more complex than this. In this chapter we will consider three important approaches to describing the self, and examine their implications for how the self may be constructed in virtual worlds and how this constructed self may relate to the 'real' self (which we will refer to as the *offline self*). We will examine some of the factors that make us choose to construct the selves we use online (referred to as *online selves*), and the consequences these have for our offline selves. Throughout the chapter, the emphasis will be on taking what is already known about the self in terms of psychological theories and evidence, and applying this to the online self. There are several reasons for this. First, there exists a set of well-developed and empirically supported theories that deal with different aspects of the self. Second, accounts of the online self are often based on specific online environments (e.g., *Second Life*, *World of Warcraft*) and while these may have a lot to say about specific aspects of particular game worlds and the experience of the self within these, they may be driven more by the details of the world than the general characteristics of self we are interested in exploring. Third, as the self turns out to be flexible, complex, multifaceted, and context-dependent, we do not believe it makes sense to discriminate between online and offline selves. The same psychosocial forces that operate in the real world operate, more or less unchanged in kind (if not degree) when we travel online. As Edward Castronova puts it, 'Place a group of people in a strange place, and they will follow their usual tendencies in pursuit of their usual objectives' (Castronova, 2005, p. 8).

7.2 Motivations and needs

At the heart of our self perception is the idea that we do things for a reason, and that our behaviour is guided by an underlying set of desires, aims, goals, and motivations. This idea has been most effectively developed in the general theory of motivation put forward by Edward Deci and Richard Ryan, and known as Self Determination Theory (**SDT**; see Deci & Ryan, 2008, and Chapter 3 of this book).

At its heart, SDT argues that there are three basic psychological needs, which all individuals strive to satisfy, and that the degree of satisfaction we experience towards each of these needs has a profound influence on our well-being and behaviour. The needs are competence, autonomy, and relatedness. **Competence** refers to our need to feel we are capable of carrying out the various tasks and actions that life presents. If information we receive from the environment and from others suggests that we are not able to achieve our goals, we experience a lack of competence. **Autonomy** relates to our need to feel in control of our own actions and goals. To the extent that our lives are controlled by external forces (or we *perceive* our lives as controlled by external forces), we feel a lack of autonomy. Finally, **relatedness** refers to the need for social contact and emotional links with others. Our species is, by its nature, a social animal and social relations are critical to normal functioning.

When these needs are satisfied we feel a sense of well-being, and when they are not, a motivation to engage in activities that might lead to satisfaction. We also experience these needs at different levels at different times. The forces that guide our motivation are thus seen as resulting from the interaction of who we are, and what we want, and the degree to which our current circumstances are able to satisfy those needs.

7.2.1 Applying self-determination theory to the online self

Self-determination theory is a general theory of human motivation which has received a considerable amount of empirical support. Its application to online behaviour has not been extensively researched, although there is some evidence that human needs for competence, autonomy, and relatedness predict how enjoyable people find games (Ryan, Rigby, & Przybylski, 2006). This suggests the framework may be useful in understanding the choices people make in virtual environments, for example how they use character creation tools, the character 'class' or role they prefer to adopt, and their style of role-play.

There are several competing accounts of motivation that have been developed from researchers whose interests are specifically about motivations for online behaviour (and in particular, within massively multiplayer online games: **MMOs**). For instance, Bartle (2004) created a typology of four kinds of gamer:

1. Gamers classified as **explorers** like to investigate and experience new places.
2. **Achievers** want to accomplish tasks.
3. **Socializers** are there for friendship and shared experiences.
4. **Killers** are interested in eliminating threats, be they computer- or human-controlled.

Any one individual is seen as being some mix of the four, though the expression of one style is assumed to inhibit the others at least temporarily. In a similar vein, Nick Yee's (Yee, 2006) survey of 3,000 MMO players, with questions based on Bartle's typology, resulted in the statistical identification of three overarching factors, which Yee labelled *Achievement*, *Social*, and *Immersion*.

The notion of a 'type' is an attractive one, touching as it does on our desire to categorize the world in different ways. Some types make intuitive sense and appeal to our pre-existing notions, but we should be wary of any system of classification that is unsupported by data. Furthermore, we should exercise caution in using systems that, although supported by data, are based on the responses of specific populations of people in specific environments (for instance, those people who play MMOs, who, despite their ever increasing number are not a representative sample of our species). Thankfully, there is a certain amount of convergence in the different accounts, with all three identifying broadly similar constructs. Some of the statistical relationships are also quite strong. In Ryan et al.'s (2006) studies, for instance, the correlation between the Relatedness component of SDT and Yee's Social motivation was 0.66, suggesting a large overlap in what the two scales were measuring. Until there is a compelling need for a model that includes details specific to the online self (and for some suggestions about this, see Section 7.7), general frameworks with established validity and a considerable base of evidence offer the most parsimonious explanation of the online self. Just as in the offline world, our online selves wish to be competent and act autonomously within networks of relatedness with others.

7.3 Perceptions of behaviour

The common sense view of a single, stable, and consistent self has also been challenged from the perspective of the accuracy of our own self knowledge. We tend to think we know who we are, and possess access to the contents of our own minds that are both privileged (only we know them) and accurate (what we think about ourselves and our knowledge is, by and large, true). After all, they are *our* minds and this is *my* self. A great deal of psychological research, however, has demonstrated that while we may have access to the *outputs* of our minds, in terms of the kinds of behaviour we engage in in different situations, our access to the *contents* of our minds is extremely limited.

For instance, in a famous series of experiments by Kruger and Dunning (1999), university undergraduates were asked to estimate their abilities relative to their peers on a number of domains (sense of humour, knowledge of grammar, and logical thinking). They were then given standardized tests of those same abilities, and their performance on the tests was mapped onto their self-perceptions. The results were astonishing—in general, there was almost no relationship between people's perceived and actual competence, an effect that was enhanced for those lowest in ability. Even when participants were asked how good they were at thinking logically, *and* how well they had performed on the specific test of logical thinking they had just taken, there was little or no correspondence between prediction and behaviour. Broadly speaking, the conclusion from this research is that people have little or no idea about their own abilities, and a person's answer to the question 'how good are you at ability X?' provides almost no information as to their actual ability.

A theory that predates these findings but effectively predicts them, is Bem's (1967) Self Perception Theory (**SPT**). Bem argues that we do not have direct access to our own beliefs, attitudes, and motivations, and are forced to infer these from observing our own behaviours. So while a common sense account might be something along the lines of 'I like playing *World of Warcraft*, so I play it a lot', Bem suggests that what is actually occurring is more like 'I notice that I play a lot of *World of Warcraft*, therefore I must like it'. In a sense these inferences become our beliefs, even though they may be incorrect (for instance, I may not enjoy playing *World of Warcraft*, but have nothing else to do). In Bem's model we are no better at knowing our own beliefs than another person who merely observes us behaving. In effect, we make up stories about ourselves that fit, to a reasonable level of consistency, the things we observe ourselves doing. The self is therefore constantly constructed from our ongoing observations, and we only know it in the way any reasonably careful observer might.

These seemingly counterintuitive ideas receive a considerable amount of support. In a famous statement that predated SPT by over 70 years, William James (1950) suggested that our common sense view of the relationship between emotion and behaviour is wrong. In a famous example, James asked, what is the sequence of events when we are out for a walk in the woods and see a bear? Our normal explanation of these events runs something along the lines of 'see a bear, experience fear, run away'. In other words, the emotion of fear *causes* us to run away. In James' formulation, that classic sequence of events is turned on its head. James argues that seeing a bear *causes* us to run, and our experience of running away having seen a bear *is* fear. In other words, our feelings are not the result of something 'out there', caused by some state of the world that makes us feel a certain way and leads us to behave in some more or less appropriate fashion, but are instead the results of our own observations of our own behaviours. In this model, emotions play no role in the generation of the behaviours we normally believe they do.

This is not to say that James' model applies to all emotional experience, and there are long running debates as to whether it generalizes to all emotions. For instance, if all emotional responses are the result of information gleaned from our bodily responses, we would not expect people with spinal lesions, which block transmission of that information from the periphery of the body to the brain, to experience emotion. While there is some evidence that such people experience a reduction in the intensity of emotional response over time (Chwalisz, Diener, & Gallagher, 1988) it seems clear that they do not experience the complete cessation of emotional responses that James' theory predicts.

However, there is considerable experimental evidence that supports James' idea. A study by Soussignan (2002), replicating and extending earlier work, showed that when participants were 'duped' into pulling a genuine smile by being asked to hold a pencil in their mouths (a manipulation that has the reliable effect of contorting the face into a smile without the participant necessarily being aware of this), humorous cartoons were rated as funnier than participants whose faces were contorted into other configurations. In short, adopting a particular facial expression, even when it has nothing to do with the stimuli that are present in the envir-onment, has a measurable effect on emotional state. It really is as if the brain is observing the behaviour of the body in which it resides and making decisions about what it feels based on those observations.

7.4 Applying self-perception theory to the online self

To the extent that we construct our selves by observing our own behaviour (and it should be emphasized that this is by no means the *only* way in which we construct our selves), we must reject the idea that the online self is simply a projection of, and identical to, the offline self. Indeed, no aspect of the self is simply a projection, as the projection feeds back into the self, dynamically updating it. If we identify with our online selves, then we are forced to acknow-ledge the existence of two-way traffic between the online and offline selves, and while we may construct the online self in some appropriate way (more on this later), the actions which that online self takes while under our control will nevertheless affect our offline beliefs and atti-tudes. This is not to say we will *become* the saints, sinners, and killers that we become online, but their actions will cross into, and form part of, our offline selves. The membrane between the real and the virtual is semi-permeable and effects move back and forth across it.

There is some limited evidence that this is the case. Nick Yee and Jeremy Bailenson (2007) assigned participants in their study either an attractive or an unattractive avatar, and asked them to interact in a virtual environment with a confederate of the experimenters (who could not see whether the avatar was attractive or not). Participants assigned attractive avatars tended to stand closer to the confederate and disclosed more personal information than those assigned an unattractive avatar. Yee and Bailenson term this the **Proteus Effect** after the Greek God by the same name who could take on many different forms. In a separate study, Fox and colleagues (Fox, Bailenson, & Tricase, 2013) further examined the Proteus effect in the context of sexualized avatars. Women participants who used a sexualized avatar (the manipu-lation was relatively simple, and involved avatars dressed either in short skirts and cropped tops or in jeans and long sleeved tops) exhibited a greater degree of **objectivization** than those using non-sexualized avatars. Objectivization refers to the experience of being treated as an object, a process that has been argued to occur to young women from an early age. Women in the sexualized condition reported both more body-related thoughts and more strongly condoned **rape myths** (beliefs about rape being more the fault of the victim, i.e., for dressing or behaving provocatively, than the perpetrator). This latter effect was enhanced when the sexualized avatar had a face that resembled that of the real participant's, suggest-ing that the Proteus effect may be enhanced where there are certain features of avatars that strongly resemble their offline counterparts.

Participants in these studies did not select their avatars, so it is impossible to draw strong con-clusions about how self-initiated decisions about the appearance of an online self might affect behaviour. The researchers also only measured online behaviour, making it difficult to extend the findings of this research to the offline self. However, it is clear that the avatar that represents our online self is not just a one way projection, but provides a channel through which the online self's actions may affect the attitudes and beliefs of the offline self. The decisions people make when they decide how to present themselves online may have wide ranging and long lasting effects.

When first logging on to an MMO, players will be asked to create a character. The character creation screen lists a variety of options that allow the player to change the look of their character. For example, facial and bodily features, accessories, and hairstyles allow the player to create a character that may be vastly different from other players within the game world, known as **identity tourism** (Nakamura, 1995). Studies have suggested that some players will create characters that are more likely to be attractive and therefore represent the 'good' side of, for example, warring factions (Ducheneaut, Yee, Nickell, & Moore, 2006), compared to choosing a less attractive character that is perceived to be ugly or 'bad'.

It is not just our own physical appearance that affects behaviour—the appearance of other online selves may affect us in comparable ways to how offline selves do. In the offline world we make rapid decisions about other people, generally driven by their appearance as this information is salient and easy to process. Some of these decisions we may feel we understand ('I don't trust tall men who smile broadly') others we might only guess at. From what has already been discussed, it should come as no surprise to learn that the causes of our responses to other people are not open to direct introspection. While we may be able to articulate certain preferences with a fair degree of accuracy, others exist at a far less conscious level. In effect, social responses are driven by two possible separate systems, one open to reflective thought (knowing that you don't like tall men who smile broadly) and one that is unconscious, automatic, and implicit (and that makes you respond in ways you may not even be aware of). Yee and Bailenson (2007) found that a character's bodily features had a behavioural and emotional effect on interaction with other players within the game. For example, those who created attractive characters were more likely to reveal personal information about themselves to others; tall characters were more likely to communicate aggressively to shorter stature player characters during negotiations, who in turn were more likely to succumb to these unfair negotiations. Therefore, a character's attractiveness and height can have an impact on how they perceive themselves, and how they are perceived by others.

Many online games, including MMOs, only provide options for players to create slim and attractive (depending on personal choice) characters. Yee and Bailenson (2007) suggested that the ability to create only slim and attractive avatars in MMOs might encourage players to be more co-operative and friendly with others. However, more recent MMOs (e.g., *Elder Scrolls Online*) provide players with the option to create slim or large, tall or short, muscular or chubby characters, in addition to adding various scars. The effects of such 'ugly' avatars on player behaviour have yet to be fully investigated.

In a fascinating study by Dotsch and Wigboldus (2008), participants (who were all Dutch and ethnically white) interacted with an avatar in a virtual environment. Some of the participants interacted with a white avatar while others interacted with an avatar that had a Moroccan face (Moroccans are a stigmatized ethnic group in the Netherlands). Participants completed both explicit and implicit measures of prejudice. Explicit measures were simple self-report questions (such as rating the statement 'I like Moroccans'), whereas implicit measures involved participants classifying Moroccan names (e.g., 'Mustafa') alongside either positive or negative words (e.g., 'love' or 'hate'). The difference in how long it takes to perform elements of this task is taken as a measure of implicit prejudice (Greenwald, McGhee, & Schwartz, 1998). When examining physical distance and social space (i.e., how far away from the target avatar the participants positioned themselves), there was no effect of explicit prejudice, but a significant effect of implicit prejudice, with more prejudiced participants preferring to stand a greater distance away from the avatar than less prejudiced participants. Interestingly, the researchers also measured skin conductance, a physiological measure that is affected by the amount of sweat on the surface of a person's skin and is taken as a fairly accurate assessment of the activity of the autonomic nervous system, that part of the nervous system associated with the 'fight or flight' response. The skin conductance measure on its own was sufficient to explain the increased distance, suggesting that this effect was almost entirely down to stronger unconscious physiological responses in some participants.

Taken together, these findings suggest that there are multiple ways in which the online self, and the encounters it has with others, affect the offline self. An avatar is not simply a vehicle people use to drive through online worlds. It is also a part of their self, influencing and being influenced by everything it comes into contact with.

7.5 Discrepancy and emotion

Simultaneous with our (perhaps somewhat illusory) perception of a consistent internal self whose values and beliefs we know, is the perception that however stable the self may be, we all play different roles that might prescribe quite different sorts of behaviours in different contexts. We might be students, parents, friends, or opponents, and these different roles permeate different aspects of our lives. Each of these might be considered another aspect of our self. To the extent that they all direct us in the same direction, and motivate us to behave in similar ways, the notion of a single self might be relatively easy to maintain. In the event that our different roles make competing demands on our behaviour at any one moment, our sense of self may come to be more conflicted and fragmented.

The distinction between an 'inner' self, the single entity that is always there and can be thought of as the 'real me', and the selves we play dependent on the roles we are required to adopt, was first outlined by the father of modern psychology, William James. James (1950) observed that a person has as many selves as there are people who know her, as each carries some internal representation of who she is, what James referred to as 'me'. In addition to these, the self that is experienced, and that is seen as consistent from moment to moment, is the 'I'.

Perhaps the clearest articulation of the complex self is that originating from the work of Higgins (1987). Higgins' Self-Discrepancy Theory (**SDST**) distinguishes between *domains* and *standpoints* of the self. The three domains are:

1. Internal representations of the person we are at the moment (called the **actual self**—who we think we are right now).
2. The person we aspire to be (the **ideal self**—who we might be in the future if everything works out well).
3. The person specified by the roles we play (the **ought self**—the person or persons we have to be contingent on our various roles).

Cutting across these domains are two standpoints, that of our own, and that of significant others in our life. This model therefore sees six components to the self, all of which change over time, and which overlap to greater or lesser degrees.

Higgins' model predicts that discrepancies between different aspects of the self will have different implications for one's well-being and emotional state. For instance, if our actual self is perceived as overlapping with our ideal self, the result will be emotions such as satisfaction and pride. If there is a large discrepancy (i.e., we are failing to live up to what we believe we should be) then the results might be anxiety or shame. A perceived difference between our own ideal self and the ideal self that an important other person sees might give rise to a different set of emotions. For instance, if we believe ourselves capable of great things, but the important people in our life repeatedly tell us we are being overly ambitious and should aim lower (i.e., a large discrepancy between the own and other ideal self, with the former being greater than the latter), we might experience depression, loss of self-esteem, and dejection. If, on the other hand, we are informed by other people that we are capable of a great deal more than we think we are (i.e., the same discrepancy, but with the own ideal self being less than the other ideal self) we might feel inspiration and excitement (as well as perhaps a little anxiety).

7.5.1 Applying self-discrepancy theory to the online self

Some discrepancies may be familiar to many. MMOs are of interest for many reasons, but one of these relates to the necessity of cooperation and teamwork if the game's greatest challenges are to be overcome. In order for teamwork to be true teamwork as opposed to a collection of individuals all doing the same thing, different roles need to be provided. As MMOs tend to focus principally on combat challenges, these roles frequently boil down to those who Kill, Irritate, or Preserve; the **KIP model** (Coulson, Barnett, Ferguson, & Gould, 2012). *Killers*, often referred to as 'DPS' for 'damage per second', a standard measure of damage output, typically make up the majority of a group and focus on damaging and eventually killing opponents. *Irritators* attract the attention of opponents, directing attacks onto themselves (and are frequently referred to as 'tanks' due to generally high durability, though their damage output tends to be low relative to Killers). Finally, in order to permit Irritators and Killers to continue to do their jobs, *Preservers* protect and heal everyone else. There is a sense in which such a division of labour is inevitable. If Killers are as durable as Irritators, there is no need for Irritators, and if Irritators are as capable of damage dealing as Killers, there is no need for Killers. If everyone can maintain their own health, Preservers are unnecessary. The end result is a reasonably clear delineation between roles that, although potentially fluid (depending on game mechanics, a player may be able to swap between roles at various points during the lifetime of the group), nonetheless sets up expectations about what each player ought to be doing at any one moment. **Irritators** who do not keep opponents' attention ('losing aggro') will quickly learn just how keen the expectations of others are. In common MMO parlance, 'If the tank dies, it's the healer's fault. If the healer dies, it's the tank's fault. If the DPS dies, it's their own damn fault'.

7.6 How the online self is represented and created

Modern online environments offer tremendous flexibility in the ways in which avatars can be customized, providing interactive tools that can create millions of possible outcomes even within the relatively constrained space of a human being. Everything from skin and hair colour through body size and shape, limb length, and thickness, and all manner of facial features can be tweaked until the online self is exactly what the user requires. The possibilities for self-representation are almost limitless.

One way of looking at this flexibility is simply to see it as window dressing. It is in the interests of companies selling a service, whether it is an MMO, an online dating website, a gambling site, or a virtual chat room, to offer as much optional flexibility as possible in the creation of avatars. Some people may legitimately not care what their online self looks like, in which case any one of a number of pre-determined avatars would likely suit them perfectly well. Others may gravitate towards a certain 'type', enjoying a small degree of customization that makes them feel unique, or one of the crowd, or identify allegiance with one group or another. Yet others may appreciate spending a considerable amount of time designing the perfect avatar for them.

There is not a great deal of research that examines how and why people create the avatars they do and this is certainly a topic that requires further investigation. Some authors have suggested that avatars tend to map onto Higgins' notion of the ideal self. In a paper wonderfully entitled 'The Ideal Elf', Bessière, Seay, and Kiesler (2007) examined the differences between participants' assessments of their own abilities and characteristics, and those of the avatar they had created in *World of Warcraft*. The authors claim that avatar characteristics were generally more positive than those of the participant who created them, and that this effect was stronger for participants who scored low on well-being. Of course, when we create an avatar in an MMO like *World of Warcraft*, we are expecting this avatar to shoot, bludgeon, or fireball its way through thousands of opponents. It is therefore entirely plausible that we instil positive characteristics in such a godlike creation. However, an actual-ideal discrepancy in avatar creation has been observed in other studies, and may be enhanced in individuals who score high on the personality dimension of agreeableness (Dunn & Guadagno, 2012).

Early studies (Ducheneaut et al., 2006) found that males who created characters who chose to play Preserver roles, which often require the wearing of light armour, were more likely to choose a female character. Other research has suggested that men tend to create avatars who are slightly thinner than their offline selves, and slightly more muscular both than their actual *and* their ideal selves (Cacioli & Mussap, 2014). Of course, many avatar creation tools offer unrealistically scaled models, with arms, shoulders, and breasts of a size that would be positively unwieldy offline.

There is a key question here about the degree of similarity between online and offline selves. We have seen evidence which suggests that people are motivated to create avatars that tend to be subtly different from their offline selves in a positive fashion. So our online selves tend towards idealized versions of our offline selves. Why only small differences? Why not create avatars that are perfect? One possible answer to this question is that for a sense of immersion to persist, there has to be some threshold level of similarity between the online and offline self. So as creators of online selves, we are subject to two opposing forces. One pushes in the direction of an idealized heroic self, the second keeps us rooted in some sense of what is realistic rather than what is possible in the avatar design engine. The end result is some compromise between these. Mar and Oatley (2008), whose work we consider again later, argue that a sense of immersion in a fictitious world (their interest lies in literary fiction rather than online worlds) is enhanced by the degree to which protagonists are perceived as being close to the self. This sense of partial identification, the notion that there are some similarities between who we are and the characters involved in the story, allows us to 'transport' ourselves into the fiction. Avatars need to be heroic and idealized, but not so heroic and idealized that we cannot see a little of ourselves in them.

Borrowing from evolutionary theory and mate selection, we propose that the online self can be defined in part by the *principle of optimal online intermediate similarity*. In evolutionary terms, the principle of optimal intermediate similarity refers to the fact that individuals choose to mate with others who are similar, but not *too* similar to themselves (so for instance, quail prefer to mate with first cousins rather than third cousins and sisters; third cousins are too different, sisters are too similar). It is thought that this optimizes genetic fitness while preventing inbreeding, which generally carries heavy costs.

This principle predicts an optimal degree of difference between offline and online selves that offers the ideal blend of immersion and identification. An online self that is too different from our offline self will not permit us to identify with its actions, interfering with the sense of ownership and opportunities for learning and development. An online self that is too similar to the offline self, in contrast, demotes our online actions to mere simulacra of 'real' life. In essence, without a little bit of escapism from who we normally are (or ought to be, or might be one day) there is little point in creating an online self.

As with any preference, there will be significant individual variation. Individuals' preferences are likely filtered through their motivations (in terms of SDT) as well as a potential host of other variables associated with motivation and personality. The increasing amount of time we spend inhabiting online selves makes understanding these relationships an important goal of research.

Another key flexibility offered by online selves concerns the sex of an avatar. Many, if not most, environments offer the opportunity to experience the virtual world as either a male or a female (and many additionally provide a range of other species as well). While there is generally not a great deal of difference between playing as a man or a woman (key characteristics that affect gameplay are rarely affected, and the difference is generally purely cosmetic), the effect on the avatar's user may be more wide reaching.

At this point it is important to distinguish the sex of an individual from its gender. Although gender is increasingly treated as synonymous with sex, its meaning refers not to the biological sex of an individual, its maleness or femaleness, but to the degree to which the individual's behaviour conforms with social and cultural expectations about what constitutes masculine and feminine behaviour. While there is very little that can be done about one's (offline) sex, gender is a far more fluid construct. Indeed, the evidence suggests that gender is a combination of both masculinity and femininity, with individuals possessing elements of both.

When faced with the opportunity to play as a member of one's own or another sex, there is some evidence for sex differences. Research in our lab (Coulson et al., 2012) investigated player preferences for avatar sex in *Dragon Age: Origins* (Bioware, 2009; http://www.imdb.com/title/tt1541718/) and found that while over 90% of women chose to play as a woman, 28% of men chose to play as women. While the study's sample size was small, and only concerned decisions taken in a single game, this is an interesting finding that suggests the two sexes may bring somewhat different motivations to avatar creation. We speculate that this may be due to the 'Lara phenomenon' (Jansz & Martis, 2007), where the eponymous Lara Croft provides a female antidote to the often male-dominated action game. The availability of a strong female avatar may be extremely attractive to women, as the physical and social power that they are often denied offline can be experienced through the actions of the avatar in the game world. The concept of a powerful woman can be novel and exciting, and there is much to be gained experientially from playing as such a woman. For men, on the other hand, although many might be denied physical and social power in the offline world, and the exercise of power in-game may be similarly attractive, the option to play as a member of the opposite sex provides greater novelty. For players of both sexes, socially and physically powerful male avatars are nothing new. As a consequence, male players frequently take on female avatars while women players are more likely to stick with avatars of the same sex when given a choice.

7.7 The nature of the online self

The tendency to create online selves that tend towards the ideal is a consequence of the additional freedom that online worlds offer. It is as if our online selves serve as rose tinted mirrors, gifting us the opportunity to look at ourselves at our best (or even hyper-best), freeing us from the constraints of our earthly bodies, complex social networks, and everyday responsibilities. Such opportunities may underpin the importance of immersion and escapism that online worlds offer.

It is tempting to think that this relates to the concept of 'losing' oneself, in a similar way to how we think of losing ourselves in a book or a movie. We suggest, however, that nothing could be further from the truth. Indeed, what online selves offer are new ways of finding and exploring the self in its many incarnations and varieties. Whether this acts in a positive or a negative way depends on the uses to which this freedom is put. We have argued that online selves allow us to explore new aspects of our selves, and experience things that we may not wish to, or may be prevented from experiencing in the real world. Our online selves perform acts with few real consequences with respect to their outcomes, but with potentially important consequences for who we are and how we choose to behave. Our online selves can lead us to experience new emotions, and examine the consequences of courses of action we would never normally be allowed to take. Ignoring for the moment the fact that most online worlds are very different from the offline world we inhabit each day, the positions our online selves occupy provide tremendous scope for experimentation. Is 'playing' an avatar in an online world therefore a useful, perhaps important aspect of personal development?

The importance of experimentation, and exploration, and the broader category of play into which they both fit, was emphasized (but subsequently somewhat ignored) by the great developmental psychologist Jean Piaget. Piaget (1926) saw an important role for play that he integrated into his famous theories of child intellectual development. For Piaget, play provided children with an opportunity to learn about things in the 'here and now' as they lack the intellectual tools necessary for abstract thought. Play was crucial in early development but increasingly less important as maturity provided children with the tools to think about things without necessitating their physical presence.

Observations across many different species suggest that play is very common in young, but tends to disappear as individuals age. Does this make adult forms of play throwbacks to immature forms of behaviour? Questions such as this are notoriously hard to disentangle from one's own views of whether playing is 'just for kids' or whether it serves a more general purpose. Two forms of evidence suggest that adult play is an important feature of our species, and in fact serves an important evolutionary advantage.

The first strand of evidence comes from the increasing penetration of games into everyday society. It appears that modern computing devices, in particular smartphones and tablet devices, have released a technological 'brake' on the proliferation of games. The evidence is that people like to play, like experiencing challenge, like constant feedback, and like competition (McGonigal, 2011). Of course different people like these things to different degrees, but the desire to play is far more widespread than we would expect if this was simply something that was useful for a brief period during our childhood. The increasing amount of evidence that gamers are not socially isolated teenage boys, but are in fact drawn from all sex, age, and socioeconomic strata, further supports the notion that play is a ubiquitous characteristic of our species.

Second, play and the positive emotions associated with it may actually serve a crucial evolutionary function. Researchers have for a long time accepted that negative emotions, for all the unpleasantness they bring with them, are actually crucial for survival (Buss, 2000). Negative emotions are *signals* that indicate that whatever the individual is engaged in at the moment, focus needs to be switched to the event or object responsible for generating the emotion. An organism that did not initiate the behaviours and corresponding emotion of fear when confronted with a predator would not live long enough to pass its genes on to the next generation. As a consequence, negative emotions are selected for by evolution.

Explaining why we have positive emotions, by contrast, is far less obvious. To be sure, positive emotion *feels* nice, but this is a long way from explaining why we have it. Evolution does not equip species with things that feel nice unless they serve a function, and if that function is not in some sense associated with the probability of passing the organism's genes on to the next generation, there is no pressure to create the function in the first place. The work of Fredrickson (2001) changed the way we think about positive emotion, and its role in evolution and development. Fredrickson's *broaden and build* theory posits that positive emotions encourage exploration and play, signalling to the organism that the current state of the environment is such that it is safe to do so. What is key about the kinds of behaviour that play induces is that playful activity can be creative, opening up new ways of responding to situations. As a result of this, organisms can *build* resources (e.g., new forms of behaviour) and *broaden* their behavioural repertoire, basically expanding the 'toolkit' of responses they can choose from in any particular situation.

Consider the standard response to threat. We are all aware of the basic 'fight or flight' response that governs whether a threatened individual will respond with aggression or fear. What is less often mentioned is that fight and flight are fairly infrequent responses to threat, and other more useful options often exist. For instance, whereas fight or flight may be the best options to choose from when confronted by a predator, most confrontations actually involve members of one's own species. Under these circumstances, it might be better to *posture* (puffing oneself up, trying to look threatening, shouting), or *appease* (acknowledge the other's position of power, adopt a submissive posture). The key element to these behaviours is that they are potentially better than fight or flight *for both parties* and are therefore likely to be selected by evolution.

By spending time in play, individuals have the opportunity to experiment with different ways of doing things in an environment where failure is not costly. If, rather than attack when confronted, our play experiences teach us that making a loud noise and snarling is an effective way to scare off a potential threat, we may adopt that behaviour in circumstances where the costs are potentially much greater. A great deal of human and animal conflict is handled in this way as it is usually in no one's best interests to actually fight. However strong and big an individual is, getting into a fight introduces the risk of some degree of injury. If you can accomplish the same goals (for instance, access to food or mates) by simply growling, everyone is better off.

The evidence in support of Fredrickson's ideas comes largely from experimental studies that demonstrate that there are associations between positive emotion and mental and physical health outcomes (Garland et al., 2010). The evidence suggests that play not only makes people happy, it also teaches them new skills and builds resilience for future challenges. Recent studies have explored the importance of play in relation to virtual therapeutic processes, mood management, and violent gameplay. Barnett, Coulson, and Foreman (2010) used *World of Warcraft* to explore players' moods before and after two hours of gameplay as a function of personality, age, gender, sex, and gameplay motivation. After two hours of gameplay, the results showed a significant reduction of negative mood and an increase in positive mood, regardless of the functional variables. These effects were most noticeable in those players who had originally reported high levels of neuroticism, and low levels of agreeableness, conscientiousness, and openness to experience. Similar results were found by Ferguson et al. (2008) who offered participants the choice of playing a violent or non-violent game. Results showed that participants did not experience aggression regardless of which type of game they chose to play. Research has also shown that the challenge and stimulation provided by playing video games can play an important role during adolescence. A sample of 16-year-old students who played video games scored more positively on factors such as positive mental health, school engagement, involving themselves in activities, less or no substance abuse, positive view of the self, and more friends, compared to those who did not play video games (Durkin & Barber, 2002).

While we do not aim to stray into the highly charged realm of video games and violence, the essentially violent nature of many games cannot be ignored. Are the potentially beneficial elements of play outweighed by the potentially destructive? We believe there is much cause for optimism. Research by Jansz, for example, has explored the relationship between adolescent males, violent video games, and emotional behaviour (Jansz, 2005). Contrary to popular belief that violent video games 'teach' gamers violent behaviour, Jansz's research showed that adolescent males always feel in control of the game, suggesting they are also in control of the emotions they experience while playing. Jansz suggests that this freedom is important because it allows adolescent males to construct their own identity at their own pace and the violent video game is used as a 'safe haven' or experimental laboratory where they can experience different, often controversial emotions (such as those perceived as non-masculine) without being judged by peers.

In a related line of research, Oatley and colleagues (Mar & Oatley, 2008; Oatley, 2012) have likened the process of reading novels or watching plays to a simulation of behaviour, morals, and emotions that runs on the computational hardware of the human brain. They outline a number of ways in which fiction can permit transportation of the reader/viewer into the world created by the author, thereby enabling experiences that might not normally be offered in the real world. Much as with Fredrickson's model, the experiences gained within these fictitious spaces provide opportunities for growth and development. Oatley's work focuses on the effects of what are effectively passive media (though he would claim that novels and plays are not passively consumed). The application of these ideas to online selves creates a rich source of opportunities not available to more traditional media. In online worlds we are not limited to observing the implications and outcomes of the protagonists' decisions, we *are* the protagonists. There is some limited evidence from Oatley's lab that people who frequently read fiction tend to be more empathic (Djikic, Oatley, & Moldoveanu, 2013), and that even a single episode of reading a short story may increase certain kinds of empathy in some participants. Much still needs to be learned about how online simulations affect psychological development.

7.8 A model of the online self

Before turning to some conclusions, we present a synthesis of the discussion we have presented in the form of a model (see Figure 7.1). In this model, the offline self is immersed in online selves, its status as special and different maintained only through its existence prior to the others. We have argued that it makes little or no sense to distinguish between offline and online, and that the same processes, concerns, emotions, and social effects exist in much the same way wherever our minds find themselves. The deck of a ferry, a starship, or a pirate's frigate; a beach

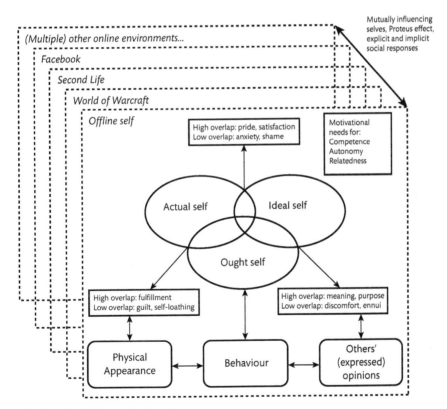

Figure 7.1 Model of offline and online selves.

in Africa, in Azeroth, or on some far flung planet; an underground car park, an underground civilization of vampires, an underground dungeon (okay we know, dungeons are always underground). Different worlds, but the same concerns about who we are, what we want to do, what we hope to accomplish, and who's around to love, hate, and form memories with.

7.9 Chapter summary

Unlike the hackneyed actor who asks the director 'what's my motivation?', online worlds provide the freedom and flexibility to suit whatever motivations we might bring with us. For example, whether it be social (making new friends), competitive (waging war against, or with, other players), exploration (discovering new areas), or role-playing (developing a character personality), or a combination of all of these, the self can find a satisfying home. Indeed, some authors (Castronova, 2007) see a developing exodus from the real into the virtual as the latter's offerings increasingly offset the frustrations and limitations of the former.

Regardless of how much time we might choose to spend in online worlds, our offline selves are dynamic and multifaceted, continuously evolving and changing in light of information about our behaviour, motivations, and the myriad discrepancies arising between our own and others' perceptions of who we are, who we should be, and who we might be. Online selves need to reflect at least some of this complexity if they are to promote understanding, growth, engagement, immersion, and enjoyment. There seems little need to provide a completely synthetic experience that is as rich as the offline one, as the impact of a simulation, whether a work of literary fiction or an online environment, depends more on abstracting and preserving key features of the self than copying it in every way.

The experience of the self online offers tremendous promise for enhancing our understanding of both the light and the dark side of our natures. The online self is unbounded in ways that can make the offline self appear hopelessly impoverished in comparison. Our offline selves imprison us in bodies of a certain size, shape, colour, and appearance, with little or no respect for our desires or attempts at change. There are few, if any, opportunities to experiment offline with the experiences afforded by alternative selves without having to pay the consequences. The creation of multiple online selves may offer us opportunities to explore and develop our own identity that are far more valuable and long lasting than the most epic battles, vistas, and loot.

 ## References

Barnett, J., Coulson, M., & Foreman, N. (2010). Examining player anger in world of warcraft. In Bainbridge, W.S. (Ed.), *Online Worlds: Convergence of the Real and the Virtual* (pp. 147–160). London: Springer.

Bartle, R.A. (2004). *Designing Virtual Worlds*. Indianapolis, IN: New Riders.

Bem, D.J. (1967). Self-perception: An alternative interpretation of cognitive dissonance phenomena. *Psychological Review*, 74(3), 183.

Bessière, K., Seay, A.F., & Kiesler, S. (2007). The Ideal Elf: Identity exploration in *World of Warcraft*. *CyberPsychology & Behavior*, 10(4), 530–535. doi:10.1089/cpb.2007.9994.

Buss, D.M. (2000). The evolution of happiness. *American Psychologist*, 55(1), 15–23. doi:10.1037//0003-066X.55.1.15.

Cacioli, J.-P. & Mussap, A.J. (2014). Avatar body dimensions and men's body image. *Body Image*. doi:10.1016/j.bodyim.2013.11.005.

Castronova, E. (2005). *Synthetic Worlds*. Retrieved from http://www.press.uchicago.edu/ucp/books/book/chicago/S/bo3620704.html (accessed 3rd September, 2014).

Castronova, E. (2007). *Exodus to the Virtual World: How Online Fun is Changing Reality*. Basingstoke & New York: Palgrave Macmillan.

Chwalisz, K., Diener, E., & Gallagher, D. (1988). Autonomic arousal feedback and emotional experience: Evidence from the spinal cord injured. *Journal of Personality and Social Psychology*, 54(5), 820–828. doi:10.1037/0022-3514.54.5.820.

Coulson, M., Barnett, J., Ferguson, C.J., & Gould, R.L. (2012). Real feelings for virtual people: Emotional attachments and interpersonal attraction in video games. *Psychology of Popular Media Culture*, 1(3), 176–184. doi:10.1037/a0028192.

Deci, E.L. & Ryan, R.M. (2008). Self-determination theory: A macrotheory of human motivation, development, and health. *Canadian Psychology/Psychologie Canadienne*, 49(3), 182–185. doi:10.1037/a0012801.

Djikic, M., Oatley, K., & Moldoveanu, M.C. (2013). Reading other minds: Effects of literature on empathy. *Scientific Study of Literature*, 3(1), 28–47. doi:10.1075/ssol.3.1.06dji.

Dotsch, R. & Wigboldus, D.H.J. (2008). Virtual prejudice. *Journal of Experimental Social Psychology*, 44(4), 1194–1198. doi:10.1016/j.jesp.2008.03.003.

Ducheneaut, N., Yee, N., Nickell, E., & Moore, R.J. (2006). Alone together?: exploring the social dynamics of massively multiplayer online games. In *Proceedings of the SIGCHI Conference on Human Factors in computing systems* (pp. 407–416). ACM Digital Library. Retrieved from http://dl.acm.org/citation.cfm?id=1124834 (accessed 3rd September, 2014).

Dunn, R.A. & Guadagno, R.E. (2012). My avatar and me—Gender and personality predictors of avatar-self discrepancy. *Computers in Human Behavior*, 28(1), 97–106. doi:10.1016/j.chb.2011.08.015.

Durkin, K. & Barber, B. (2002). Not so doomed: Computer game play and positive adolescent development. *Journal of Applied Developmental Psychology*, 23(4), 373–392.

Ferguson, C.J., Rueda, S.M., Cruz, A.M., Ferguson, D.E., Fritz, S., & Smith, S.M. (2008). Violent video games and aggression: Causal relationship or byproduct of family violence and intrinsic violence motivation?

Criminal Justice and Behavior, 35(3), 311–332. doi:10.1177/0093854807311719.

Fox, J., Bailenson, J.N., & Tricase, L. (2013). The embodiment of sexualized virtual selves: The Proteus Effect and experiences of self-objectification via avatars. *Computers in Human Behavior*, 29(3), 930–938. doi:10.1016/j.chb.2012.12.027.

Fredrickson, B.L. (2001). The role of positive emotions in positive psychology: The broaden-and-build theory of positive emotions. *American Psychologist*, 56(3), 218.

Garland, E.L., Fredrickson, B., Kring, A.M., Johnson, D.P., Meyer, P.S., & Penn, D.L. (2010). Upward spirals of positive emotions counter downward spirals of negativity: Insights from the broaden-and-build theory and affective neuroscience on the treatment of emotion dysfunctions and deficits in psychopathology. *Clinical Psychology Review*, 30(7), 849–864. doi:10.1016/j.cpr.2010.03.002.

Greenwald, A.G., McGhee, D.E., & Schwartz, J.L. (1998). Measuring individual differences in implicit cognition: the implicit association test. *Journal of Personality and Social Psychology*, 74(6), 1464.

Higgins, E. (1987). Self-Discrepancy: A theory relating self and affect. *Psychological Review*, 94(3), 319–340.

James, W. (1950). *Principles of Psychology* (Vol. 2). New York: Dover (original work published 1890).

Jansz, J. (2005). The emotional appeal of violent video games for adolescent males. *Communication Theory*, 15(3), 219–241. doi:10.1111/j.1468-2885.2005.tb00334.x.

Jansz, J. & Martis, R.G. (2007). The Lara Phenomenon: Powerful female characters in video games. *Sex Roles*, 56 (3-4), 141–148. doi:10.1007/s11199-006-9158-0.

Kruger, J. & Dunning, D. (1999). Unskilled and unaware of it: how difficulties in recognizing one's own incompetence lead to inflated self-assessments. *Journal of Personality and Social Psychology*, 77(6), 1121.

Mar, R.A. & Oatley, K. (2008). The function of fiction is the abstraction and simulation of social experience. *Perspectives on Psychological Science*, 3(3), 173–192.

McGonigal, J. (2011). *Reality Is Broken: Why Games Make Us Better and How They Can Change the World* (Reprint edition). New York: Penguin Books.

Nakamura, L. (1995). Race in/for cyberspace: Identity tourism and racial passing on the Internet. *Works and Days*, 25(26), 13.

Oatley, K. (2012). The cognitive science of fiction. *Wiley Interdisciplinary Reviews: Cognitive Science*, 3(4), 425–430. doi:10.1002/wcs.1185.

Piaget, J. (1926). *The Language and Thought of the Child*. New York: Meridian Books.

Ryan, R.M., Rigby, C.S., & Przybylski, A. (2006). The motivational pull of video games: A Self-Determination Theory approach. *Motivation and Emotion*, 30(4), 344–360. doi:10.1007/s11031-006-9051-8.

Soussignan, R. (2002). Duchenne smile, emotional experience, and autonomic reactivity: A test of the facial feedback hypothesis. *Emotion*, 2(1), 52–74. doi:10.1037/1528-3542.2.1.52.

Yee, N. (2006). Motivations for play in online games. *CyberPsychology & Behavior*, 9(6), 772–775.

Yee, N. & Bailenson, J. (2007). The Proteus effect: The effect of transformed self-representation on behavior. *Human Communication Research*, 33(3), 271–290.

Further Reading

A lot more than just a discussion of the self in online worlds, but contains important insights into what avatars represent to us once we inhabit their forms:

Castronova, E. (2005). *Synthetic Worlds*. Retrieved from http://www.press.uchicago.edu/ucp/books/book/chicago/S/bo3620704.html (accessed 3rd September, 2014).

An outline of why fictions are important. Does not explicitly discuss video games, but the work has direct relevance to how our experiences of fictitious worlds expand and develop out notions of selfhood:

Mar, R.A. & Oatley, K. (2008). The function of fiction is the abstraction and simulation of social experience. *Perspectives on Psychological Science*, 3(3), 173–192.

A nice outline of a fundamental approach to human motivation and selfhood and how these relate to gaming:

Ryan, R.M., Rigby, C.S., & Przybylski, A. (2006). The motivational pull of video games: A Self-Determination Theory approach. *Motivation and Emotion*, 30(4), 344–360. doi:10.1007/s11031-006-9051-8.

Discussion questions

1. Outline and compare theories in relation to how the self is created and experienced online.
2. Is the online representation of self different to offline presentations?
3. How do online and offline selves interact and possibly influence one another?
4. What is the Proteus Effect?
5. What roles do sex and gender play in online gaming?

Part 2

Psychological Processes and Consequences of Online Behaviour

Cybercrime and Deviance

THOMAS J. HOLT

 Learning outcomes

This chapter will introduce a number of key concepts related to cybercrime and deviance that will aid the understanding of the specific example of online deviant behaviour, cyberbullying, in Chapter 12. By the end of this chapter you should be able to:

- Define and distinguish various key concepts of cybercrime and deviance.
- Distinguish different types of system attack such as hacking and those aimed at larger groups, corporations, or individuals (e.g., malware and phishing).
- Consider implications for both perpetrators and victims of illegal online activities.
- Outline the differences between online and offline crime, and be able to explain the under-reporting of online crimes.
- Outline and discuss Wall's (2001) typology of cybercrime.

8.1 Introduction

This chapter will examine the various forms of **cybercrime** that can occur, and contextualize these acts relative to the protection and maintenance of identity online. Utilizing Wall's (2001) typology of cybercrime, this chapter will consider hacking, piracy, theft, pornography, and violent behaviour in online environments, and their intersection with real world offending behaviours. The anonymity, lack of corporeality, and temporal dynamics affecting cyberspace will be discussed to consider why and how some offenders choose to engage in crime online.

8.2 Cybercrime and deviance

Over the last 30 years, the evolution of computer technology and the Internet have dramatically changed the ways that humans interact with one another on a global scale. The World Wide Web and easy-to-use computer hardware and software enable individuals to engage in commercial transactions and personal communications at virtually any time of day (Newman & Clarke, 2003, Wall, 2007). Cellular telephony, smartphones, wireless Internet connectivity, and tablet PCs such as iPads enable individuals to go online from anywhere at any time regardless of where they are in the world. Technology use is particularly concentrated among youth, as individuals in the United States acquire their first cell phones between the ages of

12 and 13 (Lenhart, 2010), and 75% of youth own either a laptop or desktop computer and 15% own both devices (Lenhart, Madden, & Hitlin, 2005). In addition, technology use cuts across socio-economic groups as 93% of American youths between the ages of 12 and 17 use the Internet on a weekly basis.

The proliferation of technology has led to distinct changes in the ways that individuals engage with the world. Consumers are also increasingly using the Internet for entertainment purposes through the use of streaming media services like Netflix and Hulu. Social networking sites like Facebook and Twitter have become a primary mechanism for social interaction, particularly among young audiences (Socialbakers, 2011). The sheer volume of online purchases made every day (Anderson, 2010), coupled with the use of online banking systems to manage personal finances mean that our sensitive personal data are stored remotely and managed by private industry (James, 2005).

All of these technologies have created interesting opportunities for individual identity construction and management online. Individuals can be any age, gender, or race that they want, and present themselves through photos, videos, and text (DiMarco, 2003). The extent to which an online identity corresponds to that of the actual person in the real world is entirely up to that person, leading to substantial opportunities for misrepresentation (DiMarco, 2003, Brenner, 2008). As a result, technology enables myriad opportunities for crime and deviance on and offline. For instance, cell phones, digital cameras, and text messaging allow individuals to send sexually explicit pictures of themselves to others with or without their permission (Mitchell, Finkelhor, Jones, & Wolak, 2012), and even arrange sexual encounters with partners outside of their current committed relationships (Quinn & Forsyth, 2013). Individuals can also use these technologies to lure unsuspecting persons into fraudulent schemes under the guise of aiding rich foreigners (James, 2005, Holt & Graves, 2007, King & Thomas, 2009) or sell counterfeit goods (Wall & Large, 2010). Social media can also be used as a means to harass, threaten, or intimidate others who they may or may not know in the real world (Bocij, 2004, Hinduja & Patchin, 2009, Wolak, Finkelhor, & Mitchell, 2012).

The emergence of these various technologies has also led to new offences that are completely dependent on computers and the Internet (Wall, 2001). Computer hackers, for instance, are involved in activities to compromise and subvert various systems in order to gain access to sensitive information or cause harm (Taylor, 1999, Holt, 2007). Additionally, malicious software programs, such as viruses and botnet malware, can only operate on computer systems and are frequently spread through the Internet or infected files shared on flash drives and removable media (Chu, Holt, & Ahn, 2010). In turn, malware can be used to cause damage or remotely control systems, and even steal personal data and intellectual property (Choi, 2008, Bossler & Holt, 2009, Holt & Turner, 2012). The quantity of personal information now stored on servers by financial institutions and retailers are also being targeted by thieves in order to gain thousands, if not millions, of credit and debit card details and engage in fraud (Holt & Lampke, 2010, Motoyama, McCoy, Levchenko, Savage, & Voelker, 2011).

Due to the substantial impact that technology has on the ability for individuals to engage in crime and deviance, it is necessary to understand the nature of online criminality and how these offences are attractive due to the ability to manipulate an offender's identity online. Thus, this chapter will continue by providing an overview of cybercrimes, why these offences may be difficult to police, and the range of offences that constitute cybercrimes overall.

In turn, readers will understand how individual identity construction is related to the problem of cybercrime.

8.3 Defining computer misuse and abuse

Over the last three decades, there have been a number of terms used to describe computer and technology misuse (Furnell, 2002). Some terms have become particularly popular, such as cybercrime, though the meaning of these concepts can be quite distinct. In order to clarify this issue, it is vital to delineate what constitutes the abuse and misuse of technology. For instance, the term **deviance** is used to refer to a behaviour that may not be illegal, though outside of the formal and informal norms or beliefs of a prevailing culture. There are many forms of deviance, depending on societal norms and societal contexts. For instance, texting and using mobile phones while watching a movie at a cinema is not technically illegal, though it is disruptive and discouraged by the cinema and other patrons in the theatre. As a result, the use of a mobile device in this context may be considered deviant as it is considered unacceptable by the majority of people. Since texting and mobile devices are enabled by the Internet and cyberspace, it may be appropriate to refer to this behaviour as a form of **cyberdeviance**.

A more pertinent example of cyberdeviance involves the use and creation of pornographic content, or erotic, sexual materials. The Internet has made it exceedingly easy for individuals to view pornographic images and videos hosted online, or create and distribute their own content using webcams, mobile phone cameras, and WiFi networks. In fact, the term sexting was coined in the last few years to describe the process of voluntarily making and sending sexually explicit images and text to others via mobile devices (Mitchell et al., 2012). When this activity is performed by consenting individuals over the age of 18, it is technically considered legal (Mitchell et al., 2012). The majority of individuals within the community may, however, feel that such an activity is morally wrong or unjust. As a result, engaging in sexting or viewing pornography may be considered deviant in that area since it goes against local norms regarding acceptable behaviour.

Once an activity violates established legal statutes it changes from being a deviant act to a form of crime. In the context of sexting in the United States, if an individual is under the age of 18 then they are not legally allowed to either create or view pornographic images (Mitchell et al., 2012). Anyone who knowingly attempts to send pornographic materials to a minor, or solicits them, then that person is engaging in a crime because of the legal sanctions prescribed to punish individuals for engaging in this activity. In fact, there are multiple instances of adults being prosecuted at either the state or federal level for the sexual solicitation of minors or distribution of child pornography via text message (Mitchell et al., 2012).

The criminal law of most nations is complex, and recognizes a range of behaviours as criminal with sanctions that vary based on the severity of the offence. There is minimal consistency in the ways that technology-facilitated offences are classified from country to country (Wall, 2007, Brenner, 2008). Some nations utilize the term *cybercrime* to describe certain offences, while others may use the term *electronic crime* or **computer crime** to refer to the unique way that technology was used to facilitate criminal activity. Though these terms are generally used interchangeably, they actually refer to distinct phenomena (Wall, 2001, Furnell, 2002). Cybercrime refers to crimes 'in which the perpetrator uses special knowledge of cyberspace', while computer crimes occur because 'the perpetrator uses special knowledge about computer technology' (Wall, 2001, Furnell, 2002, p. 21). In the early days of computing, the difference between these terms was useful to clarify how technology was incorporated into the offence. The fact that almost every computer is now connected to the Internet in some way has diminished the need to segment these two acts (Wall, 2007). As a result, the term cybercrime will be used throughout the rest of this chapter, since a range of crimes can occur through the use of online environments and almost all computers and mobile devices now connect to the Internet (Wall, 2007).

8.4 Cybercrime and offender identity

The rise of cyberdeviance and crime over the last few decades has led some to question why virtual environments are an attractive outlet for wrongdoing. There are several prospective factors associated with the rate of cybercrime, most notably the ease with which individuals can gain access to the necessary tools. The portability and low cost of laptop computers and tablet PCs, coupled with the increased capabilities of mobile phones makes it extremely easy for individuals to get online from any location and stay online over time (Associated Press, 2005, Anderson, 2010). Individuals who cannot afford their own computer can still engage in some forms of cybercrime through the use of PCs available in Internet cafes and public libraries for free or a small cost (Holt, 2009).

Second, the technical proficiency necessary to engage in cybercrime has decreased dramatically over the last two decades. As computer technology becomes increasingly user friendly, the skills needed to engage in simple forms of computer hacking, such as password guessing and simple scams are minimal (Holt, 2007, Holt, Bossler, & May, 2012). In fact, there is some evidence that individuals use the same password for multiple email and social networking profiles enabling an attacker to gain full access to their victim's online identity. In much the same way, people can easily post hurtful messages or videos on social media sites about others in order to publicly embarrass or shame someone (Hinduja & Patchin, 2009). Activities like digital piracy have become extremely simple to complete through the use of tools and web-based file sharing services like Bit Torrent (Holt & Copes, 2010).

Third, and perhaps most important, is the fact that technology also greatly reduces an individual's level of risk while engaging in any form of crime. First, the risk of detection in online environments is much lower than in the offline world (Brenner, 2008, Denning, 2011). Should an individual choose to engage in a robbery, for instance, they may take steps to minimize the likelihood that they are recognized by their victim. Robbers often wear masks or baggy clothing to conceal their face and build, and may even try to disguise their voice by speaking in higher or lower tones of voice (Wright & Decker, 1997, Miller, 1998). Though this may help confuse victims, security cameras and passers-by may observe the incident and increase the likelihood of detection.

These issues are largely absent in online environments as individual identity is performative, based entirely on presentation of self through text and images (Wall, 2001, DiMarco, 2003). An individual can hide their gender, race, or age by falsifying information to create accounts in social networking sites like Twitter or Facebook, or email. Similarly, individuals can utilize pictures downloaded from various websites in order to visually present themselves to the world as any race, ethnicity, or gender they see fit (Cere, 2003). In addition, **proxy services** can be used to hide a person's actual location in physical space while online. There are a range of tools now available to hide the location of a person's computer, such as *Tor*, by acting as an intermediary between a computer and the servers and systems it connects to through the Internet (Brenner, 2008, Denning, 2011). As a result, an individual's online activities will be associated with the proxy service provider rather than the computer being used by the offender. Such techniques are essential to help minimize an individual's risk of identification or attribution to any form of cybercrime (Brenner, 2008).

The ability to conceal one's true identity makes it easier for individuals to express their interests and desires online. The Internet affords individuals the potential to find and connect with others who share their interests without any stigma or shame that may otherwise come from admission of interests in the real world (DiMarco, 2003, Quinn & Forsyth, 2013). In fact, that is why some argue that a range of communities focused on various forms of sexual deviance are incredibly active online (Quinn & Forsyth, 2013). There are active forums designed to connect individuals interested in sexual relationships with animals (bestiality), fictional characters (slash fiction), and more aberrant activities such as sexual activities with minors (paedophilia; Quayle & Taylor, 2002, Quinn & Forsyth, 2013).

Fourth, cyberspace makes it easy for individuals to target hundreds of prospective victims at once and in ways that are rather difficult to achieve in the offline world. For instance, most street crimes involve single victims and one or more offenders in order to intimidate or manage the victim's behaviour in an efficient fashion (Wright & Decker, 1997). The Internet completely changes this equation, as a single individual can easily target thousands of victims at once and do so largely without their knowledge. For example, individuals regularly send out unsolicited emails, called **spam**, to thousands of potential victims (Wall, 2004, Holt & Graves, 2007, King & Thomas, 2009). Spam is commonly used to send fraud schemes of all types, ranging from penny stock scams to fraudulent pharmaceuticals (Wall, 2004). Such capability is rare in the offline world, making virtual spaces ideal for certain offenders.

The increased offending capabilities provided by technology are also emboldened by the inherent difficulties in enforcing domestic laws in a transnational environment like the Internet. Though virtually all industrialized nations have created laws prohibiting cybercrimes, they are not inherently similar in their wording or definition for an activity (Brenner, 2008). As a result, if an individual violates US laws by engaging in online identity theft against victims living in Atlanta, Georgia, while they live in Moscow, Russia, there is no common legal process to prosecute the offender. Furthermore, some countries do not allow their citizens to be extradited to another country to face prosecution for crimes (Brenner, 2008). For instance, there is no treaty allowing Russian citizens who engage in attacks against US citizens to be brought to the United States for prosecution (Brenner, 2008). The inability to prosecute or extradite means that the offenders may not receive any sanctions for their actions, and encourage attacks against various nations as the offenders perceive that they face no risk of punishment for their actions (Brenner, 2008, Denning, 2011). As a result, individuals who engage in cybercrime face a much lower risk of arrest and may experience greater monetary or emotional rewards without causing any detriment to their real offline identity.

8.5 Cybercrime and its harm to victim identities

In light of the seeming benefits for offenders to engage in cybercrimes, it is also necessary to consider how their actions negatively impact victims. First, the global scope of cybercrime makes it difficult for victims to report any experience they have to law enforcement agencies. The structure of policing, particularly in the United States, establishes guidelines for the investigation of crimes at the local, state, and federal level. Offences that occur within a single jurisdictional boundary are often the responsibility of local police sheriffs or police, while those that cross state or national boundaries are handled by state or federal agencies depending on the scope of economic harm caused. Many cybercriminals may not live within the same region as their victim (Wall, 1998, Holt, 2003), and victims do not often know sufficient information to identify where their offender actually resides. As a result, victims may not know the correct police agency to contact in the event they are victimized (Wall, 2007, Bossler & Holt, 2012). It is thought that the lack of knowledge among victims may diminish the number of cybercrime incidents made known to police, which in turn creates a 'dark figure' of cybercrime, in that the true number of offences is unknown (Holt, 2003).

When considering the minimal statistics available on cybercrime offending and victimization amongst police agencies (Holt, 2003, Bossler & Holt, 2012), some argue the underrepresentation stems from victim difficulty in recognizing when a cybercrime has taken place. Physical burglaries or break-ins typically produce evidence that someone forced their way into a location to remove valuables or goods (Wright & Decker, 1997). In cyberspace, there may not be any immediate signs that a person's identity or computer has been misused. For example, failures in computer hardware and software may be either the result of an error in the equipment, or a direct result of criminal activities designed to hide their occurrence (Chu et al., 2010, Holt & Bossler, 2013). Many in the general public do not have the skills necessary to discern the root cause, making it hard to know when some sort of compromise has taken place (Bossler & Holt, 2010). Even if a person determines they were a victim of cybercrime, they may be relatively unaware of what risky online behaviour patterns exposed their system to an offender or how a compromise occurred (Bossler & Holt, 2010). Thus, incidents may go unknown simply because victims are unaware they have been harmed.

Those who recognize that they are a victim of some form of cybercrime may not, however, choose to report the incident to proper authorities. Some victims may be too embarrassed or ashamed to contact police, such as victims of a unique form of email-based fraud called a Nigerian, or **419 scam**. These messages typically present the recipient with the idea that the sender is a foreign member of royalty or bankers who need assistance in moving large sums of money (Newman & Clarke, 2003, Wall, 2004, Holt & Graves, 2007). In return for their assistance, the victim will receive a proportion of the total amount that may be hundreds of thousands of dollars or millions in some circumstances (Holt & Graves, 2007, King & Thomas, 2009). They request information from the e-mail recipients, including their name, mailing address, phone number, and in some cases bank account and routing numbers under the guise of facilitating financial transactions (Holt & Graves, 2007, King & Thomas, 2009). Victims who respond to these solicitations often lose between hundreds and thousands of dollars as they provide the fraudster with small amounts of money repeatedly over time on the basis of covering taxes, attorney fees, and other costs associated with moving the full dollar amount (Internet Crime Complaint Center, 2008). By the time these losses are incurred, victims realize that they have been defrauded but feel humiliated that they were scammed. Thus, a very small proportion of victims of this type of fraud actually contact law enforcement about their experiences.

Some victims may also believe that law enforcement agencies cannot actually help them. For instance, victims of malicious software infections or computer hacking may think that their experience is not something that law enforcement can even do anything about (Bossler & Holt, 2010, Holt & Bossler, 2013). Similarly, victims of cyberstalking and harassment may not know what information police need in order to successfully investigate the offence. They may inadvertently delete messages or contacts from their pursuer so that they do not have to see this content on a regular basis (Bocij, 2004). In turn, this may make it difficult for an investigation to successfully move a case forward.

Finally, there is substantial evidence that corporate entities are the least likely to report when a cybercrime has occurred until well after the incident has happened (Holt, 2003, Wall, 2007). For instance, the US retail giant Target announced in late December 2013 that their in-store payment systems had been compromised by hackers. They did not immediately announce how much data had been lost, only that the compromise lasted between November 27 and December 15 and that customers' names, card number, expiration date, and CVV or Credit Verification Value were acquired (Target, 2014).

Toward the end of December, it was revealed that the breach may have affected 70 million people who shopped at stores across the country. The incident was rather shocking, particularly as it appeared to have been enabled by a weakness in the point of sale terminals, or cash register systems in the stores themselves (Higgins, 2014). As a result, Target scrambled to respond to customer fears and provided detailed information on how individual victims could protect themselves in the event that their personal information was affected. It is not yet clear how this incident may affect Target over the long term, though it is clear that they lost some customers and had a slight dip in stock values after this public admission (Higgins, 2014). This is a prime demonstration of the reasons why corporations may limit public acknowledgement of any cybercrime incident they experience.

8.6 Understanding the forms of cybercrime

Since cybercrime and deviance are increasingly prevalent, it is important to consider the range of activities that constitute cybercrime. Though there are a number of typologies of cybercrime, few completely account for the diverse number of behaviours that are facilitated in part by technology (Holt & Bossler, 2014). One of the most comprehensive yet elegantly simple typology to date was devised by Wall (2001) and encapsulates behaviour into one of four categories:

1. cyber-trespass.
2. cyber-deception and theft.
3. cyber-porn and obscenity.
4. cyber-violence.

These categories encompass the wide range of deviant, criminal, and terrorist behaviours that have emerged utilizing technology and the subcultures supporting offenders throughout the world.

8.6.1 **Cyber-tresspass**

The first category, **cyber-trespass**, involves acts where individuals cross boundaries of ownership in online environments. This specifically refers to what is otherwise called *computer hacking* and the actions of computer hackers. Hackers are commonly believed to access computer systems, email accounts, or protected systems that they do not own (Jordan & Taylor, 1998, Furnell, 2002). As a result, the general public tends to associate hackers with involvement in criminal acts of trespassing sensitive boundaries of ownership (Furnell, 2002).

Not all hackers are, however, interested in causing harm or compromising computer systems without permission. A large number of individuals who hack do so as computer security professionals who identify flaws and weaknesses in systems to better protect them (Jordan & Taylor, 1998, Taylor, 1999, Holt, 2007). The ethical and legitimate computer hacker is not as well recognized among the general populace, and is often confused for those who maliciously hack (Furnell, 2002, Bossler & Holt, 2012). This misconception stems from the fact that both groups utilize the same skillsets in order to gain access; the only difference is that ethical hackers do so with permission from system owners. As a result, there is a strong rift within the hacker community based on an individual's willingness to engage in acts of cyber-trespass in support of hacking (Taylor, 1999, Schell & Dodge, 2002, Holt, 2007).

Malicious hackers are also responsible for the creation and use of viruses, trojans, worms, and other forms of malicious software, or malware (Chu et al., 2010). These tools disrupt network traffic, capture passwords for sensitive resources, delete or corrupt files, and utilize infected systems for future attacks (Symantec Corporation, 2012). In addition, they simplify the process of hacking by automating portions of an attack, making it easier for a hacker to gain access to a computer system (Chu et al., 2010). As a consequence, the use of malware is also often closely associated with acts of cyber-trespass (Wall, 2001, Holt & Bossler, 2014).

The consequences of cyber-trespass are myriad, capture headlines, and are costly on a regular basis. For example, the U.S. Government Accountability Office (2007) estimates that various forms of computer crime cost the US economy over $100 billion dollars annually. Additionally, the Internet Crime Complaint Center (IC3, 2009) found that the total dollar losses attributed to computer crime complaints was $559 million in 2009, with an average dollar loss per respondent of $575. Similarly a recent estimate placed the global effect of malware and spam on the world economy at $100 billion per year. In fact, malware is so rampant that a recent survey conducted by Consumer Reports (June 2011), found that a third of US households had active malware infections and cost them approximately $2.3 billion in damages largely due to the costs of protective software programs and computer replacements due to system errors. As a result, cyber-trespass offences are often viewed as some of the most serious forms of cybercrime around the world.

8.6.2 **Cyber-deception and theft**

The second category of cybercrime is *cyber-deception and theft*, which can extend from hacking and other forms of cyber-trespass. Deception is readily enabled by technology on the basis of the ease with which individuals can manipulate email and other forms of communication. For instance, criminals can use email messages to acquire bank account information from victims through **phishing** messages (James, 2005). In this case, criminals send messages to hundreds if not thousands of email addresses claiming that the recipient's bank or financial institution has detected fraudulent charges on their account that needs to be validated. They typically indicate that the recipient must respond to the message within 24 hours or risk their account being closed or online access restricted and provide links to the institution's website. Should the individual click through that link, they are sent to what appears to be the legitimate website, though in reality it is a site set up by the criminal to acquire the individual's bank account username, login, and other sensitive information (James, 2005). The data is then stored in a server for the offender to use later to engage in fraud, or to resell to others through online black markets for stolen data (Franklin, Paxson, Perrig, & Savage, 2007, Holt & Lampke, 2010, Motoyama et al., 2011). These crimes are extremely costly for consumers and businesses alike, and appear to cause millions of dollars in losses every year (Anti-Phishing Working Group, 2012).

In addition to traditional theft, this category also includes **digital piracy**, or the illegal copying of digital media such as computer software, sound, and video recordings without the explicit permission of the copyright holder (Gopal, Sanders, Bhattacharjee, Agrawal, & Wagner, 2004). Piracy is a rampant problem worldwide, with estimates ranging between 40 and 60% of US youth illegally downloading pirated materials every year (Hinduja, 2003, Higgins, 2005, Ingram & Hinduja, 2008, Gunter, 2009, Holt, Burruss, & Bossler, 2010). Similar rates are evident cross-nationally, with the highest estimates in Asia and Africa (Business Software Alliance, 2011). As a consequence, corporate copyright holders are thought to lose tens of millions of dollars due to piracy on a yearly basis (Business Software Alliance, 2011).

The global scope of piracy is due in large part to the subculture of pirates who break copyright protections on DVDs, Blu-Ray disks, and software, and distribute these materials online (Cooper & Harrison, 2001, Holt & Copes, 2010). A small proportion of pirates also record first run movies while in theatres using cell phones and other recording devices to disseminate them online (Holt & Copes, 2010). In turn, these materials are distributed through various outlets including file sharing services, torrents, and direct download websites (Cooper & Harrison, 2001, Holt & Copes, 2010). Torrent sharing software has become one of the most popular mechanisms for downloading content as it allows for rapid download of music or movies from multiple computers around the world in small pieces all at once.

Torrent clients became extremely popular in the mid-2000s and were thought to have accounted for over half of all pirated materials online by 2004 (Pouwelse, Garbacki, Epema, & Sips, 2005). In fact, one of the most popular resources in the torrent community is **The Pirate Bay (TPB)**, which maintains indexed torrent files for music, software, video games, and new release movies. The group operates out of Sweden and has been in existence for years despite being raided by police and having three of its key operators convicted of copyright law violations requiring one year in jail and millions of dollars in fines (Nhan, 2013). TPB still exists, and operates in order to promote the idea that copyright laws are unacceptable and only serve to make the rich richer. Similar ideas are promoted by individuals who regularly download media as they feel piracy is an acceptable behaviour that has little impact on artists or private industry (Hinduja, 2003, Ingram & Hinduja, 2008). Although legal bodies in the UK are now working with Internet providers to block access to well-known torrent sites, communities like these rapidly re-emerge when access to one of their sites is blocked. This raises the question of how we can ever control for this type of crime. Moreover, given the difficulties of cross-boundary law enforcement of more than one country, it is often difficult to police these activities in a way that ceases their existence completely.

8.6.3 Cyber-porn and obscenity

The third category in Wall's typology of cybercrime is **cyber-porn** and obscenity, representing the range of sexually expressive content online. This category is unique as some forms of sexuality online are perfectly legal. For instance, porn and obscenity may be deviant or criminal based on local laws. In the US, viewing pornographic content is not illegal for individuals over the age of 18; though accessing certain content such as violent or animal-related material may be criminal depending on local laws (Quinn & Forsyth, 2013). Since high speed Internet connectivity is relatively inexpensive and available in major cities, the adult porn industry has become extremely lucrative (Lane, 2000, Edelman, 2009). In addition, amateurs are increasingly active in the production of pornographic content out of their own homes as individuals can produce professional quality images and media through HD digital cameras, web enabled cameras, and other equipment (Lane, 2000).

The global reach of the Internet has also engendered the formation of online subcultures focused on various deviant sexual activities (DiMarco, 2003, Quinn & Forsyth, 2013). In fact, the Internet provides a venue for individuals to discuss their beliefs, interests, and attitudes in a way that does not stigmatize their identity. As a result, content related to niche sexual fetishes can be readily accessed through multiple outlets in web forums, listserves, and online groups that allow individuals to exchange information in near real time (DiMarco, 2003).

In addition, sexual subcultures can move from legal, if not deviant, behaviour through the use of technology. For instance, prostitutes increasingly utilize the Internet to advertise their services and keep in touch with clients (Cunningham & Kendall, 2010). The customers of sex workers also utilize this technology in order to discuss their experiences with escorts, prostitutes and other sex workers, provide detailed accounts of their interactions, and warn others about police activities in a given area (Sharp & Earle, 2003, Holt & Blevins, 2007). Similarly, paedophiles who seek out sexual relationships with children frequently use computer mediated communications in order to identify and share pornographic and sexual images (Jenkins, 2001, Quayle & Taylor, 2002). They may also use forums and instant messaging to connect with children in attempts to move into offline relationships (Wolak, Mitchell, & Finkelhor, 2003, Wolak, Finkelhor, & Mitchell, 2004).

8.6.4 Cyber-violence

The final category of Wall's typology is **cyber-violence**, recognizing all forms of accessing and distributing injurious, hurtful, or dangerous materials online. Acts in this category may be designed to cause emotional, psychological, or physical harm. One of the most common forms of violence involves online bullying and harassment based in part on the volume of information individuals provide about themselves through social networking sites and constant access to technology in general (Finkelhor, Mitchell, & Wolak, 2000, Finn, 2004, Hinduja & Patchin, 2009, Holt and Bossler, 2009). Individuals from various age groups compose, send, and receive threatening or sexual messages via email, instant message, or texts (Bocij, 2004, Finn, 2004). People can also use CMCs to post embarrassing videos, images, and text about another person for the public to see (Finkelhor et al., 2000, Wolak, Mitchell, & Finkelhor, 2006). In fact, there is a direct relationship between the experience of bullying in the real world and online (Hinduja & Patchin, 2009, Holt et al., 2012, Holt, Bossler, Chee, & Ng, 2013) as will be outlined in Chapter 12.

Beyond acts of violence against individuals, technology is also increasingly being employed by political and social movements to spread information about causes or beliefs, or even as a coordinating tool to engage in violence against various targets on and offline (Cere, 2003, Brenner, 2008, Denning, 2011). For instance, riots in the UK and Arab states across the Middle East over the last few years were organized through social media sites, including Twitter and Facebook (Stepanova, 2011). CMCs are also used to form **flash mobs**, or mass organizations of people to organize quickly and move rapidly through the use of online media without alerting local citizens or law enforcement (Taylor, Fritsch, Liederbach, & Holt, 2010).

The Internet has also become a critical tool for extremist and terror groups to promote their ideologies and radicalize individuals toward violence. In fact, white supremacist groups across the US use the web forum Stormfront and social media sites to promote their message and coordinate demonstrations and other hate speech events (Taylor et al., 2010). Websites also provide an important fundraising venue, such as Resistance Records where individuals could purchase CDs and merchandise for hard rock and heavy metal bands that promote hatred of other races and religions (Resistance Records, 2011). Not only did the site help to promote their ideology in a socially acceptable format like music, but also allowed individuals to make direct donations to the group the National Alliance, a well-known far right hate group. The Alliance actually operated the site, thus they could make money indirectly through the sale of media and merchandise, as well as through direct fundraising (Jipson, 2007).

Extremist groups and ideologically driven hackers have also found ways to use the Internet as a mechanism to engage in attacks against government targets across the globe. For instance, the hacker group Anonymous has engaged in a variety of **Distributed Denial of Service** (DDoS) attacks against governments, the recording industry, and private businesses (Correll, 2010, Poulsen, 2011). In a DDoS attack, individuals send multiple requests to servers that house online content repeatedly in order to overload their capabilities and render them inoperable to others. Such an attack can completely knock a website or service offline, causing companies to lose money and potentially affect customer confidence (Chu et al., 2010).

The group *Anonymous* used DDoS attacks in order to protest attempts to reduce the distribution of pirated media online. The group believes that intellectual property laws are unfair, and that governments are stifling the activities of consumers, requiring a direct response from the general public to stand up against this supposed tyranny (Correll, 2010, Poulsen, 2011). As a result, they regularly target the Recording Industry of America (RIAA), various corporations, and third-party groups who attempt to regulate and block access to pirated content (Poulsen, 2011). Thus, the use of technology has expanded the capability of extremist groups to affect populations and targets well beyond their overall capacity in the real world.

8.7 **Theories and future directions**

Prior to summarizing the current chapter, it is worth pointing out that there is a dearth of theoretical conceptualizations that could explain online criminal behaviour and deviance. There are a number of offline theories that might be useful in explaining some activities online, but given the diversity of behaviours outlined in this chapter, hopefully you will come to the conclusion that finding any single theory to account and explain all of these would be a bit of a mission impossible. Wall (2001) provides a useful typology for beginning this explanation, but the diversity of the categorized behaviours requires more activity-specific theoretical explanations. Given the differences between online and offline criminal activities, it would seem that using offline theories to explain online crimes is not the best way forward. Future research is clearly tasked with establishing new theories that can assist the understanding of the wide and varied activities that count as deviant and/or criminal online.

In light of the range of offences that can occur as a result of technology, there is a need to consider how the future of these offences may change with innovations in computers, mobile phones, and Internet connectivity generally. This is largely dependent on the success of a particular technology and its penetration into consumer markets. For example, hackers and malware writers began to target smartphone users in the mid-2000s as these devices gained popularity in the marketplace generally. Today, those hackers who target mobile phone platforms are specifically focused on the population that they have the greatest ease of access to compromise: Android phone users (Panda Security, 2013). Unlike other mobile phone platforms, the Android application market is largely unregulated and can easily serve as a vehicle to distribute malicious software under the guise of a legitimate application. In turn, hackers and data thieves can easily capture banking information and sensitive personal data and use it to their own ends (Panda Security, 2013). The success of this activity has led McAfee and other security vendors to predict that mobile malware will be the most plentiful attack tool among hackers over the next decade (McAfee Labs, 2014). This pattern will no doubt continue until such time as mobile phone users recognize the threat they face and take steps to secure their systems through antivirus software and regular updates.

Similarly, a range of wearable devices that are Internet-enabled that are being introduced to more completely integrate technology into our daily lives. Google's new Google Glass technology may have a substantive impact on the way that we record our lives and interact with the Internet (Torbert, 2013). This technology is comprised of a thin wire frame similar to traditional eyeglasses, except that it includes a wearable computer featuring a heads-up display that is voice-activated and controlled. Glass users can utilize the device to do a range of things completely hands free, including taking photos and videos, searching the Internet, checking email, and several other activities that are evolving through the creation of new applications (Torbert, 2013).

Though Glass is still in its infancy, should it become popular it may radically affect how we use technology in ways that are far beyond our current mobile phones and tablet/laptop computers. This device means we will no longer have to open or turn on a device to go online and engage in basic online activities. At the same time, this may lead people to record and stream all facets of their day-to-day lives with others to social media. In addition, the impact that this could have on both privacy and security are hard to tell, as it may further degrade our sense of personal privacy or space.

An additional concern lies in the changing nature of privacy online. Cybercrime is currently attractive to some because of the anonymity and privacy technology affords. Individuals can easily hide their identity in various ways, making it difficult to determine where they reside or their actual identity. As social media sites like Facebook and Twitter are increasingly popular among the general population and are being integrated into various websites, it has become difficult to separate one's real and virtual identities. Some forms of cybercrime, such as bullying and harassment, may become more difficult to perform due to the perception that their actual identity may be identified. Others may continue to offend, but will find increasingly sophisticated technologies to help minimize their risk of detection.

As a result, research must focus on the predictors and risk factors for both cybercrime offending and victimization (Holt & Bossler, 2014). Though criminological and psychological research have identified unique behavioural and attitudinal correlates for involvement in piracy, hacking, and other forms of crime, few have considered how an individual's identity is impacted by their experiences on and offline (see Holt, 2007, Holt & Bossler, 2014 for review). Furthermore, youth born after the year 2000 have never known life without the Internet, which may substantially impact on their perceptions of cybercrime and their general identity formation process. Given that virtually all industrialized nations have a near-ubiquitous level of technological access, research is needed that considers how the use of computers and the Internet affect adolescent development through adulthood and involvement in both on and offline offending (Holt & Bossler, 2014). The findings of such work could improve our understanding of both cybercrime and the ways that individual identities are directly impacted by offending or victimization. In turn, we can expand our knowledge of the drivers for crime in the twenty-first century.

8.8 Chapter summary

- Outlined the difference between cybercrime and deviance, paying attention to the definitions thereof and to the technology that can promote both online and offline deviance and crime. Specific examples of sexting and the distribution of pornographic material have been used to highlight an act of deviance becoming an illegal act.

- Defining the different types of behaviour as legal or illegal is complicated by the absence of laws that span more than one country. Moreover, behaviours that may be legal in the USA may not be legal elsewhere in the world, and vice versa.

- Technology-dependent and, in particular, computer-dependent crimes were discussed, with a focus on monetary and identity crimes.

- It has been highlighted that the 'face' of crime online and offline differs greatly. Crimes that are identifiable and leave evidence offline may not do so online. That does not mean that online criminal activity is faceless. It does, however, appear to be the case that people who would otherwise not engage in criminal activity offline, may do so online because of the rapidly developed ease of use of technology for most people. Also, a lot of people do not realize that they are identifiable online.

- One of the main barriers to punishing online crimes is the amount of people who can be targeted in one act. Through spamming and scams such as the 491 scam, criminals can buy and sell users' data to their heart's content! Contacting hundreds of thousands of people offline in one go would not only be time consuming, but also overly costly. If scammers send out 100,000 emails and just one 'victim' responds, they have not lost any money. Think of offline similarities, such as pyramid schemes, or scratchcards that require you to ring a telephone number to claim a prize; it is far more costly to create and run these than it is to promote similar schemes online.

- Wall's (2001) typology of online criminal behaviour has been briefly introduced in this chapter. It categorizes activities into four groups: cyber-trespass, cyber-deception and theft, cyber-porn and obscenity, and cyber-violence. Consideration has been given to each of these groups to highlight the diversity of cybercrimes.

- Attention has been paid to crimes that appear to have become socially acceptable, such as illegally downloading films and music. This represents the notion that people believe themselves to be unpunishable online; that they are anonymous and simply will not be caught or prosecuted. The use of The Pirate Bay as an example hopefully highlights this not to be the case.

- Finally, the absence of theoretical conceptualizations in this area has been addressed, with a nod of the need to future research for the development of specific theories that are associated with different types of online behaviour, rather than a global theory that attempts to explain such diverse crimes and deviances.

- Throughout this chapter, we hope that you have given some consideration to your own online behaviour. Have you ever fallen foul of any of these criminal activities? Or, have you perpetrated any of them? If so, you may not have even been aware that you were committing an illegal act. Consider your answers to these questions when pondering some of the discussion questions at the end of this chapter.

 ## References

Anderson, J. (2010). *Understanding the changing needs of the US online consumer, 2010. An empowered report: How online and mobile behaviors are changing*, Forrester Research. Retrieved from http://www.forrester.com/rb/Research/understanding_changing_needs_of_us_online_consumer%2C/q/id/57861/t/2 (accessed 3rd September, 2014).

Anti-Phishing Working Group (2012). *APWG Phishing Activity Trends Report, 2nd Quarter 2012*. Retrieved from http://docs.apwg.org/reports/apwg_trends_report_q2_2012.pdf (accessed 3rd September, 2014).

Associated Press (2005). *Average price of laptops drops to $1,000*. Retrieved from http://www.msnbc.msn.com/id/9157036/ns/technology_and_science-tech_and_gadgets/t/average-price-laptops-drops/ (accessed 3rd September, 2014).

Bocij, P. (2004). *Cyberstalking: Harassment in the Internet Age and How to Protect Your Family.* Westport, CT: Praeger.

Bossler, A.M. & Holt, T.J. (2009). Online activities, guardianship, and malware infection: An examination of routine activities theory. *International Journal of Cyber Criminology*, 3, 400–420.

Bossler, A.M. & Holt, T.J. (2010). The effect of self control on victimization in the cyberworld. *Journal of Criminal Justice*, 38, 227–236.

Bossler, A.M. & Holt, T.J. (2012). Patrol officers' perceived role in responding to cybercrime. *Policing: An International Journal of Police Strategies and Management*, 35, 165–181.

Brenner, S.W. (2008). *Cyberthreats: The Emerging Fault Lines of the Nation State*. New York: Oxford University Press.

Business Software Alliance (2011). *9th Annual BSA Global Software 2011 Piracy Study*. Retrieved from http://globalstudy.bsa.org/2011/ (accessed 3rd September, 2014).

Cere, R. (2003). Digital counter-cultures and the nature of electronic social and political movements. In Jewkes, Y. (Ed.), *Dot.cons: Crime, Deviance and Identity on the Internet* (pp. 147-163). Portland, OR: Willan Publishing.

Choi, K.C. (2008). Computer crime victimization and integrated theory: An empirical assessment. *International Journal of Cyber Criminology*, 2, 308-333.

Chu, B., Holt, T.J., & Ahn, G.J. (2010). *Examining the Creation, Distribution, and Function of Malware Online*. Washington D.C.: National Institute of Justice, 2010. NIJ Grant No. 2007-IJ-CX-0018.

Consumer Reports (2011, June). *Online exposure: Social networks, mobile phones, and scams can threatened your security*. Available at http://www.consumerreports.org/cro/magazine-archive/2011/june/electronics-computers/state-of-the-net/online-exposure/index.htm (accessed 3rd September, 2014).

Cooper, J. & Harrison, D.M. (2001). The social organization of audio piracy on the Internet. *Media, Culture, and Society*, 23, 71-89.

Correll, S.P. (2010). An interview with Anonymous. *PandaLabs Blog*. Available at http://pandalabs.pandasecurity.com/an-interview-with-anonymous/ (accessed 3rd September, 2014).

Cunningham, S. & Kendall, T. (2010). Sex for sale: Online commerce in the world's oldest profession. In Holt, T.J. (Ed.), *Crime Online: Correlates, Causes, and Context* (pp. 40-75). Raleigh, NC: Carolina Academic Press.

Denning, D.E. (2011). Cyber-conflict as an emergent social problem. In Holt, T.J. & Schell, B. (Eds), *Corporate Hacking and Technology-Driven Crime: Social Dynamics and Implications* (pp. 170-186). Hershey, PA: IGI-Global.

DiMarco, H. (2003). The electronic cloak: secret sexual deviance in cybersociety. In Jewkes, Y. (Ed.), *Dot.cons: Crime, Deviance, and Identity on the Internet* (pp. 53-67). Portland, OR: Willan Publishing.

Edelman, B. (2009). Red light states: Who buys online adult entertainment? *Journal of Economic Perspectives*, 23, 209-220.

Finkelhor, D., Mitchell, K.J., & Wolak, J. (2000). *Online victimization: A report on the nation's youth*. Washington DC: National Center for Missing and Exploited Children.

Finn, J. (2004). A survey of online harassment at a university campus. *Journal of Interpersonal Violence*, 19, 468-483.

Franklin, J., Paxson, V., Perrig, A., & Savage, S. (2007). An inquiry into the nature and cause of the wealth of Internet miscreants. Paper presented at *CCS07*, October 29-November 2, in Alexandria, VA, 2007.

Furnell, S. (2002). *Cybercrime: Vandalizing the Information Society*. London: Addison-Wesley.

Gopal, R., Sanders, G.L., Bhattacharjee, S., Agrawal, M.K., & Wagner, S.C. (2004). A behavioral model of digital music piracy. *Journal of Organizational Computing & Electronic Commerce*, 14, 89-105.

Government Accountability Office (2007). *Cybercrime: Public and Private Entities Face Challenges in Addressing Cyber Threats*. United States Government Accountability Office Report to Congressional Requesters. Available at http://www.gao.gov/new.items/d07705.pdf (accessed 3rd September, 2014).

Gunter, W.D. (2009). Internet scallywags: A comparative analysis of multiple forms and measurements of digital piracy. *Western Criminology Review*, 10, 15-28.

Higgins, G.E. (2005). Can low self-control help with the understanding of the software piracy problem? *Deviant Behavior*, 26, 1-24.

Higgins, K.J. (2014). Target, Neiman Marcus data breaches tip of the iceberg. *Dark Reading*, January 13, 2014. Available at http://www.darkreading.com/attacks-breaches/target-neiman-marcus-data-breaches-tip-o/240165363 (accessed 3rd September, 2014).

Hinduja, S. (2003). Trends and patterns among software pirates. *Ethics and Information Technology*, 5, 49-61.

Hinduja, S. & Patchin, J.W. (2009). *Bullying Beyond the Schoolyard: Preventing and Responding to Cyberbullying*. New York: Corwin Press.

Holt, T.J. (2003). Examining a transnational problem: An analysis of computer crime victimization in eight countries from 1999 to 2001. *International Journal of Comparative and Applied Criminal Justice*, 27, 199-220.

Holt, T.J. (2007). Subcultural evolution? Examining the influence of on- and off-line experiences on deviant subcultures. *Deviant Behavior*, 28, 171-198

Holt, T.J. (2009). The attack dynamics of political and religiously motivated hackers. In Saadawi, T. & Jordan, L. (Eds) *Cyber Infrastructure Protection* (pp. 161–182). New York: Strategic Studies Institute.

Holt, T.J. & Blevins, K.R. (2007). Examining sex work from the client's perspective: Assessing johns using online data. *Deviant Behavior*, 28, 333–354.

Holt, T.J. & Bossler, A.M. (2009). Examining the applicability of lifestyle-routine activities theory for cybercrime victimization. *Deviant Behavior*, 30, 1–25.

Holt, T.J. & Bossler, A.M. (2013). Examining the relationship between routine activities and malware infection indicators. *Journal of Contemporary Criminal Justice*, 29, 420–436.

Holt, T.J. & Bossler, A.M. (2014). An assessment of the current state of cybercrime scholarship. *Deviant Behavior*, 35, 20–40.

Holt, T.J. & Copes, H. (2010). Transferring subcultural knowledge online: Practices and beliefs of persistent digital pirates. *Deviant Behavior*, 31, 625–654.

Holt, T.J. & Graves, D.C. (2007). A qualitative analysis of advanced fee fraud schemes. *The International Journal of Cyber-Criminology*, 1, 137–154.

Holt, T.J. & Lampke, E. (2010). Exploring stolen data markets online: Products and market forces. *Criminal Justice Studies*, 23, 33–50.

Holt, T.J. & Turner, M.G. (2012). Examining risk and protective factors of online identity theft. *Deviant Behavior*, 33 (4), 308–323.

Holt, T.J., Burruss, G.W., & Bossler, A.M. (2010). Social learning and cyber deviance: examining the importance of a full social learning model in the virtual world. *Journal of Crime and Justice*, 33, 15–30.

Holt, T.J., Bossler, A.M., & May, D.C. (2012). Low self-control deviant peer associations and juvenile cyberdeviance. *American Journal of Criminal Justice*, 37, 378–395.

Holt, T.J., Bossler, A.M., Chee, G., & Ng, E. (2013). Exploring the consequences of bullying victimization in a sample of Singapore youth. *International Criminal Justice Review*, 23, 5–24.

Ingram, J.R. & Hinduja, S. (2008). Neutralizing music piracy: An empirical examination. *Deviant Behavior*, 29, 334–366.

Internet Crime Complaint Center (2008). *IC3 2008 Internet Crime Report*. Available at http://www.ic3.gov/media/annualreport/2008_IC3Report.pdf (accessed 3rd September, 2014).

James, L. (2005). *Phishing Exposed*. Rockland: Syngress.

Jenkins, P. (2001). *Beyond Tolerance: Child Pornography on the Internet*. New York: New York University Press.

Jipson, A. (2007). Influence of hate rock. *Popular Music and Society*, 30, 449–451.

Jordan, T. & Taylor, P. (1998). A sociology of hackers. *The Sociological Review*, 46, 757–780.

King, A. & Thomas, J. (2009). You can't cheat an honest man: Making ($$$s and) sense of the Nigerian e-mail scams. In Schmalleger, F. & Pittaro, M. (Eds), *Crime of the Internet* (pp. 206–224). Saddle River, NJ: Prentice Hall.

Lane, F.S. (2000). *Obscene Profits: The Entrepreneurs of Pornography in the Cyber Age*. New York: Routledge.

Lenhart, A. (2010). *Is the age at which teens get cell phones getting younger?* Pew Internet and American Life Project. Available at http://pewInternet.org/Commentary/2010/December/Is-the-age-at-which-kids-get-cell-phones-getting-younger.aspx (accessed 3rd September, 2014).

Lenhart, A., Madden, M., & Hitlin, P. (2005). *Teens and Technology*. Pew Internet and American Life Project. Available at http://www.pewInternet.org/~/media/Files/Reports/2005/PIP_Teens_Tech_July2005web.pdf.pdf (accessed 3rd September, 2014).

McAfee Labs. (2014). *McAfee Labs 2014 Threats Predictions*. Available at http://www.mcafee.com/us/resources/reports/rp-threats-predictions-2014.pdf (accessed 3rd September, 2014).

Miller, J. (1998). Up it up: Gender and the accomplishment of street robbery. *Criminology*, 36, 37–66.

Mitchell, K.J., Finkelhor, D., Jones, L., & Wolak, J. (2012). Prevalence and characteristics of youth sexting: A national study. *Pediatrics*, 129 (1), 13–20.

Motoyama, M., McCoy, D., Levchenko, K., Savage, S., & Voelker, G.M. (2011). An analysis of underground forums. *IMC'11*, 71–79.

Newman, G. & Clarke, R. (2003). *Superhighway Robbery: Preventing E-commerce Crime*. Cullompton: Willan Press.

Nhan, J. (2013). The evolution of online piracy: Challenge and response. In Holt, T.J. (Ed.), *Crime Online: Correlates, Causes, and Context*, 2nd edn (pp. 61–80). Raleigh, NC: Carolina Academic Press.

Panda Security (2013). *Annual Report Pandalabs 2013 Summary*. Available at http://press.pandasecurity.com/wp-content/uploads/2010/05/Annual-Report-PandaLabs-2013.pdf (accessed 3rd September, 2014).

Poulsen, K. (2011). In 'Anonymous' raids, feds work from list of top 1,000 protesters. *Wired Threat Level*. Available at http://www.wired.com/threatlevel/2011/07/op_payback/ (accessed 3rd September, 2014).

Pouwelse, J., Garbacki, P., Epema, D.H.J., & Sips, H. (2005). The bittorrent P2P file-sharing system: Measurements and analysis, In *4th International Workshop on Peer-To-Peer Systems (IPTPS'05)*, Ithaca, NY, February 2005.

Quayle, E. & Taylor, M. (2002). Child pornography and the Internet: Perpetuating a cycle of abuse. *Deviant Behavior*, 23, 331–361.

Quinn, J.F. & Forsyth, C.J. (2013). Red light districts on blue screens: A typology for understanding the evolution of deviant communities on the Internet. *Deviant Behavior*, 34, 579–585.

Resistance Records (2011). *What's New Here?* Available at http://www.metal-archives.com/labels/Resistance_Records/642 (accessed 24th September, 2014).

Schell, B.H. & Dodge, J.L. (2002). *The Hacking of America: Who's Doing it, Why, and How*. Westport, CT: Quorum Books.

Sharp, K. & Earle, S. (2003). Cyberpunters and cyberwhores: prostitution on the Internet. In Jewkes, Y. (Ed.), *Dot Cons. Crime, Deviance and Identity on the Internet* (pp. 36–52). Portland, OR: Willan Publishing.

Socialbakers (2011). *United States Facebook Statistics*. Available at: http://www.socialbakers.com/facebook-statistics/united-states (accessed 3rd September, 2014).

Stepanova, E. (2011). The role of information communications technology in the 'Arab Spring': Implications beyond the region. *PONARS Eurasia Policy Memo No. 159*. Available at http://www.gwu.edu/~ieresgwu/assets/docs/ponars/pepm_159.pdf (accessed 3rd September, 2014).

Symantec Corporation (2012). *Symantec Internet security threat report, Volume 17*. Available at http://www.symantec.com/threatreport/ (accessed 3rd September, 2014).

Target (2014). *Data breach FAQ*. Available at https://corporate.target.com/about/shopping-experience/payment-card-issue-FAQ (accessed 3rd September, 2014).

Taylor, P. (1999). *Hackers: Crime in the Digital Sublime*. London: Routledge.

Taylor, R.W., Fritsch, E.J., Liederbach, J., & Holt, T.J. (2010). *Digital Crime and Digital Terrorism*, 2nd Edn. Upper Saddle River, NJ: Pearson Prentice Hall.

Torbert, S. (2013). GoogleGlass Teardown. *TechRadar* June 12, 2013. Available at: http://www.catwig.com/google-glass-teardown/ (accessed 3rd September, 2014).

Wall, D.S. (1998). Catching cybercriminals: Policing the Internet. International review of law. *Computers & Technology*, 12, 201–218.

Wall, D.S. (2001). Cybercrimes and the Internet. In Wall, D.S. (Ed.), *Crime and the Internet* (pp. 1–17). New York: Routledge.

Wall, D.S. (2004). Digital realism and the governance of spam as cybercrime. *European Journal on Criminal Policy and Research*, 10, 309–335.

Wall, D.S. (2007). *Cybercrime: The Transformation of Crime in the Information Age*. Cambridge: Polity Press.

Wall, D.S. & Large, J (2010). Locating the public interest in policing counterfeit luxury fashion goods. *British Journal of Criminology*, 50, 1094–1116.

Wolak, J., Mitchell, K., & Finkelhor, D. (2003). *Internet Sex Crimes Against Minors: The Response of Law Enforcement*. Washington, DC: Office of Juvenile Justice and Delinquency Prevention.

Wolak, J., Finkelhor, D., & Mitchell, K. (2004). Internet-initiated sex crimes against minors: Implications for prevention based on findings from a national study. *Journal of Adolescent Health*, 35, 424.

Wolak, J., Mitchell, K., & Finkelhor, D. (2006). *Online Victimization of Youth: Five Years Later*. Washington, DC: National Center for Missing & Exploited Children.

Wolak, J., Finkelhor, D., & Mitchell, K. (2012). *Trends in Law Enforcement Responses to Technology-Facilitated Child Sexual Exploitation Crimes: The Third National Juvenile Online Victimization Study (NJOV-3)*. Durham, NH: Crimes against Children Research Center.

Wright, R.T. & Decker, S.H. (1997). *Armed Robbers In Action: Stickups and Street Culture*. Boston, MA: Northeastern University Press.

Further reading

The website for the Internet Crime Complaint Center in the US provides detail on the ways that victims of cybercrime can report their experience to law enforcement, as well as new and emergent threats to consumers and the computer using public. They also provide a breakdown of complaints of cybercrime victimization by state each year, giving one of the few available metrics on fraud and theft online:
http://www.ic3.gov/default.aspx

This is the website for the US Department of Justice Computer Crime and Intellectual Property Section, which is responsible for the prosecution of various forms of computer crime that affect the US. In addition, the site provides detail on the most recent federal prosecutions brought against individuals for their involvement in cybercrimes:
www.justice.gov/criminal/cybercrime

This site provides a link to the annual cybercrime threat assessment conducted by the security vendor Symantec. The report gives detailed information on the range of hacks and malware attack that occur globally, as well as metrics on the number of malware infections by type identified in the wild each year
http://www.symantec.com/about/news/release/article.jsp?prid=20131001_01

The website for the U.S. Computer Emergency Response Team provides up-to-the-minute information on threats to computer users, including new vulnerabilities that could increase individual risk of victimization. They also provide tips on how to improve individual computer security.
http://www.us-cert.gov/

The UK Action Fraud group is a recently created law enforcement entity designed to deal with complaints of cyber-fraud and threats online. Similar to the IC3, the group can take complaints of cybercrime victimization and direct victims to appropriate nearby law enforcement agencies to investigate.
http://www.actionfraud.police.uk/

The National Center for Missing and Exploited Children is the premier entity in the US designed to accept complaints regarding crimes against children, including sexual exploitation and child pornography use or production in online environments. The NCMEC also serves as a resource to coordinate the law enforcement response on cyber-porn crimes against youth, and can disseminate tips collected on offenders to local police agencies.
http://www.missingkids.com/home

 Discussion questions

1. Outline and discuss the differences between deviant and criminal online behaviour, cybercrime, and computer crime.
2. Critically evaluate the reasons as to why it might be easier to offend online than offline.
3. What are the main differences around awareness of when a crime has been committed online and offline?
4. Critically consider the categorizations used by Wall's (2001) typology of cybercrime.
5. Debate the illegality of illegal downloading via Bit torrent sites.
6. Critically consider how future research needs to develop our understanding of online crime and deviance.

A Focus on Online Bullying

MAGDALENA MARCZAK & IAIN COYNE

Learning objectives

Having read this chapter, we hope that you have an understanding of:

- The difficulties in defining cyberbullying.
- The differences between different types of cyberbullying based on the victims, perpetrators and their physical locations.
- Some of the main theoretical conceptualizations that have been used to try to explain cyberbullying.
- The ways in which governments and different agencies world-wide have been trying to tackle the rise of cyberbullying.
- The difficulties associated with carrying out research into online bullying and how this might affect the future directions of this work.

9.1 Introduction

For those interested in the phenomenon of online bullying (cyberbullying), it is often difficult to accept that academic research into this topic is relatively recent. In the last 13 years there has been an explosion of interest in cyberbullying, partly as a result of the surge of computers and mobile phone usage by young people (Ybarra & Mitchell, 2004, Patchin & Hinduja, 2006, Li, 2007, Kowalski, Limber, & Agatston, 2008, Shariff, 2008, Smith et al., 2008, Sourander et. al, 2010) and partly because of parental, media, or wider societal concerns surrounding negative online behaviour. While there are many advantages with the usage of mobile phones and computers for communication purposes, these can also bring some negative experiences in the form of unwanted aggressive messages (Smith et al., 2008, Vandebosch & Van Cleemput, 2008), flaming (Gillespie, 2006, Smith et al., 2008), happy slapping (Smith et al., 2008) and sexting (Gillespie, 2008, Spears, Slee, Owens, & Johnson, 2009). This chapter will debate the current research on cyberbullying, specifically the conceptualization, the prevalence, and outcomes of cyberbullying as well as contrasting it with traditional (offline) bullying. To date, theoretical explanations for cyberbullying are limited, yet we will endeavour to discuss possible explanations using ideas from computer-mediated communication (**CMC**) and work psychology. Additionally, we will discuss current approaches to reducing the problem including the legal perspective, development of policies and the proactive/reactive approaches operated by technology-based organizations (e.g., Internet service providers and mobile phone companies). Finally, we will outline a future agenda for research and practice in this area.

9.2 What is cyberbullying?

Although, we have seen an upsurge in cyberbullying research, aggressive online interactions are not a new phenomenon. Rivers, Chesney, and Coyne (2011) suggest that interactions such as flaming, flooding, kicking, and spamming were investigated before the term cyberbullying was coined. However, cyberbullying first emerged from Finkelhor et al.'s analysis of a sample of 1,501 American students (Finkelhor, Mitchell, & Wolak, 2000). This research distinguished Internet chat rooms, instant messaging, and emails as means to perpetrate bullying. In the UK the National Children's Home (NCH, now Action for Children) charity was first to report in 2002 text messaging via mobile phone as a form of bullying (NCH, 2002). Since then a number of studies have been conducted in the USA, Canada, the UK, and mainland Europe as well as Australia and Israel (Ybarra and Mitchell, 2004, Kowalski, 2005, Patchin & Hinduja, 2006, Li, 2006, 2007, Raskauskas & Stoltz, 2007, Smith et al., 2008, Ortega, Elipe, Mora-Merchán, Calmaestra, & Vega, 2009, Dooley, Gradinger, Strohmeier, Cross, & Spiel, 2010, Smith, 2011, Olenik-Shemesh, Heiman, & Eden, 2012). These studies illustrated that a considerable number of children became victims of this negative use of technology, which in turn led to heightened awareness of the seriousness of the problem of cyberbullying (Li, 2006, 2007, Willard, 2006, Dooley, Pyzalski, & Cross, 2009, Smith, 2011).

Cyberbullying can take many forms. Willard (2006) listed seven categories of behaviour depending on its content. These behaviours included flaming, online harassment, cyberstalking, denigration, masquerade, outing, and exclusion. Huang and Chou (2010) investigated types of cyberbullying across three role groups: *victims*, *aggressors*, and *bystanders*. Victims reported harassment and threats as the most common behaviour. These were followed by making jokes about the victim or fun out of the victim. The least popular behaviour included spreading rumours about the victim (Huang & Chou, 2010). In Rivers and Noret's (2010) study, ten categories of behaviour were listed: threat of physical violence, abusive or hate-related, name calling (including homophobia), death threats, ending of platonic relationships, sexual acts, demands/instructions, threats to damage existing relationships, threats to family/home, and menacing chain messages. Other new modes of cyberbullying include sexting (described as circulation of sexualized images via mobile phones or the Internet without a person's consent), trolling (described as persistent abusive comments on a website), and griefing (described as harassment of someone in a cyber-game or virtual world) (Slonje, Smith, & Frisén, 2013).

More broadly, Langos (2012) distinguished between direct and indirect cyberbullying. Direct cyberbullying occurs in the private domain and comprises electronic communications from the perpetrator aimed only at the victim (e.g., a perpetrator making direct phone calls to a victim's mobile phone, sending SMS messages to a victim's mobile phone, or emails to a victim's personal email account). Indirect cyberbullying takes place in the public cyberspace and it consists of the material that has been posted on the Internet and is easily accessible, such as posts in a public forum or a public blog (Langos, 2012).

Cyberbullying has been considered from a generic behavioural and media perspective. In some cases it is considered aggressive behaviour across different media (e.g., threats) and in other cases it involves behaviour specific to media (e.g., sexting). What is clear is that technological advances in online and virtual communication has opened up the avenue for varied types of aggressive online behaviour and therefore our understanding and conceptualizations of cyberbullying need to continually adapt and be revised in light of these advances.

9.3 Defining cyberbullying

With this in mind, it is not always easy to define what constitutes an act of cyberbullying, and to date no one universal definition is available. Initial investigations into cyberbullying based their own conceptualization on the definition of traditional bullying proposed by Olweus (1993). Many of these have now been accepted and are widely used among the researchers investigating this phenomenon (Table 9.1).

Table 9.1 Conceptual definitions of cyberbullying used in research.

Study/ Year	Definition
Finkelhor et al. (2000)	Online harassment: Threats or other offensive behaviour (not sexual solicitation) sent online to the youth or posted online about the youth for others to see (p. 9).
Belsey (2004)	Cyberbullying involves the use of information and communication technologies such as email, mobile/cell phone, and pager text messages, instant messaging, defamatory personal websites, and defamatory online personal polling websites, to support deliberate, repeated, hostile behaviour by an individual or a group that is intended to harm others (http://www.cyberbullying.ca/).
Ybarra & Mitchell (2004)	Internet harassment: An overt, intentional act of aggression towards another person online (p. 320).
Patchin & Hinduja (2006)	Wilful and repeated harm inflicted through the medium of electronic text (p. 152).
Aftab (2006)	Cyberbullying is when a child, preteen or teen is tormented, threatened, harassed, humiliated, embarrassed, or otherwise targeted by another child, preteen or teen using the Internet, interactive and digital technologies, or mobile phones. It has to have a minor on both sides, or at least have been investigated by a minor against another minor. Once adults become involved, it is plain and simple cyber-harassment or cyberstalking (http://www.stopcyberbullying.org/doc/what_is_cyberbullying_exactly.doc).
Willard (2007)	Sending or posting harmful or cruel text or images using the Internet or other digital communication devices (p. 1).
Slonje & Smith (2008)	Aggression that occurs through modern technological devices and specifically mobile phones or the Internet (p. 147).
Smith et al. (2008)	An aggressive, intentional act carried out by a group or an individual, using electronic forms of contact, repeatedly and over time against a victim who cannot easily defend him or herself (p. 376).
Juvonen & Gross (2008)	The use of the Internet or other digital communication devices to insult or threaten someone (p. 497).
Li (2008)	Bullying via electronic communication tools such as email, cell phone, personal digital assistant (PDA), instant messaging, or the World Wide Web (p. 224).
Tokunaga (2010)	Cyberbullying is any behaviour performed through electronic or digital media by individuals or groups that repeatedly communicates hostile or aggressive messages intended to inflict harm or discomfort on others (p. 278).

All of the definitions mentioned highlight the core aspects of cyberbullying: intention to harm, repetition, and power imbalance between victim and perpetrator. However, although these criteria are widely accepted (Dooley et al., 2009) some controversy among researchers remains (Nocentini et al., 2010).

9.3.1 Intention

As a result of the indirect nature of cyberbullying, it is very difficult to ascertain the intention of this behaviour (Slonje & Smith, 2008, Menesini & Nocentini, 2009). This raises questions about whether intention to cause harm is really needed because messages sent as a joke and not meant to harm have the same effects on the victim. Rather, victim perceptions of the perpetrator's intention and the impact the message(s) had on the victim should be the criterion used (Grigg, 2010).

9.3.2 Repetition

Negative behaviour has to happen on more than one occasion in order to be differentiated from a single act of aggression and this repetition criterion is decided in the same way as in the traditional bullying. However, in indirect cyberbullying it is no longer necessary for the victim to prove a course of behaviour to satisfy the criterion of repetition (Langos, 2012). Here even one single act of cyberbullying (e.g., creating a hate page) can spread rapidly reaching an unrestrained audience. It can be viewed infinitely and distributed, saved, and re-posted at a later time. Hence a single behaviour by one perpetrator may be repeated time and again by others and experienced repeatedly by the victim (Menesini & Nocentini, 2009). Therefore, as one act of cyberbullying can be experienced repeatedly and cause harm to the victim, our traditional view of repetition in bullying does not necessarily have to be met.

9.3.3 Power imbalance

Power imbalance is ubiquitous within offline bullying definitions. In cyberbullying, however, the nature of the power is different with the more technologically savvy individuals appearing to hold the power (Law, Shapka, Hymel, Olson, & Waterhouse, 2012). Indeed, both Ybarra and Mitchell (2004) and Vandebosch and Van Cleemput (2008) posit that a greater knowledge of technology may contribute to a power imbalance. Ybarra and Mitchell (2004) found that cyberbullies rate themselves as being better Internet experts compared to those who do not cyberbully others and Vandebosch and Van Cleemput (2008) report that students who had more advanced Internet skills were more likely to experience deviant Internet and mobile phone activities. This technological power is also present in virtual worlds such as *Second Life*. For example, Chesney, Coyne, Logan, and Madden (2009) concluded that a virtual world is a specific environment in which having a greater expertise may enable someone to become more powerful than others and therefore more equipped to intentionally harm others.

Looking at this issue from the victim's perspective Dooley et al. (2009) argued that power in an online environment is not necessarily based on the perpetrator's possession of power, but rather on the victim's lack of power, as once some information enters the public web, it can be circulated, saved, reposted, or edited and amended by people other than the original perpetrator. They believed that as the material exists in cyberspace, the environment itself makes it harder to remove or to avoid it, which in turn can make the victim feel more power-less (Dooley et al., 2009).

9.4 Workplace cyberbullying

The discussion so far has focused mainly on cyberbullying within adolescent samples. Within a work context research in this domain is relatively sparse. While other related concepts have been considered, to date cyberbullying per se has yet to be fully conceptualized. For example, Weatherbee and Kelloway (2006) define cyberaggression as 'aggression expressed in a communication between two or more people using ICTs, wherein at least one person in the communication aggresses against another in order to effect harm' (p. 461). Lim and Teo (2009, p. 419) suggest cyber-incivility is 'communicative behaviour exhibited in computer-mediated interactions that violate workplace norms of mutual respect'. Coyne, Axtell, Sprigg, Farley, Best, and Kwok (in review) propose that workplace cyberbullying would be expected to differ from cyberaggression because it generally does not consider the involvement of organizational outsiders and from cyber-incivility as it is focused on higher intensity behaviours.

As expected for a relatively new research area, there is continued debate on the conceptualization of cyberbullying and disagreement on how and whether we adopt the criteria of intention to harm, repetition, and power imbalance professed within traditional bullying. It is evident that current conceptualizations map closely on traditional bullying definitions, yet this assumes that both behaviours are identical. Next we consider if this is the case.

9.5 Cyberbullying versus traditional bullying

Cyberbullying, despite being viewed as similar to traditional bullying, possesses some unique features that differentiate it from its offline cousin. These include:

- *Invisibility/anonymity*—a perpetrator can choose to remain anonymous by withholding identification in text messages, which minimizes the risk of getting caught. This can foster a disinhibition effect, where individuals fail to modulate behaviour online.

- *Lack of physical and social cues*—a perpetrator is not aware of the initial victim's reaction as s/he does not witness it face-to-face and therefore is not personally confronted with the consequences of the behaviour (Postmes, Spears, & Lea, 1998).

- *Bystander's role* seems to be more complex in cyberbullying in comparison with traditional bullying as three rather than one role has been distinguished. As such a bystander can be someone who is with the victim at the time when cyberbullying takes place (i.e., when a text message is being received), with the bully (i.e., when a text message is being sent), or when an individual opens a relevant Internet site/is within the group of people the message has been circulated to.

- The *breadth of potential audience* is increased in cyberbullying.

- There is *'no place to hide'* and therefore it is difficult to escape cyberbullying. In traditional bullying the victim may feel secure at home and away from the bullying. However, with cyberbullying, the victim can be sent messages to their mobile phone or computer anywhere and at any time.

There is no doubt that the online environment has unique features that may lead us to consider cyberbullying as a different concept to offline bullying. By contrast, one would argue that differences between offline and online behaviour are reflected only in terms of the context in which the behaviour operates (e.g., the media used to bully, the reach of the perpetrators) and the impact on the victim (which we discuss later). Conceptually, they are very similar concepts—just enacted via different media. Indeed, our continued understanding of cyberbullying may actually help researchers to reconsider how we conceptualize traditional bullying, especially whether we should be so rigid in applying our definitional criteria of repetition, power imbalance, and intent.

9.6 **Prevalence rates and methodological issues**

Previous research investigating the prevalence rates of cyberbullying in adolescent samples has mainly focused on two categories of involvement, that is, cyber-victims and cyberbullies. Rates reported across a number of countries range from approximately 10 to 72% (Smith, Mandavi, Carvalho, & Tippett, 2005, Patchin & Hinduja, 2006, Agatson, Kowalski, & Limber, 2007, Li, 2007, Raskauskas & Stoltz, 2007, Williams & Guerra, 2007, Hinduja & Patchin, 2008, Hoff & Mitchell, 2008, Juvonen & Gross, 2008, Mishna, Cook, Gadalla, Daciuk, & Solomon, 2010). In the UK, Rivers and Noret's (2010) four-year study on bullying found that 15% of the 11,227 children surveyed had received nasty or aggressive texts and emails, and demonstrated a year-on-year increase in the number of children who are being cyberbullied. Limited evidence in working populations has shown that 9% (Baruch, 2005, Ford, 2013), 10.7% (Privitera & Campbell, 2009) and between 14–21% (Coyne et al., in review) of respondents had experienced some form of cyberbullying. However, research in working domains is embryonic and further investigations are needed.

Differences in methodology create problems for researchers and practitioners in comparing studies across countries and over time. For example, some studies use a very specific time frame (such as within the last year) for cyberbullying occurrence (Ybarra, 2004, Ybarra & Mitchell, 2004, 2008, Williams & Guerra, 2007, Wolak, Mitchell, & Finkelhor, 2007, DeHue, Bolman, & Völlink, 2008) whereas others do not. Additionally, the media covered in these studies varies and has included seven (e.g., mobile phone calls, text messages, picture/video clip bullying, emails, chatroom, instant messaging, and websites; Smith et al., 2008), nine (Hinduja & Patchin, 2010), and five (Wachs & Wolf, 2011) types of technology. Although with the technological evolution of smartphones, it is actually possible to access easily different online communication media using the one mobile phone (Slonje et al., 2013). Many studies were conducted in one country and may reflect cultural differences. Some attempts have, however, been made to compare the cyberbullying phenomena across different countries. These include three major projects such as the European Daphne Programme (incorporating three countries: Italy, Spain, England), EU Kids Online (33 countries) and COST Action ISO801 (30 countries in total).

While studies employ a quantitative methodology exploring the phenomenon of cyberbullying through online or face-to-face questionnaires, with many using either convenience samples or small sample sizes (Li, Smith, & Cross, 2012), they differ in whether they use a global or specific item assessment. A global item assessment asks an individual directly about his/her involvement in cyberbullying during a specific period of time, whereas a specific item assessment asks about involvement in specific forms of behaviours or usage of a specific medium to perpetrate cyberbullying (Gradinger, Strohmeier, & Spiel, 2010). One of the main problems associated with the global item assessment is its assumption that the respondent understands fully the concept of cyberbullying when answering questions. In many cases different countries may lack a comparable word for cyberbullying in their language (Gradinger et al., 2010).

However, the specific item assessment also has its limitations. The specific behaviours captured within the questionnaire are not necessarily the only ones in which cyberbullying can be perpetrated (i.e., due to the constant evolution of technology) and as the list of behaviours varies from one questionnaire to the other it makes the task of comparing the prevalence of the cyberbullying phenomenon very difficult (Kowalski & Limber, 2007). Some studies do, however, adopt both a general and the specific item assessment. Evidence here suggests higher prevalence rates for the specific measurement method with differences of 10% in perpetrator rates reported (Nocentini, Menesini, & Calussi, 2009, Gradinger et al., 2010). Interestingly, Slonje and Smith (2008) only found a small increase of 1% in the number of cyber victims identified using specific items as compared to a global item.

9.7 Outcomes of cyberbullying

The literature on children/adolescent samples reveals that being cyberbullied can ultimately result in serious physical, social, and psychological problems (Finkelhor et al., 2000; British Broadcasting Corporation, 2006). Consequences include psychosocial problems, such as social anxiety, low levels of self-esteem, and depression (Ybarra, 2004, Juvonen & Gross, 2008, Didden et al., 2009, Katzer, Fetchenhauer, & Belschak, 2009); emotional difficulties with some cyber-victims reporting sadness, hopelessness, depression, and anxiety (Raskauskas & Stoltz, 2007) and others reporting feeling angry, upset, frustrated, vulnerable, depressed, and fearful (Katzer & Fetchenhauer, 2007); a higher risk for internalizing adjustment problems (Gradinger, Strohmeier, & Spiel, 2009); development of mental health difficulties (Dyer & Teggart, 2007, Aluede, Adeleke, Omoike, & Afen-Akpaida, 2008, Brighi et al., 2012); increased substance use (Carbone-Lopez, Esbensen, & Brick, 2010); and eating disorders (Fosse & Holen, 2006, Ybarra & Mitchell, 2007, DeHue et al., 2008). The most disastrous consequence of cyberbullying is suicide (Hinduja & Patchin, 2010).

There is also a growing body of evidence that cyberbullying is associated with declined academic performance (Patchin & Hinduja, 2006, Beran & Li, 2007, Beran, Hughes, & Lupart, 2008, Katzer et al., 2009, Rothon, Head, Klineberg, & Stansfeld, 2011), inability to concentrate (Beran & Li, 2005, Juvonen & Gross, 2008), reduced school attendance (Wolak et al., 2007, Ybarra, West, & Leaf, 2007b, Ybarra, Diener-West, & Leaf, 2007a), school commitment (Ybarra & Mitchell, 2004) and a negative school climate (Williams & Guerra, 2007).

The sparse literature in working contexts, indicates a relationship between cyberbullying and anxiety, job dissatisfaction, and intention to leave (Baruch, 2005); general well-being

(Coyne et al., in review; Ford, 2013); and a loss of confidence, increased stress, and sick leave (Association of Teachers and Lecturers (ATL), 2009).

Given the unique features of the cyber-environment, some authors have argued cyber-bullying may have more severe outcomes than traditional bullying (Campbell, 2005, Dooley et al., 2009). However, impact may depend on the form of cyberbullying. Some types of cyberbullying (such as insults and threats) are perceived as less harmful than trad-itional bullying, whilst others (especially ones using images or videos and with an element of blackmail and therefore a high risk of personal injury) are considered more damaging (Smith et al., 2008).

9.8 Risk factors

Much of the previous research has attempted to identify risk factors for cyberbullying, focus-ing on demographic and behavioural factors. Few studies have examined the predictors of cyberbullying and whether these are similar or distinct from those linked to bullying in schools or at work.

Intensive use of the Internet is a risk factor for child cyber harassment (Wolak et al., 2007). For example, children and adolescents who enter chatrooms are subject to aggressive acts and psychological pressure from other chatroom guests (Ybarra & Mitchell, 2004, Li, 2006, Patchin & Hinduja, 2006, Willard, 2006). Moreover, the location of the computer within the family house has been found to be a predictive factor of cyber victimization. Sengupta and Chaudhuri (2011) found that children who use the Internet at home in private places such as their bedroom as opposed to those who use the computer located within the communal places of the house (such as lounge) were at a higher risk of being victimized. Further-more, children involved in cyberbullying were found to be less aware of some of the risks involved in the Internet use. These included sharing passwords with others and conversing with people not known to them in their offline lives (Hinduja & Patchin, 2008, Sengupta & Chaudhuri, 2011).

An additional risk factor that has been considered refers to a young person's involvement in school violence and bullying. Ybarra and Mitchell (2004) reported that students who were victims of physical bullying at school were more likely to be perpetrators of cyberbullying. Conversely, Raskauskas and Stoltz (2007) indicated that victims of traditional bullying were not more likely to cyberbully, but rather to be cyber-victims. They also found that teens who were traditional bullies were more likely to have been bullied and to cyberbully. Furthermore, Katzer et al. (2009) demonstrated an association between victimization experiences in school and in Internet chatrooms.

9.8.1 Age differences

Traditional bullying appears to peak during early adolescence, with verbal bully-ing remaining high throughout the adolescent years. Furthermore, boys are more likely to engage in physical bullying than girls (Nansel et al., 2001). Relatively little is known about the prevalence of Internet bullying and how this compares with other types of bullying for boys and girls across different ages (Willard, 2006). Although cyberbullying occurs among people of all ages in varying degrees, the majority of research investigating this phenomenon has been conducted on children and adolescents (Tokunaga, 2010). Moreover, inconsistent findings have been reported regarding age differences (Smith et al., 2008, Hinduja & Patchin, 2010). The majority of studies report the lack of a relationship between age and cyberbullying victimization (Ybarra, 2004, Patchin & Hinduja, 2006, Beran & Li, 2007, Wolak et al., 2007, Juvonen & Gross, 2008, Smith et al., 2008, Didden et al., 2009, Katzer et al., 2009, Varjas, Henrich, & Meyers, 2009), although some research does suggest an association (Kowalski & Limber, 2007, Ybarra et al., 2007b, DeHue et al., 2008, Hinduja & Patchin, 2008, Slonje & Smith, 2008, Ybarra & Mitchell, 2008). Williams and Guerra (2007) showed that physical and cyberbullying peaked in middle school and declined in high school. Indeed, Tokunaga (2010) suggested that the age trend across research shows a curvilinear relationship for victimization, with the greatest occurrence around 13–15 year olds.

9.8.2 Gender differences

Keith and Martin (2005) believe that as cyberbullying is similar to the relational form of traditional bullying, and as girls engage in more relational forms of traditional bullying (Bjorkqvist, 1994, Owens, Shute, & Slee, 2000, Nansel et al., 2001, Archer & Coyne, 2005), girls are more likely to be cyberbullies. However, inconsistent findings have also been reported regarding gender differences in cyberbullying (Smith et al., 2008, Hinduja & Patchin, 2010, Tokunaga, 2010). Some studies have shown few or no significant gender differences (Smith et al., 2008, Livingstone, Haddon, Görzig, & Ólafsson, 2011), while others report that boys are more involved than girls (Calvete, Orue, Estévez, Villardón, & Padilla, 2010, Fanti, Demetriou, & Hawa, 2012) or that girls are more involved than boys (Rivers & Noret, 2010). Further, empirical data suggests girls cyberbully boys because girls use emails and texting more than boys do (Blair, 2003), whilst other data suggests male students cyberbully both male and female students more than females do (Li, 2006, Smith, et al., 2008, Erdur-Baker, 2010). Sexuality appears to also play a role in cyberbullying. The content of bullying also appears to differ between the sexes. Whereas boys are more likely to engage in homophobic bullying towards other boys, girls are more likely to spread rumours (Bond, Katz, & Carter, 2011).

To sum up the information so far on demographic differences, inconsistencies in findings and the divergent methodologies used, make it difficult to draw firm conclusions about the role of demographics in cyberbullying (Tokunaga, 2010). Additionally, research to date has failed to consider the similarities/differences between an individual's online and offline identity (Rivers et al., 2011). As individuals can change or hide their offline identities online, it is difficult to fully understand the role that age or gender may play in cyberbullying.

9.9 Theoretical explanations

Although little consideration has been given to the theoretical ideas underpinning cyberbullying in the research conducted to date (Chesney et al., 2009) the *general strain theory* (**GST**), the *social identity deindividuation model* (**SIDE**) and the *cues-filtered out theory* are the most often referred to conceptions that could explain this phenomenon.

9.9.1 **General strain theory**

Since its introduction (Agnew, 1992) GST suggests that individuals who experience strain will, as a result, also experience some negative emotions such as anger, frustration, and resentment that may lead them to engage in criminal acts or deviant behaviours such as bullying and cyberbullying. Furthermore, bullying has been associated with other delinquent outcomes, such as vandalism, shoplifting, fighting, and substance misuse (Patchin & Hinduja, 2011). Patchin and Hinduja (2011) used the GST to investigate the factors associated with traditional and electronic forms of bullying. They found that strain and negative emotions such as anger and/or frustration were significantly related to both traditional bullying and cyberbullying (Patchin & Hinduja, 2011).

9.9.2 **Social identity model of deindividuation (SIDE)**

Zimbardo (1969) asserted that the deindividuated state is caused by a number of aspects such as anonymity, loss of individual responsibility, arousal, sensory overload, novel, or unregulated situations as well as illicit substances and alcohol. More recent studies on computer-mediated communication uphold the concept that anonymous online communication has some deindividuating effects (Joinson, 2001a). Research showed that it may, for instance, lead to an individual being less concerned about what others think about them, as well as to an individual reacting suddenly and without thinking primarily on the basis of one's present emotional state (Joinson, 2001b). Brandtzaeg, Staksrud, Hagen, and Wold (2009) claim that 'anonymity and a lack of self-awareness' (p. 362) play a major role in the deindividuation process. This assumption could further our understanding of a perpetrator's thought processes as well as of these individuals who, due to the indirect and isolated nature of online interactions, feel unpunishable.

According to the SIDE, first named by Lea and Spears in 1991, visual anonymity can increase the social influence applied by group norms and depersonalization (Spears, Postmes, Lea, & Wolbert, 2002). Moreover, SIDE suggests that collective behaviour is socially regulated as, whilst in a group situation, an individual's cognitive functioning changes from being influenced by one's identity to becoming dominated by the influence of social identity (Kugihara, 2001).

9.9.3 **Cues-filtered-out theory**

According to the cues-filtered-out theory, text-based computer-mediated communication (CMC) lacks physical and social cues and therefore fosters antinormative, uninhibited, aggressive, and impulsive behaviour (Kiesler, Siegel, & McGuire, 1984). As the direct feedback (victim's reaction) is missing, the perpetrator may be not aware of the victim's difficulties and therefore may lead to the perpetrator having fewer opportunities for remorse or empathy (Li et al., 2012). However, reduced social cues in CMC may potentially have a positive side as it significantly affects an organizational hierarchy (Kim, 2000). A relative lack of social cues due to the anonymity and depersonalization of CMC can change group dynamics as it liberates employees from rigid and hierarchical structures of their organization. These transformation differences can be shown using an example of a face-to-face interaction. It has been reported that a strong correlation exists between social hierarchy and the amount of participation in a discussion during an organizational meeting with managers voicing their opinion much more than their workers (Kim, 2000). The electronic communication becomes more open and provides an opportunity for people to voice their opinion regardless of the position they are in because of the relative lack of social status clues (Kim, 2000).

9.9.4 **Disempowerment theory**

In terms of understanding the outcomes of cyberbullying at work, Coyne et al. (in review) promote **disempowerment theory** (Kane & Montgomery, 1998) as an explanatory model. This theory suggests that an employee's appraisal of a 'polluting' work event as a violation of his/her dignity results in a perception of subjective stress, leading to negative affect, which in turn disrupts the employee's attitudes and behaviour at work. Kane and Montgomery (1998) posit that a higher volume of polluting events will lead to a stronger impact on the disempowerment process. Cyberbullying, due to its pervasive nature and its ability to stay with the victim and intrude into other life domains outside of work, has the potential to increase the volume and perceived intensity of the polluting event(s) experienced by an individual and therefore should result in a strong disempowerment process.

Empirically, Lim and Teo (2009) have supported the disempowerment process in relation to online workplace incivility. Additionally, across three studies of UK Higher Education staff, Coyne et al. (in review) find support for the model, with mediation effects seen for negative affect and interpersonal justice on the relationship between exposure to cyberbullying behaviours and job satisfaction and mental strain.

9.10 **Controlling cyberbullying**

In recognition of the severity of the impact of bullying, an increase in the development of anti-bullying legislation has been observed around the world in the past decade (Hopkins, Taylor, Bowen, & Wood, 2013). Legislation and law have fallen into one of three categories: (1) laws requiring schools to create policies or update existing bullying policies to include online bullying, (2) updating existing criminal law to include online communication, and (3) creating new laws that specifically address cyberbullying.

9.10.1 **Creation of new policies or updating existing bullying policies**

The most noticeable increase in anti-bullying legislation can be seen within the United States of America (Hopkins et al., 2013). Although there is no federal legal requirement to do so, most U.S. states (46 out of 51) have proposed or enacted laws requiring schools to create or update existing policies on bullying to include online bullying. According to these policies schools may only discipline students for incidents that occur in educational settings, for example when students are on school grounds, on the way to and from school, during school hours and during a school sponsored activity (Hinduja & Patchin, 2013).

Governmental policy in England and Wales states that every school has to construct and implement an anti-bullying policy, with the Department for Education (DfE) in England and Wales extending their definition of bullying to include cyberbullying and cyber-victimization occurring due to the use of technology '24/7, with a potentially bigger audience' (DfE, 2011,

p. 4). Schools use this definition to update the existing anti-bullying policies and to edu-cate students on what bullying involves (Hopkins et al., 2013). Further, the Education and Inspections Act (2006) allows head teachers to manage the conduct of students when not on school grounds or not under the control of a member of staff, to 'such an extent as is reason-able' (Marczak & Coyne, 2010). The act also gives school staff the power to confiscate certain items from students, such as mobile phones.

9.10.2 Updating existing criminal law to include online communication

Canada has a defamation law that protects the reputation of an individual and can be employed for serious cases of cyberbullying. Under the Criminal Code of Canada, the penalty is up to five years of imprisonment. Section 264 of the Criminal Code of Canada makes it a criminal offence to harass people through electronic devices. The Canadian government has updated its definition of cyber harassment in accordance to technology enabling it to deal with cyberbullying cases (Haykowsky, McLennan, & Lundrigan, 2013).

In Australia, under the updated Commonwealth Criminal Code, using a carriage service (such as mobile phone or the Internet) to harass others is considered a criminal offence. For those who are found guilty, the maximum sentence is three years in prison. However, at the time of writing this chapter, no cases had been brought using this law.

9.10.3 Creation of new laws addressing cyberbullying

A new anti-cyberbullying law known as the Internet real-name system was enacted in South Korea and China. This approach requires website operators to collect and keep a record of the identification of their users when they post entries online (China Communication Network, 2012). If there's a lawsuit or criminal charge related to the comments, the website operators must turn over the user information. However, many people felt that this violates their right to free speech and dissuades people from speaking out for fear of being punished.

9.10.4 Interventions

Although legislation may play a role in reducing cyberbullying, there needs to be a balance with ensuring freedom of speech. It has therefore been recognized that prevention is one of the best ways of dealing with cyberbullying (Marczak & Coyne, 2010).

Many prevention programs have been created for traditional bullying that often have good success rates (Ttofi & Farrington, 2011). It has been suggested that cyberbullying could be incorporated in some components of these programs to create a whole-school approach incorporating anti-bullying policy and awareness-raising curriculum-based activities (Slonje et al., 2013). Salmivalli, Kärnä, and Poskiparta (2011) evaluated a general anti-bullying pro-gram in Finland called the **KiVa** and showed it as effective in reducing cyberbullying as tra-ditional bullying. Another type of intervention used in traditional bullying and shown to be successful in cyberbullying is the **quality circles approach**. It involves students in small groups finding out information about a problem, using structured discussion techniques in order to discover solutions that are presented to and considered by teachers and the school (Slonje et al., 2013).

Not many intervention or prevention programs have been created specifically for cyber-bullying. A UK charity *BeatBullying* launched in 2009 a new form of an online peer-support called **CyberMentors**. Young people aged 11–17 become mentors upon receipt of an intensive face-to-face training from BeatBullying staff. This training gives them the skills and confidence to mentor both offline (in their school or community) and online (on the BeatBullying website). This initiative has been positively evaluated by Banerjee, Robinson, and Smalley (2010) as well as by Thompson and Smith (2012). New intervention and prevention resources for cyberbullying are still being developed, for example *ChildNet International* and *Child Exploitation and Online Protection* (CEOP) have created two e-safety films used by secondary schools, *Let's Fight It Together* and *Exposed*, respectively.

Although preventative interventions in cyberbullying are still in their infancy, Byron (2008) suggests five key areas, drawn from intervention approaches used for traditional bullying, which enables schools to create a comprehensive and effective prevention plan. They include (1) understanding and talking about cyberbullying, (2) updating existing policies and practices, (3) making reporting cyberbullying easier, (4) promoting positive use of technology, and (5) evaluating the impact of prevention activities.

Finally, Internet service providers, social networking sites, mobile phone companies, and so on, also need to consider what interventions they should put in place to reduce cyberbullying. Coyne and Gountsidou (2013) highlight that technical and educational features are being adopted by the technology industry to promote safer Internet use. Further, some organizations have adopted national/European self-regulatory codes of practice that promote safe online behaviour. However, it still remains to be seen how effective these codes of practice are in reducing cyberbullying.

9.11 Chapter summary

Although this is a relatively new area of research, we are starting to develop a much greater understanding of cyberbullying; its nature, its impact and its similarities and differences to traditional bullying. Research and practice is at a global level with individuals across the world coming together to debate, discuss, and to help reduce cyberbullying. Currently, this amalgamation of expertise and knowledge is focused on cyberbullying in children and adolescent samples with limited research and practice focused on adult/working populations. This latter research can only grow and if the model to look at is traditional bullying, we would expect to see an explosion of interest in workplace cyberbullying going forward. However, several challenges exist for those researchers who will continue to investigate different aspects of this phenomenon. These include:

- Incorporating different methodological approaches within the studies, such as appropriate sampling procedures (often self-selected samples participate in the online surveys) and longitudinal and experimental designs (as the majority of research is based on cross-sectional designs).

- Focusing not only on the main effects of Internet communication on the psychosocial development of adolescents, but also on the processes underlying these effects.

- More testing of theoretical models that either can be developed within the cyberbullying domain or drawn from general theories in psychology (e.g., stress and/or attributions).

- Consideration of the rapidly changing technological environment that not only may require us to change our conceptualizations of cyberbullying, but also could revise our theoretical models and intervention approaches (especially those based on a legal framework).

 ## References

Aftab, P. (2006). Stop cyberbullying: Take a stand against cyberbullying. Available online: http://www.stopcyberbullying.org/doc/what_is_cyberbullying_exactly.doc (accessed 3rd September, 2014).

Agatson, P.W., Kowalski, R., & Limber, S. (2007). Students' perspectives on cyber bullying. *Journal of Adolescent Health*, 41(6), S59–S60.

Agnew, R. (1992). Foundation for a general strain theory of crime and delinquency. *Criminology*, 30, 47–87.

Aluede, O., Adeleke, F., Omoike, D., & Afen-Akpaida, J. (2008). A review of the extent, nature, characteristics and effects of bullying behaviour in schools. *Journal of Instructional Psychology*, 35, 151–158.

Archer, J. & Coyne, S. (2005). An integrated review of indirect, relational and social aggression. *Personality and Social Psychology Review*, 9 (3), 212–230.

Association of Teachers and Lecturers, ATL (2009). 15 per cent of teachers have experienced cyberbullying. Available at: www.atl.org.uk/Images/Joint%20ATL%20TSN%20cyberbullying%20survey%202009.pdf (accessed 3rd September, 2014).

Banerjee, R., Robinson, C., & Smalley, D. (2010). *Evaluation of the Beatbullying Peer Mentoring Programme. Report for Beatbullying*. University of Sussex.

Baruch, Y. (2005). Bullying on the net: adverse behavior on e-mail and its impact. *Information & Management*, 42(2), 361–371.

Belsey, B. (2004). Cyberbullying. Available at: http://www.cyberbullying.ca/ (accessed 3rd September, 2014).

Beran, T.N. & Li, Q. (2005). Cyber-harassment: A new method for an old behavior. *Journal of Educational Computing Research*, 32(3), 265–77.

Beran, T.N. & Li, Q. (2007). The relationship between cyberbullying and school bullying. *The Journal of Student Wellbeing*, 1(2), 16–33.

Beran, T.N., Hughes, G., & Lupart, J. (2008). A model of achievement and bullying: analyses of the Canadian National Longitudinal Survey of Children and Youth data. *Educational Research*, 50(1), 25–39.

Bjorkqvist, K. (1994). Sex differences in physical, verbal, and indirect aggression: A review of recent research. *Sex Roles*, 30, 177–88.

Blair, J. (2003). New breed of bullies torment their peers on the Internet. *Education Week 2003*. Available at: www.edweek.org/ew/ewstory.cfm?slug_21cyberbully.h22 (accessed 3rd September, 2014).

Bond, E., Katz, A., & Carter, P. (2011). *The Suffolk Cybersurvey*. Youthworks Consulting Ltd.

Brandtzaeg, P.B., Staksrud, E., Hagen, I., & Wold, T. (2009). Norwegian children's experiences of cyberbullying when using different technological platforms. *Journal of Children and Media*, 3(4), 349–365.

Brighi, A., Melotti, G., Guarini, A., Genta, M.L., Ortega, R., Mora-Merchán, J., & Thompson, F. (2012). Self-esteem and loneliness in relation to cyberbullying in three European countries. In Cross, D. & Smith, P. (Eds), *Cyberbullying in the Global Playground: Research From International Perspectives* (pp. 32–56). Wiley-Blackwell.

British Broadcasting Corporation (2006). Youngsters targeted by digital bullies. Available at: http://news.bbc.co.uk/1/hi/uk/1929944.stm (accessed 3rd September, 2014).

Byron, T. (2008). *Safer Children in a Digital World: The Report of the Byron review*. Available at: http://webarchive.nationalarchives.gov.uk/20130401151715/http://www.education.gov.uk/publications/eOrderingDownload/Byron_Review_Action_Plan.pdf (accessed 3rd September, 2014).

Calvete, E., Orue, I., Estévez, A., Villardón, L., & Padilla, P. (2010). Cyberbullying in adolescents: Modalities and aggressors' profile. *Computers in Human Behavior*, 26(5), 1128–1135.

Campbell, M.A. (2005). Cyber bullying: An old problem in a new guise. *Australian Journal of Guidance and Counselling*, 15(1), 68–76.

Carbone-Lopez, K., Esbensen, F.A., & Brick, B.T. (2010). Correlates and consequences of peer victimization: Gender differences in direct and indirect forms of bullying. *Youth Violence and Juvenile Justice*, 8(4), 332–350.

Chesney, T., Coyne, I., Logan, B., & Madden, N. (2009). Griefing in virtual worlds: causes, casualties and coping strategies. *Information Systems Journal*, 19(6), 525–548.

China Communication Network (24 August, 2012). South Korea scraps law requiring use of real names online. Available at: http://www.cn-c114.net/575/a711922.html (accessed 3rd September, 2014).

Coyne, I. & Gountsidou, V. (2013). In Smith, P.K. & Steffgen, G. (Eds), *Cyberbullying Through the New Media. Findings From an International Network* (pp. 83–98). Hove, East Sussex: Psychology Press.

Coyne, I., Axtell, C., Sprigg, C.A., Farley, S., Best, L., & Kwok, O. (in review). Workplace cyberbullying, employee mental strain and job satisfaction: A dysempowerment perspective. *The International Journal of Human Resource Management*.

DeHue, F., Bolman, C., & Völlink, T. (2008). Cyberbullying: Youngsters' experiences and parental perception. *CyberPsychology & Behavior*, 11(2), 217–223.

Didden, R., Scholte, R.H., Korzilius, H., de Moor, J.M., Vermeulen, A., O'Reilly, M., & Lancioni, G.E. (2009). Cyberbullying among students with intellectual and developmental disability in special education settings. *Developmental Neurorehabilitation*, 12(3), 146–151.

Dooley, J.J., Pyzalski, J., & Cross, D. (2009). Cyberbullying versus face-to-face bullying: A theoretical and conceptual review. *Zeitschrift fur Psychologie/Journal of Psychology*, 217, 182–188.

Dooley, J.J., Gradinger, P., Strohmeier, D., Cross, D.S., & Spiel, C. (2010). Cyber-victimisation: The association between help seeking behaviours and self-reported emotional symptoms in Australia and Austria. *Australian Journal of Guidance and Counselling*, 20(2), 194–209.

Dyer, K. &Teggart, T. (2007). Bullying experiences of child and adolescent mental health service-users: A pilot survey. *Child Care in Practice*, 13(4), 351–365.

Erdur-Baker, Ö. (2010). Cyberbullying and its correlation to traditional bullying, gender and frequent and risky usage of Internet-mediated communication tools. *New Media & Society*, 12(1), 109–125.

Fanti, K.A., Demetriou, A.G., & Hawa, V.V. (2012). A longitudinal study of cyberbullying: Examining risk and protective factors. *European Journal of Developmental Psychology*, 9(2), 168–181.

Finkelhor, D., Mitchell, K.J., & Wolak, J. (2000). *Online Victimization: A Report on the Nation's Youth* (6-00-020). Alexandria, VA: National Center for Missing and Exploited Children.

Ford, D.P. (2013). Virtual harassment: media characteristics' role in psychological health. *Journal of Managerial Psychology*, 28(4), 408–428.

Fosse, G.K. & Holen, A. (2006). Childhood maltreatment in adult female psychiatric outpatients with eating disorders. *Eating Behaviours*, 7, 404–409.

Gillespie, A.A. (2006). Cyber-bullying and Harassment of Teenagers: The Legal Response. *Journal of Social Welfare & Family Law*, 28(2), 123–136.

Gillespie, A. (2008). *Child Exploitation and Communication Technologies*. Lyme Regis: Russell House Publishing.

Gradinger, P., Strohmeier, D., & Spiel, C. (2009). Traditional bullying and cyberbullying. *Zeitschrift für Psychologie/Journal of Psychology*, 217(4), 205–213.

Gradinger, P., Strohmeier, D., & Spiel, Ch. (2010). Definition and Measurement of Cyberbullying. *Cyberpsychology: Journal of Psychosocial Research on Cyberspace*, 4(2), article -1.

Grigg, D.W. (2010). Cyber-aggression: Definition and concept of cyberbullying. *Australian Journal of Guidance and Counselling*, 20, 143–156.

Haykowsky, T.R., McLennan R., & Lundrigan, S. (2013). *Search For Solutions To Cyber-Bullying Continues*. Canada: Alberta School Boards Association.

Hinduja, S. & Patchin, J.W. (2008). Cyberbullying: An exploratory analysis of factors related to offending and victimization. *Deviant Behavior*, 29(2), 129–156.

Hinduja, S. & Patchin, J.W. (2010). Bullying, cyberbullying, and suicide. *Archives of Suicide Research*, 14(3), 206–221.

Hinduja, S. & Patchin, J.W. (2013). Social influences on cyberbullying behaviors among middle and high school students. *Journal of Youth and Adolescence*, 1–12.

Hoff, D.L. & Mitchell, S.N. (2008). Cyberbullying: Causes, effects, and remedies. *Journal of Educational Administration*, 47(5), 652–665.

Hopkins, L., Taylor, L., Bowen, E., & Wood, C. (2013). A qualitative study investigating adolescents' understanding of aggression, bullying and violence. *Children and Youth Services Review*, 35(4), 685–693.

Huang, Y.Y. & Chou, C. (2010). An analysis of multiple factors of cyberbullying among junior high school students in Taiwan. *Computers in Human Behavior*, 26(6), 1581–1590.

Joinson, A.N. (2001a). Self-disclosure in computer-mediated communication: The role of self-awareness and visual anonymity. *European Journal of Social Psychology*, 31, 177–192.

Joinson, A.N. (2001b). Knowing me, knowing you: Reciprocal self-disclosure in Internet-based surveys. *Cyberpsychology & Behavior*, 4, 587–591.

Juvonen, J. & Gross, E.F. (2008). Extending the school grounds?—Bullying experiences in cyberspace. *Journal of School Health*, 78(9), 496–505.

Kane, K. & Montgomery, K. (1998). A framework for understanding dysempowerment in organizations. *Human Resource Management*, 37(34), 263–275.

Katzer, C. & Fetchenhauer, D. (2007). Aggression und sexuelle Viktimisierung in Chatrooms. In Gollwitzer, M., Schneider, V., Ulrich, C., Steffke, T., Schulz, A., & Pfetsch, J. (Eds), *Gewalt—praevention bei Kindern und Jugendlichen. Aktuelle Erkenntnisse aus Forschung und Praxis*. Goettingen: Hogrefe.

Katzer, C., Fetchenhauer, D., & Belschak, F. (2009). Cyberbullying: Who are the victims? *Journal of Media Psychology: Theories, Methods, and Applications*, 21(1), 25–36.

Keith, S. & Martin, M.E. (2005). Cyberbullying: creating a culture of respect in a cyber world. *Reclaiming Children & Youth*, 13, 224–228.

Kiesler, S., Siegel, J., & McGuire, T.W. (1984). Social psychological aspects of computer-mediated communication. *American Psychologist*, 39, 1123–1132.

Kim, J.-Y. (2000). Social interaction in computer-mediated communication. *Bulletin of the American Society for Information Science and Technology*, 26(3), 15–17.

Kowalski, R. (August, 2005). Electronic bullying among school-aged children and youth. Poster presented at the *Annual Meeting of the American Psychological Association*. Washington, DC.

Kowalski, R.M. & Limber, S.P. (2007). Electronic bullying among middle school students. *Journal of Adolescent Health*, 41, 22–30.

Kowalski, R.M., Limber, S.P., & Agatston, P.W. (2008). *Cyber Bullying. Bullying in the Digital Age*. Oxford: Blackwell.

Kugihara, N. (2001). Effects of aggressive behaviour and group size on collective escape in an emergency: A test between a social identity model and deindividuation theory. *British Journal of Social Psychology*, 40(4), 575–598.

Langos, C. (2012). Cyberbullying: The challenge to define. *Cyberpsychology, Behavior, and Social Networking*, 15(6), 285–289.

Law, D.M., Shapka, J.D., Hymel, S., Olson, B.F., & Waterhouse, T. (2012). The changing face of bullying: An empirical comparison between traditional and Internet bullying and victimization. *Computers in Human Behavior*, 28, 226–232.

Lea, M. & Spears, R. (1991). Computer-mediated communication, de-individuation and group decision-making. *International Journal of Man Machine Studies*, 34, 283–301.

Li, Q. (2006). Cyberbullying in schools: A research of gender differences. *School Psychology International*, 27(2), 157–170.

Li, Q. (2007). New bottle but old wine: A research of cyberbullying in schools. *Computers in Human Behavior*, 23(4), 1777–1791.

Li, Q. (2008). A cross-cultural comparison of adolescents' experience related to cyberbullying. *Educational Research*, 50(3), 223–234.

Li, Q., Smith, P.K., & Cross, D. (2012). Research into cyberbullying context. In Li, Q., Cross, D., & Smith, P.K. (Eds), *Cyberbullying in the Global Playground. Research from International Perspectives* (p. 1–12). Oxford: Wiley-Blackwell.

Lim, V.K.G. & Teo, T.S.H. (2009). Mind your E-manners: Impact of cyber incivility on employees' work attitude and behavior. *Information and Management*, 46(8), 419–425.

Livingstone, S., Haddon, L., Görzig, A., & Ólafsson, K. (2011). *EU Kids Online: final report, 2011*.

Marczak, M. & Coyne, I. (2010). Cyberbullying at school: Good practice and legal aspects in the United Kingdom. *Australian Journal of Guidance and Counselling*, 20(2), 182–193.

Menesini, E. & Nocentini, A. (2009). Cyberbullying definition and measurement. *Zeitschrift für Psychologie/Journal of Psychology*, 217(4), 230–232.

Mishna, F., Cook, C., Gadalla, T., Daciuk, J., & Solomon, S. (2010). Cyber bullying behaviors among middle and high school students. *American Journal of Orthopsychiatry*, 80(3), 362–374.

Nansel, T.R., Overpeck, M., Pilla, R.S., Ruan, W.J., Simons-Morton, B., & Scheidt, P. (2001). Bullying behaviors among US youth. *JAMA: the journal of the American Medical Association*, 285(16), 2094–2100.

NCH (2002). Available at: http://www.actionforchildren.org.uk/.

Nocentini, A., Menesini, E., & Calussi, P. (August, 2009). Cyberbullying measurement: A comparison between different strategies. Poster presented at the *Postconference of the European Society for Developmental Psychology (ESDP) on Cyberbullying: Definition and Measurement Issues*, Vilnius, Lithuania, August, 22–23.

Nocentini, A., Calmaestra, J., Schultze-Krumbholz, A., Scheithauer, H., Ortega, R., & Menesini, E. (2010). Cyberbullying: labels, behaviours and definition in three European countries. *Australian Journal of Guidance and Counselling*, 20(02), 129–142.

Olenik-Shemesh, D., Heiman, T., & Eden, S. (2012). Cyberbullying victimization in adolescence: The relationships with loneliness and depressive mood. *Emotional Behavioral Difficulties Journal*, 17(3–4), 361–374.

Olweus, D. (1993). *Bullying at School: What We Know and What We can Do*. Cambridge, MA: Blackwell.

Ortega, R., Elipe, P., Mora-Merchán, J.A., Calmaestra, J., & Vega, E. (2009). The emotional impact on victims of traditional bullying and cyberbullying. *Zeitschrift für Psychologie/Journal of Psychology*, 217(4), 197–204.

Owens, L., Shute, R., & Slee, P. (2000). 'Guess what I just heard!': Indirect aggression among teenage girls in Australia. *Aggressive Behavior*, 26, 67–83.

Patchin, J.W. & Hinduja, S. (2006). Bullies move beyond the schoolyard: A preliminary look at cyberbullying. *Youth Violence and Juvenile Justice*, 4(2), 148–169.

Patchin, J.W. & Hinduja, S. (2011). Traditional and nontraditional bullying among youth: A test of general strain theory. *Youth and Society*, 43(2), 727–751.

Postmes, T., Spears R., & Lea, M. (1998). Breaching or building social boundaries? Side-effects of computer-mediated communication. *Communication Research*, 25, 689–715.

Privitera, C. & Campbell, M.A. (2009). Cyberbullying: the new face of workplace bullying? *CyberPsychology & Behavior*, 12(4), 395–400.

Raskauskas, J. & Stoltz, A.D. (2007). Involvement in traditional and electronic bullying among adolescents. *Developmental Psychology*, 43(3), 564.

Rivers, I. & Noret, N. (2010). 'I h8 u': findings from a five-year study of text and email bullying. *British Educational Research Journal*, 36(4), 643–671.

Rivers, I., Chesney, T., & Coyne, I. (2011). Cyberbullying. In Monks, C.P. & Coyne, I. (Eds), *Bullying in Different Contexts* (pp. 211–230). Cambridge: Cambridge University Press.

Rothon, C., Head, J., Klineberg, E., & Stansfeld, S. (2011). Can social support protect bullied adolescents from adverse outcomes? A prospective study on the effects of bullying on the educational achievement and mental health of adolescents at secondary schools in east London. *Journal of Adolescence*, 34(3), 579–588.

Salmivalli, C., Kärnä, A., & Poskiparta, E. (2011). Counteracting bullying in Finland: The KiVa program and its effects on different forms of being bullied. *International Journal of Behavioral Development*, 35(5), 405–411.

Sengupta, A. & Chaudhuri, A. (2011). Are social networking sites a source of online harassment for teens? Evidence from survey data. *Children and Youth Services Review*, 33(2), 284–290.

Shariff, S. (2008). *Cyber-Bullying: Issues and Solutions for the School, the Classroom and the Home*. New York, NY: Routledge.

Slonje, R. & Smith, P.K. (2008). Cyberbullying: Another main type of bullying? *Scandinavian Journal of Psychology*, 49(2), 147–154.

Slonje, R., Smith, P.K., & Frisén, A. (2013). The nature of cyberbullying, and strategies for prevention, *Computers in Human Behavior*, 2, 26–32.

Smith, P.K. (2011). Why interventions to reduce bullying and violence in schools may (or may not) succeed: Comments on this Special Section. *International Journal of Behavioral Development*, 35(5), 419–423.

Smith, P., Mahdavi, J., Carvalho, M., & Tippett, N. (2005). *An Investigation into Cyberbullying, its Forms, Awareness and Impact, and the Relationship Between Age and Gender in Cyberbullying* (A Report to the Anti-Bullying Alliance). University of London,

Goldsmiths College, Unit for School and Family Studies.

Smith, P.K., Mahdavi, J., Carvalho, M., Fisher, S., Russell S., & Tippett, N. (2008). Cyberbullying: Its nature and impact in secondary school pupils. *Child Psychology and Psychiatry*, 49(4), 376–85.

Sourander, A., Brunstein-Klomek, A., Ikonen, M., Lindroos, J., Luntamo, T., Koskelainen, M., Ristkari, T., & Helenius, H. (2010). Psychosocial risk factors associated with cyberbullying among adolescents: a population-based study. *Archives of General Psychiatry*, 67, 720–728.

Spears, B., Slee, P., Owens, L., & Johnson, B. (2009). Behind the scenes and screens: Insights into the human dimension of covert and cyberbullying. *Zeitschrift für Psychologie/Journal of Psychology*, 217(4), 189.

Spears, R., Postmes, T., Lea, M., & Wolbert, A. (2002). When are net effects gross products? The power of influence and the influence of power in computer-mediated communication. *Journal of Social Issues*, 58, 91–107.

The Department for Education (2011). *Preventing and tackling bullying: What is bullying?* Available at: http://www.education.gov.uk/aboutdfe/advice/f0076899/preventing-and-tackling-bullying/what-is-bullying (accessed 4th September, 2014).

The Education and Inspections Act, 2006 [89]:1b, 3, 5. Available at: http://www.legislation.gov.uk/ukpga/2006/40/contents (accessed 4th September, 2014).

Thompson, F. & Smith, P.K. (2012). Anti-bullying strategies in schools: what is done and what works. *British Journal of Educational Psychology*, Monograph Series II, 9, 154–173.

Tokunaga, R.S. (2010). Following you home from school: A critical review and synthesis of research on cyberbullying victimization. *Computers in Human Behavior*, 26(3), 277–287.

Ttofi, M.M. & Farrington, D.P. (2011). Effectiveness of school-based programs to reduce bullying: A systematic and meta-analytic review. *Journal of Experimental Criminology*, 7(1), 27–56.

Vandebosch, H. & Van Cleemput, K. (2008). Defining cyberbullying: A qualitative research into the perceptions of youngsters. *CyberPsychology & Behavior*, 11(4), 499–503.

Varjas, K., Henrich, C.C., & Meyers, J. (2009). Urban middle school students' perceptions of bullying, cyberbullying, and school safety. *Journal of School Violence*, 8(2), 159–176.

Wachs, S. & Wolf, K.D. (2011). Über den Zusammenhang von Bullying und Cyberbullying. Erste Ergebnisse einer Selbstberichtsstudie. *Praxis der Kinderpsychologie und Kinderpsychiatrie*, 60(9), 735–744.

Weatherbee, T.G., & Kelloway, E.K. (2006). A case of cyberdeviancy: CyberAggression in the workplace. In Kelloway, E.K., Barling, J. & S Hurrell, J.J. (Eds), *Handbook of Workplace Violence* (pp. 445–487). Thousand Oaks, CA: Sage Publications, Inc.

Willard, N.E. (2006). *Cyberbullying and Cyberthreats: Responding to the Challenge of Online Social Cruelty, Threats, and Distress*. Center for Safe and Responsible Internet Use (available at: https://www.internetsafetyproject.org/wiki/center-safe-and-responsible-internet-use).

Williams, K. & Guerra, N. (2007). Prevalence and predictors of Internet bullying. *Journal of Adolescent Health*, 41, 14–21.

Wolak, J., Mitchell, K.J., & Finkelhor, D. (2007). Does online harassment constitute bullying? An exploration of online harassment by known peers and online-only contacts. *Journal of Adolescent Health*, 41(6), S51–S58.

Ybarra, M.L. (2004). Linkages between depressive symptomatology and Internet harassment among young regular Internet users. *CyberPsychology & Behavior*, 7(2), 247–257.

Ybarra, M.L. & Mitchell, K.J. (2004). Youth engaging in online harassment: Associations with caregiver–child relationships, Internet use, and personal characteristics. *Journal of Adolescence*, 271(3), 319–336.

Ybarra, M.L. & Mitchell, K.J. (2007). Prevalence and frequency of Internet harassment instigation: Implications for adolescent health. *Journal of Adolescent Health*, 41, 189–195.

Ybarra, M.L. & Mitchell, K.J. (2008). How risky are social networking sites? A comparison of places online where youth sexual solicitation and harassment occurs. *Pediatrics*, 121I(2), e350–e357.

Ybarra, M.L., Diener-West, M., & Leaf, P.J. (2007). Examining the overlap in Internet harassment and school bullying: Implications for school intervention. *Journal of Adolescent Health*, 41(6), S42–S50.

Ybarra, M.L., West, M.D., & Leaf, P. (2007). Examining the overlap in Internet harassment and school bullying: implications for school intervention. *Journal of Adolescent Health*, 1, 42–50.

Zimbardo, P.G. (1969). The human choice: Individuation, reason, and order versus deindividuation, impulse, and chaos. In *Nebraska Symposium on Motivation*. University of Nebraska Press.

Further reading

Berne, S., Frisén, A., Schultze-Krumbholz, A., Scheithauer, H., Naruskov, K., Luik, P., Katzer, C., Erentaite, R., & Zukauskiene, R. (2013). Cyberbullying assessment instruments: A systematic review. *Aggression and Violent Behavior*, 18, 320–334.

Kowalski, R.M., Limber, S.P., & Agatston, P.W. (2012). *Cyber Bullying. Bullying in the Digital Age*, 2nd Edn. Chichester: Wiley-Blackwell.

Kowalski, R.M., Giumetti, G.W., Schroeder, A.N., & Lattanner, M.R. (2014). Bullying in the digital age: A critical review and meta-analysis of cyberbullying research among youth. *Psychological Bulletin*, 140(4), 1073–1137.

Low, S. & Espelage, D. (2013). Differentiating cyber bullying perpetration from non-physical bullying: Commonalities across race, individual and family predictors. *Psychology of Violence*, 3(1), 39–52.

Smith, P.K. & Steffgen, G. (2013) (Eds), *Cyberbullying Through the New Media. Findings from an International Network*. Hove, East Sussex: Psychology Press.

 ## Discussion questions

1. Critically consider some of the difficulties associated with carrying out research into cyberbullying.
2. Are bullying and cyberbullying the same or different? Discuss.
3. What types of bullying occur online? Discuss different factors that affect different types of cyberbullying.
4. Discuss the ways in which bodies and agencies worldwide are trying to tackle cyberbullying.
5. Should the technology industry do more to reduce cyberbullying? Discuss.
6. Critically compare and contrast different theoretical approaches to understanding cyberbullying.

10 Health Psychology Online

GRÁINNE H. KIRWAN

Learning objectives

Having read this chapter, you should be able to:

- Provide a brief overview of the main areas of research within health psychology.

- Describe why individuals might seek medical information online and how this relates to the concept of cyberchondria.

- Explain the role of social support in coping and provide explanations for why individuals might seek such support online instead of offline.

- Evaluate the impact of technology on health, particularly in relation to stress induced by email overload, harmful content online, and the effect of sedentary activities on well-being.

- Assess the efficacy of technological interventions in improving health, with particular focus on active videogames and virtual reality.

10.1 Introduction

While sometimes overlooked in **cyberpsychology** texts, there is a substantial body of research considering the links between technology and health psychology, particularly in relation to information and support seeking online, how negative aspects of online activity can impact on our health, and the ways in which technology can be used to enhance our health. This chapter aims to provide an overview of some of the key research within the field.

The chapter firstly provides a brief overview of some of the key research areas within health psychology, such as health beliefs, illness cognitions, severe illnesses, communication with healthcare professionals, pain, and placebos. This section is included to provide some background for readers who have not previously studied health psychology—those who have some background in the area may prefer to skip this section and proceed straight to the remainder of the chapter, which focuses specifically on health psychology online. The role of the Internet in coping mechanisms is considered, with particular focus on how it is used for both information seeking and support seeking during illness and injury. The concept of cyberchondria is described, and its relationship to general information seeking online, and recognized psychological disorders, is explained. The importance of social support in coping with illness, injury, and other medical conditions is outlined, along with the benefits and risks involved in using online support groups for such conditions with particular focus on how communication theories might encourage individuals to make use of such online groups. This work is extended in Chapter 12, which is a focus chapter on online support seeking behaviour in times of illness. This chapter then proceeds to consider the negative influences that technology can have on our lives, using as examples pro-eating disorder websites, the stress that can be induced by always being available for work emails due to the prevalence of mobile devices, and the effect that sedentary activities such as Internet use and gaming might have on our health. Finally, the chapter examines how technology can be used to improve our health, considering the efficacy of various technological interventions such as active videogames and virtual reality, with Chapter 13 offering a thorough consideration of online counselling and therapies.

10.2 Health psychology: A very brief overview

Thanks to the research conducted by doctors, pharmacists, and other health professionals, medicine is constantly improving. When we visit our doctor, we expect that most ailments that we may be suffering from can be cured with some medication or a minor surgical procedure. Medications such as antibiotics mean that illnesses that were life-threatening only a few decades ago are now little more than an inconvenience. We often attend our doctor with the expectation that they will *make* us well—we describe our symptoms, while they conduct an examination and prescribe the cure. But what happens when the doctor does not provide a prescription, instead suggesting other approaches to remedying the problem, such as making changes to our daily behaviours? They may feel that the problem will reduce or disappear if we stop smoking, or exercise more, or eat a healthy diet, or get enough rest and sleep. Such a response by the medical practitioner might result in varied reactions from their patients—while some patients may accept the advice and attempt to implement it, others may feel that their visit to the doctor is incomplete without a prescription for what would ultimately be a non-beneficial treatment. The unnecessary use and prescription of medication can have serious consequences for society as well as the individual (e.g., incorrect use of antibiotics can result in antibiotic-resistant strains of infection, which threaten all of society), while the costs of such treatments and diagnosis may eventually fall to the taxpayer. Also, unnecessary procedures and diagnostic tests may extend hospital and clinic waiting times for those who genuinely need them. Despite these drawbacks, some medical practitioners may prescribe treatments or courses of diagnostic enquiry that they know will be ineffective because of the pressures presented by the patient. The doctor may fear that should they fail to do so, it may result in confrontation and a reduction in the quality of their relationship with the patient (Brett & McCullough, 2012). The physician recognizes that their role is more complex than simply dispensing a 'cure'—their relationship with the patient is also an important factor in the long-term health of the individual.

This scenario illustrates some (though not all!) of the key areas of research in health psychology. It considers the relationship between the patient and the caregiver, particularly in terms of the roles that each hold within that relationship. For example, the patient who feels underserving by the practitioner who refuses to write a prescription may hold the belief that it is the responsibility of the health professional to cure them, and that their own role as a patient is a relatively passive one. On the other hand, the doctor may feel that the relationship is more collaborative, requiring effort from both the doctor and the patient to improve the individual's health. The scenario also shows an example of **illness cognitions** or **illness**

representations—what the patient believes about their own illness (Leventhal, Diefenbach, & Leventhal, 1992). Illness cognitions or representations are sometimes seen as part of a larger model of understanding patient responses and reactions to illnesses and other health problems (such as the Commonsense Model—see for example Leventhal, Bodnar-Deren, Breland, Hash-Converse, & Phillips, 2012). In this case, the patient who demands a prescription believes that their illness is best addressed through medication, rather than other responses. A related concept is the beliefs that the individual has about health in general—do they feel that their actions have an effect on how healthy they are, and if necessary, do they think that they are capable of changing their behaviours? Our *health beliefs* and illness cognitions are particularly obvious to us when we come across a case where they have been violated. For example, we may feel sympathy, but little surprise, if an older, overweight man who smokes, drinks to excess, and has a highly stressful job is struck with a heart attack. But if a young woman with a healthy lifestyle is similarly struck down, then we may be very shocked—our health beliefs and illness cognitions determine our perception of who will suffer a heart attack, and we find it difficult to understand cases that do not fit our beliefs.

Health psychologists have developed and evaluated many different models that incorporate health beliefs and illness cognitions, as these form a fundamental basis of understanding not only why an individual may or may not engage in healthy behaviours, but also what they perceive to be their own risk of falling ill, and how they will react given a diagnosis of an illness. These concepts can also help us to comprehend why an individual might change their behaviours to become more or less healthy in response to various stimuli. Understanding why an individual might change their behaviours can help greatly in the development of interventions designed to promote healthier lifestyles and may allow predictions to be made regarding which patients will adhere to treatment regimes, and why such regimes may not be followed by others. Similarly, such models can help us to understand peoples' attitudes regarding screening—why do some people avoid routine tests that may provide early indications of problems (thus preventing a swifter, and possibly more effective medical response), while others avoid seeking medical attention despite worrying symptoms, and others still seek unnecessary or invasive diagnostic tests despite a lack of medical necessity?

While any illness or condition can be considered in light of research in health psychology, there has understandably been a focus on chronic and severe conditions. As well as heart disease, many serious illnesses and ailments such as HIV and cancer are researched, alongside other conditions, such as obesity, fertility, and pregnancy. The role of stress is examined, including how stress may lead to short-term and long-term illness, how we cope with stress, or how stress may affect the prognosis and/or duration of a medical condition. The psychological aspects of the ageing process are also studied, while research is also conducted into addictions such as smoking, drinking, and substance abuse. Another key area of research in health psychology examines how we experience pain—why do different people seem to experience pain to varying extents, and why do we feel pain more under certain conditions than others? Several different theories of pain have been proposed, with Melzack and Wall's *gate control theory of pain* (Melzack & Wall, 1965, Melzack, 1996) probably being the most famous (although it is not without critique). Health psychologists examine how chronic pain can be treated, and what can be done to manage severe or ongoing pain.

A final topic that is frequently researched within health psychology is the phenomenon of **placebos**—inert substances that nonetheless have an effect on an individual's condition. If that effect is a negative one, the substance may be called a **nocebo**. Placebos might reduce the sensation of pain, increase energy, or lessen the symptoms of anxiety or depression, amongst many other outcomes. The use of placebos is very important for clinical trials, helping to ensure that a specific medication or treatment actually has the desired outcome, but the mechanisms behind the effectiveness of placebos are of particular interest to health psychologists—why should an inert substance impact biological processes? The use of placebos in treatment also has ethical implications, which need to be carefully deliberated (Finniss, Kaptchuk, Miller, & Benedetti, 2010).

By necessity, this section has only briefly outlined a small number of the concepts and research areas within health psychology. These topics, and many others, are considered in much more detail in many textbooks, readers, and journals in the area. A good starting place for more information is Jane Ogden's textbook, *Health Psychology* (2012—currently in its fifth edition), or Baum, Revenson, and Singer's, *Handbook of Health Psychology* (2012—currently in its second edition).

10.3 Coping and online resources

Humans have developed a wide variety of coping mechanisms that can help to moderate the stressful effects of illness, injury, and other problems in life. The combination of stress, health, and coping has been widely covered in the research literature (Folkman, 2011), and this section considers how individuals might use online resources as part of a suite of coping strategies during illness or injury. Why individuals might use the Internet as a coping mechanism has been addressed by some researchers. For example, Lee and Hawkins (2010) identified a key reason as being unmet needs—those 'which have not been satisfied' (p. 152). Whether the unmet need was information or emotional support showed correlation with likelihood of using specialized health information or social support services respectively, and these are the two online coping strategies that will be reviewed here. Of course there are many other coping strategies that individuals employ, both online and offline, but most research concerning online strategies has examined these two topics.

10.3.1 The Internet as a source of information

Prior to the popularity of the Internet and World Wide Web, most people had very little access to medical information. If they found themselves ill or injured, and wished to research the condition, they were generally limited to seeking information from the healthcare professionals treating them and any other sources available to them, such as libraries, television, friends, and so on. Today it is easy to be overwhelmed by the medical information available online. Individuals may choose to seek a diagnosis online after experiencing one or more symptoms, or they may wish to identify a new approach to treating a condition that they have already been diagnosed with. Searching for any symptom or condition returns extensive lists of information websites, although it must be considered that these sources are of varying quality. While some information is provided by recognized government entities with remit for public health, others are created by lay people with an interest in the area, or even individuals or groups who wish to profit by selling unproven treatments or medicines to patients who are desperately in need of cure, or who cannot afford to seek treatment through mainstream clinics.

There has been substantial research examining the use of the Internet as a source of medical information by patients. Diaz et al. (2002) found that over half of respondents to a mail survey stated that they used the Internet for this purpose, and that 60% of those felt that the information provided was the same, or better than, the information that they received from their doctors. Only 41% shared the information that they had found with their doctor. The Internet has increased in popularity since Diaz et al.'s research, and more recent work by Li, Orrange, Kravitz, and Bell (2014) found a much higher rate amongst individuals seeking information after a doctor's visit—specifically 80%. The main source used for information was forum posts (91%), and searching was associated with individuals who had increased worry because of the visit or had experienced lower levels of patient-centred communication from their providers. A substantial minority (40%) were motivated by being dissatisfied with the physician's performance. These findings are concerning, particularly as forum posts are frequently written by lay individuals with no medical qualifications. However, the participants were recruited from members of online support groups, and this membership may disproportionally affect the number of individuals who use forum posts for information seeking. In a similar study, Hu, Bell, Kravitz, and Orrange (2012) asked online support group members about their use of online and offline resources in advance of a medical appointment. They found that online information seeking before such appointments was extensive in the group members, but that this was usually supplemented by offline information. Those who believed that they had control over their illness were more likely to use the online resources, while trust in their physician was unrelated to such advance online information seeking.

Similarly to Li et al. (2014), Tustin (2010) identified dissatisfaction amongst cancer listserv users as being associated with using the Internet to find health information, particularly noting that healthcare provider empathy and quality of time spent with the patient were related to preferred information source (oncologist or the Internet). The importance of this is considered by Tustin—if a patient is dissatisfied with their healthcare provider, then they are more likely to rate the information online as better than that provided by the doctor, and this may have an effect on their compliance with treatment approaches prescribed by the doctor. Similarly, Brett and McCullough (2012) describe how Internet sources might encourage patients to challenge their physician, making requests for specific treatments or diagnostic tests that may not be appropriate for their case. While it is without doubt that such patient research may be beneficial to their prognosis in many cases, Brett and McCullough outline how it is sometimes difficult for the practitioner to deny such requests where benefits are unlikely.

Research has also examined how the type of search conducted can affect the sources returned. For example, Wang et al. (2012) compared the results returned by four search engines for the keyword *breast cancer*, as well as the usability of the search results. They found that the search engines emphasized different types of content (such as websites that are aimed at the general population or those aimed at professionals or researchers), but that all four identified six well-known websites on the topic, pre-identified by a medical expert, within the top 30 results.

A related concept is **cyberchondria**, defined by White and Horvitz (2009) as 'the unfounded escalation of concerns about common symptomatology, based on the review of search results and literature on the web' (p. 23). However, other researchers use broader definitions—Smith, Fox, Davies, and Hamidi-Manesh (2006) refer to cyberchondriacs as 'anyone who seeks health-related information on the Internet' (p. 209). Definitions and consideration of cyberchondria in the literature were frequently based on an adaptation of hypochondriasis as defined by the DSM-IV-TR (American Psychiatric Association, 2000). However, the fifth edition of the DSM (American Psychiatric Association, 2013a) removes the disorder, amongst other somatoform disorders, replacing them with other conditions, such as **Somatic Symptom Disorder (SSD)** and **Illness Anxiety Disorder**. For SSD, the somatic symptoms need not lack medical explanation, but they must be 'significantly distressing or disruptive to daily life and must be accompanied by excessive thoughts, feelings or behaviours' (American Psychiatric Association, 2013b, p. 1). If an individual has high health anxiety but no somatic symptoms, the diagnosis of Illness Anxiety Disorder might be given (American Psychiatric Association, 2013c). As such, although cyberchondria has attracted considerable interest from researchers (Berezovska, Buchinger, & Matsyuk, 2010, Fergus, 2013, Aiken & Kirwan, 2014, McElroy & Shevlin, 2014), the use of the term as a diagnosis in itself must be carefully handled, particularly as the anxiety experienced would not, in most cases, meet the criteria of being distressing or disruptive to daily life. In the same way that an individual may feel sad from time to time without meeting the criteria for a depressive disorder, it is highly unlikely that most individuals who seek medical information online would meet the criteria for Somatic Symptom Disorder or Illness Anxiety Disorder.

10.3.2 The Internet as a source of social support

Wills and Ainette (2012) describe how social support (or the perceived availability of it) can have many beneficial relationships for an individual, including 'lower likelihood of morbidity or mortality . . . higher levels of psychological well-being, and . . . lower levels of health-risk behaviour' (p. 465). This occurs through various means—for example, social support may encourage people to exercise appropriately, go for regular check-ups, or complete other health promoting behaviours. It may also encourage people to follow any treatment procedures that have been prescribed, or to avoid substance abuse. Revenson and Lepore (2012) review the literature relating to how coping occurs within a social context, and how social support can promote coping abilities. For example, they describe the social-cognitive processing (SCP) model (Lepore, Silver, Wortman, & Wayment, 1996), which describes how people wish to discuss major stressors or traumas with others, and that this is especially so during the early stages of the experience. This may help with both cognitive and emotional adaptation, but it is dependent on the reactions of the confidante. For example, if the confidante is perceived as being bored of the topic, or non-caring, or as not understanding the complexity of the problem, the benefits may be minimal. The availability of specific support groups online for individuals with certain illnesses and injuries may help individuals in sharing their situation and experience, while feeling that the other members of the group are not bored and have a more thorough understanding of their condition.

   While the social supports outlined by Wills and Ainette (2012) and Revenson and Lepore (2012) were primarily offline supports (such as spouses, families, friends, and so on), some research has examined the role of online social support groups. For example, Tanis (2007) describes how online social support groups have a great deal of potential, but that users should be cautious. He describes how the anonymity and lack of physical visibility provided by online groups mean that these may provide a useful form of support. This may be particularly the case where an individual feels that their actual selves deviate from the ideal or ought self in some way. An example of this could relate to obesity—an individual may experience a degree of shame or guilt that their perceived **actual self**-state is larger than their ideal or **ought self**-state (Castonguay, Brunet, Ferguson, & Sabiston, 2012) (see Chapter 2 for more on the different types of online self). Online support mechanisms allow such individuals to join support groups for weight loss (or for unrelated health matters) without feeling the same level of shame or guilt that they would if they sought support from offline groups. Such anonymity and lack of physical visibility may then be crucial factors in encouraging individuals to seek support while they normally would not do so. Tanis also suggests that the anonymity and lack of physical visibility might be combined with the lack of traditional barriers such as geographical distance, thus allowing users to join groups not previously available to them. However, Tanis warns that the groups are not without risks, such as flaming, cyberstalking, dependence on the online community, exchange of misinformation, and encouragement of a belief that a person's situation is hopeless, perhaps leading to a fatalistic perspective regarding their illness or condition.

Nevertheless, there has been considerable research examining the use of online social supports for health related topics. Studies have examined the use of online forums as supports for many different conditions and illnesses, such as cancer (Orgad, 2006, Love et al., 2012, Sillence, 2013), pregnancy (Sherman & Greenfield, 2013), miscarriage and threatened pregnancy loss (Gold, Boggs, Mugisha, & Lancaster Palladino, 2012, Betts, Dahlen, & Smith, 2014), recovery from hysterectomy (Bunde, Suls, Martin, & Barnett, 2007), irritable bowel syndrome (Coulson, 2005), and infertility (Welbourne, Blanchard, & Wadsworth, 2013), amongst many others (see Chapter 12 for a focus on online support groups).

As Tanis outlined, there are many reasons why online communication might be particularly attractive as a method of seeking support. In addition to the anonymity and lack of physical visibility mentioned by Tanis, other theories of online and offline communication can aid our understanding of such an approach. For example, Walther's concept of **hyperpersonal communication** (1996, 2007) describes how online communication may result in higher perceived levels of affection and emotion. Other theories relating to communication may also be relevant—such as Altman and Taylor's (1973) **social penetration theory** and the importance of reciprocity (Altman, 1973). Herb Clark's theories regarding shared knowledge and grounding in communication may also be relevant (Clark & Marshall, 1978, Clark & Schaefer, 1989, Clark & Brennan, 1991)—as many individuals in the support organizations would already hold a great deal of information about the specific condition, communication becomes easier and less explanation is required when seeking support or advice.

A related concept is Suler's (2004) **online disinhibition effect**. He argues that individuals may disclose more personal information online than they would offline. Suler argues that there are several factors that contribute to such self-disclosure, including 'anonymity, invisibility, asynchronicity, solipsistic introjection, dissociative imagination, and minimisation of authority' (p. 321). While many references to Suler's theory focus on how the disinhibition can be *toxic*, thus leading to negative behaviours such as cyberbullying, he also refers to *benign disinhibition*, where individuals show high levels of kindness or altruism online. In many online support forums it is this benign disinhibition that is more evident, as users attempt to support and provide advice for each other. It is possible that online anonymity and invisibility might also allow users to more easily seek information or advice on what they might normally consider too embarrassing to mention, even to a medical practitioner.

Finally, any users of online support forums should be cognizant of the risks to privacy and security that are inherent in sharing information online. Over-disclosure is possible, especially when discussing what may be highly personal information, and it is sometimes easy to overlook the public nature of many online forums, believing that the audience for a comment is limited to the respondents, when it may be visible to any Internet user who happens across the forum. Concepts and advice relating to privacy, security, and trust are also relevant to support seeking online. Research on privacy, security, and trust, and why over-disclosure can occur online, is described in more detail in Chapter 14.

10.4 Technology as a risk factor for health

Thus far, this chapter has primarily focused on technological support for individuals with health conditions. However, media reports about the impact of technology on our health are common, and this section considers how technology might have a detrimental effect on our well-being. In particular, it examines how the proliferation of mobile devices can result in an 'always on' mentality, the role of websites that promote harmful activities, and the impact of sedentary lifestyles on health.

10.4.1 Stress and the 'always on' mentality

In 2014, many news websites reported that France had initiated a new law banning work email communication before 9 am and after 6 pm. It quickly emerged that many of these reports were incorrect—it was clarified that it was a labour agreement rather than a new law, and it only applied to a small minority of the workforce ('France's 6 pm e-mail ban,' 2014). Nevertheless, it should be considered if being constantly available to employers via computer mediated communication has an effect on employee health.

Prior to the development of the Internet, most work-related communication ceased after the employee left their workplace for the day (with the exception of those who continued to take telephone calls or similar communications through non-work hours). Internet connections in the home, followed relatively swiftly by WiFi, mobile data, smartphones, and tablet devices have led to a different mentality regarding work-related communication, and email in particular. It is now common for people to have access to such communication at all times, including at night, and there are fears that there is a growing expectation for employees to respond to emails during non-working hours.

Rennecker and Derks (2013) provide an overview of the research to date regarding **email overload**, but argue that it is not just the number of emails sent/received, nor the time spent doing so, that causes difficulties. Perceptions of overload can result from other factors, such as time pressure in responding, lack of control over incoming messages, interruptions, and the generation of unexpected tasks (p. 14). Rennecker and Derks suggest that email overload can be of three types—**information overload**, **work overload**, and **social overload**. Information overload refers to the processing requirements of the information received, while work overload refers to unreasonable expectations regarding the ability to deal with messages within the available time. Social overload comes from being overwhelmed by the diversity of interactions and role demands.

Such stress may not simply emerge from email and work-related communications. Maier, Laumer, Eckhardt, and Weitzel (2012) argue that social networking sites may also result in emotional exhaustion. Nevertheless, email overload is not an unavoidable aspect of life for most people—Park and Jex (2011) indicate that employees can create beneficial boundaries around such communications to maintain a balance between work and family life.

10.4.2 Internet sources harmful to health

As described previously, individuals may explore the Internet seeking information about medical issues and concerns. While doing so they may, intentionally or unintentionally, come across Internet sources that provide products or information that are actually harmful to the user. There are many examples of such negative content, such as the 'Silk Road', one of several online marketplaces that sell illegal or counterfeit drugs (Siva, 2010, Christin, 2013, Barratt, Ferris, & Winstock, 2014). Much psychological research regarding online content harmful to health investigates online communities and websites that promote eating disorders.

The nature of the Internet is to connect people, including those with minority or harmful interests and perspectives. As the World Wide Web grew, individuals with eating disorders were drawn to it to seek support and advice, but more sinister websites with **pro-ana** (pro-anorexia) and/or **pro-mia** (pro-bulimia) content also emerged. Norris, Boydell, Pinhas, and Katzman (2006) analysed the content of 20 pro-ana websites, many of which included tips and 'thinspiration' ('inspirational photo galleries and quotes that aim to serve as motivators for weight loss', p. 443). Prevalent themes on these websites included control, success, and perfection. A more recent study investigating 180 active websites found similar results (Borzekowski, Schenk, Wilson, & Peebles, 2010). Such content is indicative of the sufferers' desire for an ideal self that is different to the actual self, but also a desire for their actual self to be accepted and for their goals to be reinforced through the evidence of similar goals being held by others. Nevertheless, Boero and Pascoe (2012) describe how members of pro-anorexia groups online can find it difficult to build communities due to fear of inauthenticity of potential members—particularly individuals who are not anorexic, but who may wish to be—with tensions forming as a result.

Dias (2003) suggests that the Internet provides a space where individuals suffering from anorexia can express thoughts that they are not able or ready to share with others, but, as with many communities, there seem to be varied responses to members on such sites. Brotsky and Giles (2007) found both hostile and supportive responses from community members when one of the researchers covertly posed as a participant on a site, leading them to suggest that the communities are like cliques that offer 'temporary relief from offline hostility' (p. 93), but are unlikely to provide any therapeutic value beyond this. Yeshua-Katz and Martins (2013) interviewed pro-ana bloggers, who cited their motivations as seeking social support, coping with a stigmatizing illness, and employing a means of self-expression, although they indicated a fear of revealing their eating disorder should the blog be exposed, as well as a concern that their blog encouraged disordered eating in others.

10.4.3 Sedentary lifestyles and health

In 2012, newspapers reported the death of a teenager in Taiwan who collapsed and died after spending 40 consecutive hours in a sedentary position playing an online game called Diablo 3 ('Taiwan teen dies,' 2012). Police investigating speculated that the gaming marathon had caused cardiovascular problems. While this is an extreme case, it is not the only reported instance of an individual dying during lengthy gaming sessions. Much more common are less extreme, but still worrying, conditions that appear to be correlated with prolonged sedentary activity in the form of technology use. For example, Calvert, Staiano, and Bond (2013) describe how electronic gaming is often associated with the problem of childhood obesity (although they note that such games may also increase the physical activity of children, while exposing them to healthier foods). Similarly, Melchior, Chollet, Fombonne, Surkan, and Dray-Spira (2014) found that young adults aged 22–35 years who played video games more than once per week were more likely to be overweight than those who did not, and Lepp, Barkley, Sanders, Rebold, and Gates (2013) found that cell phone use was negatively related to cardio respiratory fitness, with high frequency users giving up opportunities to engage in physical activity so that they could use their phone instead.

While there are many further examples of the types of studies outlined here indicating a negative correlation between technology use and health measures, conversely Scharrer and Zeller (2014) found that there was no correlation between body mass index (BMI) and levels of time spent with video games by 13–15 year olds. They also found no correlation between BMI and relative time in active and sedentary types of game. In addition to this, games developers have placed increasing focus on alternative methods of interaction, and the potential for games to increase our well-being is attracting more interest from authors and researchers (McGonigal, 2011, Ferguson, 2012). This potential for technology to be used to improve user health is examined in the next section.

10.5 Technology in treatment and health promotion

Research on technology as a health promotion strategy has focused on many areas, such as the use of telepresence for medical consultations, online diagnosis, the use of mobile phones and smartphones in promoting adherence to treatment schedules, the development of software that promotes healthy activity (particularly in relation to smartphone applications), gamification as a method of making healthy activities more interesting, and the use of virtual reality to treat conditions such as eating disorders and addictions, as well as providing distraction from pain.

10.5.1 Gaming, gamification, and smartphone apps in health promotion

Over the past ten years, traditional, sedentary gaming controllers have been increasingly supplemented with or replaced by motion sensitive devices that encourage physical activity while playing ('active video games'). A more recent development is the design and provision of health promotion applications for smartphones. These have many different goals, including helping users develop better sleep rhythms, encouraging healthier eating patterns, setting targets for weight loss and fitness levels, and aiding users in meditative practices. Many of these technologies and applications can be augmented by the use of wearable technologies, such as smartwatches that monitor heart rate and activity levels. While the use of cellular phones for health promotion is not new (Merrell and Doarn, 2014), these wearable technologies provide a more accurate mechanism for tracking progress. Smartphone apps (and other software designed to increase well-being) sometimes employ a strategy known as **gamification** to increase efficacy. Gamification is 'the use of video game elements in non-gaming systems to improve user experience (UX) and user engagement' (Deterding, Sicart, Nacke, O'Hara, & Dixon, 2011, p. 2425). Such elements may include the use of leaderboards, or the awarding of badges or prizes when users complete certain goals.

While there has been limited research conducted to date on the efficacy of smartphone apps, there are mixed findings regarding the value of active videogames in increasing physical activity amongst users. Some studies and papers have suggested that such technological interventions have shown success in the treatment or management of various conditions, including stress management and resilience (Rose, 2014), obesity (Castelnuovo & Simpson, 2011), and tinnitus (Hesser et al., 2012). Similarly, Straker, Abbott, and Smith (2013) discovered that replacement of sedentary games with active ones had a similar, positive effect on physical activity in 10–12 year olds as removal of all electronic games. Other studies found more limited results, for example, Joseph et al. (2014), who did not find a reduced BMI in young adult African American women who accessed a physical activity promotion website over the course of three months, although they did find that users decreased their sedentary screen time and increased their self-regulation for physical activity. Other studies, such as Carr et al. (2013), have found that such interventions designed to improve physical activity are effective in the short-term, but improvement is not maintained over time.

Sufficient research has been conducted to allow some authors to prepare reviews of the studies conducted. These reviews tend to show some efficacy, although the results are somewhat limited. While LeBlanc et al. (2013) found that active video games increased acute energy expenditure in children and young people in a review of previous literature, they concluded that the effects on habitual physical activity are less certain and so they may not be useful in increasing daily physical activity. Parisod et al. (2014) conducted a 'review of reviews' regarding digital games in children's health, concluding that there appears to be an increase in physical activity, but only to light/moderate levels, and particularly for games that involve both upper and lower body movements. Parisod et al. also note that even sedentary games had potential, particularly for asthma and diabetes related behaviours and diet.

For any health promotion intervention, designers need to be cognizant of how health psychology and human-computer interaction should be used to inform the structure, design and content of the intervention. Riley et al. (2011) note that health behaviour theories could be employed to a greater extent in interventions, particularly those promoting adherence and disease management (rather than those targeting smoking or weight loss). However, they accept that health behaviour theories may need to be adapted due to the interactivity that mobile interventions allow. Other factors, such as security, usability and technical difficulties, must also be carefully integrated into the design of such interventions (Yuen, Goetter, Herbert, & Forman, 2012). Finally, the importance of appropriate research design, implementation, and procedures has also been highlighted (Baranowski & Frankel, 2012, Baranowski, Baranowski, O'Connor, Lu, & Thompson, 2012).

Technologies such as smartphone apps and active videogames are primarily developed as 'self-help' interventions, where the user follows the instructions on screen, and often proceeds through the intervention stages with little or no professional help. However, technology in the form of virtual reality has also been used as interventions based on principles of health psychology, most notably for addictions and pain management, and these will be considered in the following, final, section.

10.5.2 **Virtual Reality and health psychology**

Virtual Reality (**VR**) is experiencing a resurgence in popularity, primarily due to the development of relatively low-cost, yet innovative, headsets. However, researchers have been exploring the potential of VR in clinical and health psychology for several years, establishing it as a potential supplementary mechanism for the therapy of many disorders. While research examining the use of VR in the treatment and management of anxiety disorders is probably the most dominant body of literature in the field, the potential for VR to be used in therapy for addictions and eating disorders has also been explored. Another researched application of VR has been distraction from pain.

While there are various mechanisms employed in VR therapies, one of the most prevalent in terms of addiction and obesity treatments is cue exposure and response extinction. A sizeable number of papers first examine if clients react to virtual cues in the same way that they do to real situations (e.g., if an individual usually associates a desire for an alcoholic drink with eating out in a restaurant, the VR environment being considered as a treatment aid must replicate a restaurant in sufficient detail to generate such a desire in the individual, despite being entirely computer generated). Further research then attempts to determine if the individual who is given skills for managing their addiction in the virtual world can then transfer those skills to real environments in their daily life. Many studies and papers have proposed or investigated the ability of VR to generate cravings and/or be beneficial in the treatment of individuals with nicotine addiction, alcohol use disorders, obesity, and addictions to illegal substances, often with promising results (Bordnick et al., 2008, Bordnick, Carter, & Traylor, 2011, Paris et al., 2011, Riva, 2011, Culbertson, Shulenberger, De La Garza, Newton, & Brody, 2012, Ferrer-Garcia, Gutierrez-Maldonado, & Riva, 2013, Wiederhold, Riva, & Wiederhold, 2014, among many others).

While most treatment applications of VR rely on the user's attention to cues and environments within the virtual world, the use of VR as a distractor for pain solely requires the individual to immerse themselves in the environment, irrespective of the content of the world. The nature of the content is often irrelevant, once the user finds the stimuli engaging and distracting. However, in some cases, worlds have been chosen or developed with particular consideration of the type of pain that the participant is experiencing. Extensive research has examined the use of VR as a distractor for pain, with considerable support for its applicability in a wide variety of contexts (Malloy & Milling, 2010, Hoffman et al., 2011, Maani et al., 2011, Schmitt et al., 2011, Keefe et al., 2012, Faber, Patterson, & Bremer, 2013, Hoffman et al., 2014). Virtual reality has been demonstrated to be a more effective distractor than many other techniques, and can be used as an alternative or supplement to pharmacological analgesics, but much of the research in this area has included very small participant numbers (sometimes only one or two case studies), and large scale experimental studies are fewer in number.

10.6 Chapter summary

- Health psychology examines many different aspects of human behaviour and conditions affecting health and well-being.

- An individual may hold various health beliefs and illness cognitions that may affect their behaviours when they are well or ill. A greater understanding of these can help health psychologists and other professionals to promote healthier behaviours.

- Other common research areas in health psychology include treatment and effects of serious/long-term illnesses and medical conditions, communication with healthcare professionals, screening, the ageing process, stress, placebos, and the experience and management of pain.

- The Internet may be used as part of a suite of coping techniques by individuals experiencing illness or injury.

- Patients may seek medical information online, sometimes due to dissatisfaction with their experiences with a medical professional. The reliability of these online sources is highly variable.

- There has been considerable research into a condition termed *cyberchondria*, although definitions of the condition vary by researchers and it is not included as a specific condition in the American Psychiatric Association's DSM-5.

- Social support has been linked with various positive health related behaviours and outcomes.

- Various factors may lead individuals to seek social support online, including anonymity, lack of visibility, disinhibition, reciprocity, and a shared knowledge of conditions.

- Disclosure of personal information online may be perilous, and care should be taken by users of online support groups to protect their personal information as necessary.

- The ways in which we use the Internet may cause health problems. These include stress induced by email overload and obesity and cardiovascular problems due to sedentary lifestyles.

- Some online communities promote and encourage unhealthy behaviours and conditions, such as eating disorders.

- However, technology has also been used to increase well-being through a variety of means, including smartphone apps, mobile interventions, and active videogames. These applications may require further evaluation to determine their long-term efficacy, and the interactivity of such interventions may require adaptation or updating of existing theories of health behaviour.

- Virtual Reality (VR) has been demonstrated to have a number of benefits to health, including use as a therapeutic tool for addictions and as a distractor for pain.

References

Aiken, M. & Kirwan, G. (2014). The psychology of cyberchondria and 'cyberchondria by proxy'. In Power, A. & Kirwan, G. (Eds), *Cyberpsychology and New Media: A Thematic Reader* (pp. 158–169). Hove /New York: Psychology Press.

Altman, I. (1973). Reciprocity of interpersonal exchange. *Journal for the Theory of Social Behaviour*, 3 (2), 249–261.

Altman, I. & Taylor, D.A. (1973). *Social Penetration: The Development of Interpersonal Relationships*. New York: Holt, Rinehart & Winston.

American Psychiatric Association (2000). *Diagnostic and Statistical Manual of Mental Disorders*, 4th edn, text rev. Washington DC: Author.

American Psychiatric Association (2013a). *Diagnostic and Statistical Manual of Mental Disorders*, 5th edn. Arlington, VA: American Psychiatric Publishing.

American Psychiatric Association (2013b). *Somatic Symptom Disorder*. Retrieved from American Psychiatric Association DSM 5 website http://www.dsm5.org/Documents/Somatic%20 Symptom%20Disorder%20Fact%20Sheet.pdf (accessed 4th September, 2014).

American Psychiatric Association (2013c). *Highlights of changes from DSM-IV-TR to DSM-5*. Retrieved from American Psychiatric Association DSM 5 website http://www.dsm5.org/Documents/ changes%20from%20dsm-iv-tr%20to%20dsm-5. pdf (accessed 4th September, 2014).

Baronowski, T. & Frankel, L. (2012). Let's get technical! Gaming and technology for weight control and health promotion in children. *Childhood Obesity*, 8, 34–37.

Baranowski, T., Baranowski, J., O'Connor, T., Lu, A.S., & Thompson, D. (2012). Is enhanced physical activity possible using active videogames? *Games for Health Journal*, 1, 228–232.

Barratt, M.J., Ferris, J.A., & Winstock, A.R. (2014). Use of Silk Road, the online drug marketplace, in the United Kingdom, Australia and the United States. *Addiction*, 109 (5), 774–783.

Baum, A., Revenson, T.A., & Singer, J. (Eds) (2012). *Handbook of Health Psychology* 2nd edn. New York: Psychology Press.

Berezovska, I., Buchinger, K., & Matsyuk, O. (2010, July). Evolving facets of cyberchondria: Primum non nocere 'First do no harm'. Paper presented at the *Seventh International Conference on Hands-on Science*, Rethymno, Greece.

Betts, D., Dahlen, H.G., & Smith, C.A. (2014). A search for hope and understanding: an analysis of threatened miscarriage Internet forums. *Midwifery*, 30 (6), 650–656.

Boero, N. & Pascoe, C.J. (2012). Pro-anorexia communities and online interaction: Bringing the pro-ana body online. *Body Society*, 18 (2), 27–57.

Bordnick, P.S., Traylor, A., Copp, H.L., Graap, K.M., Carter, B., Ferrer, M., & Walton, A.P. (2008). Assessing reactivity to virtual reality alcohol based cues. *Addictive Behaviours*, 33, 743–756.

Bordnick, P.S., Carter, B.L., & Traylor, A.C. (2011). What virtual reality research in addictions can tell us about the future of obesity assessment and treatment. *Journal of Diabetes Science and Technology*, 5 (2), 265–271.

Borzekowski, D.L.G., Schenk, S., Wilson, J.L., & Peebles, R. (2010). e-Ana and e-Mia: A content analysis of pro-eating disorder web sites. *American Journal of Public Health*, 100 (8), 1526–1534.

Brett, A.S. & McCullough, L.B. (2012). Addressing requests by patients for nonbeneficial interventions. *Journal of the American Medical Association*, 307 (2), 149–150.

Brotsky, S.R. & Giles, D. (2007). Inside the 'pro-ana' community: A covert online participant observation. *Eating Disorders: The Journal of Treatment & Prevention*, 15 (2), 93–109.

Bunde, M., Suls, J., Martin, R., & Barnett, K. (2007). Online hysterectomy support: Characteristics of website experiences. *Cyberpsychology & Behaviour*, 10 (1), 80–85.

Calvert, S.L., Staiano, A.E., & Bond, B.J. (2013). Electronic gaming and the obesity crisis. In Blumberg, F.C. & Fisch, S.M. (Eds), *Digital Games: A Context for Cognitive Development* (pp. 51–57). San Francisco: Wiley.

Carr, L.J., Dunsiger, S.I., Lewis, B., Ciccolo, J.T., Hartman, S., Bock, B., Dominick, G., & Marcus, B.H. (2013). Randomised controlled trial testing an Internet physical activity intervention for sedentary adults. *Health Psychology*, 32 (3), 328–336.

Castelnuovo, G. & Simpson, S. (2011). Ebesity— Ehealth for Obesity—New technologies for the treatment of obesity in clinical psychology and medicine. *Clinical Practice & Epidemiology in Mental Health*, 7, 5–8.

Castonguay, A.L., Brunet, J., Ferguson, L., & Sabiston, C.M. (2012). Weight-related actual and ideal self-states, discrepancies, and shame, guilt, and pride. Examining associations within the process model of self-conscious emotions. *Body Image*, 9, 488–494.

Christin, N. (2013). Travelling the Silk Road: A measurement analysis of a large anonymous online marketplace. *Proceedings of the 22nd International Conference on World Wide Web, Brazil*, 213–224.

Clark, H.H. & Brennan, S.A. (1991). Grounding in communication. In Resnick, L.B., Levine, J.M., & Teasley, S.D. (Eds), *Perspectives on Socially Shared Cognition* (pp. 127–149). Washington: APA Books.

Clark, H.H. & Marshall, C.R. (1978). Reference diaries. In Waltz, D.L. (Ed.), *Theoretical Issues in Natural Language Processing*, Vol. 2. (pp. 57–63). New York: Association for Computing Machinery.

Clark, H.H. & Schaefer, E.F. (1989). Contributing to discourse. *Cognitive Science*, 13, 259–294.

Coulson, N.S. (2005). Receiving social support online: An analysis of a computer-mediated support group for individuals living with irritable bowel syndrome. *Cyberpsychology & Behaviour*, 8 (6), 580–584.

Culbertson, C.S., Shulenberger, S., De La Garza, R., Newton, T.F., & Brody, A.L. (2012). Virtual reality cue exposure therapy for the treatment of tobacco dependence. *Journal of CyberTherapy & Rehabilitation*, 5 (1), 57–64.

Deterding, S., Sicart, M., Nacke, L., O'Hara, K., & Dixon, D. (2011). Gamification: Using game-design elements in non-gaming contexts. *Proceedings of the CHI EA '11, Vancouver*, 2425–2428. doi: 10.1145/1979742.1979575.

Dias, K. (2003). The Ana sanctuary: Women's pro-anorexia narratives in cyberspace. *Journal of International Women's Studies*, 4 (2), 31–45.

Diaz, J.A., Griffith, R.A., Ng, J.J., Reinert, S.E., Friedmann, P.D., & Moulton, A.W. (2002). Patients' use of the Internet for medical information. *Journal of General Internal Medicine*, 17 (3), 180–185.

Faber, A.W., Patterson, D.R., & Bremer (2013). Repeated use of immersive virtual reality therapy to control pain during wound dressing changes in paediatric and adult burn patients. *Journal of Burn Care & Research*, 34 (5), 563–568.

Fergus, T.A. (2013). Cyberchondria and intolerance of uncertainty: Examining when individuals experience health anxiety in response to Internet searches for medical information. *Cyberpsychology, Behaviour and Social Networking*, 16 (10), 735–739.

Ferguson, B. (2012). The emergence of games for health. *Games for Health Journal*, 1, 1–2.

Ferrer-Garcia, M., Gutierrez-Maldonado, J., & Riva, G. (2013). Virtual reality based treatments in eating disorders and obesity: A review. *Journal of Contemporary Psychotherapy*, 43 (4), 207–221.

Finniss, D.G., Kaptchuk, T.J., Miller, F., & Benedetti, F. (2010). Placebo effects: Biological, clinical and ethical advances. *The Lancet*, 375 (9715), 686–695.

Folkman, S. (2011). Stress, health and coping: An overview. In Folkman, S. (Ed.), *The Oxford Handbook of Stress, Health and Coping* (pp. 3–11). Oxford: Oxford University Press.

France's 6 pm e-mail ban: Not what it seemed (2014, April 14). *The Economist: Charlemagne European Politics*. Retrieved from http://www.economist.com/blogs/charlemagne/2014/04/frances-6pm-e-mail-ban#sthash.zYhUBxoP.dpbs (accessed 4th September, 2014).

Gold, K.J., Boggs, M.E., Mugisha, E., & Lancaster Palladino, C. (2012). Internet message boards for pregnancy loss: Who's online and why? *Women's Health Issues*, 22 (1), e67–e72.

Hesser, H., Gustafsson, T., Lundén, C., Henrikson, O., Fattahi, K., Johnsson, E., Westin, V.W., Carlbring, P., Mäki-Torkko, E., & Kaldo, V. (2012). A randomised controlled trial of Internet-delivered cognitive behaviour therapy and acceptance and commitment therapy in the treatment of tinnitus. *Journal of Counselling and Clinical Psychology*, 80 (4), 649–661.

Hoffman, H.G., Chambers, G.T., Meyer, III, W.J., Arceneaux, L.L., Russell, W.J., Seibel, E.J., Richards, T.L., Sharar, S.R., & Patterson, D.R. (2011). Virtual reality as an adjunctive non-pharmacologic analgesic for acute burn pain during medical procedures. *Annals of Behavioural Medicine*, 41, 183–191.

Hoffman, H.G., Meyer, III, W.J., Ramirez, M., Roberts, L., Seibel, E.J., Atzori, B., Sharar, S.R., & Patterson, D.R. (2014). Feasibility of articulated arm mounted Oculus Rift virtual reality goggles for adjunctive pain control during occupational therapy in paediatric burn patients. *Cyberpsychology, Behaviour and Social Networking*, 17 (6), 397–401.

Hu, X., Bell, R.A., Kravitz, R.L., & Orrange, S. (2012). The prepared patient: Information seeking of online support group members before their medical appointments. *Journal of Health Communication: International Perspectives*, 17 (8), 960–978.

Joseph, R.P., Pekmezi, D., Dutton, G.R., Cherrington, A.L., Kim, Y., Allison, J.J., & Durrant, N.H. (2014). Results of a culturally adapted Internet-enhanced physical activity pilot intervention for overweight and obese young adult African American women. *Journal of Transcultural*

Nursing. Advance online publication. doi: 10.1177/1043659614539176.

Keefe, F.J., Huling, D.A., Coggins, M.J., Keefe, D.F., Rosenthal, M.Z., Herr, N.R., & Hoffman, H.G. (2012). Virtual reality for persistent pain: A new direction for behavioural pain management. *Pain*, 153 (11), 2163–2166.

LeBlanc, A.G., Chaput, J.P., McFarlane, A., Colley, R.C., Thivel, D., Biddle, S.J.H., Maddison, R., Leatherdale, S.T., & Tremlay, M.S. (2013). Active video games and health indicators in children and youth: A systematic review. *PLOS One*. doi: 10.1371/journal.pone.0065351.

Lee, S.Y. & Hawkins, R. (2010). Why do patients seek an alternative channel? The effects of unmet needs on patients' health-related Internet use. *Journal of Health Communication: International Perspectives*, 15 (2), 152–166.

Lepore, S.J., Silver, R.C., Wortman, C.B., & Wayment, H.A. (1996). Social constraints, intrusive thoughts, and depressive symptoms among bereaved mothers. *Journal of Personality and Social Psychology*, 70 (2), 271–282.

Lepp, A., Barkley, J.E., Sanders, G.J., Rebold, M., & Gates, P. (2013). The relationship between cell phone use, physical and sedentary activity, and cardiorespiratory fitness in a sample of U.S. college students. *International Journal of Behavioural Nutrition and Physical Activity*, 10 (79). Retrieved from http://www.biomedcentral.com/content/pdf/1479-5868-10-79.pdf (accessed 4th September, 2014).

Leventhal, H., Diefenbach, M., & Leventhal, E.A. (1992). Illness cognition: Using common sense to understand treatment adherence and affect cognition interactions. *Cognitive Therapy and Research*, 16 (2), 143–163.

Leventhal, H., Bodnar-Deren, S., Breland, J.Y., Hash-Converse, J., & Phillips, L.A. (2012). Modeling health and illness behaviour: The approach of the Commonsense Model. In Baum, A., Revenson, T.A., & Singer, J. (Eds), *Handbook of Health Psychology*, 2nd edn (pp. 3–35). New York: Psychology Press.

Li, N., Orrange, S., Kravitz, R.L., & Bell, R.A. (2014). Reasons for and predictors of patients' online health information seeking following a medical appointment. *Family Practice*. Advance online publication. doi: 10.1093/fampra/cmu034.

Love, B., Crook, B., Thompson, C.M., Zaitchik, S., Knapp, J., LeFebvre, L., Jones, B., Donovan-Kicken, E., Eargle, E., & Rechis, R. (2012). Exploring psychosocial support online: A content analysis of messages in an adolescent and young adult cancer community. *Cyberpsychology, Behaviour and Social Networking*, 15 (10), 555–559.

Maani, C.V., Hoffman, H.G., Fowler, M., Maiers, A.J., Gaylord, K.M., & DeSocio, P.A. (2011). Combining ketamine and virtual reality pain control during severe burn wound care: One military and one civilian patient. *Pain Medicine*, 12 (4), 673–678.

Maier, C., Laumer, S., Eckhardt, A., & Weitzel, T. (2012). When social networking turns to social overload: Explaining the stress, emotional exhaustion and quitting behaviour from social network sites' users. *ECIS 2012 Proceedings of the European Conference on Information Systems (ECIS), Spain, Paper 71*. Retrieved from http://aisel.aisnet.org/ecis2012/71/ (accessed 4th September, 2014).

Malloy, K.M. & Milling, L.S. (2010). The effectiveness of virtual reality distraction for pain reduction: A systematic review. *Clinical Psychology Review*, 30 (8), 1011–1018.

McElroy, E. & Shevlin, M. (2014). The development and initial validation of the cyberchondria severity scale (CSS). *Journal of Anxiety Disorders*, 28 (2), 259–265.

McGonigal, J. (2011). *Reality is Broken: Why Games Make us Better and How They Can Change the World*. London: Vintage.

Melchior, M., Chollet, A., Fombonne, E., Surkan, P.J., & Dray-Spira, R. (2014). Internet and video game use in relation to overweight in young adults. *American Journal of Health Promotion*, 28 (5), 321–324.

Melzack, R. (1996). Gate control theory: On the evolution of pain concepts. *Pain Forum*, 5 (2), 128–138.

Melzack, R. & Wall, P.D. (1965). Pain mechanisms: a new theory. *Science*, 150 (3699), 971–979.

Merrell, R.C. & Doarn, C.R. (2014). m-Health. *Telemedicine and e-Health*, 20, 99–101.

Norris, M.L., Boydell, K.M., Pinhas, L., & Katzman, D.K. (2006). Ana and the Internet: A review of pro-anorexia websites. *International Journal of Eating Disorders*, 39 (6), 443–447.

Ogden, J. (2012). *Health Psychology: A Textbook*, 5th edn. Maidenhead: Open University Press/McGraw Hill Education.

Orgad, S. (2006). The cultural dimensions of online communication: A study of breast cancer patients' Internet spaces. *New Media & Society*, 8 (6), 877–899.

Paris, M.M., Carter, B.L., Traylor, A.C., Bordnick, P.S., Day, S.X., Armsworth, M.W., & Cinciripini,

P.M. (2011). Cue reactivity in virtual reality: The role of context. *Addictive Behaviours*, 36 (7), 696–699.

Parisod, H., Pakarinen, A., Kuhanen, L., Aromaa, M., Leppänen, V., Liukkonen, T.N., Smed, J., & Salanterä, S. (2014). Promoting children's health with digital games: A review of reviews. *Games for Health Journal*, 3 (3), 145–156.

Park, Y. & Jex, S.M. (2011). Work-home boundary management using communication and information technology. *International Journal of Stress Management*, 18 (2), 133–152.

Rennecker, J. & Derks, D. (2013). Email overload: Fine tuning the research lens. In Derks, D. & Bakker, A. (Eds), *The Psychology of Digital Media at Work* (pp. 14–38). Hove: Psychology Press.

Revenson, T.A. & Lepore, S.J. (2012). Coping in a social context. In Baum, A., Revenson, T.A., & Singer, J. (Eds), *Handbook of Health Psychology*, 2nd edn (pp. 193–217). New York: Psychology Press.

Riley, W.T., Rivera, D.E., Atienza, A.A., Nilsen, W., Allison, S.M., & Mermelstein, R. (2011). Health behaviour models in the age of mobile interventions: Are our theories up to the task? *Translational Behavioural Medicine*, 1 (1), 53–71.

Riva, G. (2011). The key to unlocking the virtual body: Virtual reality in the treatment of obesity and eating disorders. *Journal of Diabetes Science and Technology*, 5 (2), 283–292.

Rose, R.D. (2014). Self-guided multimedia stress management and resilience training. *Journal of Positive Psychology*. Advance online publication. doi: 10.1080/17439760.2014.927907.

Scharrer, E. & Zeller, A. (2014). Active and sedentary video game time: Testing associations with adolescents' BMI. *Journal of Media Psychology: Theories, Methods and Applications*, 26 (1), 39–49.

Schmitt, Y.S., Hoffman, H.G., Blough, D.K., Patterson, D.R., Jensen, M.P., Soltani, M., Carrougher, G.J., Nakamura, D., & Sharar, S.R. (2011). A randomised, controlled trial of immersive virtual reality analgesia during physical therapy for paediatric burn injuries. *Burns*, 37 (1), 61–68.

Sherman, L.E. & Greenfield, P.M. (2013). Forging friendship, soliciting support: A mixed-method examination of message boards for pregnant teens and teen mothers. *Computers in Human Behaviour*, 29, 75–85.

Sillence, E. (2013). Giving and receiving peer advice in an online breast cancer support group. *Cyberpsychology, Behaviour and Social Networking*, 16 (6), 480–485.

Siva, N. (2010). Tackling the booming trade in counterfeit drugs. *The Lancet*, 376 (9754), 1725–1726.

Smith, P.K., Fox, A.T., Davies, P., & Hamidi-Manesh, L. (2006). Cyberchondriacs. *International Journal of Adolescent Medicine and Health*, 18 (2), 209–213.

Straker, L.M., Abbott, R.A., & Smith, A.J. (2013). To remove or to replace traditional electronic games? A crossover randomised controlled trial on the impact of removing or replacing home access to electronic games on physical activity and sedentary behaviour in children aged 10–12 years. *BMJ Open*, 3 (6), doi: 10.1136/bmjopen-2013-002629.

Suler, J. (2004). The online disinhibition effect. *Cyberpsychology & Behaviour*, 7 (3), 321–326.

Taiwan teen dies after gaming for 40 hours (2012, August 2). *The Australian*. Retrieved from http://www.theaustralian.com.au/news/latest-news/taiwan-teen-dies-after-gaming-for-40-hours/story-fn3dxix6-1226428437223?nk=6ca5aa7bd2a9deee8d431bdc67b894a2 (accessed 4th September, 2014).

Tanis. M. (2007). Online social support groups. In Joinson, A., McKenna, K., Postmes, T., & Reips, U. (Eds), *The Oxford Handbook of Internet Psychology* (pp. 139–153). Oxford: Oxford University Press.

Tustin, N. (2010). The role of patient satisfaction in online health information seeking. *Journal of Health Communication: International Perspectives*, 15 (1), 3–17.

Walther, J.B. (1996). Computer-mediated communication: Impersonal, interpersonal and hyperpersonal interaction. *Communication Research*, 23, 3–43.

Walther, J.B. (2007). Selective self-presentation in computer-mediated communication: Hyperpersonal dimensions of technology, language and cognition. *Computers in Human Behaviour*, 23, 2538–2557.

Wang, L., Wang, J., Wang, M., Li, Y., Liang, Y., & Xu, D. (2012). Using Internet search engines to obtain medical information: A comparative study. *Journal of Medical Internet Research*, 14 (3), e74.

Welbourne, J.L., Blanchard, A.L., & Wadsworth, M.B. (2013). Motivations in virtual health communities and their relationship to community, connectedness and stress. *Computers in Human Behaviour*, 29, 129–139.

White, R.W. & Horvitz, E. (2009). Cyberchondria. *ACM Transactions on Information Systems*, 27 (4), Article 23. Retrieved from http://research.

microsoft.com/en-us/um/people/ryenw/papers/whitetois2009.pdf (accessed 4th September, 2014).

Wiederhold, B.K., Riva, G., & Wiederhold, M.D. (2014). How can virtual reality interventions help reduce prescription opioid drug misuse? *Cyberpsychology, Behaviour and Social Networking*, 17 (6), 331–332.

Wills, T.A. & Ainette, M.G. (2012). Social networks and social support. In Baum, A., Revenson, T.A.,

& Singer, J. (Eds), *Handbook of Health Psychology*, 2nd edn (pp. 465–492). New York: Psychology Press.

Yeshua-Katz, D. & Martins, N. (2013). Communicating stigma: The pro-ana paradox. *Health Communication*, 28 (5), 499–508.

Yuen, E.K., Goetter, E.M., Herbert, J.D., & Forman, E.M. (2012). Challenges and opportunities in Internet-mediated telemental health. *Professional Psychology: Research and Practice*, 43 (1), 1–8.

Further reading

This paper examines how perceptions of unmet needs by patients may influence their use of online medical information seeking and online support groups such as discussion forums:

Lee, S.Y. & Hawkins, R. (2010). Why do patients seek an alternative channel? The effects of unmet needs on patients' health-related Internet use. *Journal of Health Communication: International Perspectives*, 15 (2), 152–166.

Sillence's article examines how individuals ask for and give advice in an online breast cancer support forum. In particular, it examines the disclosure of personal experience and the searching for other individuals in the same medical position:

Sillence, E. (2013). Giving and receiving peer advice in an online breast cancer support group. *Cyberpsychology, Behaviour and Social Networking*, 16 (6), 480–485.

This chapter examines the different types of overload that can be associated with emails, and how each might be addressed. It classifies email overload into information overload, work overload and social overload:

Rennecker, J. & Derks, D. (2013). Email overload: Fine tuning the research lens. In Derks, D. & Bakker, A., (Eds), *The Psychology of Digital Media at Work* (pp. 14–38). Hove: Psychology Press.

This article describes a content analysis of pro-anorexia and pro-bulimia websites, describing the strategies employed to promote eating-disordered behaviours:

Borzekowski, D.L.G., Schenk, S., Wilson, J.L., & Peebles, R. (2010). e-Ana and e-Mia: A content analysis of pro-eating disorder web sites. *American Journal of Public Health*, 100 (8), 1526–1534.

Parisod et al. conduct an extensive review of research examining children's health and digital games, determining the characteristics of games that can help to increase physical activity in children and the extent of the evidence supporting these claims:

Parisod, H., Pakarinen, A., Kuhanen, L., Aromaa, M., Leppänen, V., Liukkonen, T.N., Smed, J., & Salanterä, S. (2014). Promoting children's health with digital games: A review of reviews. *Games for Health Journal*, 3 (3), 145–156.

This article examines the use of mobile interventions in health care, determining that current theories of health behaviour may be inadequate in aiding the development of such interventions due to the increased interactivity that these interventions allow:

Riley, W.T., Rivera, D.E., Atienza, A.A., Nilsen, W., Allison, S.M., & Mermelstein, R. (2011). Health behaviour models in the age of mobile interventions: Are our theories up to the task? *Translational Behavioural Medicine*, 1 (1), 53–71.

Discussion questions

1. Should patients avoid searching for medical information about their condition online, or is this ultimately beneficial to their treatment and psychological well-being?

2. Support seeking online may be beneficial to an individual's health, but care must be taken to protect privacy and avoid over-disclosure of personal information. What precautions should users of online support forums take to protect themselves from online threats?

3. Should workers be required to access and respond to emails outside of their core working hours? What types of restrictions and/or guidelines should be put in place to ensure an appropriate work-life balance?

4. Are active video games the solution to gaming and technology related health problems? What are the best methods to evaluate their contribution to child, adolescent, and adult well-being, and can we be confident that their benefits will be long-term?

5. Does the potential of virtual reality in pain distraction and the treatment of addictions and obesity warrant the research conducted in the area?

The Psychology of Online Addictive Behaviour

MARK D. GRIFFITHS

 Learning objectives

By the end of this chapter, you should be able to:

- Debate the existence of online addictive behaviours.
- Outline criteria that need to be fulfilled to diagnose an addiction and consider whether these apply to online behaviours.
- Describe different subtypes of online addictive behaviours.
- Provide an overview of recent research into online gaming behaviours and social networking behaviours.

11.1 Introduction

The popularity of technology as a leisure phenomenon has become ever-increasing in the lives of both adults and adolescents. Coupled with this, there have been a growing number of reports in the media about excessive use of technology (e.g., video games, mobile phones, the Internet, etc.). Although the concept of technological addictions appears to have its supporters in the media, there is much scepticism amongst the academic community—not least among those working in the field of addiction research. It is not hard to understand such attitudes. For many, the concept of technological addictions seems far-fetched, particularly if their concepts and definitions of addiction involve the taking of psychoactive drugs. Despite the predominance of drug-based definitions of addiction, there is now a growing movement that views a number of behaviours as potentially addictive including many behaviours that do not involve the ingestion of a psychoactive drug (e.g., gambling, computer game playing, exercise, sex, Internet use) (Griffiths, 2005). Such diversity has led to new all-encompassing definitions of what constitutes addictive behaviour.

11.2 Defining addiction: Technological addiction as a behavioural addiction

I have consistently argued that behaviours such as problematic gambling and problematic video game playing are no different from (say) alcoholism or heroin addiction in terms of the core components of addiction (Griffiths, 2005). If it can be shown that a behaviour such as excessive gambling can be a *bona fide* addiction then there is a precedent that any behaviour that can provide continuous rewards in the absence of a psychoactive substance can be potentially addictive (i.e., a behavioural as opposed to a chemical addiction). Such a precedent 'opens the floodgates' for other excessive behaviours to be theoretically considered as potential addictions (such as Internet and videogame use) (Griffiths, 2005).

For many years, it has been alleged that pathologies exist among excessive Internet users and video game players. For instance, as early as 1983, Soper and Miller claimed 'video game addiction' was like any other addiction and consisted of a compulsive behavioural involvement, a lack of interest in other activities, association mainly with other addicts, and physical and mental symptoms when attempting to stop the behaviour (e.g., the shakes). Griffiths (1996a) and Young (1998) argued a similar case for excessive Internet users. Such addictions have been termed 'technological addictions' (Griffiths, 1995, 1996a) and have been operationally defined as non-chemical (behavioural) addictions that involve excessive and problematic human-machine interaction. Technological addictions can either be passive (e.g., television), or active (e.g., video games) and usually contain inducing and reinforcing features that may contribute to the promotion of addictive tendencies (Griffiths, 1995). Technological addictions can thus be viewed as a subset of behavioural addictions (Marks, 1990) and feature core components of addiction first outlined by Brown (1993) and modified by Griffiths (1996b, 2005), that is, salience, mood modification, tolerance, withdrawal, conflict, and relapse.

Research into the area of technological and online addictions is underpinned by three fundamental questions:

1. What is addiction?
2. Do technological and online addictions actually exist?
3. If technological and online addictions exist, what are people actually addicted to?

The first question continues to be a much-debated question both amongst psychologists within the field of addiction research as well as those working in other disciplines. For many years, I have operationally defined addictive behaviour as any behaviour that features all the core components of addiction. It is my contention that any behaviour (e.g., video game playing, social networking, mobile phone use) that fulfils these six criteria is therefore operationally defined as an addiction. In the case of a technological addiction it would be:

- **Salience**: This occurs when some kind of technology use (e.g., video game playing, Internet use, mobile phone use) becomes the most important activity in the person's life and dominates their thinking (preoccupations and cognitive distortions), feelings (cravings) and behaviour (deterioration of socialized behaviour). For instance, even if the person is not actually playing on a video game they will be thinking about the next time that they will be.

- **Mood modification**: This refers to the subjective experiences that people report as a consequence of engaging in their chosen technological behaviour and can be seen as a coping strategy (i.e., they experience an arousing 'buzz' or a 'high' or paradoxically tranquilizing feel of 'escape' or 'numbing').

- **Tolerance**: This is the process whereby increasing amounts of time engaged in a technological behaviour is required to achieve the former mood modifiying effects. This basically means that for someone engaged in Internet use or video game playing, they gradually build up the amount of time they spend engaged in the behaviour.

- **Withdrawal symptoms**: These are the unpleasant feeling states and/or physical effects that occur when the technological behaviour is discontinued or suddenly reduced (e.g., the shakes, moodiness, irritability).

- *Conflict*: This refers to the conflicts between the technology user and those around them (interpersonal conflict), conflicts with other activities (job, schoolwork, social life, hobbies, and interests), or from within the individual themselves (intrapsychic conflict and/or subjective feelings of loss of control), which are concerned with spending too much time engaged in activities such as Internet use or video game play.

- *Relapse*: This is the tendency for repeated reversions to earlier patterns of technology use to recur and for even the most extreme patterns typical of the height of excessive technology use to be quickly restored after periods of abstinence or control.

Having operationally defined addiction, it is my belief that technological and online addictions exist but that it affects only a small minority of users. There appear to be many people who use technology excessively but are not addicted as measured by these (or any other) criteria (Griffiths, 2010a). The third question is perhaps the most interesting and the most important when it comes to researching in this field. What are people actually addicted to when they use the Internet, mobile phone, or play video games excessively? Is it the interactive medium of playing? Aspects of its specific style (e.g., an anonymous and disinhibiting activity)? The specific types of games (aggressive games, strategy games, etc.)? This has led to much debate amongst those of us working in this field. Research being carried out into Internet addiction may lead to insights about other technological addictions such as video game addiction and mobile phone addiction (and vice versa). For instance, Young (1999) has claimed that Internet addiction is a broad term covering a wide variety of behaviours and impulse control problems. This is categorized by five specific subtypes:

1. Cybersexual addiction: Compulsive use of adult websites for cybersex and cyberporn.

2. Cyber-relationship addiction: over-involvement in online relationships.

3. Net compulsions: Obsessive online gambling, shopping, or day-trading.

4. Information overload: Compulsive web surfing or database searches.

5. Computer addiction: Obsessive computer game playing (e.g., Doom, Myst, Solitaire, etc.).

In reply to Young, I have argued that many of these excessive Internet users are not 'Internet addicts' but just use the Internet excessively as a medium to fuel other addictions (Griffiths, 1999, 2000a). Put very simply, a gambling addict or a video game addict who engages in their chosen behaviour online is not addicted to the Internet. The Internet is just the place where they engage in the behaviour. However, in contrast to this, there are case study reports of individuals who appear to be addicted to the Internet itself (Griffiths, 1996a, 1998, 2000b, Young, 1998). These are usually people (and very often adolescents in their late teenage years) who use Internet chat rooms or play fantasy role playing games—activities that they would not engage in except on the Internet itself. These individuals to some extent are engaged in text-based virtual realities and take on other social personae and social identities as a way of making users feel good about themselves (Griffiths, 2000b). In these cases, the Internet may provide an alternative reality to the user and allow them feelings of immersion and anonymity that may lead to an altered state of consciousness. This in itself may be highly psychologically and/or physiologically rewarding. Obviously for those playing online computer games (theoretically a combination of both Internet use and video game play), these speculations may provide insights into the potentially addictive nature of video games for those playing in this medium.

To date, there have been many types of excessive and/or problematic activity that have been conceptualized as a technological and/or online addiction. This has included television addiction (McIlwraith, Jacobvitz, Kubey, & Alexander, 1991, Sussman & Moran, 2013), mobile phone addiction (Choliz, 2010, Billieux, 2012, Carbonell et al., 2012), video game addiction (Lemmens, Valkenburg, & Peter, 2009, Griffiths, Kuss, & King, 2012), Internet addiction (van den Eijnden, Spijkerman, Vermulst, van Rooij, & Engels, 2010, Kuss, Griffiths, & Binder, 2013), social networking addiction (Andraessen, Tosheim, BrunBerg, & Pallesen, 2012, Turel & Serenko, 2012), online auction addiction (Turel, Serenko, & Giles, 2011), online sex addiction (Cooper, Delmonico, Griffin-Shelley, & Mathy, 2004, Griffiths, 2012a), and online gambling addiction (Griffiths, 2010b, Wardle, Moody, Griffiths, Orford, & Volberg, 2011). Due to space restraints, a review of all of these different types of technological addiction is beyond the scope of this chapter. Therefore, the rest of this chapter will briefly overview the empirical research on two online addictions—online gaming addiction and social networking addiction.

11.3 A brief overview of online gaming addiction

Following the release of the first commercial video games in the early 1970s, it took until the 1980s for the first reports of video game addiction to appear in the psychological and psychiatric literature (Nilles, 1982, Soper & Miller, 1983, Egli & Meyers, 1984, Kuczmierczyk, Walley, & Calhoun, 1987, Shotton, 1989, Keepers, 1990). However, these studies were somewhat observational, anecdotal, and/or case studies, primarily based on samples of teenage males, mostly based on a particular type of video game using a particular medium (i.e., 'pay-to-play' arcade video games). The 1990s saw a small but significant increase of research into video game addiction with all of these studies being carried out in the UK and on adolescents typically surveying children in school settings (Brown & Robertson, 1993, Fisher, 1994, Griffiths & Hunt, 1995, 1998, Phillips, Rolls, Rouse, & Griffiths, 1995, Griffiths, 1997). In contrast to the early 1980s studies, these studies mainly examined non-arcade video game playing (i.e., home console games, handheld games, PC gaming). However, all of these studies were self-report surveys, relatively small scale and the main problem was that all of them assessed video game addiction using adapted versions of the DSM-III-R or DSM-IV criteria for pathological gambling. Although there are clearly many similarities between gambling and video gaming, they are different behaviours and specific video game screening instruments should have been developed. Based on further analysis of the adapted DSM criteria used, these studies were later criticized as being more likely to be assessing video game preoccupation rather than video game addiction (Charlton, 2002).

The 2000s saw a substantial growth in the number of studies on video game addiction particularly as gaming expanded into the new online medium where games could be played as part of a gaming community (i.e., massively multiplayer online role playing games [**MMORPG**s] such as *World of Warcraft* and *Everquest*). According to a number of systemic reviews (Kuss & Griffiths, 2012, Sublette & Mullan, 2012) approximately 60 studies were published on gaming addiction between 2000 and 2010 and a vast majority of these examined MMORPG addiction and was not limited to the study of adolescent males. Furthermore, many of these studies collected their data online and a significant minority of studies examined various other aspects of video game addiction using non-self-report methodologies. These include studies using polysomnographic measures and visual and verbal memory tests (Dworak, Schierl, Bruns, & Struder, 2007), medical examinations including the patient's history, and physical, radiologic, intraoperative, and pathologic findings (Cultrara & Har-El, 2002), functional Magnetic Resonance Imaging (Hoeft, Watson, Kesler, Bettinger, & Reiss, 2008, Ko, et al., 2009, Han, Hwang, & Renshaw, 2010), and electroencephalography (Thalemann, Wölfling, & Grüsser, 2007).

When looking at estimated prevalence rates of problematic video gaming, they range from 1.7% (Rehbein, Kleimann, & Mossle, 2010), to 8–10% among general samples (Gentile, et al., 2011). Prevalence rates among video game players were in some cases much higher (Grüsser, Thalemann, & Griffiths, 2007, Hussain, Griffiths, & Baguley, 2012). These studies also indicate that, in general, males are significantly more likely than females to report problems relating to their gaming. According to King and colleagues (2012, 2013), the differences in methods of assessing game-based problems may partly account for differences in prevalence rates. Furthermore, many studies fail to assess prior problems (i.e., lifetime prevalence). King et al. (2012, 2013) also noted that some studies do not consider subclinical cases (i.e., meeting some but not all criteria for problematic use), and the presence of co-morbid psychopathology is not routinely assessed.

From a substantive perspective, there are some generalizations that can be made with regard to the demographic characteristics of gamers and problem gamers. The literature, to date, suggests that adolescent males and young male adults appear to be at greater risk of experiencing problematic video game play. However, the course and severity of these problems is not well known and the finding that this group is more at risk may be a consequence of sampling bias as well as the fact that this group plays video games more frequently than other socio-demographic groups (Griffiths et al. 2012). It has also been suggested that university students may be especially vulnerable to developing problematic video gaming. Reasons for this include their flexible tuition and study hours, ready access to high-speed broadband on a 24/7 basis, and multiple stressors associated with adjusting to new social obligations and/or living out-of-home for the first time (King, Delfabbro, & Griffiths, 2012).

Irrespective of whether problematic video game play can be classed as an addiction, there is now a relatively large number of studies all indicating that excessive video game play can lead to a wide variety of negative psychosocial consequences for a minority of affected individuals. These were summarized by Griffiths et al. (2012) and include sacrificing work, education, hobbies, socializing, time with partner/family, and sleep, increased stress, an absence of real life relationships, lower psychosocial well-being and loneliness, poorer social skills, decreased academic achievement, increased inattention, aggressive/oppositional behaviour and hostility, maladaptive coping, decreases in verbal memory performance, maladaptive cognitions, and suicidal ideation. This list of potential psychosocial consequences clearly indicates that excessive gaming is an issue irrespective of whether it is an addiction.

A number of studies have examined the role of different personality factors, comorbidity factors, and biological factors, and their association with gaming addiction. In relation to personality traits, gaming addiction has been shown to have association with neuroticism (Peters & Malesky, 2008, Mehroof & Griffiths, 2010), aggression and hostility (Chiu, Lee, & Huang, 2004, Kim, Namkoong, Ku, & Kim, 2008, Caplan, Williams, & Yee, 2009, Mehroof & Griffiths, 2010), avoidant and schizoid interpersonal tendencies (Allison, von Wahlde, Shockley, & Gabbard, 2006), loneliness and introversion (Caplan et al., 2009), social inhibition (Porter, Starcevic, Berle, & Fenech, 2010), boredom inclination (Chiu et al., 2004), sensation-seeking (Chiu et al., 2004, Mehroof & Griffiths, 2010), diminished agreeableness (Peters & Malesky, 2008), diminished self-control and narcissistic personality traits (Kim et al., 2008), low self-esteem (Ko, Yen, Chen, & Yen, 2005), state and trait anxiety (Mehroof & Griffiths, 2010), and low emotional intelligence (Parker, Taylor, Eastabrook, Schell, & Wood, 2008). It is hard to assess the etiological significance of these associations with gaming addiction as they may not be unique to the disorder. Further research is therefore needed. Research has also shown gaming addiction to be associated with a variety of comorbid disorders. This includes attention deficit hyperactivity disorder (Allison et al., 2006, Chan & Rabinowitz, 2006, Batthyány, Müller, Benker, & Wölfling, 2009, Han et al., 2009, Haghbin, Shaterian, Hosseinzadeh, & Griffiths, 2013), symptoms of generalized anxiety disorder, panic disorder, depression, social phobia (Allison et al., 2006), school phobia (Batthyány et al., 2009), and various psychosomatic symptoms (Batthyány et al., 2009).

Through use of fMRI, biological research has shown that gaming addicts show similar neural processes and increased activity in brain areas associated with substance-related addictions and other behavioural addictions, such as pathological gambling (significant activation in the left occipital lobe, parahippocampal gyrus, dorsolateral prefrontal cortex, nucleus accumbens, right orbitofrontal cortex, bilateral anterior cingulate, medial frontal cortex, and the caudate nucleus (Hoeft et al., 2008, Ko et al., 2009, Han et al. 2010). It has also been reported that gaming addicts (like substance addicts) have a higher prevalence of two specific polymorphisms of the dopaminergic system (i.e., Taq1A1 allele of the dopamine D2 receptor and the Val158Met in the catecholamine-o-methyltransferase) (Han et al., 2007), which suggests that among some players there might be some genetic predisposition to develop video game addiction.

As a consequence of this upsurge in research over the last decade, the Substance Use Disorder Work Group (**SUDWG**) recommendeded that the DSM-5 (American Psychiatric Association, 2013) include a sub-type of 'Internet gaming disorder' (**IGD**) in Section 3 ('Emerging Measures and Models'). According to Petry and O'Brien (2013), IGD will not be included as a separate mental disorder in the DSM until the (1) defining features of IGD have been identified, (2) reliability and validity of specific IGD criteria have been obtained cross-culturally, (3) prevalence rates have been determined in representative epidemiological samples across the world, and (4) etiology and associated biological features have been evaluated.

One of the key reasons that IGD was not included in the main text of the DSM-5 was that the SUDWG concluded that no standard diagnostic criteria were used to assess gaming addiction across these many studies. A recent review of instruments assessing problematic, pathological and/or addictive gaming by King, Haagsma, Delfabbro, Gradisar, and Griffiths (2013) reported that 18 different screening instruments had been developed, and that these had been used in 63 quantitative studies comprising 58,415 participants. This comprehensive review identified both strengths and weaknesses of these instruments. The main strengths of the instrumentation included the: (1) brevity and ease of scoring, (2) excellent psychometric properties such as convergent validity and internal consistency, and (3) robust data that will aid the development of standardized norms for adolescent populations. However, the main weaknesses identified in the instrumentation included: (1) core addiction indicators being inconsistent across studies, (2) a general lack of any temporal dimension, (3) inconsistent cut-off scores relating to clinical status, (4) poor and/or inadequate inter-rater reliability and predictive validity, and (5) inconsistent and/or dimensionality. It has also been noted by a number of authors that the criteria for IGD assessment tools are theoretically based on a variety of different potentially problematic activities including substance use disorders, pathological gambling, and/or other behavioural addiction criteria. There are also issues surrounding the settings in which diagnostic screens are used as those used in clinical practice settings may require a different emphasis than those used in epidemiological, experimental, and neurobiological research settings.

The fact that IGD was included in Section 3 of the DSM-5 appears to have been well received by researchers and clinicians in the gaming addiction field (and by those individuals that have sought treatment for such disorders and had their experiences psychiatrically validated and feel less stigmatized). However, for IGD to be included in the section on 'Substance-Related and Addictive Disorders' along with 'Gambling Disorder', the gaming addiction field must unite and start using the same assessment measures so that comparisons can be made across different demographic groups and different cultures. For epidemiological purposes, Koronczai and colleagues (2011) asserted that the most appropriate measures in assessing problematic online use (including Internet gaming) should meet six requirements. Such an instrument should have: (1) brevity (to make surveys as short as possible and help overcome question fatigue), (2) comprehensiveness (to examine all core aspects of IGD), (3) reliability and validity across age groups (e.g., adolescents vs. adults), (4) reliability and validity across data collection methods (e.g., online, face-to-face interview, paper-and-pencil), (5) cross-cultural reliability and validity, and (6) clinical validation. It was also noted that an ideal assessment instrument should serve as the basis for defining adequate cut-off scores in terms of both specificity and sensitivity. To fulfill all these requirements, future research should adjust the currently used assessment tools to the newly accepted DSM-5 criteria and take much more efforts to reach and study clinical samples, which is an unequivocal shortcoming of Internet gaming research.

11.4 A brief overview of social networking addiction

Social Networking Sites (**SNS**s) are virtual communities where users can create individual public profiles, interact with real-life friends, and meet other people based on shared interests. SNS usage patterns from both consumer research and empirical research indicate that overall, regular SNS use has increased substantially over the last few years (Kuss & Griffiths, 2011). SNSs are predominantly used for social purposes, mostly related to the maintenance of established offline networks, relative to individual ones (Kuss & Griffiths, 2011). However, recent evidence suggests that individuals may feel compelled to maintain their online social networks in a way that may, in some circumstances, lead to using SNSs excessively.

Based on the relatively sparse literature to date, it would appear that in some individuals, SNS addiction incorporates the experience of the 'classic' addiction symptoms, namely mood modification (i.e., engagement in SNSs leads to a favourable change in emotional states), salience (i.e., behavioural, cognitive, and emotional preoccupation with the SNS usage), tolerance (i.e., ever increasing use of SNSs over time), withdrawal symptoms (i.e., experiencing unpleasant physical and emotional symptoms when SNS use is restricted or stopped), conflict (i.e., interpersonal and intrapsychic problems ensue because of SNS usage), and relapse (i.e., addicts quickly revert back to their excessive SNS usage after an abstinence period).

It is generally accepted that a combination of biological, psychological, and social factors contributes to the etiology of addictions that may also hold true for SNS addiction (Griffiths, Kuss, & Demetrovics, 2014). From this it follows that SNS addiction shares a common underlying etiological framework with other substance-related and behavioural addictions. However, due to the fact that the engagement in SNSs is different in terms of the actual expression of (Internet) addiction (i.e., pathological use of SNSs rather than other Internet applications), the phenomenon may be worthy of individual consideration, particularly when considering the potentially detrimental effects of both substance-related and behavioural addictions on individuals who experience a variety of negative consequences because of their addiction.

According to a recent review (Griffiths et al., 2014), the 20 or so empirical studies examining SNS addiction fall into one of four types:

1. Self-perception studies of social networking addiction.
2. Studies of social networking addiction utilizing a social networking addiction scale.
3. Studies examining the relationship between social networking and other online addictions.
4. Studies examining social networking addiction and interpersonal relationships.

The review noted that all the studies suffered from a variety of methodological limitations. Many of the studies attempted to assess SNS addiction, but mere assessment of addiction tendencies does not suffice to demarcate real pathology. Most of the study samples were generally small, specific, self-selected, convenient, and skewed with regards to young adults and female gender (Cabral, 2011, Elphinston & Noller, 2011, Sofiah, Zobidah, Bolong, & Osman, 2011, Alabi, 2012, Andraessen et al., 2012, Cam & Isbulan, 2012, Olowu & Seri, 2012, Turel & Serenko, 2012, Koc & Gulyagci, 2013). This may have led to the very high addiction prevalence rates (up to 34%) reported in some studies as individuals from these socio-demographic groups are likely to be more heavy social networking users. Consequently, empirical studies need to ensure that they are assessing addiction rather than excessive use and/or preoccupation.

I recently noted that for many researchers, Facebook addiction has become almost synonymous with social networking addiction (Griffiths, 2012b). However, Facebook is just one of many websites where social networking can take place. Most of the scales that have been developed have specifically examined excessive Facebook use such as the Bergen Facebook Addiction Scale (Andraessen et al., 2012), the Facebook Addiction Scale (Cam & Isbulan, 2012), and the Facebook Intrusion Questionnaire (Elphinston & Noller, 2011), that is, addiction to one particular commercial company's service (i.e., Facebook) rather than the whole activity itself (i.e., social networking). The real issue here concerns what people are actually addicted to and what the new Facebook addiction tools are measuring.

For instance, Facebook users can play games like *Farmville* (Griffiths, 2010c), can gamble on games like poker (Griffiths & Parke, 2010), can watch videos and films, and can engage in activities such as swapping photos or constantly updating their profile and/or messaging friends on the minutiae of their life (Kuss & Griffiths, 2011, Griffiths, 2012b). Therefore, 'Facebook addiction' is not synonymous with 'social networking addiction'—they are two fundamentally different things as Facebook has become a specific website where many different online activities can take place—and may serve different purposes to various users. What this suggests is that the field needs a psychometrically validated scale that specifically assesses 'social networking addiction' rather than Facebook use. In the aforementioned scales, social networking as an activity is not mentioned, therefore, the scale does not differentiate between someone potentially addicted to *Farmville* or someone potentially addicted to constantly messaging Facebook friends.

Whether social networking addiction exists is debatable depending upon the definition of addiction used, but there is clearly emerging evidence that a minority of social network users experience addiction-like symptoms as a consequence of their excessive use (Griffiths, et al., 2014). Studies endorsing only a few potential addiction criteria are not sufficient for establishing clinically significant addiction status. Similarly, significant impairment and negative consequences that discriminate addiction from mere abuse have (to date) generally not been assessed in published studies. Thus, future studies have great potential in addressing the emergent phenomenon of SNS addiction by means of applying better methodological designs, including more representative samples, and using more reliable and valid addiction scales so that current gaps in empirical knowledge can be filled.

11.5 Chapter summary

This chapter has demonstrated that research into technological and online addiction is becoming an increasingly studied phenomenon. Clearly more research is needed on whether activities such as video game addiction and Internet addictions such as social networking addiction are distinct clinical entities. From the research, it is evident that excessive technology use appears to be at least potentially addictive. With respect to video games, there is also a need for a general taxonomy of video games as it could be the case that particular types of games are more addictive than others. Another major problem is that video games can be played in lots of different ways including handheld consoles, on a personal computer, home video game consoles, on arcade machines, on the Internet, and on other portable devices (e.g., mobile phones, iPods). It may be the case that some of these media for playing games (such as in an arcade or on the Internet) may be more addictive because of other factors salient to that medium (e.g., disinhibition on the Internet). Therefore, future research needs to distinguish between excessive play in different media.

There is also the question of developmental effects, that is, does video game playing or social networking have the same effect regardless of age? It could well be the case that playing video games and social networking have a more pronounced addictive effect in young children but less of an effect (if any) once they have reached their adult years. There is also the social context of playing, that is, does playing in groups or individually, with or against each other affect potential addictiveness of games in any way. These all need further empirical investigation.

It does appear that excessive technology use can have potentially damaging effects upon a minority of individuals who display compulsive and addictive behaviour, and who will do anything possible to 'feed their addiction'. Using these individuals in research would help identify the roots and causes of addictive playing and the impact of such behaviour on family and school life. It would be clinically useful to illustrate problem cases even following them longitudinally and recording developmental features of technological addictions. This would help determine the variables that are salient in the acquisition, development, and mainten- ance of such behaviours.

There is no doubt that technology usage among the general population will continue to increase over the next few years and that if social pathologies (including video game addic- tion and social networking addiction) do exist then this is certainly an area for development that should be of interest and concern to all those involved in the addiction research field. Until there is an established body of literature on the psychological, sociological, and physio- logical effects of technological addiction, directions for education, prevention, intervention, and treatment will remain limited in scope.

There is clearly a need to distinguish between addictions *to* the Internet and addictions *on* the Internet. As noted in the introduction, gambling addicts who choose to engage in online gambling, as well as computer game addicts who play online are not Internet addicts—the Internet is just the place where they conduct their chosen (addictive) behaviour. These people display addictions *on* the Internet. However, there is also the observation that some behav- iours engaged on the Internet (e.g., cybersex, cyberstalking, etc.) may be behaviours that the person would only carry out on the Internet because the medium is anonymous, non face- to-face, and disinhibiting (Griffiths, 2000c, 2001).

In contrast, it is also acknowledged that there are some case studies that seem to report an addiction to the Internet itself (e.g., Young, 1996, Griffiths, 2000b). Most of these individuals use functions of the Internet that are not available in any other medium, such as chat rooms or various role playing games. These are people addicted *to* the Internet. However, despite these differences, there seem to be some common findings, most notably reports of the negative consequences of excessive technology use (neglect of work and social life, relationship break- downs, loss of control, etc.), which are comparable to those experienced with other, more established addictions. Overall, I would strongly argue that based on the empirical research to date—and based on my own operational definition of addiction—technological addictions do exist. However, how prevalent they are remains highly debatable.

 ## References

Alabi, O.F. (2012). A survey of Facebook addiction level among selected Nigerian university undergraduates. *New Media and Mass Communication*, 10, 70–80.

Allison, S.E., von Wahlde, L., Shockley, T., & Gabbard, G.O. (2006). The development of the self in the era of the Internet and role-playing fantasy games. *American Journal of Psychiatry*, 163, 381–385.

American Psychiatric Association (2013). *Diagnostic and Statistical Manual of Mental Disorders—Text Revision*, 5th Edn. Washington, D.C.: American Psychiatric Association.

Andraessen, C.S., Tosheim, T., BrunBerg, G.S., & Pallesen, S. (2012) Development of a Facebook Addiction Scale. *Psychological Reports*, 110, 501–517.

Batthyány, D., Müller, K.W., Benker, F., & Wölfling, K. (2009). Computer game playing: clinical characteristics of dependence and abuse among adolescents. *Wiener Klinsche Wochenschrift*, 121, 502–509.

Billieux, J. (2012). Problematic use of the mobile phone: a literature review and a pathways model. *Current Psychiatry Reviews*, 8, 299–307.

Brown, R.I.F. (1993). Some contributions of the study of gambling to the study of other addictions. In Eadington, W.R. & Cornelius, J.A. (Eds), *Gambling Behavior and Problem Gambling* (pp. 241–272). Reno: University of Nevada Press.

Brown, R.I.F. & Robertson, S. (1993). Home computer and video game addictions in relation to adolescent gambling: Conceptual and developmental aspects. In Eadington, W.R. & Cornelius, J.A. (Eds), *Gambling Behavior and Problem Gambling* (pp. 451–471). Reno: University of Nevada Press.

Cabral, J. (2011). Is Generation Y Addicted to social media? *Elon Journal of Undergraduate Research in Communications*, 2 (1), 5–13.

Cam, E. & Isbulan, O. (2012). A new addiction for teacher candidates: Social networks. *Turkish Online Journal of Educational Technology*, 11 (3), 14–19.

Caplan, S.E., Williams, D., & Yee, N. (2009). Problematic internet use and psychosocial well-being among MMO players. *Computers in Human Behavior*, 25, 1312–1319.

Carbonell, X., Chamarro, A., Beranuy, M., Griffiths, M.D., Obert, U., Cladellas, R., & Talarn, A. (2012). Problematic Internet and cell phone use in Spanish teenagers and young students. *Anales de Psicologia*, 28, 789–796.

Chan, P.A. & Rabinowitz, T. (2006). A cross-sectional analysis of video games and attention deficit hyperactivity disorder symptoms in adolescents. *Annals of General Psychiatry*, 5 (1), 16–26.

Charlton, J.P. (2002). A factor analytic investigation of computer 'addiction' and engagement. *British Journal of Psychology*, 93, 329–344.

Chiu, S.I., Lee, J.Z., & Huang, D.H. (2004). Video game addiction in children and teenagers in Taiwan. *CyberPsychology and Behavior*, 7, 571–581.

Choliz, M. (2010). Mobile phone addiction: A point of issue. *Addiction*, 105, 373–374.

Cooper, A., Delmonico, D.L., Griffin-Shelley, E., & Mathy, R.M. (2004). Online sexual activity: An examination of potentially problematic behaviors. *Sexual Addiction & Compulsivity*, 11, 129–143.

Cultrara, A. & Har-El, G. (2002). Hyperactivity-induced suprahyoid muscular hypertrophy secondary to excessive video game play: a case report. *Journal of Oral and Maxillofacial Surgery*, 60, 326–327.

Dworak, M., Schierl, T., Bruns, T., & Struder, H.K. (2007). Impact of singular excessive computer game and television exposure on sleep patterns and memory performance of school-aged children. *Pediatrics*, 120, 978–985.

Egli, E.A. & Meyers, L.S. (1984). The role of video game playing in adolescent life: Is there a reason to be concerned? *Bulletin of the Psychonomic Society*, 22, 309–312.

Elphinston, R.A. & Noller, P. (2011). Time to face it! Facebook intrusion and the implications for romantic jealousy and relationship satisfaction. *Cyberpsychology, Behavior, and Social Networking*, 14, 631–635.

Fisher, S.E. (1994). Identifying video game addiction in children and adolescents. *Addictive Behaviors*, 19, 545–553.

Gentile, D.A., Choo, H., Liau, A., Sim, T., Li, D., Fung, D., & Khoo, A. (2011). Pathological video game use among youths: A two-year longitudinal study. *Pediatrics*, 127, 319–329.

Griffiths, M.D. (1995). Technological addictions. *Clinical Psychology Forum*, 76, 14–19.

Griffiths, M.D. (1996a). Internet 'addiction': An issue for clinical psychology? *Clinical Psychology Forum*, 97, 32–36.

Griffiths, M.D. (1996b). Behavioural addictions: An issue for everybody? *Journal of Workplace Learning*, 8 (3), 19–25.

Griffiths, M.D. (1997). Computer game playing in early adolescence. *Youth and Society*, 29, 223–237.

Griffiths, M.D. (1998). Internet addiction: Does it really exist? In Gackenbach, J. (Ed.), *Psychology and the Internet: Intrapersonal, Interpersonal and Transpersonal Applications* (pp. 61–75). New York: Academic Press.

Griffiths, M.D. (1999). Internet addiction: Internet fuels other addictions. *Student British Medical Journal*, 7, 428–429.

Griffiths, M.D. (2000a). Internet addiction—Time to be taken seriously? *Addiction Research*, 8, 413–418.

Griffiths, M.D. (2000b). Does internet and computer 'addiction' exist? Some case study evidence. *CyberPsychology and Behavior*, 3, 211–18.

Griffiths, M.D. (2000c). Excessive Internet use: Implications for sexual behavior. *CyberPsychology and Behavior*, 3, 537–552.

Griffiths, M.D. (2001). Sex on the Internet: Observations and implications for sex addiction. *Journal of Sex Research*, 38, 333–342.

Griffiths, M.D. (2005). A 'components' model of addiction within a biopsychosocial framework. *Journal of Substance Use*, 10, 191–197.

Griffiths, M.D. (2007). *Gambling Addiction and its Treatment Within the NHS*. London: British Medical Association.

Griffiths, M.D. (2010a). The role of context in online gaming excess and addiction: Some case study evidence. *International Journal of Mental Health and Addiction*, 8, 119–125.

Griffiths, M.D. (2010b). Gambling addiction on the Internet. In Young, K. & Nabucode Abreu, C. (Eds), *Internet Addiction: A Handbook for Evaluation and Treatment* (pp. 91–111). New York: Wiley.

Griffiths, M.D. (2010c). Gaming in social networking sites: A growing concern? *World Online Gambling Law Report*, 9, 12–13.

Griffiths, M.D. (2012a). Internet sex addiction: A review of empirical research. *Addiction Research and Theory*, 20, 111–124.

Griffiths, M.D. (2012b). Facebook addiction: Concerns, criticisms and recommendations. *Psychological Reports*, 110 (2), 518–520.

Griffiths, M.D. & Hunt, N. (1995). Computer game playing in adolescence: Prevalence and demographic indicators. *Journal of Community and Applied Social Psychology*, 5, 189–194.

Griffiths, M.D. & Hunt, N. (1998). Dependence on computer games by adolescents. *Psychological Reports*, 82, 475–480.

Griffiths, M.D. & Parke, J. (2010) Adolescent gambling on the Internet: A review. *International Journal of Adolescent Medicine and Health*, 22, 58–75.

Griffiths, M.D., Kuss, D.J., & King, D.L. (2012). Video game addiction: Past, present and future. *Current Psychiatry Reviews*, 8, 308–318.

Griffiths, M.D., Kuss, D.J., & Demetrovics, Z. (2014). Social networking addiction: An overview of preliminary findings. In Rosenberg, K. & Feder, L. (Eds), *Behavioral Addictions: Criteria, Evidence and Treatment* (pp. 119–141). New York: Elsevier.

Grüsser, S.M., Thalemann, R., & Griffiths, M.D. (2007). Excessive computer game playing: Evidence for addiction and aggression? *CyberPsychology and Behavior*, 10, 290–292.

Haghbin, M., Shaterian, F., Hosseinzadeh, D., & Griffiths, M.D. (2013). A brief report on the relationship between self-control, video game addiction and academic achievement in normal and ADHD students in Iran. *Journal of Behavioral Addictions*, 2, 239–243.

Han, D.H., Lee, Y.S., Yang, K.C., Kim, E.Y., Lyoo, K., & Renshaw, P.F. (2007). Dopamine genes and reward dependence in adolescents with excessive internet video game play. *Journal of Addiction Medicine*, 1 (3), 133–138.

Han, D.H., Lee, Y.S., Na, C., Ahn, J.Y., Chung, U.S., Daniels, M.A., et al. (2009). The effect of methylphenidate on Internet video game play in children with attention-deficit/hyperactivity disorder. *Comprehensive Psychiatry*, 50, 251–256.

Han, D.H., Hwang, J.W., & Renshaw, P.F. (2010). Bupropion sustained release treatment decreases craving for video games and cue-induced brain activity in patients with Internet video game addiction. *Experimental and Clinical Psychopharmacology*, 18, 297–304.

Hoeft, F., Watson, C.L., Kesler, S.R., Bettinger, K.E., & Reiss, A.L. (2008). Gender differences in the mesocorticolimbic system during computer game-play. *Journal of Psychiatric Research*, 42, 253–258.

Hussain, Z., Griffiths, M.D., & Baguley, T. (2012). Online gaming addiction: classification, prediction and associated risk factors. *Addiction Research and Theory*, 20, 359–371.

Keepers, G.A. (1990). Pathologicical preoccupation with video games. *Journal of the American Academy of Child and Adolescent Psychiatry*, 29, 49–50.

Kim, E.J., Namkoong, K., Ku, T., & Kim, S.J. (2008). The relationship between online game addiction and aggression, self-control and narcissistic personality traits. *European Psychiatry*, 23, 212–218.

King, D.L., Delfabbro, P.H., & Griffiths, M.D. (2012). Clinical interventions for technology-based problems: Excessive Internet and video game use. *Journal of Cognitive Psychotherapy: An International Quarterly*, 26, 43–56.

King, D.L., Haagsma, M.C., Delfabbro, P.H., Gradisar, M.S., & Griffiths, M.D. (2013). Toward a consensus definition of pathological video-gaming: A systematic review of psychometric assessment tools. *Clinical Psychology Review*, 33, 331–342.

Ko, C. H., Yen, J. Y., Chen, C. C., Chen, S. H., & Yen, C. F. (2005). Gender differences and related factors affecting online gaming addiction among Taiwanese adolescents. *Journal of Nervous and Mental Disease*, 193, 273–277.

Ko, C.H., Liu, G.C., Hsiao, S.M., Yen, J.Y., Yang, M.J., Lin, W.C., et al. (2009). Brain activities associated with gaming urge of online gaming addiction. *Journal of Psychiatric Research*, 43, 739–747.

Koc, M. & Gulyagci, S. (2013). Facebook addiction among Turkish college students: The role of psychological health, demographic, and usage characteristics. *Cyberpsychology, Behavior, and Social Networking*, 16, 279–284.

Koronczai, B., Urban, R., Kokonyei, G., Paksi, B., Papp, K., Kun, B., & Demetrovics, Z. (2011). Confirmation of the three-factor model of problematic internet use on off-line adolescent and adult samples. *Cyberpsychology, Behavior and Social Networking*, 14, 657–664.

Kuczmierczyk, A.R., Walley, P.B., & Calhoun, K.S. (1987). Relaxation training, in vivo exposure and response-prevention in the treatment of compulsive video-game playing. *Scandinavian Journal of Behaviour Therapy*, 16, 185–190.

Kuss, D.J. & Griffiths, M.D. (2011). Online social networking and addiction: A literature review of empirical research. *International Journal of Environmental and Public Health*, 8, 3528–3552.

Kuss, D.J. & Griffiths, M.D. (2012). Online gaming addiction: A systematic review. *International Journal of Mental Health and Addiction*, 10, 278–296.

Kuss, D.J., Griffiths, M.D., & Binder, J. (2013). Internet addiction in students: Prevalence and risk factors. *Computers in Human Behavior*, 29, 959–966.

Lemmens, J.S., Valkenburg, P.M., & Peter, J. (2009). Development and validation of a game addiction scale for adolescents. *Media Psychology*, 12, 77–95.

Marks, I. (1990). Non-chemical (behaviourial) addictions. *British Journal of Addiction*, 85, 1389–1394.

McIlwraith, R., Jacobvitz, R.S., Kubey, R., & Alexander, A. (1991). Television addiction: Theories and data behind the ubiquitous metaphor. *American Behavioral Scientist*, 35, 104–121.

Mehroof, M. & Griffiths, M.D. (2010). Online gaming addiction: the role of sensation seeking, self-control, neuroticism, aggression, state anxiety, and trait anxiety. *CyberPsychology and Behavior*, 13, 313–316.

Nilles, J.M. (1982). *Exploring the World of the Personal Computer*. Englewood Cliffs, NJ: Prentice Hall.

Olowu, A.O. & Seri, F.O. (2012). A study of social network addiction among youths in Nigeria. *Journal of Social Science and Policy Review*, 4, 62–71.

Parker, J.D.A., Taylor, R.N., Eastabrook, J.M., Schell, S.L., & Wood, L.M. (2008). Problem gambling in adolescence: relationships with internet misuse, gaming abuse and emotional intelligence. *Personality and Individual Differences*, 45, 174–180.

Peters, C.S. & Malesky, L.A. (2008). Problematic usage among highly-engaged players of massively multiplayer online role playing games. *CyberPsychology and Behavior*, 11, 480–483.

Petry, N.M. & O'Brien, C.P. (2013). Internet gaming disorder and the DSM-5. *Addiction*, 108, 1186–1187.

Phillips, C.A., Rolls, S., Rouse, A., & Griffiths, M.D. (1995). Home video game playing in schoolchildren: A study of incidence and patterns of play. *Journal of Adolescence*, 18, 687–691.

Porter, G., Starcevic, V., Berle, D., & Fenech, P. (2010). Recognizing problem video game use. *The Australian and New Zealand Journal of Psychiatry*, 44, 120–128.

Rehbein, F., Kleimann, M., & Mossle, T. (2010). Prevalence and risk factors of video game dependency in adolescence: results of a German nationwide survey. *CyberPsychology, Behavior and Social Networking*, 13, 269–277.

Shotton, M. (1989). *Computer Addiction?: A Study of Computer Dependency*. London: Taylor & Francis.

Sofiah S., Zobidah O.S., Bolong J.N., & Osman, M. (2011). Facebook addiction among female university students. *Public Administration and Social Policy Review*, 2, 95–109.

Soper, W.B. & Miller, M.J. (1983). Junk time junkies: An emerging addiction among students. *School Counsellor*, 31, 40–43.

Sublette, V.A. & Mullan, B. (2012). Consequences of play: A systematic review of the effects of online gaming. *International Journal of Mental Health and Addiction*, 10, 3–23.

Sussman, S. & Moran, M. (2013). Hidden addiction: Television. *Journal of Behavioral Addictions*, 2, 125–132.

Thalemann, R., Wölfling, K., & Grüsser, S.M. (2007). Specific cue reactivity on computer game-related cues in excessive gamers. *Behavioral Neuroscience*, 12, 614–618.

Turel, O. & Serenko, A. (2012). The benefits and dangers of enjoyment with social networking websites. *European Journal of Information Systems*, 21, 512–528.

Turel, O., Serenko, A., & Giles, P. (2011). Integrating technology addiction and use: An empirical investigation of online auction users. *MIS Quarterly*, 35 (4), A1–A18

van den Eijnden, R.J., Spijkerman, R., Vermulst, A.A., van Rooij, A.J., & Engels, R.C.M.E. (2010). Compulsive Internet use among adolescents: Bidirectional parent-child relationships. *Journal of Abnormal Child Psychology*, 38, 77–89.

Wardle, H., Moody, A., Griffiths, M.D., Orford, J., & Volberg, R. (2011). Defining the online gambler and patterns of behaviour integration: Evidence from the British Gambling Prevalence Survey 2010. *International Gambling Studies*, 11, 339–356.

Young, K. (1996). Psychology of computer use: XL. Addictive use of the Internet: A case that breaks the stereotype. *Psychological Reports*, 79, 899–902.

Young, K. (1998). *Caught in the Net: How to Recognize the Signs of Internet Addiction and a Winning Strategy for Recovery*. New York: Wiley.

Young K. (1999). Internet addiction: Evaluation and treatment. *Student British Medical Journal*, 7, 351–352.

 ## Further reading

If you would like to read further around this topic, the following texts are recommended for further reading:

This book provides an excellent overview of behavioural addictions including chapters on internet addiction, online gaming addiction and social networking addiction:
Rosenberg, K. & Feder, L. (Eds), *Behavioral Addictions: Criteria, Evidence and Treatment*. New York: Elsevier.

This paper provides a systematic review of all 18 instruments that have been developed to assess problematic gaming and/or gaming addiction:
King, D.L., Haagsma, M.C., Delfabbro, P.H., Gradisar, M.S., & Griffiths, M.D. (2013). Toward a consensus definition of pathological video-gaming: A systematic review of psychometric assessment tools. *Clinical Psychology Review*, 33, 331–342.

This paper provides a comprehensive and systematic review of all studies on Internet addiction with a minimum sample size of 1000 participants:
Kuss, D.J., Griffiths, M.D., Karila, L., & Billieux, J. (2014). Internet addiction: A systematic review of epidemiological research for the last decade. *Current Pharmaceutical Design*, 20, 4026-4052.

This book provides an excellent introduction to addictions on and to the Internet covering both empirical research and treatment:
Young, K. & Nabuco de Abreu, C. (Eds), *Internet Addiction: A Handbook for Evaluation and Treatment*. New York: Wiley.

 ## Discussion questions

1. Using the criteria outlined in this chapter, critically consider whether people can be addicted to the Internet.

2. If you consider the information and criteria provided in this chapter in terms of online addictive behaviours, do you think that people carry out addictive behaviours online that they would not engage in in their offline worlds?

3. Can all online beahviours be addictive or are there differences between certain types of online activities? Consider the differences between gaming and social networking to answer this question.

12 A Focus on Use of Online Support

NEIL COULSON & RICHARD SMEDLEY

 Learning objectives

Having read this chapter, we hope that you will be able to:

- Outline the different types of support sought online across diverse Internet arenas.
- Consider the unique characteristics of online support groups and outline why people are motivated to seek support online.
- Explore the barriers and advantages to seeking support online.
- Develop an understanding of the types of things that people discuss online and consider whether there are certain themes that are more prevalent in online discussion groups.
- Consider whether there is a call for the development of more therapeutic applications on the Internet.
- Understand the difficulties and needs that face future work in this area.

12.1 Introduction

The Internet plays an increasingly important role across a diverse array of everyday activities ranging from online shopping, banking, learning new things, keeping in touch with family and friends, and leisure activities such as playing games and listening to music, through to seeking help and support for health-related problems (Leung, 2008). There are so many health-related resources on the Internet that it has been described as the world's largest medical library, providing access to a huge number of health-related websites as well as government health sites, professional organizations, academic journals, medical citation databases, mailing lists, online support communities, and also health-related information that is received through targeted advertising and e-mail spam messages (Morahan-Martin, 2004).

Health-related Internet use originally involved three main types of activity: searching for information, taking part in online support communities, and interacting directly with healthcare professionals (Cline & Haynes, 2001). Subsequent technological developments have expanded this into a more diverse range of activities that also includes buying medications, ordering prescriptions, and booking appointments online (Andreassen et al., 2007), accessing medical records over the Internet (Pyper, Amery, Watson, & Crook, 2004), and using social networking Internet sites like Facebook to follow the health status of friends (Thackeray, Crookston, & West, 2013).

In this chapter, we shall consider the use of online support communities and the reasons why people may turn to them in times of need. As we shall see, there are a number of unique characteristics that are likely to be associated with their increased popularity. In addition, the rapidly changing social media landscape means that there are growing opportunities for people living with long-term conditions or facing some acute health crisis to seek out and access support online. As a consequence, it is important to consider whether participation in online support communities confers any benefits, or indeed whether there is any risk of harm, and this chapter will explore both these issues. In addition, it will explore the topics that are discussed between members of such online support communities drawing on examples from the literature and across various health issues. However, in considering the role of online support for those in time of need we must not forget the important role of the volunteer moderators who spend a considerable amount of time facilitating and supporting the development and activities of these groups. We will take a look at moderators and explore both the challenges to their role as well as the benefits they may accrue through their ongoing involvement.

12.2 What are online support communities?

Online support communities (also referred to as *online support groups* or *online self-help groups*) are a type of virtual community with a health-related focus, which provide an online environment where individuals can connect and interact with other people who have had similar experiences to exchange information, social support or advice.

The vast majority of online support communities are provided for patients who are living with a specific medical condition such as diabetes (Loader, Muncer, Burrows, Pleace, & Nettleton, 2002), hearing loss (Cummings, Sproull, & Kiesler, 2002), Parkinson's disease (Attard & Coulson, 2012), Complex Regional Pain Syndrome (Rodham, McCabe, & Blake, 2009) or Irritable Bowel Syndrome (Coulson, 2013). However, there are also online support communities covering a range of other topics including bereavement communities that help individuals to overcome the death of a loved one (van der Houwen, Stroebe, Schut, Stroebe, & van den Bout, 2010), health behaviour communities that focus on behaviour change such as helping people lose weight (Bane, Haymaker, & Zinchuk, 2005), parent communities for individuals who are raising children with disorders like autism (Carter, 2009), and communities to support caregivers like those who run childcare groups (Worotynec, 2000), or who provide unpaid support to elderly or ill relatives, friends, and neighbours who are unable to perform tasks for themselves (Tanis, Das, & Fortgens-Sillmann, 2011).

Online support communities can be based on several different technologies including World Wide Web discussion forums (Attard & Coulson, 2012), Usenet newsgroups (Loader et al., 2002), e-mail LISTSERV (Cummings et al., 2002), and chat rooms (Letourneau et al., 2012). Web forums have become the most prevalent type of online support community, and have numerous advantages like being easy to access, the ability to search through archives of previous messages that have been posted, and the straightforward use of emoticons (Barak, Boniel-Nissim, & Suler, 2008).

It is also possible to distinguish between online support communities that are **synchronous** and **asynchronous** in time (Murray, 2000, Robinson, 2001). Synchronous communities provide a dynamic environment with content that is constantly changing and evolving from one moment to the next, allowing individuals to engage in live, real-time conversation with other members who are logged on. Examples of this include chat rooms, instant messaging, and online virtual reality environments (Robinson, 2001, Beard, Wilson, Morra, & Keelan, 2009). In contrast, asynchronous communities provide a more static environment with content that changes less frequently. For example, after posting a message it can take anything from a few minutes to several days or perhaps weeks before receiving a reply. It is not possible to engage in live conversation within asynchronous communities, but instead they provide people with the opportunity to read messages when it is convenient and allow individuals to take their time while composing replies. Examples of this include discussion forums or bulletin boards, e-mail LISTSERV, and Usenet newsgroups (Robinson, 2001).

Discussions are typically organized into **threads** where one person starts a new discussion by posting an initial message asking a question, describing a problem or talking about an experience that they want to share, and other members post replies to that message. Members might then post additional messages in response to these replies, thus building up a hierarchical thread of messages that stem from the original posting (Cummings et al., 2002, Petrovcic, Vehovar, & Ziberna, 2012).

12.3 Why do people access online support communities?

12.3.1 Unique characteristics

There are a number of communication features that have arguably underpinned the rise in popularity of online support communities. Indeed, for many individuals living with long-term conditions or facing some other problem or personal crisis (e.g., bereavement), they may in fact be preferable to traditional face-to-face sources of support because of their asynchronous nature. That is to say, communication is not in real-time (e.g., face-to-face conversation) but rather unfolds over time. As a result, one of the most obvious features of online support that may appeal to an individual is its availability. Online support is available to those who need it seven days per week, 24 hours per day and this stands in contrast to traditional face-to-face support groups that may meet once per week or less and at a fixed time and venue (e.g., local church hall). Thus, for individuals seeking support through these times, online support groups may offer a viable and useful means through which to obtain much needed help and support. In addition, online support may be especially helpful to those who may have limited mobility (e.g., people living with a disability) or cannot access traditional face-to-face support group meetings (e.g., those caring for children, working shifts, etc.) since they are not restricted by temporal, geographical, or spatial barriers.

An additional feature of online support groups that arises from the asynchronous nature of the communication is the fact it offers members the means to engage and participate at a speed and level appropriate for them. For example, a new member may wish to simply read messages to begin with before deciding to write a message and post it for fellow members of the community to read. Similarly, the asynchronous nature of the communication means that members can take their time and consider carefully what it is they wish to say. Indeed, it has been argued that asynchronous communication reduces the pressure associated with real-time communication thereby, allowing participants time to carefully construct their messages before contributing to the community (Joinson, 2003).

The ability to reach out to people from geographically diverse locations also increases the chances of finding others with similar experiences (White & Dorman, 2001). This is particularly helpful for individuals with rare conditions who may be unable to locate people with the same problem in their geographical area. At the same time, due to their diversity, online support communities are popular because they can offer participants a wide variety of different perspectives, viewpoints, and experiences on issues related to their condition (Wright, 1999, 2000).

Online support communities often allow individuals to participate in such a way that they can retain their anonymity. This, in turn, may be helpful to those individuals who may feel embarrassed, ashamed or feel their problem carries a social stigma. Moreover, it allows the individual the means to discuss and share their thoughts on personal and sensitive matters without fear of a negative reaction or rejection. Much has been written within the literature around the fact that individuals online are able to share and discuss things more freely than might be the case face-to-face. Indeed, this **online disinhibition effect** (Suler, 2004) has been found to be especially relevant and helpful in the context of help-seeking within online communities (Coulson, 2013).

12.3.2 What motivates members to engage with online support groups?

A number of studies have explored the reasons behind the decision to engage with an online support community. For example, Coulson (2013) surveyed 249 patients that were drawn from 35 asynchronous online support communities (i.e., web forums) supporting those living with Inflammatory Bowel Disease. The results of this study illustrate the various reasons and motives behind the decision to engage with online support. Among the most widely endorsed was the need to connect to similar others in a similar situation, a finding that has been echoed across studies exploring engagement across a range of online support communities. In addition, respondents reported a range of reasons reflecting altruistic motives (i.e., share experiences or offer support) and a desire to obtain advice, information, and emotional support. For others, there had been a change in symptoms, or new symptoms had begun, or they wanted to understand medical terminology better.

Across the vast majority of research studies that have explored why patients seek support online, the need to connect, to share, and to seek support resonate clearly. It seems then that regardless of the specific focus of the community, the reasons behind the decision to access them is reasonably consistent: support.

12.4 Is there a downside?

A number of disadvantages associated with receiving social support over the Internet have been identified in recent years (Finfgeld, 2000, White & Dorman, 2001), some of which again appear to arise because of the computer-mediated nature of virtual communities (Coulson & Knibb, 2007). We shall now consider some of the most commonly discussed problematic issues.

12.4.1 **Access requirements**

In order to participate in online support communities it is essential for individuals to have access to a computer, tablet, smartphone, or some other device with an Internet connection. Internet usage statistics show that overall only 34.3% of the world population are Internet users (Internet World Stats, 2012), so only a minority of people have potential access to these online support communities. Even in countries that have high levels of Internet use like the United Kingdom, Internet user typologies suggest that the majority of the population can still be categorized as either non- or occasional-users of the Internet (Selwyn, Gorard, & Furlong, 2005, Brandtzæg, Heim, & Karahasanović, 2011), which again suggests that only a minority of people are likely to use these communities. Furthermore, it is also essential to know how to use a computer, to understand whichever language the online support community uses, and to have adequate literary skills to read and write messages. Despite the potential worldwide membership of online support communities, these barriers may mean that only a small proportion of the world's population are likely to use them.

12.4.2 **Time-consuming**

Some online support communities have a large and active group membership where many people read messages and post replies every day. This can produce a high volume of messages, making it time-consuming for an individual to read messages and compose replies. Individuals who have family, work, or other commitments may sometimes find it difficult to make time to read all the messages. Additionally, medical conditions like Parkinson's disease can make it difficult for members to actively participate in online support communities because of the nature of the symptoms from which they suffer, which may cause members to disappear unexpectedly or produce long delays between posting a message and receiving a reply (Attard & Coulson, 2012). Members may respond to information overload by only replying to simple messages, by posting simpler replies, or by withdrawing from active participation in the community (Jones, Ravid, & Rafaeli, 2004).

12.4.3 **Lack of social cues or face-to-face contact**

Social cues like facial expressions, body language, and tone of voice are not present within online support communities, which can sometimes present difficulties (Coulson & Knibb, 2007). This can lead to misunderstandings when individuals misinterpret what others have said, or produce feelings of awkwardness when people make incorrect assumptions about other members (Attard & Coulson, 2012). Members often include smiley-face emoticons or excessive punctuation in their messages as a substitute for these missing social cues (van Uden-Kraan et al., 2008a).

    The lack of physical proximity on the Internet can make it difficult to develop a meaningful face-to-face relationship with other members, and also makes it impossible to offer physical affection like touching, holding hands, or giving the other person a hug (Malik & Coulson, 2010b, Coulson, 2013). Members sometimes report that they feel isolated and alone in their real lives after logging off from their computer (Coulson, 2013).

12.4.4 **Antisocial behaviour**

Although some online support communities are 'closed' and have membership requirements that control who is allowed to join (Malik & Coulson, 2011), many communities are 'open' and allow anyone to read messages or anonymously register a username so they can post replies. This can lead to antisocial behaviour where some individuals harass others or behave in ways that disrupt the community (Burnett, 2000). The fear of receiving aggressive or inappropriate replies is one of the reasons why some members become '**lurkers**' who read messages without posting replies of their own (Preece, Nonnecke, & Andrews, 2004). Despite these concerns, research indicates that the messages posted to online support communities are overwhelmingly positive with very few instances of negative or abusive messages (van Uden-Kraan et al., 2008a, Malik & Coulson, 2010a, 2011).

12.4.5 **Misleading advice**

Some members of online support communities have expressed concerns that the relative anonymity of the Internet can make it difficult to judge the accuracy and trustworthiness of information (Coulson & Knibb, 2007). For example, there is a possibility that some messages might be posted by imposters who are not genuine patients. These individuals might pretend to be patients who are sharing their experiences when they are really employees of a drug company or some other organization with a vested interest in wanting to promote a particular treatment (Coulson, 2013).

When a member posts a reply offering information or advice, others will often join in to share their own opinions and these responses may help the individual to assess the credibility of the initial advice (Malik & Coulson, 2011). Messages containing inaccurate or misleading information may be more common in communities with low levels of activity (Hwang et al., 2007), but overall it appears that few postings contain misleading information and in those instances where misleading or inaccurate information is posted then this is often corrected by other members or moderators (Esquivel, Meric-Bernstam, & Bernstam, 2006). Fears about the possibility of exposure to dangerous information may therefore be unfounded (van Uden-Kraan et al., 2008a).

12.5 Engagement with online support communities

Most individuals discover online support communities in one of three ways (van Uden Kraan et al., 2008b):

1. By chance while looking for health information on the Internet.
2. By hearing about them from patient organizations or family members.
3. By direct marketing by active members of the online support community.

People join online support communities for a variety of reasons including wanting to obtain or exchange social support (38.2% of respondents), obtaining information and sharing insights with others (38.2%), and for friendship (17.1%) (Ridings & Gefen, 2004). Other reasons for joining are reflected in the benefits of community membership, like being able to access support at any time, to alleviate feelings of isolation, and to use the community as a vehicle through which individuals can discuss coping strategies and feel better about themselves (Coulson & Knibb, 2007).

A small number of studies have investigated who uses online support communities, with research typically focusing on socio-demographic predictors like those used to investigate the **digital divide**. It appears that individuals who use online support communities are broadly similar to those who use the Internet for other health-related purposes (Mo & Coulson, 2010b). Online support community use is associated with being better educated, having a higher income, using complimentary or alternative therapies, and having worse health status (Owen et al., 2010). Individuals with certain health conditions like depression or anxiety, stroke, diabetes, cancer, or arthritis are more likely to use online support communities (Owen et al., 2010), and online support community use may be higher among people with rare, stigmatized, or socially isolating illnesses because those conditions make it harder to obtain support within the local community (White & Dorman, 2001). It appears that 54% of online support community users have never used a face-to-face support group (Owen et al., 2010), suggesting that online support helps people to obtain support that might otherwise be inaccessible or difficult to obtain (White & Dorman, 2001). Barriers to using online support communities include difficulty finding a suitable group, having to write about and discuss health problems online, and needing to sit at a computer for long periods of time (van Uden-Kraan, Drossaert, Taal, Seydel, & van de Laar, 2010).

Unfortunately, like with 'digital divide' studies, socio-demographic statistics might not reveal the full picture regarding who uses online support communities. Research indicates that there are several different types of Internet user, reflecting qualitatively different patterns in how individuals use the Internet (Selwyn et al., 2005, Brandtzæg et al., 2011). Little is known about how these different types of Internet user engage with online support communities. It is possible that *instrumental* (i.e., moderate level of Internet use for goal oriented tasks such as online banking) or *advanced Internet users* (i.e., high level of Internet use covering a wide and varied range of purposes primarily oriented towards instrumental rather than leisure activities) might be more likely to join online support communities than *sporadic* or *entertainment users*, and different types of Internet user might use online support communities in different ways and hence derive different benefits from community membership. It might be possible for future research to produce a typology of online support community users, reflecting different patterns of use along similar lines to typologies of Internet users and social networking website users (Brandtzaeg & Heim, 2011).

It is estimated that 29.4% of the population suffer from some form of chronic illness, with chronic disease becoming more prevalent as people grow older (Knottnerus, Metsemakers, Höppener, & Limonaro, 1992). Despite the advantages and potential benefits associated with online support communities, research indicates that online support community use is low among both the general public and those with a chronic illness. One study reported that only 1.5% of the general population have used an online support community for health-related purposes compared with 12.5% who have used face-to-face support groups, and only 1.8% of individuals with a chronic illness have used online support communities compared with 15.2% who have used face-to-face support groups (Owen et al., 2010). Another study obtained similar findings, indicating that only 4.4% of breast cancer, arthritis, and fibromyalgia patients have used online support communities compared with 5.3% who have attended face-to-face support groups (van Uden-Kraan et al., 2010).

Little is known about why so few people use online support communities, particularly when chronic illness is so prevalent in society. However, it might be possible to obtain a tentative insight into this from studies that have investigated why some people do not use popular social networking websites like Facebook. One study found that, among teenagers, the primary reasons for not using Facebook are because of lack of motivation (they can't be bothered or don't see the point), poor use of time (the sites are too time-consuming and detract from other activities), preference for doing other things (such as reading or watching television), cyber-safety concerns (risk of bullying or not wanting identifiable photos online), and a dislike of self-presentation online (not wanting to be rated against others or not having many friends), with secondary reasons of limited access (no Internet access at home), parental concerns (their parents think it is unsafe), and friends' influence (their friends don't use it) (Baker & White, 2011). Another study indicated that Facebook non-users are more likely to be older, less socially active, and shyer, or lonely compared to Facebook users (Sheldon, 2012).

Social networking sites like Facebook are sometimes used for health-related purposes, but research suggests that only 15.2% of Internet users post health-related information on social networking sites compared with 31.6% who use them as a source of information (Thackeray et al., 2013). The reasons why most people don't use online support communities remain unclear. Research is needed to investigate why overall usage levels are so low, and whether any of these explanations for the non-use of social networking might also be important in the non-use of online support communities.

Furthermore, there have been few longitudinal studies investigating online support communities (for an exception, see Wen, McTavish, Kreps, Wise, & Gustafson, 2011). Little is known about what happens when online support communities are initially launched, how they become established, or how support processes develop and evolve over time. Future longitudinal research will be needed to investigate these types of questions.

12.6 What do people talk about?

Several studies have investigated what members talk about within online support communities. Some of these studies provide a broad overview of discussion areas, while others use thematic analysis (Braun & Clarke, 2006) to identify recurring themes and go into much greater depth about specific health-related issues that arise within these communities.

Finn (1999) examined and categorized the messages posted in an online support community for individuals with physical or mental health disabilities, and found that discussions were focused around health (38.2% of messages), relationships (28.4%), off-topic subjects like pets and entertainment (22.3%), legal issues (7.8%), and political issues (3.4%). Ravert, Hancock, and Ingersoll (2004) examined the questions asked by adolescents in a type-1 diabetes community and identified six themes. The first of these was 'life tasks', where individuals asked questions relating to normal adolescent development like relationships, how to fit in, going to college, and being more independent. The second theme was 'social support', comprising messages that request support in various ways such as asking to talk to others who have had the same experiences. The third theme was 'medical care', where members ask about the kind of healthcare they receive. Common queries of this kind included wanting to know if they should seek a second opinion, questioning the knowledge or competence of doctors, and asking about health insurance. The fourth theme was 'factual information', which involved asking the kind of questions that would normally be directed towards a healthcare professional. Examples of this included asking how to cope with symptoms like hypogly-caemia, questions about drugs and other aspects of their treatment regime, and whether suffering from diabetes has any implications for travelling. The fifth theme was 'management', where individuals requested advice about how to successfully control their diabetes, such as providing glucose readings and asking what they should do. The sixth theme was 'intra-psychic concerns' and related to questions about emotions, attitudes, and state of mind, not just in relation to diabetes but also covering other topics like eating disorders. Even though some members expressed strong frustrations, the overall tone of messages was supportive and postings remained focused on coping and disease management.

Rodham et al. (2009) examined messages posted by adults in a Complex Regional Pain Syn-drome (CRPS) community and identified four themes. The first of these was 'focusing on the positive', where individuals encouraged other members to concentrate on the things they can still do despite suffering from this debilitating illness, instead of dwelling on the things they are no longer able to do. Individuals shared their goals and achievements, celebrated positive experiences, and emphasized how seemingly trivial accomplishments were actually major tri-umphs in light of the restrictions caused by this illness. The second theme was 'venting', where members shared their frustrations about everyday difficulties. The online community pro-vided a safe environment where members could express their true feelings about living with CRPS instead of needing to maintain a socially desirable pretence that they are coping with the illness. They described the impact of living with CRPS and discussed their disappointment that friends and colleagues failed to understand the illness and the limitations it creates. The third theme was 'support', which showed that members found it important to provide support as well as receiving it from others. Individuals responded to venting with sympathy and practical advice, and often used humour or sarcasm to express their feelings. Sharing advice helped oth-ers, demonstrated the progress individual members were making, and also created a sense of pride in the online community. The fourth theme was 'the hospital as a cure', showing that the need for hope was closely related to hospital appointments. Members expressed their anxiety about whether they would be offered hospital referrals, built up unreasonably high expecta-tions that the hospital would provide a cure, and then had to cope with the disappointing realization that hospitals could only help them learn how to cope with the illness.

Attard and Coulson (2012) examined messages posted by adults in a Parkinson's disease com-munity and identified six themes, comprising three positive themes and three negative ones. The first positive theme was 'what's your problem you tell me yours and I'll tell you mine', where the community acted as a valuable source of support and advice. It was perceived as a lifeline dur-ing times of emotional distress, with members expressing their gratitude to others for thinking of them and providing encouragement as they battled with the illness. Sharing personal stories and information about symptoms, medication, and treatment formed part of the community, which provided a wealth of knowledge on a wide range of issues. The second positive theme was 'welcome to the land of the Parky people', where members found comfort in knowing they are not alone. The high level of empathy and understanding meant that individuals did not need to provide detailed explanations for others to understand what they were going through, and helped to create a safe environment where sensitive topics could be discussed. This also made it easy for friendships to develop within the community. The third positive theme was 'there is always light at the end of the tunnel', where members encouraged each other to remain positive about their lives. They emphasized the importance of being resilient and living life as fully as possible instead of letting the illness dominate their lives, and used humour to dissolve negative thoughts. The first negative theme was 'it's like a graveyard at the moment', with individuals expressing their concern about the lack of replies to messages. Sometimes there could be delays of months before receiving a reply, with members describing how their Parkinson's symptoms hindered their ability to participate in discussions. Some individuals expressed their disappointment that the lack of personal information in the community made it difficult getting to know people beyond their illness. The second negative theme was 'time to migrate and take a break from the computer', where individuals would sometimes leave the community without warning. Others struggled to cope with these sudden and unexpected departures, they continued to feel lonely in their real lives, and they found it difficult to adjust to any changes in how the website operated. The third negative theme was 'did I miss something?' where the text-based nature of online communities sometimes led to misunderstandings. Incorrect assumptions about other members could produce feelings of awkwardness, and messages sometimes came across as being more negative than intended. The disagreements that arose from having a diverse community membership could sometimes have a negative impact on the overall community.

Malik and Coulson (2008b) examined messages posted by men in a fertility treatment community and identified five themes. The first of these was 'supporting dearest partner is our key role', with many men believing that their key role in fertility treatment is to support their partner, and wanting to be seen as a source of strength. This led some men to suppress their emotions, with the community serving as an important outlet for men to express their feelings. Men often described experiencing feelings of helplessness, which led other members to respond with reassurance and encouragement. Members drew on their own experiences to share advice on the best way for men to support their partners. The second theme was 'is this a good or bad pain?' where members discussed medical issues regarding fertility treatment. Men found it difficult to differentiate between symptoms caused by fertility treatment and those caused by other unrelated symptoms, so the community became an important source of information to compensate for a perceived lack of information from healthcare professionals. The third theme was 'us blokes are mere spectators in most people's eyes', where men described feeling neglected and unimportant in the fertility treatment process and complained that healthcare professionals did not appreciate that infertility affects men as well as women. This was further exacerbated when family and friends failed to recognize what men go through during fertility treatment, making the community an important place for men to vent and express their feelings without fear of upsetting anyone. The fourth theme was 'sometimes a male perspective is needed', with men emphasizing the importance of being able to interact with others who have been through similar emotions and experiences. Community members were able to draw on their own first-hand experiences while providing a male perspective on information and emotional support. The fifth theme was 'I don't want to get my hopes up but I can't help it', where the community was important for discussing hopes, aspirations, and fears about the outcomes of fertility treatment. Men often expressed mixed and contradictory emotions by wishing for success while at the same time fearing that treatment may be unsuccessful. To avoid being carried away by optimistic feelings, men would suppress their hopes for a positive result to protect themselves from the pain it would cause if the fertility treatment failed to provide a successful outcome.

A number of broad, recurring themes emerge from these studies:

1. First, they emphasize the importance of being able to communicate with others who can understand them and have been through similar experiences.

2. Second, they demonstrate how people benefit from having a safe environment where they can vent and express their true feelings without the risk of hurting others or damaging social relationships.

3. Third, they highlight the frustrations caused by misconceptions about what each illness is and how it affects sufferers.

4. Fourth, the information, social support, and advice shared within these communities can have a profound impact on members by helping them to feel less alone and develop more effective coping strategies to overcome the issues unique to each illness.

12.7 The therapeutic potential of online support communities

Participating in online support communities is associated with numerous real-world benefits. They can help to reduce the strain on relationships with partners or family members who might otherwise be the main source of support, they can reduce feelings of isolation by helping individuals to recognize that they are not alone in their distress, and they can also act as a source of information and empowerment (Malik & Coulson, 2008a). Empowerment is difficult to define but generally refers to having a sense of power or control, where personal empowerment directly benefits the individual, group empowerment arises from the mutual benefits of shared knowledge, and community empowerment arises from the social and political activities of the group (Roberts, 1999). Online support communities can boost empowerment through processes like sharing information, obtaining emotional support, finding recognition and understanding, and sharing experiences and helping others. This empowers members by helping them to feel better informed so they know more about their illness and can make better decisions, making them feel more confident when interacting with healthcare professionals so they can prepare for appointments and feel more comfortable asking questions or discussing treatment options, finding it easier to accept the disease, feeling more confident divulging their illness to others in their social environment, increased optimism about the future after hearing about the positive experiences of others, enhanced self-esteem, and improved social well-being by increasing their number of social contacts and feeling less isolated (van Uden-Kraan et al., 2008b).

How individuals benefit from online social support may be influenced by the strength of real-world social ties. Stronger social ties are associated with relationships with family and close friends, whereas weaker social ties are linked to colleagues and online support community members. Individuals without social ties, perhaps because they have no social network, a dysfunctional network, or a condition that makes it difficult for them to obtain support due to having a rare, unseen, or stigmatized illness, benefit from the weak ties that come with online support community membership (Cummings et al., 2002). However, one of the advantages of online support is that it can supplement support that is received from other sources (White & Dorman, 2001). Individuals with strong social ties may derive greater benefits from online social support and be more likely to help others if real-life family and friends also join the online support group, which helps to integrate their online and real-world support networks (Cummings et al., 2002).

12.7.1 **Levels of engagement**

Historically, it was thought there are two main levels of interaction within online support communities: 'active participation' and 'lurking' (Burnett, 2000, Preece et al., 2004, Tanis et al., 2011). Active participants read messages that have been written by other community members and contribute to the discussions by posting replies of their own, to provide support and share their knowledge and experiences with other members. In contrast, lurking is a form of non-interactive behaviour where individuals browse through the group, reading messages without posting replies. Lurking can sometimes have negative connotations because it is associated with free-riding and benefitting from the contributions of others without contributing anything yourself (Tanis et al., 2011). However, research indicates that 86.8% of lurkers start out with good intentions to contribute to the online community but find themselves deterred from taking part for a complex variety of reasons including not feeling the need to contribute, wanting to learn more about the community before posting messages, feeling that they do not have anything worthwhile to offer, not being able to post messages because of technical problems like not being able to make the software work, and disliking certain aspects of the community because they feel shy, are worried about receiving aggressive responses, or are concerned about how new members are treated (Preece et al., 2004).

Lurkers are thought to make up the majority of online community membership (Burnett, 2000). While lurking might be an effective strategy for obtaining information or distracting yourself from a stressful situation without needing to disclose yourself to the group, it appears that individuals who actively contribute to online support communities derive greater benefits from community membership (Tanis et al., 2011). There are two theories that might explain why active participation is important. First, actively posting messages should make it easier to find people to talk to as well as speeding up the process of obtaining information and support to help them deal with a problem. Second, the act of writing a message might itself have a beneficial effect on coping because it involves needing to construct an understandable account of what they are experiencing, which might lead the individual to have a clearer understanding of the problem or prompt better ways of coping with it (Tanis et al., 2011). Research indicates that lurkers tend to be older than active participants, they spend less time using online support communities, and they receive less social support and less useful information (Mo & Coulson, 2010a).

According to Burnett and Bonnici (2003), behaviour within online communities is influenced by explicit and implicit norms. Social norms define the attitudes and behaviours that are considered to be acceptable for members of an online community, and can vary from one community to another. Explicit norms refer to rules that are outlined in formal documents like **Frequently Asked Questions (FAQs)** that explain the purpose of the community and what standards of behaviour are expected from members. Implicit norms are not formally outlined and can only be learned and understood by observing the day-to-day interactions of established members. Newly joined members are sometimes advised to lurk in a community before actively joining in so they can learn the implicit rules and avoid sanctions or expulsion from the group for violating those norms. Core members of the community appear to play an important role in this process because they are defining members who reinforce community norms.

12.8 Helping the self to help others: The example of online support community moderators

In comparison to traditional online community members, there has been significantly less research that has explored the experiences of **moderators**. Moderators play a pivotal role in the activities and dynamics of online communities but their voice has seldom been heard with respect to their motivations for undertaking the role as well as what they may get out of the experience. Similarly, undertaking such a role may have negative consequences and these have yet to be fully identified and explored. However, work in this area is slowly beginning and early work by van Uden-Kraan et al. (2010) used a qualitative approach to examine the experiences of 23 Dutch patients who moderated three broad types of online support community (i.e., breast cancer, fibromyalgia, and arthritis). The findings of this work suggested that moderators have a range of intrinsic and altruistic motives for initiating an online support community. Since then, exploration of the experiences of community moderators has continued and work by Coulson and Shaw (2013), spanning a far broader range of health conditions, has illustrated the motives that underpin the decision to set up communities. For example, a number of moderators described the impact of their own diagnosis and the ability to share their thoughts and experiences was the catalyst to setting up a community. In so doing, this helped to validate their experiences and feelings and in helping others they felt personally empowered. More broadly, the moderators felt that online communities served to offer a 'communal brain' into which members could tap for information and advice. Whilst the positive virtues of online support were discussed, however, so too were the potential disadvantages, notably an over-reliance on the community by some members. Moderators also shared their experiences of the challenges associated with supporting an online community and described the factors that they considered to be relevant in securing a successful dynamic and shared space. For example, clear rules of engagement, trust, organizational skills, compassion, and kindness were considered as vital in helping the moderator to take the community forward.

12.9 Future directions

It is approximately 25 years since the Internet opened its doors to the masses and since then we have witnessed an explosion in relation to health-related online resources, including support communities. Indeed, as technology has advanced and new functionality has been developed and rolled out (i.e., Web 2.0), the nature of online support has changed. As a consequence, researchers face many challenges in terms of understanding and building a complete picture of how online support communities work and impact on the experience of health and illness. Moreover, these challenges are faced by a broad range of discipline areas and therein rests part of the problem. That is to say, online support spans many potential areas and one challenge going forward is to try and unite and draw together experts in various areas to consider a shared strategy for research. In my opinion, multi-disciplinary research is the key to successful research and only through such endeavours can a truly integrative account of online support be offered. So, for computer scientists, health psychologists, linguistic analysts and the many other potentially relevant disciplines, the challenge rests in coming together to fully examine the process, impact, and outcomes associated with online support communities.

12.10 Chapter summary

In this chapter we have outlined some key pieces of research that have considered online support from various different angles. Our overriding conclusion is that there is much work still to be done in this area, but what we have established thus far is:

- That not all discussions online in relation to health-seeking behaviours occur on the same types of Internet arena. These are varied in terms of synchronicity, type of discussions, and often illness-related.

- There are a number of characteristics that make online information seeking preferable to offline support groups, including the round-the-clock availability of online support.

- That there are a number of barriers to seeking online support, including antisocial behaviour, and wrong advice.

- That there are a number of papers from which themes emerge as to why people seek help online.

- That the notion of online therapeutic applications of information seeking online raises a number of points for future empirical consideration.

 References

Andreassen, H., Bujnowska-Fedak, M., Chronaki, C., Dumitru, R., Pudule, I., Santana, S., & Wynn, R. (2007). European citizens' use of E-health services: A study of seven countries. *BMC Public Health*, 7 (1), 53.

Attard, A. & Coulson, N.S. (2012). A thematic analysis of patient communication in Parkinson's disease online support group discussion forums. *Computers in Human Behavior*, 28 (2), 500–506.

Baker, R.K. & White, K.M. (2011). In their own words: why teenagers don't use social networking sites. *Cyberpsychology, Behavior, and Social Networking*, 14 (6), 395–398.

Bane, C.M.H., Haymaker, C.M.B., & Zinchuk, J. (2005). Social support as a moderator of the big-fish-in-a-little-pond effect in online self-help support groups. *Journal of Applied Biobehavioral Research*, 10 (4), 239–261.

Barak, A., Boniel-Nissim, M., & Suler, J. (2008). Fostering empowerment in online support groups. *Computers in Human Behavior*, 24 (5), 1867–1883.

Beard, L., Wilson, K., Morra, D., & Keelan, J. (2009). A survey of health-related activities on second life. *Journal of Medical Internet Research*, 11 (2), e 17.

Brandtzaeg, P.B. & Heim, J. (2011). A typology of social networking sites users. *International Journal of Web Based Communities*, 7 (1), 28–51.

Brandtzæg, P.B., Heim, J., & Karahasanović, A. (2011). Understanding the new digital divide—A typology of Internet users in Europe. *International Journal of Human-Computer Studies*, 69 (3), 123–138.

Braun, V. & Clarke, V. (2006) Using thematic analysis in psychology. *Qualitative Research in Psychology*, 3 (2), 77–101.

Burnett, G. (2000). Information exchange in virtual communities: a typology. *Information Research*, 5 (4). Retrieved from http://informationr.net/ir/5-4/paper82.

Burnett, G. & Bonnici, L. (2003). Beyond the FAQ: Explicit and implicit norms in Usenet newsgroups. *Library & Information Science Research*, 25 (3), 333–351.

Carter, I. (2009). Positive and negative experiences of parents involved in online self-help groups for autism. *Journal on Developmental Disabilities*, 15 (1), 44–52.

Cline, R.J.W. & Haynes, K.M. (2001). Consumer health information seeking on the Internet: the state of the art. *Health Education Research*, 16 (6), 671–692.

Coulson, N.S. (2013). How do online patient support communities affect the experience of inflammatory bowel disease? An online survey. *JRSM Short Reports*, 4 (8), 1–8.

Coulson, N.S. & Knibb, R.C. (2007). Coping with food allergy: Exploring the role of the online support group. *CyberPsychology, Behavior & Social Networking*, 10 (1), 145–148.

Coulson, N.S. & Shaw, R.L. (2013). Nurturing health-related online support groups: Exploring the experiences of patient moderators. *Computers in Human Behavior*, 29, 1695–1701.

Cummings, J.N., Sproull, L., & Kiesler, S.B. (2002). Beyond hearing: Where the real-world and online support meet. *Group Dynamics: Theory, Research, and Practice*, 6 (1), 78–88.

Esquivel, A., Meric-Bernstam, F., & Bernstam, E.V. (2006). Accuracy and self correction of information received from an internet breast cancer list: content analysis. *British Medical Journal*, 332 (7547), 939–942.

Finfgeld, D.L. (2000). Therapeutic groups online: the good, the bad, and the unknown. *Issues in Mental Health Nursing*, 21 (3), 241–255.

Finn, J. (1999). An exploration of helping processes in an online self-help group focusing on issues of disability. *Health and Social Work*, 24, 220–231.

Hwang, K.O., Farheen, K., Johnson, C.W., Thomas, E.J., Barnes, A.S., & Bernstam, E.V. (2007). Quality of weight loss advice on internet forums. *The American Journal of Medicine*, 120 (7), 604–609.

Internet World Stats (2012). *World Internet Usage and Population Statistics*. Retrieved Feb 6, 2014, from http://www.internetworldstats.com/stats.htm.

Joinson, A. (2003). *Understanding the Psychology of Internet Behaviour: Virtual Worlds, Real Lives*. New York, NY: Palgrave Macmillan.

Jones, Q., Ravid, G., & Rafaeli, S. (2004). Information overload and the message dynamics of online interaction spaces: A theoretical model and empirical exploration. *Information Systems Research*, 15 (2), 194–210.

Knottnerus, J., Metsemakers, J., Höppener, P., & Limonaro, C. (1992). Chronic Illness in the Community and the Concept of 'Social Prevalence'. *Family Practice*, 9 (1), 15–21.

Letourneau, N., Stewart, M., Masuda, J.R., Anderson, S., Cicutto, L., McGhan, S., & Watt, S. (2012). Impact of online support for youth with asthma and allergies: pilot study. *Journal of Pediatric Nursing*, 27 (1), 65–73.

Leung, L. (2008). Internet embeddedness: links with online health information seeking, expectancy value/quality of health information websites, and Internet usage patterns. *CyberPsychology, Behavior & Social Networking*, 11 (5), 565–569.

Loader, B.D., Muncer, S., Burrows, R., Pleace, N., & Nettleton, S. (2002). Medicine on the line? Computer-mediated social support and advice for people with diabetes. *International Journal of Social Welfare*, 11 (1), 53–65.

Malik, S.H. & Coulson, N.S. (2008a). Computer-mediated infertility support groups: An exploratory study of online experiences. *Patient Education and Counseling*, 73 (1), 105–113.

Malik, S.H. & Coulson, N.S. (2008b). The male experience of infertility: a thematic analysis of an online infertility support group bulletin board. *Journal of Reproductive and Infant Psychology*, 26 (1), 18–30.

Malik, S.H. & Coulson, N.S. (2010a). Coping with infertility online: An examination of self-help mechanisms in an online infertility support group. *Patient Education and Counseling*, 81 (2), 315–318.

Malik, S.H. & Coulson, N.S. (2010b). 'They all supported me but I felt like I suddenly didn't belong anymore': an exploration of perceived disadvantages to online support seeking. *Journal of Psychosomatic Obstetrics and Gynecology*, 31 (3), 140–149.

Malik, S.H. & Coulson, N.S. (2011). The therapeutic potential of the internet exploring self-help processes in an internet forum for young people with Inflammatory Bowel Disease. *Gastroenterology Nursing*, 34 (6), 439–448.

Mo, P.K.H. & Coulson, N.S. (2010a). Empowering processes in online support groups among people living with HIV/AIDS: A comparative analysis of 'lurkers' and 'posters'. *Computers in Human Behavior*, 26 (5), 1183–1193.

Mo, P.K.H. & Coulson, N.S. (2010b). Living with HIV/AIDS and use of online support groups. *Journal of Health Psychology*, 15 (3), 339–350.

Morahan-Martin, J.M. (2004). How internet users find, evaluate, and use online health information: a cross-cultural review. *CyberPsychology, Behavior & Social Networking*, 7 (5), 497–510.

Murray, D.E. (2000). Protean communication: The language of computer-mediated communication. *TESOL Quarterly*, 34 (3), 397–421.

Owen, J.E., Boxley, L., Goldstein, M.S., Lee, J.H., Breen, N., & Rowland, J.H. (2010). Use of health-related online support groups: population data from the california health interview survey complementary and alternative medicine study. *Journal of Computer-Mediated Communication*, 15 (3), 427–446.

Petrovcic, A., Vehovar, V., & Ziberna, A. (2012). Posting, quoting, and replying: a comparison of methodological approaches to measure communication ties in web forums. *Quality & Quantity*, 46 (3), 829–854.

Preece, J., Nonnecke, B., & Andrews, D. (2004). The top five reasons for lurking: improving community experiences for everyone. *Computers in Human Behavior*, 20 (2), 201–223.

Pyper, C., Amery, J., Watson, M., & Crook, C. (2004). Patients' experiences when accessing their on-line electronic patient records in primary care. *British Journal of General Practice*, 54 (498), 38–43.

Ravert, R.D., Hancock, M.D., & Ingersoll, G.M. (2004). Online forum messages posted by adolescents with type 1 diabetes. *Diabetes Educator*, 30 (5), 827–834.

Ridings, C.M. & Gefen, D. (2004). Virtual community attraction: why people hang out online. *Journal of Computer-Mediated Communication*,10 (1), 00–00.

Roberts, K.J. (1999). Patient empowerment in the United States: a critical commentary. *Health Expectations*,2 (2), 82–92.

Robinson, K.M. (2001). Unsolicited narratives from the Internet: a rich source of qualitative data. *Qualitative Health Research*, 11 (5), 706–714.

Rodham, K., McCabe, C., & Blake, D. (2009). Seeking support: An interpretative phenomenological analysis of an Internet message board for people with Complex Regional Pain Syndrome. *Psychology & Health*, 24 (6), 619–634.

Selwyn, N., Gorard, S., & Furlong, J. (2005). Whose Internet is it anyway? Exploring adults' (non)use of the Internet in everyday life. *European Journal of Communication*, 20 (1), 5–26.

Sheldon, P. (2012). Profiling the non-users: Examination of life-position indicators, sensation seeking, shyness, and loneliness among users and non-users of social network sites. *Computers in Human Behavior*, 28 (5), 1960–1965.

Suler, J. (2004). The online disinhibition effect. *Cyberpsychology, Behavior & Social Networking*, 7 (3), 321–326.

Tanis, M., Das, E., & Fortgens-Sillmann, M. (2011). Finding care for the caregiver? Active participation in online health forums attenuates the negative effect of caregiver strain on wellbeing. *Communications-European Journal of Communication Research*, 36 (1), 51–66.

Thackeray, R., Crookston, T.B., & West, H.J. (2013). Correlates of health-related social media use among adults. *Journal of Medical Internet Research*, 15 (1), e 21.

van der Houwen, K., Stroebe, M., Schut, H., Stroebe, W., & van den Bout, J. (2010). Online mutual support in bereavement: An empirical examination. *Computers in Human Behavior*, 26 (6), 1519–1525.

van Uden-Kraan, C.F., Drossaert, C.H.C., Taal, E., Lebrun, C.E.I., Drossaers-Bakker, K.W., Smit, W. M., & van de Laar, M. A. F. J. (2008a). Coping with somatic illnesses in online support groups: Do the feared disadvantages actually occur? *Computers in Human Behavior*, 24 (2), 309–324.

van Uden-Kraan, C.F., Drossaert, C.H.C., Taal, E., Shaw, B.R., Seydel, E.R., & van de Laar, M.A.F.J. (2008b). Empowering processes and outcomes of participation in online support groups for patients with breast cancer, arthritis, or fibromyalgia. *Qualitative Health Research*, 18 (3), 405–417.

van Uden-Kraan, C., Drossaert, C.H.C., Taal, E., Seydel, E.R., & van de Laar, M.A.F.J. (2010). Patient-initiated online support groups: motives for initiation, extent of success and success factors. *Journal of Telemedicine and Telecare*, 16, 30–34.

Wen, K.-Y., McTavish, F.M., Kreps, G., Wise, M., &
Gustafson, D.H. (2011). From diagnosis to death:
A case study of coping with breast cancer as
seen through online discussion group messages.
Journal of Computer-Mediated Communication,
16 (2), 331–361.

White, M. & Dorman, S.M. (2001). Receiving social
support online: implications for health education.
Health Education Research, 16 (6), 693–707.

Worotynec, Z.S. (2000). The good, the
bad and the ugly: Listserv as support.

CyberPsychology, Behavior & Social Networking,
3 (5), 797–810.

Wright, K.B. (1999). Computer-mediated support
groups: An examination of relationships among
social support, perceived stress and coping
strategies. *Communication Quarterly*, 47, 402–414.

Wright, K.B. (2000). The communication of social
support within an online community for older
adults: A qualitative analysis of the SeniorNet
community. *Qualitative Research Reports in
Communication*, 1, 33–43.

Further reading

A nice example of the various ways in which patients may engage with *online support communities* at various points of their illness journey is provided by this article:

Coulson, N.S. (2013). How do online patient support communities affect the experience of inflammatory bowel disease? An online survey. *JRSM Short Reports*, 4 (8), 1–8.

This is an important paper that reflects a far broader range of *negative consequences* of participation within online support communities than previous research has shown.

Malik, S.H. & Coulson, N.S. (2010). 'They all supported me but I felt like I suddenly didn't belong anymore': An exploration of perceived disadvantages to online support seeking. *Journal of Psychosomatic Obstetrics and Gynecology*, 31 (3), 140–149.

This paper provides a fascinating insight into the various motivations that may account for *lurking behaviour* within online communities:

Preece, J., Nonnecke, B., & Andrews, D. (2004). The top five reasons for lurking: improving community experiences for everyone. *Computers in Human Behavior*, 20 (2), 201–223.

This is a key paper in the development of research that considers the *empowering potential* of active participation within online support communities:

van Uden-Kraan, C.F., Drossaert, C.H.C., Taal, E., Shaw, B.R., Seydel, E.R., & van de Laar, M.A.F.J. (2008). Empowering processes and outcomes of participation in online support groups for patients with breast cancer, arthritis, or fibromyalgia. *Qualitative Health Research*, 18 (3), 405–417.

Discussion questions

1. Outline and critically consider the different ways in which people seek support online.
2. Discuss the roles of the information seeker, information provider, lurker, and moderator in online support groups.
3. What benefits and disadvantages are there to seeking support online?
4. Critically consider what people discuss in online support groups. What are their underlying motivations for these discussions?
5. Outline and critically consider why different types of Internet user might join online support communities for different reasons.

Online Therapies and Counselling

MELANIE NGUYEN

 Learning objectives

At the conclusion of this chapter, we hope that you will be able to:

- Describe the different types of psychological interventions delivered through the Internet.
- Discuss factors that moderate the effectiveness of online psychological interventions.
- Articulate the nature of the therapeutic relationship in online counselling and its effect on treatment outcomes.
- Discuss the current knowledge around the characteristics of online clients, counsellors and the logistics of online counselling.
- Evaluate the ethical and legal considerations of cross-border delivery of health services.
- Summarize current research about self-disclosure in online counselling.

13.1 Introduction

If you are reading this as a currently enrolled university student then it's likely that your world has always been connected by the Internet. This network allows you to quickly search for information about any topic, including psychological phenomena and concerns; watch videos about health procedures previously available only to those in the operating theatre; and connects you to other people at all times and in all places. In this context, health professionals have started offering their services through the Internet.

Online counselling can be self-directed or facilitated by a trained clinician. Both contexts represent changes in conceptualizing the 'self' in therapy and challenges to traditional methods of counselling. This chapter will examine the different types of psychological services available online, the characteristics of clients and counsellors using the Internet and the challenges and benefits associated with this practice. We review literature on the effectiveness of online counselling in facilitating a treatment outcome and a positive therapeutic relationship, and discuss changes in counselling self-disclosure according to communication medium and time. In short, we will explore the 'who' of the online self, how this online self communicates in counselling and what questions still need to be answered for effective treatment of this online self.

13.2 Psychological interventions delivered online

Whether it is said that technology has permeated, infiltrated, or embedded itself into twenty-first century lifestyle, its influence on human communication and interaction must be acknowledged. This is demonstrated in the more than 500 million active Facebook users (Facebook, 2011), the fact that 'Google' is now a verb (Oxford English Dictionary, 2011), and the widespread use of email in education, workplace, and health settings (Jarvenpaa, Tractinsky, & Vitale, 2000, Moon, 2000, Branon & Essex, 2001, Johnson, 2006).

Health consumers are frequently employing the Internet in their search for mental health information and support programs (Ybarra & Eaton, 2005). Computer-mediated psycho-education (Griffiths, Christensen, Jorm, Evans, & Groves, 2004), online support groups and group therapy (Houston et al., 2001), online self-directed therapy (Sethi, Campbell, & Ellis, 2010), and online counselling (Kraus, Zack, & Stricker, 2004) are different examples of psychological interventions available on the Internet. The growth of this field has also seen a range of new terms emerge, often used inconsistently. This is partly due to the lack of leadership or governing body as well as the diverse ways in which the Internet (accessed through computers, laptops, and mobile devices including phones and tablets) can be used to support psychological interventions.

Following a review of the field, Barak, Klein, and Proudfoot (2009) proposed a four-group classification of Internet-based interventions according to the approach used. These were:

1. Web-based interventions.
2. Online counselling and therapy.
3. Internet-operated therapeutic software.
4. Other online activities.

Together, web-based interventions were programs that provided health-based activities and/or information through a website. The aim of these programs is to improve users' understanding, knowledge, and awareness of health and mental-health issues. With this definition, **web-based interventions** were further divided into:

a. web-based education interventions,
b. self-guided web-based therapeutic interventions, and
c. human-supported web-based therapeutic interventions.

Web-based education interventions are usually static websites containing information about mental health. They require no interaction with the user and are aimed at providing information. On the other hand, both self-guided and human-supported web-based therapeutic interventions are interactive and involve structured content based on therapeutic models. Their aim is to facilitate cognitive and/or behavioural changes. The key difference is whether the interventions require additional human support or not. *Self-guided web-based therapeutic interventions* typically consist of modules that the user can interact with on their own, for example, MoodGym (https://moodgym.anu.edu.au/welcome). *Human-supported therapeutic interventions* involve some human support that can range from reminders to emails with a psychologist to participation in a discussion forum or bulletin board.

Online counselling is the delivery of therapeutic interventions by a trained professional to a client through the Internet. This can include using email, instant messaging and videoconference for delivering counselling. It is a computer-supported human-to-human interaction aimed at providing psychological interventions to promote positive cognitive and/or behavioural change.

Internet-operated therapeutic software, on the other hand, provides therapy through robotic simulation, rule-based systems, games, or 3D virtual environments. Human support is absent or minimal as responses to the client are automated and built into the system. Robotic simulations include *Eliza*, a 1966 devised program that will respond to text-input by identifying key words and responding with a question. Increasingly, virtual environments such as *Second Life* (http://secondlife.com/) have been used as platforms for treating anxiety and phobias.

Finally, the *other online activities* category encompasses psychological support derived from social networks and online support groups, blogs, podcasts, or online assessments. Social networks, support groups, and blogs allow individuals to share personal experiences and receive peer support. The popularity of online social networking sites such as Facebook has led to the development of health-based social networking sites such as *PatientsLikeMe* (http://www.patientslikeme.com). On this site, people with different health problems (physical and psychological) can connect to support each other by sharing stories and resources. Research on the effectiveness of these sites is emerging (Wicks et al., 2010). Examples of online assessments include the online administration of the K-10 (a measure of anxiety and depression) by BeyondBlue (http://www.beyondblue.org.au/the-facts/depression/signs-and-symptoms/anxiety-and-depression-checklist-k10). For an extensive discussion of these interventions, see Barak et al. (2009).

Of the interventions noted above, online counselling and therapy allows for the greatest exploration of the concept of the online self in a help-seeking situation. The 'self' in Internet-supported psychological interventions is best understood through discussions about the client-counsellor relationship when moved from an in-person to online environment. In this chapter, *eTherapy*, *online therapy*, and *online counselling* will be used interchangeably to refer to the delivery of psychological interventions by a trained mental health professional to a client via Internet-mediated communication. This type of Internet-supported psychological intervention will be the focus of this chapter.

13.3 Effectiveness of online therapeutic interventions

Online therapeutic interventions can encompass the delivery of psychological treatments through self-directed modules where the client works through structured therapeutic activities or online counselling where a trained professional delivers therapy through the Internet as they would face-to-face. The effectiveness of these interventions is usually evaluated in stand-alone research projects. To provide an audit of what we currently know about the effectiveness of online interventions, Barak, Hen, Boniel-Nissim, and Shapira (2008) conducted a meta-analysis of studies published until March 2006. Overall, they found a medium effect size for online interventions (combining self-help packages and online counselling) on symptom improvement. This suggests that Internet-based therapies are effective in creating positive health changes. Interestingly, the meta-analysis also identified several moderating factors. These include the types of problems clients present with and theoretical approach of the clinician.

Online therapeutic interventions have been designed to treat a range of symptoms and conditions. These include physical (e.g., weight loss) and psychological (e.g., anxiety, depression). The results showed that eTherapy was more effective in treating psychological problems than physical symptoms. If the therapies aimed at supporting physiological changes were removed, online interventions would show a high (rather than moderate) effect size. This suggests that there may be some conditions for which online treatment is more suitable than others. The most positive change, that is, the largest effect sizes, was found for patients receiving online treatment for post-traumatic stress disorder (PTSD).

The most common therapeutic approaches used by online counsellors was **cognitive behavioural therapy (CBT)** (Dowling & Rickwood, 2014) followed by *psychoeducation* and *behavioural strategies*. Barak et al. (2008) found that CBT was most effective and behavioural strategies the least effective for online counselling. This reinforces the findings here and supports the notion that the online environment is better suited to addressing psychological rather than physical symptoms.

There is an assumption that web-based interventions are more effective when a counsellor or trained professional is present. That is, that online, structured self-help modules are not as effective as online counselling. This meta-analysis showed no statistically significant differences in effect sizes of self-directed web-based therapeutic interventions and eTherapy (Barak et al., 2008). What might have been critical is whether the web-based modules were interactive or not. Static websites had a significantly smaller effect size than websites that required the users to interact with the information. A potential confounding factor is that interactive modules tended to be structured around CBT principles whereas static websites were psychoeducational in nature. Further investigation into this issue is required.

More recent research has compared the effectiveness of combined face-to-face and online counselling for reducing depression and anxiety symptoms in young adults (Sethi et al., 2010). Sethi et al. (2010) randomly allocated participants to one of four groups: *face-to-face therapy, therapist-supported web-based CBT, a combination of the online and offline interventions,* and *control*. The results showed that a combination of online and in-person support yielded the most positive outcomes for participants presenting symptoms of anxiety and/or depression. This suggests that there are benefits with using online psychological interventions that can value-add to face-to-face therapy.

In terms of online counselling specifically, Barak et al. (2008) found no effect of synchronicity on treatment outcomes. Interestingly, there was an effect of communication medium—audio therapy showed the greatest effect sizes for treatment outcome, then instant messaging and email with similar effect sizes, and lastly video conferencing and discussion forum-based therapy with similar, and the smallest, effect sizes. It is unclear why audio therapy is better than video conferencing and what the similarities are between video conferencing and web forums. The researchers note that for synchronicity and communication medium, there were a few studies with smaller sample sizes. It may be that more extensive research with larger sample sizes could yield further clarification.

Overall, online psychological interventions show positive effects beyond the conclusion of the treatment (Barak et al., 2008). The meta-analysis found that there were no statistical differences between treatment outcomes at the end of therapy and follow-up periods ranging from one month to one year post-treatment. Online interventions, therefore, have demonstrated positive treatment outcomes that are sustained beyond the conclusion of the therapeutic process.

So, based on this research we've established that online psychological interventions can be effective for treating a range of mental health concerns. What remains to be seen, though, is whether the dynamics of the client-clinician relationship change when counselling is moved from a face-to-face context to a mediated, online one. Is it possible to have the same kind of relationship with your counsellor or client online as you would face-to-face?

13.4 Characteristics of online counselling clients

Key to understanding the online counselling relationship is knowing who the clients are. There is limited research investigating the characteristics of clients using online counselling (and comparing them to characteristics of face-to-face clients). However, the findings of published studies present a consistent profile of eTherapy users. Clients of online counselling are mostly female (approximately 80–85%), Caucasian, young to mid-adults (aged 20–40 years), and had previously engaged in face-to-face therapy (DuBois, 2004, Leibert, Archer, Munson, & York, 2006). Consistently, the most common presenting problem was relationship issues. Depending on the service provider, other common problems included mood disorders, anxiety, and work-related issues. Leibert et al. (2006) surveyed participants and found that of the demographic variables measured (including age, time spent online, income, and educational attainment), only general Internet use predicted use of online counselling. Specifically, the more hours a person spent online, the more likely they would be to engage in online counselling if required. This is likely due to being more familiar or comfortable with interacting in the online space.

Early research into the characteristics of online therapy clients have attempted to draw comparisons between users of online and face-to-face counselling. These earlier studies identified the characteristics in their sample of online counselling clients and compared these characteristics (e.g., age, gender distribution) to published literature about face-to-face clients. They found no statistical differences between clients using online and face-to-face counselling (DuBois, 2004, Leibert et al., 2006). A limitation of this method, however, is its inability to account for the role of sociocultural context. The data about the two groups being compared were collected at different time points and subject to different social and cultural influences that may have affected a person's willingness to engage in therapy of any kind and participation in the survey study.

To address this issue, Murphy, Mitchell, and Hallett (2011) conducted a study where they simultaneously collected data about clients currently engaged in either online or in-person counselling. The results showed no statistically significant differences between the two samples on average age, gender, average service hours, and marital status. On the other hand, significantly more face-to-face clients presented with grief than online clients. Also, more online clients refused to disclose their referral source (even though for both groups, self-referral was the most common source). The authors proposed that the anonymous nature of online counselling provided clients with greater opportunity to refuse disclosure. Moreover, response to the question about referral source was optional whereas other questions in the survey were not. Overall, this study is consistent with previous research comparing characteristics of online and offline counselling clients. Together, the current literature suggests that there are no major differences between people seeking online and in-person counselling.

13.4.1 **Online counselling preferences**

The research cited here, however, has examined the demographic features (e.g., age, gender) of online counselling clients. Understanding other factors that may affect an individual's decision to engage in eTherapy could extend the scope of online counselling. The literature has consistently reported email (in the first instance) and instant messaging or chat as the preferred media for online counselling. The reasons stated for using eTherapy include convenience, affordability, privacy, and anonymity (DuBois, 2004, Leibert et al., 2006). Online counselling, particularly via asynchronous email, can transcend time and physical boundaries. Clients can access services within the privacy of their own homes and at a time convenient for them.

Anonymity could create a safe environment for people who would otherwise not participate in counselling. These people include men and young people, groups that have consistently reported negative help-seeking attitudes, particularly for mental health issues (Addis & Mahalik, 2003, Gulliver, Griffiths, & Christensen, 2010). Rochlen, Land, and Wong (2004a) asked 191 men to rate the perceived value of online counselling after reviewing vignettes of online or offline counselling sessions. Participants were divided into either high or low restrictive emotionality based on their scores on the Gender Role Conflict Scale (O'Neil, Helms, Gable, David, & Wrightsman, 1986). Restrictive emotionality is one component of gender role conflict and refers to the difficulty and fear associated with expressing emotions. A person with high restrictive emotionality would find expressing their feelings more challenging than a person with low restrictive emotionality. Rochlen et al. (2004a) found that men with high restrictive emotionality showed more positive attitudes towards online counselling than in-person therapy. These findings are encouraging and suggest that the online environment might facilitate more use of counselling in men.

Applied to a clinical setting, the benefits of complete anonymity—for example, increased self-disclosure (Joinson, 2001, Chiou & Wan, 2006, Joinson, Woodley, & Reips, 2007) and reduced social desirability biases (Joinson, 1999)—need to be evaluated against ethical, legal, and practical concerns (Rochlen, Zack, & Speyer, 2004b). Dowling and Rickwood (2014) were interested in clinicians' perception of their 12–25 year old clients attending an online mental health service. Clinicians' description of their clients centred around three themes:

1. The problems their clients presented with.
2. The type of service contact encountered in this context.
3. The role of anonymity in the client-therapist relationship.

Clinicians reported that clients presented with a range of concerns including clinical problems (primarily depression, anxiety, self-harm, and suicidal ideation) and psychosocial and environmental issues (particularly around relationships with family members, peer groups, and partners). Most clients required immediate, short-term support and only used the service once or twice. Others were long-term clients for whom clinicians provided ongoing support. Some also used online counselling to support their face-to-face counselling. Regarding anonymity, clinicians reported greater disinhibition, particularly in the form of increased aggression (e.g., swearing at practitioners). Anonymity also allowed clients greater control over personal information. This meant that clients could choose what information to disclose and withhold (e.g., personal and family members' contact details). So, the online environment has features that could attract young people to help-seeking (e.g., anonymity) but there are challenges to maintaining long-term engagement with young clients who often seek more immediate, short-term interventions. There are several implications of this that need to be considered when developing guidelines for supporting clinicians delivering therapy online.

13.5 Characteristics of online counsellors

The other half of the counselling equation is the counsellors themselves. There is even more limited research on the characteristics of counsellors than clients and the focus seems to be more on the operational side of online counselling. Heinlen, Welfel, Richmond, and Rak (2003) conducted a search for websites offering online counselling. They reviewed 136 sites using common search engines available to consumers. As identified on these websites, online counsellors were primarily based in the United States and practising as individual providers (20% were group practices). There were slightly more male than female practitioners and qualifications varied with over one third not trained in mental health. To build on and update this data, Chester and Glass (2006) surveyed counsellors who had experience delivering eTherapy. Unlike the previous study, there was an even distribution of gender among Chester and Glass' (2006) participants. This could be explained by the different recruitment strategies. Where Heinlen et al. (2003) identified gender from names listed on websites, participants volunteered to complete Chester and Glass' (2006) survey. Counsellor ages ranged from 28 to 69 years with an average age of 47 years (SD = 9 years). Most participants surveyed were highly educated, reporting a Masters or Doctorate level education, and were licensed to practice counselling. Consistent with previous research, most practitioners were from the United States, then the United Kingdom and Australia.

Finn and Barak (2010) surveyed online counsellors on their eTherapy practices. Over 90% of counsellors surveyed reported that their formal counselling/psychological training did not include an eTherapy component. Most participants reported that their professional development in this area came from personal reading and informal discussions with colleagues. Some attended formal workshops or training programmes. Despite this, counsellors reported mixed opinions when asked whether formal training should include an online counselling component. Forty four percent of participants agreed that formal eTherapy training should be enforced whereas 26% disagreed and 30% neither agreed nor disagreed (Finn & Barak, 2010). This could be reflective of the counsellors' personal experiences, as professionals who had attended formal training were more likely to say that it should be standardized and offered to all who intend on practising online. It should be noted that in the UK, counsellors intending to practise eTherapy are required to have postgraduate training. This is not the case in the US and could contribute to the responses presented here.

To date, our understanding of online counsellor demographics remain limited. There is scant research comparing the characteristics of practitioners who will and will not engage in online counselling. However, several challenges of eTherapy are cited as potential reasons for counsellors' hesitancy in using online counselling. These include the risks associated with anonymity (particularly with crisis intervention), lack of familiarity with technology (enough to ensure confidentiality of information), and reduced non-verbal cues leading to misinterpretation (Rochlen et al., 2004a,b).

13.5.1 Logistics of online counselling

DuBois (2004) analysed data from her own online private practice and found that clients used several search terms to access her website. These included 'counselling/counseling', 'online', 'free', and 'therapy'. Traffic to the site was highest on Tuesdays and from 4–5 p.m. most days. No proposed explanation was provided and further research is required to determine whether this pattern of engagement is widespread and what the implications of it are for practice. In their survey of online counselling practitioners, Chester and Glass (2006) found that session length ranged from single sessions to several months. On average, counsellors delivered five sessions for each client and a little over half the clients received sessions for less than one month. This reinforces the earlier finding that engagement with online counselling tends to be short-term, though for young adults, this may be shorter.

The cost for online psychological services varied according to practitioner. Billing rates ranged from being correspondence based (e.g., per email) to time dependent (e.g., per minute or per hour). Some clinicians offered their first email or chat session free of charge and others did not charge at all for their services (Heinlen et al., 2003). On average, emails cost either US$1 per minute or US$49.20 per hour; chat sessions were also US$1 per minute or US$58 per hour; and video conferencing sessions were charged at US$54 per hour (Chester & Glass, 2006).

13.5.2 Some ethical and legal considerations of online counselling

Ethical and legal considerations are usually at the forefront of objections to remote delivery of health services, including psychological interventions. It should be noted, however, that governments and regulatory bodies are developing and refining guidelines to untangle the myriad of issues associated with Internet-facilitated and cross-boundary service delivery (Rochlen et al., 2004b). Several studies have reported that online counsellors offer services to clients who physically reside outside the country or state that clinicians were licensed or registered to practice in (DuBois, 2004, Chester & Glass, 2006). Practitioners have a duty to notify authorities if their client is likely to cause harm to themselves or others (Shaw & Shaw, 2006, APS, 2007). If pseudonyms are employed or identifiable information not sought, questions of legal responsibility arise.

So, does the counsellor need to be registered to practise in the state or country where their client is located? In the European Union (EU), the answer is, 'no' (Ionescu-Dima, 2013). Directive 2011/24/EU provides guidelines and regulation of cross-border healthcare in the

EU. It allows patients/clients the opportunity to access healthcare (including psychological services) in other countries and states, including the right to be reimbursed for the treatment. Online counselling is considered part of this and is considered to be the equivalent of the patient/client travelling to the location of the counsellor to receive treatment. As such, the health practitioner must be licensed in their home state but need not be in the state or country of their client. At present, this type of cross-border agreement is limited to EU but online counselling and its growing popularity opens the conversation for more globalized, international, and equitable healthcare. Where services are unavailable in a person's home state or country but can be delivered remotely, the Internet can facilitate access to the relevant care. We recommend you read Ionescu-Dima (2013) for a more in-depth discussion of this issue in the EU context. Her work includes information about financial reimbursement and conflict of laws that is beyond the scope of this chapter.

In the United States, the National Board of Certified Counselors (NBCC) provides guidelines for the ethical practice of delivering professional services (including counselling) via distance (NBCC, 2012). This policy outlines the specific actions required by National Certified Counselors when delivering online counselling. They include a requirement for encryption of all therapeutic records and clear explanations to clients about procedures for technical failures. In a review of websites offering online counselling, Heinlen et al., (2003) found that less than a quarter of the sites described the encryption methods for therapeutic communication, many more emphasized the security of credit card details for payment. Moreover, only 3% of sites outlined potential technical problems and strategies for addressing them. Building on this, surveys of online clinicians also have poor compliance regarding communication encryption and discussions about managing technical failures (Chester & Glass, 2006). Some might say that this research is about ten years old. With the growth in use and awareness of technology and online counselling, it may be that compliance with NBCC guidelines has increased. More research is required to examine the alignment of current practice with international, national, and regulatory body policies for online healthcare delivery.

13.6 Working alliance in online counselling

In face-to-face counselling, the therapeutic relationship explained more variance in treatment outcomes than any specific component of the therapy itself (for a review, see Lambert & Barley, 2001). For example, Krupnick et al. (1996) found that the therapeutic relationship was a significant predictor of treatment effectiveness for depression, independent of the type of counselling the client received (CBT, interpersonal psychotherapy, and pharmacotherapy). Given the anonymous nature of the online environment, questions have arisen regarding whether a therapeutic relationship can be established in remotely delivered psychological interventions.

The therapeutic relationship is often operationalized as the 'working alliance' between a counsellor and their client. According to Bordin (1979), working alliance consists of three components: *tasks*, *bonds*, and *goals*. The tasks of counselling are the behavioural and cognitive work that forms the content of the therapy. If the client accepts these tasks as relevant and helpful then they will more likely engage with the counselling work. The bonds of counselling refer to the positive personal relationship between a client and counsellor. It includes mutual trust, acceptance, and confidence in the therapist. Finally, for an effective working alliance, both parties must value and endorse the goals or outcomes of the therapeutic process. This theoretical conceptualization of working alliance has informed the development of the Working Alliance Inventory. This is a self-report measure of working alliance commonly used to assess the therapeutic relationship in face-to-face and online counselling.

Research has consistently shown that a positive therapeutic relationship can be established during online counselling (Murphy et al., 2009). A systematic review showed that working alliance in online therapy is either not statistically different to, or significantly greater than, that of face-to-face counselling (Sucala et al., 2012). Cook and Doyle (2002) found that working alliance scores were higher in online therapy compared to those reported in published studies about in-person counselling. Moreover, the agreement between client and counsellor on the goals subscale of the *Working Alliance Inventory* was also greater for online than face-to-face therapy. Although agreement on the other subscales (bonds and tasks) was higher in online therapy, there was no statistical difference. An oft-cited limitation of this study, though, is its small sample size (15 participants). To build on this, Reynolds, Stiles, and Grohol (2006) asked participants (clients and practitioners) to rate their evaluation of online counselling sessions and the therapeutic relationship. Overall, satisfaction and perceptions of working alliance were positive for online relationships. The average satisfaction and working alliance scores were found to be within the range of published means of face-to-face therapy.

Although valuable, the comparisons of data collected about online counselling participants and previously published findings about face-to-face relationships are limited. To better assess the differences between online and in-person working alliance, participants should be randomly allocated to conditions. This would reduce the risk of confounding variables affecting the findings. Kiropoulos et al. (2008) conducted a randomized control trial comparing working alliance amongst clinicians and patients diagnosed with panic disorder or agoraphobia in online and offline therapeutic relationships. Working alliance was not statistically different between the two conditions. However, the generalization of these findings to our discussion about online counselling should be done with caution. The online 'therapy' in this study consisted of the client working through self-help modules with some email support from a trained psychologist. This is more of an example of a human-supported web-based therapeutic intervention than online counselling based on the classification system described in Section 13.2.

Preschl, Maercker, and Wagner (2011) adapted an eight-week CBT module for asynchronous online delivery and randomly allocated participants to receive either the online or in-person therapy for depression. This controlled for more variables and was able to experimentally compare the working alliance in online and offline counselling. Clients were asked to rate the working alliance twice, mid-, and post-treatment. Therapists rated working alliance once at the conclusion of the treatment. There was no statistical difference in working alliance at either time point from both perspectives. In addition, client alliance ratings significantly predicted depression scores post-treatment. This is consistent with previous research on the therapeutic relationship and shows that working alliance can be formed online and can predict some measures of treatment outcomes.

Other research, however, suggests that working alliance might have more impact on treatment outcomes in face-to-face compared to online therapy. *Kids Help Line* is a telephone and online counselling service offered across Australia. King, Bambling, Reid, and Thomas

(2006) surveyed Kids Help Line clients over 12 days and found that therapeutic alliance was not a significant predictor of session outcomes in either telephone or online counselling. This is contrary to the evidence found in studies of face-to-face therapy. A potential explanation is that this particular online service is usually accessed in once-off sessions. It may be that for the therapeutic alliance to have an impact on outcome, multiple sessions are required. However, King et al.'s (2006) study cannot draw conclusions about the contribution of working alliance in online and offline therapy as no offline counselling control group was used. This is an area for future research.

At present, the research suggests that satisfaction with online counselling is high (Richards & Viganó, 2013). In addition, the fears of not being able to form positive therapeutic relationships do not seem to be supported by current literature. Further studies are needed to examine the role of working alliance in treatment outcomes and whether there is a different effect of therapeutic relationship according to communication medium.

13.7 Self-disclosure in online counselling

Psychotherapy is premised on client disclosure to a mental health professional. The divulgence of intimate personal information—such as emotions, thoughts, fears, family history, habits—has been shown to facilitate positive therapeutic outcomes (Farber, 2003). As such, the adaptation of offline therapy to the online environment should take into account changes in disclosure patterns across communication media.

Online interactions have been described as being analogous to the **stranger-on-the-train effect**. Imagine that you're sitting on a train on the way to work or study and a stranger sits next to you when they arrive on the train. You acknowledge them with a friendly nod and they start sharing intimate information about their family, concerns, or excitement with you. They're likely to never see you again, there's no risk in telling you these things. You won't know their family or friends, the information can't be 'used against' them. This is an example of the stranger-on-the-train effect. This term refers to the tendency for individuals to reveal extensive personal information to someone they have not met previously and are unlikely to encounter again (Rubin, 1975). Online counselling, however, shows that Internet-based communication can occur over several interactions. Therefore, this explanation does not suffice.

The existence of Internet relationships leads us to question the ecological validity of experimental studies in online self-disclosure. This literature examined strangers communicating in a single session and is not completely representative of online counselling practice. Research from over 15 years ago examined changes in self-disclosure over time but not in counselling contexts. For example, Dindia, Fitzpatrick, and Kenny (1997) compared self-disclosure of three 10-minute sessions and found that only intimate self-disclosure increased over time. Won-Doornink (1985) assessed differences in self-disclosure across different romantic relationship stages (length of relationships were either less than one month, between 3-12 months, and longer than 12 months). There was no significant effect of relationship stage on self-disclosure; however, when disclosures were separated according to intimacy level, differences arose. So, it seems that time has an effect on the frequency of intimate disclosures, not all self-disclosures. Both these studies tell a story about self-disclosure across time but whether these findings can be applied to online counselling requires further investigation.

Self-disclosure is also context and audience specific. Social norms governing interactions between friends are different to that of the client–professional relationship. Previous research examined self-disclosure amongst peers in social (Antheunis, Valkenburg, & Peter, 2007) and task-based (Coleman, Paternite, & Sherman, 1999) contexts. In each scenario, participants interact with each other as peers. A therapeutic relationship, on the other hand, is notably different. In particular, clients expect, and are expected, to disclose to mental health professionals without reciprocated self-disclosure. This different relationship dynamic suggests that research findings in social interactions may not be completely relevant to therapeutic relationships.

Nguyen (2011) conducted a study systematically examining the effect of synchronicity and time on self-disclosure in goal-based counselling (coaching) and social contexts. Sixty participants were randomly allocated one of six conditions: to communicate either face-to-face, via instant messaging or email, and either in a social or professional relationship context once a week over four weeks. Participants were communicating with the researcher who was a female graduate student in psychology. We acknowledge that male–female and female–female conversations are different and analysed the differences between male and female participant responses to determine whether gender was a confounding variable. There were no statistical differences between males and females on disclosure frequency in all sessions. All conversations were coded for the number of information units communicated by the participant. Information units were defined as utterances aimed at providing knowledge to the recipient. This knowledge could be about the participant (i.e., self-disclosure) or non-personally relevant facts (e.g., 'the Golden Gate Bridge is in San Francisco'). A total self-disclosure score was calculated for each participant in each of the four sessions. The results showed that for online self-disclosure research to be validly applied to online counselling practices, the studies need to take into account the therapeutic context. Look at the results for total self-disclosure shown in Figure 13.1, you can see that participants revealed significantly more personal information via email, then instant messaging, and least face-to-face. The differences between each of these media are statistically significant. Take a look at the differences between the columns representing social and coaching groups in Figure 13.1. As you can see, the difference between these two media is reduced as the medium becomes more asynchronous even though participants consistently disclose more in the professional context.

Let's look first at the findings about communication media. Face-to-face and instant messaging conversations are both synchronous. They occur over real-time where the reactions of the person who you are speaking with are immediately perceivable. Face-to-face, you can see if someone is frowning, smiling, or smirking at what you are saying. Based on this reaction, you would modify what you choose to say next and how you will say it. Through instant messaging, you still get an immediate reaction. It may not be seen (as in the case of facial expressions) but it is still perceivable through the words the other person uses, any emoticons they share or the delay in their response. Communication via email, though, can span several days or weeks. It is not expected that the other person provides an immediate response so their 'presence' while you are composing your email to them is not as strong as it would be in synchronous communication. This study highlights the importance of synchronicity over and

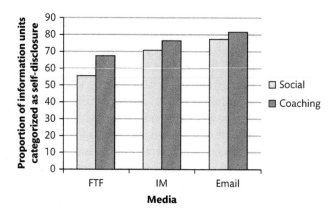

Figure 13.1 Graph showing the proportion of total self-disclosure according to media and context.
Reproduced with permission from Nguyen (2011).

above communication medium in influencing self-disclosure. The distinction is not merely online or offline because if this were the case, we would not expect to see a difference in self-disclosure between email and instant messaging. This suggests that online counsellors should consider the effect of their choice of medium on client disclosure. These findings also suggest that self-disclosure is affected by the context of the conversation in addition to the medium of communication. Participants in the coaching psychology groups disclosed significantly more than those in the social groups. This could be due to the fact that a client in a therapeutic relationship expects to disclose and therefore does so more willingly. The reasons could also be more practical. A conversation occurs within a finite amount of time. In a social situation, etiquette suggests that peers would disclose equally due to the principle of reciprocity (Altman & Taylor, 1973). On the other hand, in a counselling relationship, the client would disclose much more frequently than the counsellor. So, within an hour, for example, there should be more disclosure in a counselling context than a friendship one because the time for disclosure does not need to be shared.

A limitation of this study, however, is that it only examines frequency of self-disclosure. Self-disclosure is a multi-faceted concept, often studied along three dimensions: *frequency*, *breadth*, and *depth*. Frequency of self-disclosure refers to the amount of information revealed (how much information are you telling someone about yourself?); disclosure breadth is the range or diversity of self-disclosure topics (how many different types of information are you revealing about yourself?); and depth is the intimacy of personal information divulged (how personal is the information that you're disclosing about yourself?) (Altman & Taylor, 1973). Nguyen, Bin, and Campbell (2012) conducted a systematic review of studies comparing online and offline self-disclosure. They identified that perceived (how much you think you disclose) and actual (how much you actually reveal) self-disclosure could be differentially affected by communication medium. Findings measuring actual self-disclosure showed greater online disclosure but studies comparing perceived self-disclosure showed greater frequencies in face-to-face conversations than computer-mediated ones. It seems that people think they disclose more in 'real' life but actually disclose more online. So, although disclosure frequency is often researched, further studies are required to determine which dimension/s of self-disclosure (perceived or actual; depth, breadth, or frequency) best predicts treatment outcomes through online and face-to-face therapy. Despite the limitations, however, Nguyen (2011) showed that research about self-disclosure in non-counselling contexts should be generalized to online counselling with caution. This study has shown that there is an effect of relationship norms that needs to be considered.

13.8 Future research in online counselling

The field of online counselling is an exciting space to be working in whether we are clinicians or researchers. Existing literature points to positive directions for online counselling in both the treatment outcomes and therapeutic relationship. There is much more work to be done before an evidence-based, comprehensive framework for online counselling is widely accepted. Part of the challenge in developing this foundation of evidence is the constantly changing technological landscape. The pace at which technical advances are being made outstrips the rate at which research is being conducted and disseminated.

One example is the growth of videoconferencing. Most of the research cited in this chapter has focused on the text-based online delivery of psychological interventions. This is because, at the time these studies were being conducted, email and instant messaging were the more technically stable and widely available tools. Consumers and practitioners knew how to use email and instant messaging; they knew where to get technical support and most had access to these communication media. With the emergence of video-enabled mobile devices, videoconferencing is becoming a more accessible, supported, and increasingly used tool for communication (Manley & Publications, 2007). Preliminary research has started; for example Germain, Marchand, Bouchard, Guay, and Drouin (2010) examined working alliance in CBT for post traumatic stress disorder delivered face-to-face or through video conferencing. The results showed that working alliance increased over time and that there was no significant difference in the therapeutic alliance between online and offline groups. Consistent with research on text-based online therapy, there were no statistical differences in treatment outcomes between video conferencing and in-person counselling. More studies evaluating video conferencing as a tool for treating different health conditions would validate this research.

The current literature has mostly focused on counselling in a single modality. Increasingly, people are using multiple communication channels (in addition to in-person interactions) for conversing with each other. Online counselling could also move in this direction given the current findings. Some studies have shown that communicating via multiple channels leads to more positive treatment outcomes (Sethi et al., 2010) and therapeutic relationships (Cook & Doyle, 2002). However, these studies are few in number and contain small sample sizes. Moreover, findings by Cook and Doyle (2002) could be attributable to engaging in more therapeutic conversations (i.e., actually talking more with the counsellor) rather than there being inherent value in using two different media. Further investigation is needed.

At present, our understanding of the processes of online counselling is still developing (Rochlen et al., 2004b). The research into self-disclosure in therapeutic contexts is new and requires more nuanced measures of frequency, depth, and breadth of disclosure. Hand-in-hand with this is a theory of online communication that is able to account for the similarities and differences in how we interact with each other face-to-face and through different levels of computer-mediation. Regarding counselling, consistent, empirically supported links between the treatment processes, therapeutic relationships, and outcomes are yet to be established. So, despite the work that has been done, there are still more exciting questions to be answered in the context of modern technology and human interactions.

13.9 Chapter summary

- There is a diverse range of psychological support and interventions available through the Internet from one-on-one counselling with a trained professional to self-directed therapeutic modules to virtual reality treatments and online peer-support groups.
- Online therapy and self-directed web-based therapeutic interventions are effective in reducing physical symptoms as well as symptoms of psychological distress. This effectiveness lasts up to at least one year after the conclusion of therapy.
- The effectiveness of online psychological interventions varies according to the presenting problem, therapeutic approach, and amount of interactivity the programme contains.
- Clients of online counselling tend to be female, Caucasian and aged 20–40 years. This profile is not statistically different to that of face-to-face counselling clients.
- Online counselling clients prefer email and instant messaging as the main mode of delivery for online therapy.
- There is little research about the characteristics of online counsellors. Consistently, counsellors are mostly from the US, UK, and Australia, prefer using cognitive-behavioural approaches online and most have not received formal training in eTherapy.
- The working alliance developed in online counselling is, on the whole, not different to that of face-to-face therapeutic relationships.
- One potential difference between online and offline therapy is that working alliance may have a stronger effect on treatment outcomes in face-to-face than online counselling. This requires further investigation.
- Research into online self-disclosure shows that frequency of disclosure in counselling relationships over time are statistically different to that of social interactions. This suggests that to understand the nature of online self-disclosure in counselling, research needs to be conducted in a counselling context.
- Current research about self-disclosure in eTherapy focuses on frequency of disclosure. Future research should examine changes in disclosure depth and breadth as well.
- Future research about online counselling needs to investigate the link between the processes of online therapy and its outcome.
- The role of new technologies such as mobile technology and video conferencing requires further research.

References

Addis, M.E. & Mahalik, J.R. (2003). Men, masculinity, and the contexts of help seeking. *American Psychologist*, 58(1), 5–14.

Altman, I. & Taylor, D.A. (1973). *Social Penetration: The Development of Interpersonal Relationships*. New York: Holt, Rinehart and Winston.

Antheunis, M.L., Valkenburg, P.M., & Peter, J. (2007). Computer-mediated communication and interpersonal attraction: An experimental test of two explanatory hypotheses. *Cyberpsychology & Behavior*, 10(6), 831–836. doi:10.1089/cpb.2007.9945.

APS (2007). Australian Psychological Society Code of Ethics. Retrieved from http://www.psychology.org.au/Assets/Files/Code_Ethics_2007.pdf (accessed 8th September, 2014).

Barak, A., Hen, L., Boniel-Nissim, M., & Shapira, N. A. (2008). A comprehensive review and a meta-analysis of the effectiveness of internet-based psychotherapeutic interventions. *Journal of Technology in Human Services*, 26(2), 109–160.

Barak, A., Klein, B., & Proudfoot, J. (2009). Defining Internet-supported therapeutic interventions. *Annals of Behavioral Medicine*, 38(1), 4–17. doi:10.1007/s12160-009-9130-7.

Bordin, E.S. (1979). The generalizability of the psychoanalytic concept of the working alliance. *Psychotherapy: Theory, Research & Practice*, 16(3), 252–260. doi:10.1037/h0085885.

Branon, R. & Essex, C. (2001). Synchronous and asynchronous communication tools in distance education. *TechTrends*, 45 (1), 36–36. doi:10.1007/bf02763377.

Chester, A. & Glass, C.A. (2006). Online counselling: a descriptive analysis of therapy services on the Internet. *British Journal of Guidance & Counselling*, 34(2), 145–160.

Chiou, W.-B. & Wan, C.-S. (2006). Sexual self-disclosure in cyberspace among Taiwanese adolescents: Gender differences and the interplay of cyberspace and real life. *Cyberpsychology & Behavior*, 9(1), 46–53. doi:10.1089/cpb.2006.9.46.

Coleman, L.H., Paternite, C.E., & Sherman, R.C. (1999). A reexamination of deindividuation in synchronous computer-mediated communication. *Computers in Human Behavior*, 15(1), 51–65. doi: 10.1016/S0747-5632(98)00032-6.

Cook, J.E. & Doyle, C. (2002). Working alliance in online therapy as compared to face-to-face therapy: preliminary results. *Cyberpsychology & Behavior*, 5(2), 95–105.

Dindia, K., Fitzpatrick, M.A., & Kenny, D.A. (1997). Self-disclosure in spouse and stranger interaction: a social relations analysis. *Human Communication Research*, 23(3), 388–412. doi: 10.1111/j.1468-2958.1997.tb00402.x.

Dowling, M.J. & Rickwood, D.J. (2014). Experiences of counsellors providing online chat counselling to young people. *Australian Journal of Guidance and Counselling*, FirstView, 1–14. doi:10.1017/jgc.2013.28.

DuBois, D. (2004). Clinical and demographic features of the online counselling client population. *Counselling and Psychotherapy Research: Linking Research With Practice*, 4(1), 18–22.

Facebook (2011). Retrieved 10 March, 2011, from http://www.facebook.com (accessed 8th September, 2014).

Farber, B.A. (2003). Patient self-disclosure: A review of the research. *Journal of Clinical Psychology*, 59(5), 589–600. doi: 10.1002/jclp.10161.

Finn, J. & Barak, A. (2010). A descriptive study of e-counsellor attitudes, ethics, and practice. *Counselling and Psychotherapy Research*, 10(4), 268–277. doi: 10.1080/14733140903380847.

Germain, V., Marchand, A., Bouchard, S., Guay, S., & Drouin, M.S. (2010). Assessment of the therapeutic alliance in face-to-face or videoconference treatment for post traumatic stress disorder. *Cyberpsychology, Behavior and Social Networking*, 13(1), 29–35.

Griffiths, K.M., Christensen, H., Jorm, A.F., Evans, K., & Groves, C. (2004). Effect of web-based depression literacy and cognitive-behavioural therapy interventions on stigmatising attitudes to depression: Randomised controlled trial. *The British Journal of Psychiatry*, 185(4), 342–349. doi:10.1192/bjp.185.4.342.

Gulliver, A., Griffiths, K., & Christensen, H. (2010). Perceived barriers and facilitators to mental health help-seeking in young people: a systematic review. *BMC Psychiatry*, 10(1), 113.

Heinlen, K.T., Welfel, E.R., Richmond, E.N., & Rak, C.F. (2003). The scope of webcounseling: A survey of services and compliance with NBCC Standards for the ethical practice of webcounseling. *Journal of Counseling & Development*, 81(1), 61–69. doi: 10.1002/j.1556-6678.2003.tb00226.x.

Houston, T.K., Cooper, L.A., Vu, H.T., Kahn, J., Toser, J., & Ford, D.E. (2001). Screening the public for depression through the internet. *Psychiatric Services*, 52(3), 362–367. doi: 10.1176/appi.ps.52.3.362.

Ionescu-Dima, C. (2013). Legal challenges regarding telemedicine services in the European Union. In George, C., Whitehouse, D., & Duquenoy, P. (Eds), *eHealth: Legal, Ethical and Governance Challenges* (pp. 107–133). Berlin/Heidelberg: Springer.

Jarvenpaa, S., Tractinsky, N., & Vitale, M. (2000). Consumer trust in an Internet store. *Information Technology and Management*, 1(1), 45–71. doi: 10.1023/a:1019104520776.

Johnson, G. (2006). Synchronous and asynchronous text-based CMC in educational contexts: A review of recent research. *TechTrends*, 50(4), 46–53. doi: 10.1007/s11528-006-0046-9.

Joinson, A.N. (1999). Social desirability, anonymity and internet-based questionnaires. *Behavior Research Methods, Instruments and Computers*, 31(3), 433–438.

Joinson, A.N. (2001). Self-disclosure in computer-mediated communication: The role of self-awareness and visual anonymity. *European Journal of Social Psychology*, 31, 177–192.

Joinson, A.N., Woodley, A., & Reips, U.-D. (2007). Personalization, authentication and self-disclosure in self-administered Internet surveys. *Computers in Human Behavior*, 23(1), 275–285. doi: 10.1016/j.chb.2004.10.012.

King, R., Bambling, M., Reid, W., & Thomas, I. (2006). Telephone and online counselling for young people: A naturalistic comparison of session outcome, session impact and therapeutic alliance. *Counselling and Psychotherapy Research*, 6(3), 175–181. doi: 10.1080/14733140600874084.

Kiropoulos, L.A., Klein, B., Austin, D.W., Gilson, K., Pier, C., Mitchell, J., & Ciechomski, L. (2008). Is Internet-based CBT for panic disorder and agoraphobia as effective as face-to-face CBT? *Journal of Anxiety Disorders*, 22(8), 1273–1284. doi: 10.1016/j.janxdis.2008.01.008.

Kraus, R., Zack, J., & Stricker, G. (Eds) (2004). *Online Counseling: A Handbook for Mental Health Professionals*. London: Academic Press.

Krupnick, J.L., Sotsky, S.M., Simmens, S., Moyer, J., Elkin, I., Watkins, J., & Pilkonis, P.A. (1996). The role of the therapeutic alliance in psychotherapy and pharmacotherapy outcome: findings in the National Institute of Mental Health Treatment of Depression Collaborative Research Program.

Journal of Consulting and Clinical Psychology, 64(3), 532–539.

Lambert, M.J. & Barley, D.E. (2001). Research summary on the therapeutic relationship and psychotherapy outcome. *Psychotherapy: Theory/Research/Practice/Training Winter*, 38(4), 357–361.

Leibert, T., Archer Jr, J., Munson, J., & York, G. (2006). An exploratory study of client perceptions of internet counseling and the therapeutic alliance. *Journal of Mental Health Counseling*, 28(1), 69–83.

Manley, J. & Publications, K.N. (2007). *Videoconferencing: Market Report 2007*. London: Key Note Limited.

Moon, Y. (2000). Intimate exchanges: Using computers to elicit self-disclosure from consumers. *Journal of Consumer Research*, 26(4), 18.

Murphy, L., Parnass, P., Mitchell, D.L., Hallett, R., Cayley, P., & Seagram, S. (2009). Client satisfaction and outcome comparisons of online and face-to-face counselling methods. *British Journal of Social Work*. doi: 10.1093/bjsw/bcp041.

Murphy, L., Mitchell, D., & Hallett, R. (2011). A comparison of client characteristics in cyber and in-person counseling. *Studies in Health Technology and Informatics*, 167, 149–153.

NBCC (2012). *National Board for Certified Counselors (NBCC) Policy Regarding the Provision of Distance Professional Services*. Greensboro, NC.

Nguyen, M. (2011). *Exploring online self-disclosure: synchronicity, time, trust and relationship context*. Doctor of Philosophy, University of Sydney, Sydney.

Nguyen, M., Bin, Y.S., & Campbell, A.J. (2012). Comparing online and offline self-disclosure: a systematic review. *Cyberpsychology, Behavior and Social Networking*, 15(2), 103–111. doi: 10.1089/cyber.2011.0277.

O'Neil, J., Helms, B., Gable, R., David, L., & Wrightsman, L. (1986). Gender-role conflict scale: College men's fear of femininity. *Sex Roles*, 14I (5-6), 335–350. doi: 10.1007/bf00287583.

Oxford English Dictionary (2011) Retrieved 20 March, 2011, from http://www.oed.com/ (accessed 8th September, 2014).

Preschl, B., Maercker, A., & Wagner, B. (2011). The working alliance in a randomized controlled trial comparing online with face-to-face cognitive-behavioral therapy for depression. *BMC Psychiatry*, 11(1), 1–10. doi: 10.1186/1471-244x-11-189.

Reynolds, D.A.J., Stiles, W.B., & Grohol, J.M.
(2006). An investigation of session impact
and alliance in Internet based psychotherapy:
Preliminary results. *Counselling and
Psychotherapy Research*, 6(3), 164–168. doi:
10.1080/14733140600853617.

Richards, D. & Viganó, N. (2013). Online Counseling:
A Narrative and Critical Review of the Literature.
Journal of Clinical Psychology, 69(9), 994–1011.
doi: 10.1002/jclp.21974.

Rochlen, A.B., Land, L.N., & Wong, Y.J. (2004a). Male
restrictive emotionality and evaluations of online
versus face-to-face counseling. *Psychology of
Men & Masculinity*, 5(2), 190–200.

Rochlen, A.B., Zack, J.S., & Speyer, C. (2004b).
Online therapy: Review of relevant definitions,
debates, and current empirical support. *Journal
of Clinical Psychology*, 60(3), 269–283. doi:
10.1002/jclp.10263.

Rubin, Z. (1975). Disclosing oneself to a stranger:
Reciprocity and its limits. *Journal of Experimental
Social Psychology*, 11, 233–260.

Sethi, S., Campbell, A.J., & Ellis, L.A. (2010). The use
of computerized self-help packages to treat

adolescent depression and anxiety. *Journal of
Technology in Human Services*, 28(3), 144–160.

Shaw, H.E. & Shaw, S.F. (2006). Critical ethical issues
in online counseling: assessing current practices
with an ethical intent checklist. *Journal of
Counseling & Development*, 84(1), 41–53.

Sucala, M., Schnur, J.B., Constantino, M.J., Miller, S.J.,
Brackman, E.H., & Montgomery, G. H. (2012). The
therapeutic relationship in e-therapy for mental
health: a systematic review. *Journal of Medical
Internet Research*, 14(4), e110. doi: 10.2196/
jmir.2084.

Wicks, P., Massagli, M., Frost, J., Brownstein, C.,
Okun, S., Vaughan, T., & Heywood, J. (2010).
Sharing health data for better outcomes on
PatientsLikeMe. *Journal of Medical Internet
Research*, 12(2), e19. doi: 10.2196/jmir.1549.

Won-Doornink, M.J. (1985). Self-disclosure and
reciprocity in conversation: A cross-national
study. *Social Psychology Quarterly*, 48(2), 97–107.

Ybarra, M.L. & Eaton, W.W. (2005). Internet-based
mental health interventions. *Mental Health
Services Research*, 7(2), 75–87. doi: 10.1007/
s11020-005-3779-8.

 # Further reading

The terminology used in the online psychological interventions landscape can be quite confusing.
Barak et al. (2009) provide a classification system to help clarify the different types of therapeutic
interventions available and a consistent naming system. This is a good starter reference to build your
awareness of what is available in the online mental health space.

**Barak, A., Klein, B., & Proudfoot, J. (2009). Defining internet-supported therapeutic interventions.
Annals of Behavioral Medicine, 38(1), 4–17.**

For an excellent review of the literature examining online therapy effectiveness, see Barak et al. (2008).
This paper presents a detailed analysis of all the studies published (until 2006) investigating the
effectiveness of psychological therapies delivered online.

**Barak, A., Hen, L., Boniel-Nissim, M., & Shapira, N. A. (2008). A comprehensive review and a meta-
analysis of the effectiveness of internet-based psychotherapeutic interventions. *Journal of
Technology in Human Services*, 26(2), 109–160.**

There is limited research available with information about the practical aspects of online therapy.
Chester and Glass (2006) present findings about the logistics of delivering therapy online for the client
and practitioner. It is a good summary of how online counselling works on a practical level.

**Chester, A. & Glass, C.A. (2006). Online counselling: a descriptive analysis of therapy services on
the Internet. *British Journal of Guidance & Counselling*, 34(2), 145–160.**

Although this chapter is about telehealth (the delivery of health services, not specifically counselling,
via the Internet), the discussions about the legal and ethical challenges apply to online counselling. It

presents an in-depth response to the challenges by the European Union and starts to answer some questions that have been posed by academics, researchers, and clinicians since eTherapy began.

Ionescu-Dima, C. (2013). Legal challenges regarding telemedicine services in the European Union. In George, C., Whitehouse, D., & Duquenoy, F P. (Eds), *eHealth: Legal, Ethical and Governance Challenges* (pp. 107–133). Berlin/Heidelberg: Springer.

This systematic review provides an easy to read summary of existing research about the working alliance in online counselling. It discusses findings that compare online and offline therapeutic relationships as well as how this alliance affects treatment outcomes.

Sucala, M., Schnur, J.B., Constantino, M.J., Miller, S.J., Brackman, E.H., & Montgomery, G.H. (2012). The therapeutic relationship in e-therapy for mental health: a systematic review. *Journal of Medical Internet Research*, 14(4), e110.

 ## Discussion questions

1. According to the current research evidence, are online therapeutic interventions effective in reducing psychological distress?

2. There has been recent discussion about screening potential online counselling clients to ensure that they and their presenting problems are 'appropriate' for this treatment mode. Discuss the evidence for or against this proposal.

3. The therapeutic relationship is important to treatment outcomes in face-to-face counselling; however, research about online therapy is still developing. Evaluate the existing research and outline areas that require further investigation.

4. A recent study showed that self-disclosure patterns are different in social and counselling contexts. Does this mean that we should ignore any research into self-disclosure not conducted in a counselling situation? Why or why not?

14 Privacy and Security Risks Online

ANDREW POWER & GRÁINNE KIRWAN

 Learning objectives

At the end of this chapter, you should be able to:

- Describe the concept of online privacy.
- Discuss how trust relates to online privacy.
- Describe the characteristics of individuals with higher online privacy concerns.
- Advise on methods to improve online security and privacy related behaviours.
- Describe how theories inform our understanding of privacy and security.

14.1 Introduction

Increasingly we are encouraged by the popular media to believe that we are under both threat and surveillance by a range of forces. Virus makers are producing malware and distributing it using a wide variety of mechanisms. Cybercriminals infiltrate the websites and databases of the companies we depend on and fraudsters skim our credit card details. Still others might gain access to our computers and steal our files. Meanwhile, state intelligence services are reading our texts and checking what we are looking at on the Internet. Our employers are collecting data about our browsing habits. The companies we shop with are tracking our purchases and profiling our lifestyles. Unknown others are reading our email and we do not know who our children are talking to on social media. Is this true, even in part? In the case of our online life perhaps a little paranoia is a good thing.

In addition to those who are actively or passively seeking out our data, we also need to be aware of how much of our information we share willingly online. We might perceive that we are sharing this information with only a small number of individuals (perhaps only the person who we are sending a message to), but we might also be sharing it with a group of friends via a Social Networking Site (**SNS**) or publicly, via an online profile or website. We regularly give up certain aspects of our privacy to benefit from certain services or technological advances. Even in the case that we only share our information with a select few, there is always the possibility that the information could be forwarded by them to other parties, in which case the trust we place in our confidante might be significantly compromised. This chapter considers our concepts of online *privacy*, the sacrifices we make to our privacy in order to make other perceived gains, the role of *trust*, the types of individuals who are the most and least concerned about online privacy and the important theories in the field that inform our understanding of privacy and *security*. It also offers suggestions of methods that may increase our online security.

14.2 **What is privacy?**

The word privacy can mean different things to different people and can also vary depending on the nature of the information that a person wishes to keep private. The subject of privacy is also related to a number of other areas of our online life, these include: cyberbullying, gossip, defamation, data security breaches, improper disclosure, breach of confidentiality, unreasonable searches, and surveillance. A comprehensive explanation of the term is given by Clarke (2006). Privacy can have a particular legal meaning but also a more generally understood meaning. Clarke (2006) defines it as 'the interest that individuals have in sustaining a 'personal space', free from interference by other people and organisations' (Privacy, p. 3). Clarke goes on to break down the meaning of privacy into several related dimensions (Privacy, p. 4):

- *Privacy of the person*: concerned with the integrity of an individual's body. Issues include compulsory immunization, blood transfusion without consent, compulsory provision of samples of body fluids and body tissue, and compulsory sterilization.

- *Privacy of personal behaviour*: sexual preferences and habits, political activities, and religious practices, both in private and in public places. It includes what is sometimes referred to as *media privacy*.

- *Privacy of personal communications*: the ability of individuals to communicate among themselves, using various media, without routine monitoring of their communications by other persons or organizations.

- *Privacy of personal data*: the desire that data about an individual should not be automatically available to other individuals and organizations, and that, even where data is possessed by another party, the individual must be able to exercise a substantial degree of control over that data and its use.

A number of reasons are advanced to argue the need for, or importance of, privacy. Psychologically, people feel a need for private space. Sociologically, people need to be free to behave, and to associate with others without the fear of being observed. Economically, people need to be free to innovate; both individuals and commercial organizations need to feel secure that their innovations are free from industrial spying. Finally, politically, people need to be free to think, and argue, and act in order to preserve democracy.

For some the notion of privacy is an outdated concept. According to Facebook founder Mark Zuckerberg, privacy is no longer a social norm (Barnett, 2010). He expands on this by positing that 'people have really gotten comfortable not only sharing more information and different kinds, but more openly and with more people' (p. 1). Given this, perhaps privacy in no longer a concern; in the words of one writer, we just don't care any more (Casey, 2013, title). For Cashmore (2009) the culprit in this change in our attitude to privacy was clear when he wrote, 'Privacy is dead, and social media hold smoking gun [*sic*]' (p. 5). Social media is just one of a range of Web 2.0 applications, many of which are now accessed through mobile devices. Much of the benefit derived from these applications necessitates the sharing of some information in order for them to function effectively. We are regularly exchanging privacy for convenience. The simplest example is navigation applications. If we want our smartphone app to tell us how to get somewhere we have to first tell it where we are. Thus we are providing the service provider and unknown others with details of our location and movements.

14.3 Privacy, personality, and characteristics

Privacy is important to people in different ways. When we think about the people who we meet on a regular basis, we can probably identify several different types of individuals. There are those who 'overshare', telling everyone around them what might appear to others to be information best kept to themselves. There are those who are deeply private, rarely interacting with others at anything more than a superficial level, choosing to keep their information to themselves. There are others who may seem friendly and open to most, but on closer inspection, we can see that they only share deeply personal information with a few key individuals in their lives. Each of these individuals has different perspectives on privacy.

Certainly, individuals with higher privacy concerns are less likely to disclose personal information (Joinson, Reips, Buchanan, & Paine-Schofield, 2010), but several other traits are also linked to disclosure activities. Chen and Marcus (2012) found that certain types of individuals are more likely to disclose less-honest and more audience-relevant information online, most notably collectivistic individuals who were low on extraversion. Fogel and Nehmad (2009) found that information disclosure concerns can vary by social networking site and by gender, with men demonstrating greater risk-taking attitudes than women. Wu, Huang, Yen, and Popova (2012) found relationships between culture, the content of privacy policies, privacy concern, and the willingness to provide personal information. The differences between individual users of social networking sites in terms of their privacy behaviours was also noted by Litt (2013), who notes that certain groups take advantage of the technology to protect their privacy more than others do, and as such, some individuals are more at risk than others.

Of course, online it is not always possible to determine who will see our information. Initially most social networking sites did not allow an individual to subdivide their contacts into groups—an individual was either a contact or they were not, and if they were a contact then they could see everything that a user shared on that site. This meant that work colleagues, family, friends, current and past romantic partners, former school friends, and even casual acquaintances were all privy to the same information. However, it is rare that we want to share the same information with all of these groups, unless of course it is information that we do not really value. Realistically, there is information that we do not mind sharing with everyone who we have ever met (and some who we have never met!), and there is other information that we prefer to limit to those closest to us. The importance of these conflicting **social spheres** is described by Marder, Joinson, and Shankar (2012). They outline how different social spheres may have different norms and expectations about an individual, and that when not carefully managed, online social networking can cause tension. Similarly, Chen and Marcus (2012) note that student users of social networking sites selectively used privacy settings to control how they portrayed themselves online.

14.3.1 Communication Privacy Management (CPM) theory

Many of the aspects of online privacy discussed here are considered by **Communication Privacy Management (CPM)** theory. There are several basic principles of CPM, as outlined by Petronio (2002). These include that users (individuals or collectives) believe that they own their private information, and hold the right to control how this information is disseminated. The users also decide on rules to determine how much information is shared, and the methods used to share it, and presume that other holders of the information will also follow these rules. Finally, if this information is shared without permission, then turbulence will ensue. Communication Privacy Management theory has been applied to many aspects of online communication (Child, Haridakis, & Petronio, 2012, Jin, 2012, Kisekka, Bagchi-Sen, & Rao, 2013).

14.4 How did we give up our privacy?

Brenner (2006) argues that there have been six particular developments that have at the least facilitated us in giving up our privacy. These he lists as: Google, social networking, RFID (Radio-Frequency IDentification) tags, loyalty cards, Government action, and tools like the Kindle.

In the case of Google, Brenner is referring in particular to apps such as Gmail and Google calendar, which allow us to organize our schedules and communication. However, this is giving up a great deal of information as we, out of convenience, use the same tools for scheduling business and personal appointments. How this information is used and who has access to it is no longer in our control.

The explosion in social networking means that just about everyone is on LinkedIn, Facebook, or Twitter. The convenience and attractiveness of these tools as ways of communicating has induced us all to give up a lot of our privacy every day, willingly, and even happily. The type of personal information if used or seen by those we would not wish could have consequences from the mildly embarrassing to the risk of blackmail.

The growth in the use of RFID tags and loyalty cards has led to the ability to map our movements and buying behaviour to an enormous and growing degree. The RFID tag on our car saves us the inconvenience of struggling to find change for the toll road, but in exchange maps our location and movement. The loyalty card in our local shops may save us a percentage of our shopping bill, but it gives the store access to our buying habits and lifestyle choices and changes.

In the aftermath of terrorist attacks such as 9/11, governments around the world sought to increase their powers of surveillance in order to prevent such acts of terror recurring. Inevitably this has led to a potential for conflict between the right to privacy and the security of the state, between the desire to uphold civil liberties and the desire to protect citizens.

The widespread adoption of GPS navigation technologies in cars and smartphones means that the providers of this technology now have a simple tracking device on all of us, all of the time. This of course we have freely signed up to, and every time the little dialogue box pops up on our screen saying 'this app would like to use your location' we reconfirm our acceptance of this diminishing of our privacy. Other apps require access to our social networking accounts in order to sign up for them, so we are presented with a message like: 'This App' would like to access your basic profile information and list of friends.

Other less obvious applications are making inroads on our privacy. The Kindle keeps track of what you read, how quickly you read it. Various walking apps are tracking how much you exercise and how fit you are. Health motivated apps are used by us to manage our diet or lose weight. Who might be interested in this data: health insurance companies, employers, retailers? More people than you might at first think!

14.5 **Trust**

We have seen the characteristics that might lead to an individual sharing details of themselves with others, but a core aspect of personal disclosure does not relate solely to the individual disclosing the information, but instead relates to their relationship with the person or organization who the information is being disclosed to—in other words, the trust that the individual has in the recipient of the information. This may be the key factor for the individual above who is generally friendly and warm, but only discloses what they consider to be deeply personal information to a small number of others—they trust those others not to share the information with other people. Should one of those others share personal information without the permission of the individual, then it is very likely that the trust will break, possibly irrevocably.

The same principle applies online—we trust those individuals and organizations that we think will not share our information with third parties. We expect them to take care with our information, to not give it to others, and to protect it from cybercriminals who may try to steal it. If we think that this trust has been broken, that the information recipient has willingly or unwillingly disclosed our information to a third party without our permission, we may find that we are hesitant to share further information with them unless absolutely necessary. For some online organizations we have limited choice and may be forced to return to them (e.g., for government agencies). However, for many online organizations we do have a choice—we can choose to close our accounts and move to competitors. As such, trust is an important element of online commerce.

There are certain features of online communication that may result in a heightened tendency to disclose personal information. For example, Walther (1996, 2007) noted that the mechanisms inherent in online communication can result in heightened perceived levels of affection and emotion. Walther dubbed this **hyperpersonal communication**, and the resulting increased personal disclosures (Jiang, Bazarova, & Hancock, 2011) may not have occurred in offline settings. Indeed, since Rubin's (1974, 1975) early research on self-disclosure, there have been many insights into how and why individuals share information with others, even those who they don't necessarily know very well.

The trust that we hold in the individual who we are sharing our information with plays a key role in our likelihood of disclosing information (Joinson et al., 2010)—with high trust compensating for low privacy. The importance of such trust also relates to our interactions with organizations online, such as governments (Beldad, de Jong, & Steehouder, 2011). However, the type of communication tool used for discussion of private information is also important to users, particularly those with low levels of trust and those who were less frequent technology users (Frye & Dornisch, 2010).

14.6 Privatization of online data

The growth in global participation in the online and digital world has meant that an increasing amount of information is being uploaded, stored, and shared. Individuals have at best a limited knowledge of or concern about how private this information may or may not be. Access to the Internet is not only widespread but it has become a primary source of personal data about the user. The combining of social networking technologies and mobile telephony means that the Internet has moved from the desktop to the pocket. Being constantly online and constantly connected, social networking has become portable and omnipresent. The concept of the Internet has moved from a useful reference tool and a place we went to visit, to an alternate form of communication always available, never more than an arm's reach away.

Consequently there has been a huge increase in the volume of digital data routinely generated, collected, and stored about individuals' purchases, communications, relationships, movements, finances, and almost every aspect of peoples' lives. In addition, technologies have an ever growing power to collect, store, and mine such data. Most data is collected and stored by private companies: service providers, telecoms operators, social networks, and so on. Sometimes this is to enable them to provide a better service, in more cases it is for marketing, research, or other forms of monetization. Cate, Dempsey, and Rubinstein (2012) believe that rather than seeing this as a threat to their power, or to democracy, governments view these third parties as a ready, efficient, and cost-effective source of data about individuals and organizations.

For many years governments have required businesses to collect, retain, and share data about their customers and clients to assist in curtailing money laundering, drug trafficking, tax evasion, terrorism, and other offences. Governments seek access to personal information held by the private sector not only by asking companies to produce specific records about a single target or a small number of people at a time but increasingly via what Cate et al. (2012) call *systematic* government access. The advent of cloud computing and the resultant storage of data in large shared facilities that are accessible around the world provides advantages in terms of efficiency, data security, and cost. However, fear of broad government access to this data has slowed the deployment and use of some cloud services. Cate et al. (2012) cite the example of the Dutch Minister of Safety and Justice who, in July 2012, blocked US providers of cloud computing services from bidding on Dutch government contracts because of a fear that US law permits too much government access to personal information held by the private sector. As a further example, the fact that US law enforcement officials made at least 1.3 million demands for text messages, caller locations, and other subscriber information from cell phone carriers in 2011 is further cited.

Brown (2012) and Cate et al. (2012) argue that companies like Facebook are more than willing to provide private data to governments through a system called **systematic volunteerism**. By this they mean that in the UK, all that is required is for the government to ask. According to Brown (2012, p. 237) Facebook and BlackBerry comply with requests from UK public authorities for specific subscriber data under the Regulation of Investigatory Powers Act 2000 procedures, although neither are providing a public telecommunication system and so are not bound by the law.

14.7 **The privacy paradox**

The number of Facebook profiles and status updates, Twitter tweets, and Foursquare 'check ins' of a typical social network user might create the impression that young people in particular do not care about privacy. Tene (2011) argues that this is not the case and that young adults (aged 18–29) are more likely than older users to limit the amount of information available about them online, and are the most proactive in customizing their privacy settings and restricting who can see various updates. In 2006 Susan Barnes wrote about the **privacy paradox**. By this she meant that privacy seemed to be a concern of many using the Internet and yet their behaviour, in terms of sharing data, was in opposition to this view. It also seemed from her research that the view of younger Internet users was that their information was secure if their parents could not see it.

A further paradox is the distinction between what is seen as public information and private information. In fact Tene (2011) argues that there has been an erosion of the distinction between what is public and private. He cites the example of once anonymous cities like London that are now increasingly monitored by an intricate web of surveillance cameras backed up by face recognition software. When this is considered in the context of social media sites, where information is partially broadcast to the world and partially shared with friends, the question of public and private is no longer black and white. We are increasingly living in a 'semi-public' sphere.

There seems to be an uneasy alliance developing between the public and private. The private sector is gathering a huge amount of information and the state appears to see this as a tool of governance rather than as a threat. At the same time politicians and governments are seeing that participation on these same social networks and a sharing of their own information and data is a way of bridging the gap between themselves and their electorate. The digital divide, where it remains, limits online participation and while the private sector will continue to slowly gather the disconnected minority if there is a perceived market benefit, it should be recognized that the public sector is in the best position in regards to both authority and funding to address this problem. If social networks are to cast themselves in the light of an infrastructural service provider then closer cooperation with government to close this divide may be required.

Users are also beginning to gain a greater awareness of the potential negative issues surrounding the use of Facebook, including issues of privacy and security. Gross and Acquisti (2005) highlighted risks such as stalking, identity theft, price discrimination, or blackmailing. Boyd and Ellison (2007) identified privacy risks such as damaged reputations, unwanted contacts, and surveillance-like structures due to backtracking functions, harassment, and use of personal data by third-parties. Skeels and Grudin (2009) studied SNS use in the workplace and identified tensions due to the mixing of users' personal and professional circles. Wang et al. (2011) extended this work by looking at the issue of regret amongst users of Facebook. While well-evolved norms guide socialization and self-disclosure in the offline world, in the online world it can be more difficult to identify one's audience, control the scope of one's actions, and predict others' reactions to them. For many Facebook users they might not anticipate the negative consequences of their online activities, and may engage in actions that they later regret. Wang et al. (2011) found that the things people most regret posting about related to alcohol or drug use, sex, religion, politics, profanity, and personal, family, or work related issues. In examining why users make such posts, responses included: it's cool, it's funny, venting frustration, they had a good intention at the time, they didn't think about it, or being in an emotional state. Even a single act of indiscretion can have serious consequences, as in the case of a school teacher who was forced to resign because she posted a picture of herself on her Facebook page holding a glass of wine and a mug of beer (Moriarty, 2011). Incidents like these show the negative impact that a single act can have on an SNS user.

14.8 Getting back some privacy

The first step in recovering some privacy is to understand the environment we are now living in and ensure that the privacy/convenience deal that we make for ourselves is a conscious one. Understanding the nature of the information we are giving away is a first step.

The first and most straightforward way to improve privacy and keep government and commercial monitoring of your activities out of your life is to withdraw as much as possible from the online world. Of course that means giving up your smartphone, or at least turning it off and removing the battery when you are not using it. Otherwise it continues to broadcast your location. You could also consider the possibility of not doing business online, not sending email and never posting anything on social media that you don't consider public information. According to the Electronic Frontier Foundation (EFF, 2013, p. 1), 'due to a combination of legal and technical factors, face-to-face conversations and conversations using landline telephones are more secure against wiretapping than cell phone or Internet communications.' They go on to say:

> Cell phone conversations are more vulnerable both technically and legally, while SMS text messaging appears for now to be very insecure both technically and legally. Cell phones also create the risk of location tracking, and the only way to eliminate that risk entirely is to not carry a cell phone or to remove the battery.

For most of us the convenience of the technology that now surrounds us so pervasively is so integral to the way we work and play that this approach is not realistic. We have for the most part decided that the convenience of the technology in our pocket is worth the diminished privacy of our lives. Armerding (2013) offers some practical advice for those of us not willing to give up our technology but hoping to minimize the intrusion of other forces into our lives, including the use of encryption technologies, blocking technologies, and private networks.

A related point is the ability or right of someone to remove data about themselves from the online world. In January 2012 the European Commissioner for Justice, Fundamental Rights, and Citizenship, Viviane Reding (Reding, 2012), announced the European Commission's proposal to create a new privacy right: the **right to be forgotten**. In theory this would mean that companies like Facebook and Google would be liable for the cost (if it is even possible) of removing all data that we might post online and later regret. Rosen (2012) makes the point that this thinking comes from a fundamental difference between European and American conceptions of the balance between privacy and free speech. Europe is influenced by the law in France, which recognizes *le droit à l'oubli*—or the 'right of oblivion'—a right that allows a convicted criminal who has served his time and been rehabilitated to object to the publication of the facts of his conviction and incarceration. In America, the publication of someone's criminal history is protected by the First Amendment. Although debate around the appropriateness of this right ensues, Google recently implemented it having had backing from the European top court. Upon doing so, they received on average seven requests per second within the first 24 hours of its implementation. There are many reports of the statistics of these requests, but these are media and newspaper reports rather than statistics founded on Google's own research or academic insight.

14.9 Privacy and big data

The collection and analysis of big data sets create enormous value for the economy. It drives innovation, productivity, efficiency, and growth. However, it is also a privacy concern that could stir a regulatory backlash, dampening the data economy and stifling innovation (Tene & Polonetsky 2012). One example of an unexpected, or at least unplanned, positive outcome of the availability of big data is Google Flu Trends. Each week, millions of us from all around the world search for health information online. There are flu-related searches during flu season and sunburn-related searches in the summer. Google have found a close relationship between how many people search for flu-related topics and how many people actually have flu symptoms. This allows them to graph and predict outbreaks of flu around the world.

However, the harvesting of large data sets and the use of powerful analytic tools raises many privacy concerns. Information about our health, location, electricity use, and online activity is exposed to scrutiny, raises concerns about profiling, discrimination, exclusion, and loss of control. Some organizations use software tools in order to de-identify users. This is variously known as anonymization, pseudonymization, encryption, key-coding, and data sharding. The goal is to mask real identities yet allow analysis of the data. Unfortunately research has shown that even anonymized data can often be re-identified and attributed to specific individuals (Narayanan & Shmatikov, 2008, Ohm, 2010).

14.10 Security and risk management

Essentially, any time that we disclose information about ourselves, we are making a decision to do so, bearing in mind that such disclosure carries a certain risk. It is possible that the information that we share may be abused by the individual that we disclose it to (e.g., they may share it with others, or use it to obtain our compliance in particular actions). Also, simply by sharing the information and not holding it entirely private, we are running a risk of the information being overheard or obtained by a third party. There are several theories that consider why we engage in risky behaviours, and what influences our decision making under such risky conditions, with the most famous research in this area being conducted by Kahneman and Tversky (Kahneman & Tversky, 1979). In essence, how the potential risks and benefits of a certain interaction are framed and perceived by an individual affect how likely they are to engage in a certain risky behaviour, or choose one type of risky behaviour over another. Should we feel that the potential advantages of a behaviour outweigh the risks involved, and the information about such gains and losses are presented in specific ways, then we may decide that the disclosure of information is worth the risks involved. For example, we may choose that the advantages of having our bank balance and transactions constantly available via a smartphone app outweigh the risks of our smartphone being stolen and these details becoming available to a third party. An individual with a lower propensity to risk, or if the information about the risk and gains is presented in a different way, may result in a decision to restrict our access to information about banking to in-person transactions at our local branch, or reviewing statements when they arrive through the letterbox. It is important to note that our perceptions of risk are not always accurate, and we have a tendency to hold the belief that undesirable events (such as serious illness) are less likely to happen to us than to most other people, while desirable events (such as winning a prize) are more likely to happen to us than to others. This **optimism bias** (Weinstein, 1980, 1987) is a noted phenomenon across many aspects of life, but has also been noted to apply to perceptions of online privacy risks (Cho, Lee, & Chung, 2010).

However, it is also possible that we have a good awareness of risks, and yet decide to behave in risky ways. Bryce and Fraser (2014) conducted focus groups with young people aged 9–19 years, finding that the participants were aware of the risks of their online behaviour, but that they perceived the benefits of disclosing personal information and interacting with strangers online as outweighing the risks involved. Similarly, Heirman, Walrave, and Ponnet (2013) noted that adolescents were influenced by perceived social pressure from significant others when deciding to disclose personal information. It would seem that many current strategies to promote safer online behaviours in this group are therefore misdirected—the young people are aware of the risks, but choose to engage in such behaviours nonetheless. The solution may be in determining methods to achieve the young peoples' goals without requiring them to disclose such information in the first instance.

Elsewhere in this volume (see Chapter 6), a discussion is made of **Protection Motivation Theory** and its application to online safety behaviours. Protection Motivation Theory was devised by Rogers (1975, 1983) and has been applied to online safety in numerous ways (Lee, Larose, & Rifon, 2008, O'Connell & Kirwan, 2014). In essence, the theory describes how the user's perceptions of the threat and potential preventative measures influence their likelihood to engage in risk management behaviours. For example, the component 'Perceived severity of the threatened event' refers to the individual's beliefs about how severe the repercussions of the loss of privacy might be, while the component 'Perceived probability of the threat' refers to how likely that individual feels that the event might occur. In general, it could be expected that the higher the expected probability and severity, the more likely it is that an individual will take preventative measures (although this could be mediated by other factors, such as the individual's beliefs that they can effectively use preventative measures). Recent developments regarding the acquisition of personal information and correspondence by government agencies may have an interesting interaction with this model—if an individual feels that their information is not secure irrespective of what measures they take, and the user feels that the third party may be overwhelmed by the amount of information available to them, they may lower their risk aversive tendencies again, due to the belief that the information will be shared regardless of what precautions that they take, and that the likelihood of any individual person seeing this information and taking the steps of identifying the user themselves is minimal, as those involved in the surveillance have limited interest in the individual's communications. As such, in relation to Protection Motivation Theory, the user may feel that they have limited self-efficacy in preventing the incident (as their communications may be shared irrespectively), but that the perceived severity of the incident will be so low as to be negligible. Indeed, it is possible that Protection Motivation Theory has potential in the development of effective interventions to prevent security lapses (Workman, Bommer, & Straub, 2008). Nevertheless, it should be remembered that in many cases individuals know what they should be doing to increase security and protect privacy, but do not engage in such behaviours, a discrepancy sometimes referred to as the **knowing-doing gap** (Cox, 2012).

14.10.1 **Deleting the evidence**

There is a Jewish tale that tells of a man who went around his community spreading lies and gossip. When he went to his rabbi seeking forgiveness, the rabbi instructed him to take a feather pillow, to open it, and to scatter the feathers. The feathers spread—some remained close to the man, but some were taken away by the wind. The rabbi then told the man to gather all the feathers again. When the man indicated that this was impossible, the rabbi told him that it was equally impossible to undo the damage done by spreading lies and gossip.

Online we might not find ourselves lying or gossiping, but the story of the feather pillow has echoes nonetheless. What is disclosed or written online cannot be fully withdrawn—the possibility of its continued existence remains, even when the original disclosure has long since been erased. Some applications use a transitory element of information as a selling point, offering to delete the information (often a photograph) within seconds of being viewed. However, there are methods of retaining this information, with other applications being designed to recover the file, or the possibility of taking screenshots of the image or information always remaining.

Even when our information has been available online for some time, we might choose to adjust our privacy settings, perhaps in response to a cyberstalking event (see next) or another incident that makes us question our online security. Child, Petronio, Agyeman-Budu, and Westermann (2011) examined such behaviours in bloggers, finding that 'impression management triggers, personal safety identity triggers, relational triggers, and legal/disciplinary triggers' (p. 2017) can result in a blogger altering individual privacy rules, resulting in them 'scrubbing' their blog site and engaging in greater protective measures. Later, Child et al. (2012) identified various motives for deleting information that had previously appeared on bloggers' sites, including: protection of personal identity/safety, conflict management, employment security, fear of retribution, impression management, emotional regulation, and relational cleansing.

Similar research has been completed on social networking sites, with Stieger, Burger, Bohn, and Voracek (2013) examining **Virtual Identity Suicide**. This refers to leaving social networking sites and deleting the accounts. Stieger et al. noted that those who deleted their accounts had higher conscientiousness levels and were significantly more cautious about privacy than those who remained on the social networking site, with privacy concerns being stated as the most likely reason given by participants for their departure.

14.10.2 **Stalking and cyberstalking**

A relatively rare outcome of our sharing of information, but one that must be considered due to its severity, is stalking and cyberstalking. Because we now have opportunities to share information about ourselves at a regularity and immediacy previously impossible, due to the presence of smartphones with geolocation technology, we also have the ability to inform many individuals about our current and intended locations. In some cases we might select who we share this information with, selecting specific groups or individuals who will be able to view this information, but in some cases we might unintentionally share the information with individuals who would cause us harm or distress without realizing their intent. In other instances the availability of information via technology might mean that our location is known to others with little control left to us—for example, if we are registered on a specific university course, and the timetable of classes for that course is publicly available via the university website, then it is likely that anyone can determine where we will be for significant portions of the academic year.

Mishra and Mishra (2008) define cyberstalking as 'when a person is followed and pursued online. Their privacy is invaded, their every move watched. It is a form of harassment and can disrupt the life of the victim and leave them feeling very afraid' (p. 216). However, it is possible that an individual may not know that they are being stalked (Kirwan & Power, 2013)—their stalker may limit their behaviours to monitoring their activities using the Internet, and occasionally appearing wherever they know that the victim will be. Nevertheless, there are some estimates that over 40% of college students had experienced cyberstalking victimization, while almost 5% had perpetrated it (Reyns, Henson, & Fisher, 2012).

There are various responses to cyberstalking, outlined by Kirwan and Power (2013), including avoiding engaging with the stalker and reporting serious incidents to the police. However, the more information that is available online for a stalker to access, and the more methods that there are to communicate with a victim (e.g., via text messaging, instant messaging, social networking sites, email, etc.) the more difficult it becomes for a victim to avoid the stalker, and the greater impact that a stalker can have on their lives, both online and offline. It is also notable that the reduced privacy experienced online might result in individuals becoming cyberstalkers when they would never engage in offline stalking behaviours—for example, they may repeatedly visit their victim's social networking profiles, or message them late at night, whereas they would not consider following the victim to their home or approaching them in person.

14.11 **Chapter summary**

In this chapter we have addressed a number of factors in relation to privacy and trust concerns when using the Internet. The main points arising from this exploration are that:

- Privacy is a relative term, with different meanings and levels of importance for different people.
- For some, the notion of privacy is an outdated concept.
- Many modern technologies and applications require the sharing of information by the user in order to function effectively, thus eroding privacy.

- This data, gathered by organizations and companies, may be shared with third parties, such as governments.
- Certain types of individuals disclose different types and amounts of information online.
- Trust is an important component of online information sharing.
- We may choose or desire to share certain information with specific 'social spheres', and not with other individuals or groups.
- Communication Privacy Management theory has useful application to online information sharing.
- The 'privacy paradox' refers to a concern amongst individuals using the Internet about their privacy, while their behaviour is in opposition to this concern.
- There are various negative issues regarding the erosion of privacy, including identity theft, damaged reputations, surveillance, and increased tension between personal and professional lives.
- Research on decision making under uncertainty can provide us with insights about security and risk management.
- Protection Motivation Theory can be applied to privacy protection behaviours, and may be useful in encouraging the development of effective interventions to prevent security lapses.
- Once released into the Internet, it is extremely difficult to withdraw information.
- The increased data about ourselves presented online can make us vulnerable to cyberstalking.

 References

Armerding, T. (2013, July). 8 tips to enhance your online privacy. *CSO Online*. Retrieved from http://www.csoonline.com/article/736886/8-tips-to-enhance-your-online-privacy (accessed 9th September, 2014).

Barnes, S. (2006, September). A privacy paradox: Social networking in the United States. *First Monday*, 11 (9). Retrieved from http://firstmonday.org/htbin/cgiwrap/bin/ojs/index.php/fm/article/viewArticle/1394/1312%23note4 (accessed 9th September, 2014).

Barnett, E. (2010, January). Facebook's Mark Zuckerberg says privacy is no longer a 'social norm'. *The Telegraph*. Retrieved from http://www.telegraph.co.uk/technology/facebook/6966628/Facebooks-Mark-Zuckerberg-says-privacy-is-no-longer-a-social-norm.html (accessed 9th September, 2014).

Beldad, A., de Jong, M., & Steehouder, M. (2011). I trust not therefore it must be risky: Determinants of the perceived risks of disclosing personal data for e-government transactions. *Computers in Human Behavior*, 27, 2233–2242.

boyd, d. & Ellison, N. (2007). Social network sites: Definition, history, and scholarship. *Journal of Computer-Mediated Communication*, 13 (1). Retrieved from http://jcmc.indiana.edu/vol13/issue1/boyd.ellison.html (accessed 9th September, 2014).

Brenner, B. (2006, October). 6 ways we gave up our privacy. *CSO Online*. Retrieved from http://www.csoonline.com/article/504793/6-ways-we-gave-up-our-privacy (accessed 9th September, 2014).

Brown, I. (2012). Government access to private-sector data in the United Kingdom. *International Data Privacy Law*, 2 (4), 230–238.

Bryce, J. & Fraser, J. (2014). The role of disclosure of personal information in the evaluation of risk and trust in young peoples' online interactions. *Computers in Human Behavior*, 30, 299–306.

Casey, K. (2013). Online privacy: We just don't care. *Information Week*. Retrieved from http://www.informationweek.com/security/privacy/online-privacy-we-just-dont-care/240157369 (accessed 9th September, 2014).

Cashmore, P. (2009) Privacy is dead, and social media hold smoking gun. *CNN Opinion*. Retrieved from http://edition.cnn.com/2009/OPINION/10/28/cashmore.online.privacy/ (accessed 9th September, 2014).

Cate, F.H., Dempsey, J.X., & Rubinstein, I.S. (2012). Systematic government access to private-sector data. *International Data Privacy Law*, 2 (4), 195–199.

Chen, B. & Marcus, J. (2012). Students' self-presentation on Facebook: An examination of personality and self-construal factors. *Computers in Human Behavior*, 28, 2091–2099.

Child, J.T., Petronio, S., Agyeman-Budu, E.A., & Westermann, D.A. (2011). Blog scrubbing: Exploring triggers that change privacy rules. *Computers in Human Behavior*, 27, 2017–2027.

Child, J.T., Haridakis, P.M., & Petronio, S. (2012). Blogging privacy rule orientations, privacy management and content deletion practices: The variability of online privacy management activity at different stages of social media use. *Computers in Human Behavior*, 28, 1859–1872.

Cho, H., Lee, J.S., & Chung, S. (2010). Optimistic bias about online privacy risks: Testing the moderating effects of perceived controllability and prior experience. *Computers in Human Behavior*, 26, 987–995.

Clarke, R. (2006). *Introduction to Dataveillance and Information Privacy, and Definitions of Terms*. Available at http://www.rogerclarke.com/DV/Intro.html#Priv (accessed 9th September, 2014).

Cox, J. (2012). Information systems user security: A structured model of the knowing-doing gap. *Computers in Human Behavior*, 28, 1849–1858.

EFF (2013). Surveillance self-defence. *Electronic Frontier Foundation*. Retrieved from https://ssd.eff. org/wire/protect/summing-up (accessed 9th September, 2014).

Fogel, J. & Nehmad, E. (2009). Internet social network communities: Risk taking, trust and privacy concerns. *Computers in Human Behavior*, 25, 153–160.

Frye, N.E. & Dornisch, M.M. (2010). When is trust not enough? The role of perceived privacy of communication tools in comfort with self-disclosure. *Computers in Human Behavior*, 26, 1120–1127.

Gross, R. & Acquisti, A. (2005). Information revelation and privacy in online social networks. *WPES '05: Proceedings of the 2005 ACM Workshop on Privacy in the Electronic Society*, 71–80.

Heirman, W., Walrave, M., & Ponnet, K. (2013). Predicting adolescents' disclosure of personal information in exchange for commercial incentives: An application of an extended Theory of Planned Behavior. *Cyberpsychology, Behavior and Social Networking*, 16, 81–87.

Jiang, C.L., Bazarova, N.N., & Hancock, J.T. (2011). The disclosure–intimacy link in computer-mediated communication: An attributional extension of the hyperpersonal model. *Human Communication Research*, 37, 58–77.

Jin, S.-A.A. (2012). 'To disclose or not to disclose, that is the question': A structural equation modelling approach to communication privacy management in e-health. *Computers in Human Behavior*, 28, 69–77.

Joinson, A.N., Reips, U.-D., Buchanan, T., & Paine-Schofield, C.B. (2010). Privacy, trust and self-disclosure online. *Human Computer Interaction*, 25, 1–24.

Kahneman, D. & Tversky, A. (1979). Prospect Theory: An analysis of decision under risk. *Econometrica*, 47, 263–292.

Kirwan, G. & Power, A. (2013). *Cybercrime: The Psychology of Online Offenders*. Cambridge: Cambridge University Press.

Kisekka, V., Bagchi-Sen, S., & Rao, H.R. (2013). Extent of private information disclosure on online social networks: An exploration of Facebook mobile phone users. *Computers in Human Behavior*, 29, 2722–2729.

Lee, D., Larose, R., & Rifon, N. (2008). Keeping our network safe: a model of online protection behaviour. *Behaviour & Information Technology*, 27, 445–454.

Litt, E. (2013). Understanding social network site users' privacy tool use. *Computers in Human Behavior*, 29, 1649–1656.

Marder, B., Joinson, A., & Shankar, A. (2012). Every post you make, every pic you take, I'll be watching you: Behind social spheres on Facebook. In *45th Hawaii International Conference on System Science (HICSS)*, IEEE, pp. 859–868.

Mishra, A. & Mishra, D. (2008). Cyber Stalking: A challenge for web security. In Janczewski, L.J. & Colarik, A.M. (Eds), *Cyber Warfare and Cyber Terrorism* (pp. 216–225). Hershey, PA: Information Science Reference.

Moriarty, E. (2011). Did the Internet kill privacy? Facebook photos lead to a teacher losing her job; what expectations of privacy exist in the digital era? *CBS Interactive*. Retrieved from http://www.cbsnews.com/stories/2011/02/06/sunday/main7323148.shtml (accessed 9th September, 2014).

Narayanan, A. & Shmatikov, V. (2008). Robust de-anonymization of large sparse datasets. In *Proceedings of the 2008 IEEE Symposium on Security and Privacy*, pp. 111-125. ISBN: 978-0-7695- 3168-,7doi: 10.1109/SP.2008.33. Retrieved from http://www.cs.utexas.edu/~shmat/shmat_oak08netflix.pdf (accessed 9th September, 2014).

O'Connell, R. & Kirwan, G. (2014). Protection motivation theory and online activities. In Power, A. & Kirwan, G. (Eds), *Cyberpsychology and New Media: A Thematic Reader* (pp.139-148). Hove/New York: Psychology Press.

Ohm, P. (2010) Broken promises of privacy: Responding to the surprising failure of anonymization. *UCLA Law Review*, 57, 1701–1777. Retrieved from http://www.uclalawreview.org/pdf/57-6-3.pdf (accessed 9th September, 2014).

Petronio, S. (2002). *Boundaries of Privacy: Dialectics of Disclosure*. Albany, NY: SUNY Press.

Reding, V. (2012, January). The EU Data Protection Reform 2012: Making Europe the standard setter for modern data protection rules in the digital age. Speech presented at the *Innovation Conference Digital, Life, Design*. Munich. Retrieved from http://europa.eu/rapid/press-release_SPEECH-12-26_en.htm (accessed 9th September, 2014).

Reyns, B.W., Henson, B., & Fisher, B.S. (2012). Stalking in the Twilight Zone: Extent of cyberstalking victimization and offending among college students. *Deviant Behaviour*, 33, 1-25.

Rogers, R.W. (1975). A protection motivation theory of fear appeals and attitude change. *The Journal of Psychology*, 91, 93-114.

Rogers, R.W. (1983). Cognitive and physiological processes in fear appeals and attitude change: a revised theory of protection motivation. In Cacioppo, J. & Petty, R. (Eds), *Social Psychophysiology* (pp. 153-176). New York: Guildford Press.

Rosen, J. (2012). The right to be forgotten. *Stanford Law Review Online*, 64 (88), 88-92. Retrieved from http://www.stanfordlawreview.org/sites/default/files/online/topics/64-SLRO-88.pdf (accessed 9th September, 2014).

Rubin, Z. (1974). Lovers and other strangers: The development of intimacy in encounters and relationships. *American Scientist*, 62, 182-190.

Rubin, Z. (1975). Disclosing oneself to a stranger: Reciprocity and its limits. *Journal of Experimental Social Psychology*, 11, 233-260.

Skeels, M.M. & Grudin, J. (2009). When social networks cross boundaries: A case study of workplace use of Facebook and LinkedIn. In Teasley, S. & Havn, E. (Chairs), *Group 2009: Proceedings, Sanibel Island, Florida, 10-13 May*, pp. 95-104. Retrieved from http://research.microsoft.com/en-us/um/people/jgrudin/publications/newwave/socialnetworking2009.pdf (accessed 9th September, 2014).

Stieger, S., Burger, C., Bohn, M., & Voracek, M. (2013). Who commits virtual identity suicide? Differences in privacy concerns, Internet addiction and personality between Facebook users and quitters. *Cyberpsychology, Behavior and Social Networking*, 16, 629-634.

Tene, O. (2011). Privacy: The new generations. *International Data Privacy Law*, 1 (1), 15–27.

Tene, O. & Polonetsky, J. (2012). Privacy in the Age of Big Data: A time for big decisions. *Stanford Law Review Online*, 64 (63), 64–69. Retrieved from http://www.stanfordlawreview.org/sites/default/files/online/topics/64-SLRO-63_1.pdf (accessed 9th September, 2014).

Walther, J.B. (1996). Computer-mediated communication: Impersonal, interpersonal and hyperpersonal interaction. *Communication Research*, 23, 3-43.

Walther, J.B. (2007). Selective self-presentation in computer-mediated communication: Hyperpersonal dimensions of technology, language and cognition. *Computers in Human Behaviour*, 23, 2538-2557.

Wang, Y., Komanduri, S., Leon, P.G., Norcie, G., Acquisti, A., & Cranor L.F. (2011). I regretted the minute I pressed share: A qualitative study of regrets on Facebook. In Cranor, L.F. (Chair), *Proceedings of the 7th Symposium on Usable Privacy and Security (SOUPS)*, Pittsburgh, PA 20-22 July.

Weinstein, N.D. (1980). Unrealistic Optimism about Future Life Events. *Journal of Personality and Social Psychology*, 39, 806-820.

Weinstein, N.D. (1987). Unrealistic optimism about susceptibility to health problems: Conclusions from a community-wide sample. *Journal of Behavioral Medicine*, 10, 481-500.

Workman, M., Bommer, W.H., & Straub, D. (2008). Security lapses and the omission of information security measures: A threat control model and empirical test. *Computers in Human Behavior*, 24, 2799–2816.

Wu, K.W., Huang, S.Y., Yen, D.C., & Popova, I. (2012). The effect of online privacy policy on consumer privacy concern and trust. *Computers in Human Behaviour*, 28, 889–897.

 ## Further reading

Barnes, S.B. (2006). A Privacy Paradox: Social networking in the United States, *First Monday*, http://firstmonday.org/htbin/cgiwrap/bin/ojs/index.php/fm/article/viewArticle/1394/1312%23note4. This looks at how children think that the information they share on the Internet is safe from danger as long as their parents do not see it. They appear unaware that this information can be tracked and that there are dangers in sharing personal information. Social networking is cited as particularly dangerous.

Child, J.T., Petronio, S., Agyeman-Budu, E.A., & Westermann, D.A. (2011). Blog scrubbing: Exploring triggers that change privacy rules. *Computers in Human Behavior*, 27, 2017–2027. This paper examines how individuals adjust their privacy settings in response to 'critical incidents'.

Fogel, J. & Nehmad, E. (2009). Internet social network communities: Risk taking, trust, and privacy concerns. *Computers in Human Behavior*, 25 (1), 153–160. doi:10.1016/j.chb.2008.08.006. This is a study of male and female students' behaviours on social networks and their comparative privacy settings. It expresses the view that when people share this information, they are very vulnerable to putting themselves in danger. The Internet possesses many dangers that most do not take into account.

Joinson, A.N., Reips, U.-D., Buchanan, T., & Paine-Schofield, C.B. (2010). Privacy, trust and self-disclosure online. *Human Computer Interaction*, 25, 1–24. This paper examines the links between dispositional privacy concerns, trust in an information requestor and perceived privacy during an interaction on disclosure of personal information using two studies.

Livingstone, S. (2008). Taking risky opportunities in youthful content creation: teenagers' use of social networking sites for intimacy, privacy and self-expression. *New Media & Society*, 10 (3), 393–411. doi:10.1177/1461444808089415. Livingstone breaks down teenagers' behaviours when using social networking sites, how they use social networking, friend people, and are these people really friends?

Marder, B., Joinson, A., & Shankar, A. (2012). Every post you make, every pic you take, I'll be watching you: Behind social spheres on Facebook. In *45th Hawaii International Conference on System Science (HICSS)*, IEEE, pp. 859–868. This paper examines how disclosures to different 'social spheres' on social networking sites can cause tension due to varying norms and expectations among user groups.

 ## Discussion questions

1. In the age of interconnected digital communication, is privacy a realistic expectation?
2. Is the perceived lack of privacy concerns amongst Internet users a result of ignorance, carelessness, or indifference?
3. What security measures is it reasonable to expect users to comply with?
4. How can individuals be encouraged to maintain greater privacy settings?

Cognitive Factors in Online Behaviour

LEE HADLINGTON

⊙ Learning objectives

By the end of this chapter we hope that the reader will have a basic understanding of the following issues:

- How the activities we engage in on the Internet affect the way in which we process information.
- How reading online is different to offline reading with the ability to explore the key impact such a difference can have on learning.
- How memory is changing to reflect our dependence on search engines to locate relevant material.
- How research has demonstrated that our attentional system is not as accurate at representing the online visual environment as we might expect.
- How the activities we engage in on the Internet serve to increase cognitive load to a point where errors are incurred.
- How interruptions to our working patterns are brought about as a result of our use of the Internet hinders performance.
- How using the Internet, specifically social networking sites, may provide a mechanism for improving aspects of cognition.

15.1 Introduction

As a tool, the Internet has become a key feature of our daily lives. We shop online, we chat online, we do business online, we date online, and we seek information online. These activities have become so commonplace in our daily lives that many of us take for granted the ease with which they can be accomplished. Our engagement in these activities becomes even more interesting when we consider that the environments through which such interactions take place are not *physically* real. Nonetheless, they do present an arena for psychological experiences that serve to replicate many of the things we do in the offline world. Key to the management of these interactions is a set of cognitive processes that govern aspects such as learning, memory, attention, and problem solving. In the context of the current discussion these processes allow us to manipulate key aspects of the digital environment in which we find ourselves immersed.

The focus for this chapter is an exploration of the research that highlights the possible downside to our interactions on the Internet. This could be in the form of misguided or faulty attentional processes, distractions, and interruptions or associated problems with memory recall and encoding. These processes are fundamental for our everyday lives yet most of us take them for granted, particularly when they work so well for the vast majority of time. For the most part those processes we use in the 'offline' environment are pretty good. As a function of our daily lives we can remember most things, we can learn new skills and acquire new facts and information, and we can pay attention to a variety of things at any one time. There are occasions when we forget, when learning a new skill or solving a problem is hard, or when our attention is distracted away from our current goal objectives. The current issue is to which extent our online lives serve to aid similar failures in cognitive processes. We perhaps assume that if we are given a simple webpage presented on a computer screen, we can easily pay attention to all of the information that is contained within it (Varakin, Levin, & Fidler, 2004). This assumption is an oversimplification of the ways in which humans can interact with the online digital environment. Furthermore, as we will see throughout this chapter, the processes we use in the online world are every bit as fragile as their offline counterparts.

15.2 So, how many golf balls are on the Moon?

Things evolve and things change. This is an evitable consequence of the passage of time. If you had been asked the question that serves as a title for this section any time before the advent of the Internet, you would have perhaps done a variety of different things. You could have asked someone in your social group, perhaps a relative or a friend whom you believe could provide you with an answer to that question. The problem here is that of corroboration—how do you know that the information you are being provided with is correct? On the other hand, you could have visited your local library where you could explore the archives of information, perhaps stored in the form of newspaper articles, books, microfiche, encyclopaedias, journal articles, and so on. Such a process takes a great deal of time and requires the expenditure of a great deal of resources in terms of time and effort. This is never a good thing, particularly as humans have a reputation for being miserly when it comes to expending mental effort on something, especially when there is another easier and quicker mechanism for finding the answer. If we do find information through this mechanism, the bonus is that we do not really have to verify the information that we have found; if someone has published the information in a book it must be credible, right? There are some further subsidiary benefits from engaging in this process, things that we might not initially think about when we are looking for information. Asking questions in a social context increases our interpersonal skills, particularly when verbalizing information and gaining confidence. We also develop communication skills that in turn help reflect well on our self-efficacy. Research by Ybarra, Winkielman, Yeh, Burnstein, and Kavanagh (2010) has demonstrated that aspects of social interaction are actually beneficial for aspects of our cognitive functioning such as executive control, the overarching process that governs what we pay attention to and when. There is also the actual search for the information itself, which builds learning, and improves problem solving and decision making. The process of searching for information is not just about the piece of information itself, the semantic or the factual. It is also about the autobiographical aspects of the search, what we did, how and where we found that information.

This is important in anchoring the memory we have for that material deeper (this concept of autobiographical memory is a long and controversial story but Conway & Pleydell-Pearce (2000) present an excellent discussion of the key points).

Moving forward to the present day, the mechanisms by which an individual would go about searching for the answer to the very same question have changed somewhat. What has changed? Well, to select an uncontroversial example, the tools we can use to search for information have changed. They have changed so rapidly that we are still attempting to understand the impact such changes may be having on the human information processing system. In one of my recent lectures on memory the topic of general knowledge came up and I broached the question of how many golf balls are actually on the Moon? Initially, as is the case in a few of my lectures, students questioned my sanity and dismissed the question as being a trick, suggesting there were indeed no golf balls on the Moon. As the discussion continued, a member of the group shouted out the answer to this question. As we explored the process through which this answer had been obtained, it was clear that the student had used a smartphone connected to the Internet to Google key phrases from the question, for example, 'Moon' and 'golf balls' (the answer is two, for those readers without a smartphone handy, taken from the official transcript of the Apollo 14 mission to the moon where Alan Shepard used a modified sampling tool to hit two golf balls just before the astronauts returned to Earth). This almost instant access to information belies a key change in our relationship, not only with that information, but also with the technology that governs our interactions with it. Moreover, this relationship is developing at speed, with research already demonstrating the impact of cyberspace on the cognitive processes we use to manage situations such as the golf balls question.

Aspects such as attention, memory, reading and problem-solving/decision making are all basic cognitive processes that we are only just beginning to understand in the offline world. Throw the individual into a world of hypermedia, viral advertising, online social networks, and blogs, and the toll that such environments have on these processes and their limited resources is only just becoming a matter of interest for researchers.

15.3 'Google knows'

The previous example of utilizing a search engine to answer a question involves the notion of **transactive memory**. This is a term that is taken from the realm of social cognition and describes the way in which aspects of memory are 'offloaded' to elements within the immediate environment (Sparrow, Liu, & Wegner, 2011). The capacity to store pieces of information 'externally' is not something that is new or different. As any group structure or information-transferring relationship develops there will be the creation of a transactive memory. This social memory includes not only the sum of all the memories we possess as an individual but also the cumulative knowledge that the group as a whole possesses in terms of their own particular memories. If we do not know the information, we might know someone else who does (Wegner, Giuliano, & Hertel, 1985, Wegner, 1987, Sparrow et al., 2011). The crucial aspect of the research conducted by Sparrow et al. (2011) is an exploration of whether the search engines that we interact with have now become members of this social memory. The research concluded that we are indeed offloading part of our transactive memory to search engines in the belief that the Internet will 'know' the answer to any question we can throw at it. As a consequence it appears that, rather than remembering the actual pieces of information, we are increasingly remembering (only) the sources for that information. So rather than having a factual piece of information embedded in our long-term memory we have a procedural memory that tells us where to go if we need to find similar information again. This mimics the previous social context of transactive memory where, if we did not know the answer to a question then at least we would know the location of someone who might. Perhaps the other downside to this process, as Sparrow et al. (2011) pointed out, is that in order to know whatever 'Google knows' means that we must be connected to it in some way, with the consequences that 'disconnection' results in a loss of this resource.

There is an inevitability regarding the progress of technology and its impact on the individual as well as the processes that govern our interactions with the world. It is important for us not to take these developments for granted, but to understand how such developments are influencing the processes that determine our cognitive selves.

15.4 Online interaction and evolving cognitions

Let's not get too disheartened straight away. The Internet itself is a brilliant tool, allowing us to search, surf, download, tweet, chat, and play in a number of ways. Where areas such as human–computer interaction have highlighted the ways in which we interact with technology using the Internet is not the same as using a computer. Being engaged in activities within cyberspace places various cognitive demands on the individual compared to just using a computer (Johnson, 2006). The key difference between the use of the Internet and the use of a computer is the connectivity we have when engaged in the former. Johnson and Johnson (2008) noted that the Internet serves to connect us to a whole realm of different forms of media, all of which we can interact with and more importantly some of which can interact with us. In most cases using a non-networked computer is a static experience constrained by the limitations of the installed software and the connected devices such as mouse, keyboard, and monitor. The interactions we have are in isolation and are not governed by any external forces. Once that computer is connected to the Internet something different starts to happen, and the cognitive load we experience increases (Johnson & Johnson, 2008).

Early work in this area conducted by Tarpley (2001) alluded to the complexity of Internet use in contrast to more conventional forms of media interaction. If you read a book or a newspaper, watch TV, or listen to the radio, you are for the most part a passive consumer of information. Yes, you can shout at the television or sing along to music on the radio, but what you do has little direct impact on the media conveying that message. In the context of the Internet we go from being passive to very much an active consumer. We can play games, interact with material and media, communicate in real time, and leave people messages. The cognitive mechanisms underlying these processes mean that the primary way of interacting with our environment, particularly that which is Internet based, has moved away from being mostly verbal to one of visual (Subrahmanyam, Greenfield, Kraut, & Gross, 2001). Whereas previously we would talk or chat, we now look, type, and click in order to manipulate elements on the screen in front of us.

15.5 Could the Internet be improving the way we think?

In an initial foray into exploring how using the Internet affects our cognitive abilities Johnson and Johnson (2008) explored differences in reasoning skills between those people who reported being frequently online versus those who were infrequent users of the Internet. The findings demonstrated that frequent users differed from their not-so-frequent counterparts in an important aspect of cognition, that of non-verbal reasoning. The notion of non-verbal reasoning relates to something that has been termed **visual intelligence** (Subrahmanyam et al., 2001). This aspect of cognition requires individuals to manipulate aspects of problem space using visual mechanisms for example, size, difference, and identification of relationships amongst objects or remembering/recognizing sequences. Those who spent more time engaged in online activities demonstrated a clear advantage in this form of reasoning, suggesting that being subjected to media of this type had influenced this improvement. Perhaps we should interpret these results with a degree of caution before we send people out to sit in front of the Internet for 16 hours. There is no prior test in this study to establish the levels at which such skills existed in the participants before they took part. It could be suggested that increased levels of non-verbal reasoning skills existed prior to the testing taking place and that the differences noted are not due to an increase in performance as a result of using the Internet. It could be that people who displayed these differences in non-verbal communication are simply seeking out these communication mechanisms to match their disposition, rather than any underlying 'improvement' in this form of intelligence.

Further research has highlighted a potential link between the use of social networking sites (**SNS**) and an impact on cognitive abilities. In initial research by Kirschner and Karpinski (2010) it was suggested that there is a detrimental link between academic test scores and frequent use of a social networking website (in the instance of this study, Facebook). Associated findings also suggested frequent Facebook users reported spending significantly less time studying and poorer self-reported time management skills linked into a propensity for using Facebook as a tool for procrastination. There is a suggestion that perhaps the link to poor academic performance and the use of Facebook may tap into an underlying personality trait for distractibility rather than indicating an actual relationship between social networking and low academic attainment (Alloway, Horton, Alloway, & Dawson, 2013). Further research by Junco (2012) explored this idea and highlighted a dichotomy according to the tasks engaged in on Facebook as well as the associated impacts on objective measures of academic attainment. As much of this research has taken place in America, the objective measure used for academic attainment is the grade point average (GPA). Those students who engaged in aspects of social monitoring (sharing links or reading friends' status updates) lead to higher GPA scores versus active social activities such as posting status updates and engaging in instant messaging chat. Here, the spectre of multitasking may be responsible for such a difference, specifically where studying activities and those being engaged in on SNSs have a significant cross over. Where there is a high degree of similarity between studying and social networking activity, competition for limited cognitive resources would occur. This could provide a situation where information being learned is either not committed to memory at all, or the links that are established between concepts are confused with material from the social networking activity. Obviously such a process could clearly impact on poorer GPA scores, especially where links to key information and concepts are required (Junco, 2012).

Alloway et al. (2013) explored an interesting question related to the use of SNSs and a link to improved cognitive abilities. The authors posed a variety of research questions with the main one asking if engagement with different types of social networking has a direct impact on cognitive skills and academic attainment. The results demonstrated a significant difference in scores on measures of working memory, verbal ability, and spelling in participants who used Facebook for a year or more compared to those who infrequently engaged in Facebook. The authors suggest a possible explanation for this improvement that relates to the similarity of cognitive processes being used in both tasks. In a typical Facebook activity, most individuals will log on and be faced with a plethora of detailed information that they must access, process, and manipulate. They must also determine (using complex cognitive decision-making processes) how relevant the accessed information is to them before executing any number of processes based on the result of this decision-making process. Such a process clearly links to activities associated with working memory function, including aspects of visual attention, verbal coding, and decision making. Reasons proposed for the positive effect of Facebook on spelling and verbal ability relate to a training effect, with individuals regularly engaging in reading posts or commenting on status updates having more practice in verbal communication. Such a benefit is apparent when contrasted with scores on mathematical-related concepts, which demonstrated no significant differences between high and low engagers in social networking activity, with such tasks not generally featured on sites such as Facebook (Alloway et al., 2013).

This collection of research seems to suggest that just using the Internet or engaging in social networking activities online does not present a magic pill to improve flagging cognitive skills. Instead it would indicate that the *type* of activity an individual engages in online has a residual training effect, helping the development of a skill through engagement and experience rather than just being subjected to passive information. Clearly, activities we engage in can form a distraction and for those who have a subtle predisposition to procrastinate, the use of the Internet or social networking sites more specifically may be seen as a 'constructive' diversion.

15.6 Reading and the Internet

Whilst you are reading this, think about the cognitive effort that you are exerting. For most humans reading is an automatic process to which we need to devote little conscious effort. Now, consider the average webpage containing a variety of text. On the surface this would appear innocuous enough. In most cases you would assume that any form of text, whether online or offline requires the same level of cognitive processing. Research suggests, however, that this assumption is an erroneous one. **Hypertext** is a commonly used mechanism for presenting electronic text and is used quite frequently in a variety of contexts from e-reading to web-based text. The thing that sets hypertext apart from more traditional offline text is that it contains active links (or **hyperlinks**) embedded within the text. These links permit users to access a wide variety of information from the current text that they are reading (Destefano & LeFevre, 2007). Researchers such as Destefano and LeFevre (2007) and Smart (2010) point out that the enhanced experience that is offered by hypertext could be increasing the **cognitive load** (for a full discussion of this, see Section 15.8 in this chapter) we experience in comparison to offline text. As the flexibility and the amount of options available to users increases, it is assumed that so too does the cognitive load faced by the individual. The use of hyperlinks is a great tool providing the user with the benefit of connecting the reader with a plethora of further information. This functionality may come at a price, and as Carr (2010) notes, the use of hyperlinks encourages us to move away from the initial point of interest and become subjected to additional (possibly irrelevant) information.

Carr (2010) highlights key contrasts between on and offline text processing, noting that the cognitive process of offline reading involves two essential senses: haptic (touch) and sight (Mangen, 2008, Carr, 2010). According to the work conducted by Mangen (2008) reading is a multi-sensory process where we have to establish the relative links between the *context* in which the text is introduced as well as the *content* (understanding) of the text (Carr, 2010). Reading also requires a set of visual–spatial processes to be engaged that help us keep track of where we are in the text whilst guiding us through a pre-determined route across the page. In contrast, reading hypertext opens up new ways for material to be navigated as well as altering the amount of attention we devote to each new piece of information (Carr, 2010). The propensity for individuals to become lost in a cascade of hyperlinks that follow on from each other could become a real possibility, particularly where that individual possesses low-level proficiency in navigating the Internet. On the surface, the use of hyperlinks appears no different to reading a textbook and then looking up a reference in the back of the book, or reading a table of contents and then moving to the required page. The difference with hypertext is related to the ease and speed with which such information can be chosen, accessed, scanned, and then by-passed (Carr, 2010).

Carr (2010) suggests that when we are engaged in reading material online we appear to be seeing the 'twigs and the leaves' of the online forest (Carr, 2010, p. 91), suggesting that we get so involved in the links between different sources that we often only experience the superficial aspects of the material being conveyed through the hypertext environment. Consequently there is a real possibility that we are failing to piece together a *global* picture of the material with which we are engaging. This could include missing key connections between pieces of information that have been collected, or failing to pay attention sufficiently to the material we are reading. This global view is seen as being critical to both planning (where to go next for information) and understanding (what does the information mean in context). Similarly, there is a real chance of people becoming distracted by irrelevant material accessed through a hyperlink and suffering from a fragmentation of the original goals from which they disengaged.

15.7 Learning in the online environment

The importance of trying to make connections between individual concepts gleaned from our environment is seen as being critical in one core cognitive skill: learning. Sweller (1994) highlighted the notion that aspects of learning involve the construction of what we term **schemas**. Schemas, a term originally used by Bartlett (1932), can be thought of as 'online' active scripts that serve to store pieces of information grouped together around a particular topic or subject. We might, for example, have a schema that relates to the topic of holidays that could include how you define a holiday, what you need to take on holiday, your previous holiday experiences, and so on. This process of transferring information into a more long-term and durable format allows us the capacity to build an experience of the real world. This process is, however, never as clear-cut as we might assume, and the mechanism through which information is transferred from a temporary store (e.g., short-term memory) into the schema located in a more permanent store (long-term memory) is fraught with obstacles. We can view the route between these two stores as being analogous to a busy one-way road that has only one very small feeder lane. Only a small number of cars can get onto this main route at any one time, meaning that those that do not make it onto the road are stuck. This process of being 'stuck' equates to processes that affect the memories we try to form, such as the process of **decay** (a loss of information over time) or **interference** (other material gets in the way of the actual material we want to remember). In an analogy used by Carr (2010), the process of transferring material from short-term memory into long-term memory was akin to 'filling a bath with a thimble' (Carr, 2010, p. 124).

Both Sweller (1994) and Carr (2010) consider this to be a key issue related to cognitive load, a term that was introduced earlier on in Chapter 13, Section 13.7. The notion of cognitive load has been used as an objective measure to explore how much information and material we can attend to and then encode by transferring it from short-term to long-term memory. The associated notion of cognitive overload is the situation where we have a higher amount of information coming in from the environment that is not being met or sustained by our capacity to transfer this information into schemas contained in long-term memory. If we have a situation in which material is being lost and not encoded, this will obviously weaken memory formation leading to poorer retention and learning (Carr, 2010).

So what has this got to do with cognition, the Internet and us? Well let's take the example mentioned previously of reading. For most of us we read at our own pace when given a written book or article in the offline world. This is the process that controls the way in which material is transferred from short-term to long-term memory, and if we find ourselves not remembering information or we are getting a bit lost (perhaps a complicated plot or a complex idea is being conveyed) then we can re-read the material or take more time to digest the information. In the context of the Internet this process is slightly different in terms of the speed at which material is conveyed and the sheer number of sources via which information can be presented. For some of these sources we have an overt control on the way in which we engage with them and can meter our understanding of them accordingly. For other sources or streams of material (e.g., an animated advertisement, auditory commentary, or alert) there is no such way to prevent us being subjected to them and individuals often find themselves being bombarded with information they do not want.

Small, Moody, Siddarth, and Bookheimer (2009) made the suggestion that the use of the Internet, or more specifically the action of searching the Internet, could lead to measurable changes in the levels of brain activation. The researchers aimed to demonstrate this by comparing the performance of two groups, those who were experienced in the use of the Internet (Internet-savvy) and those who had less experience using the Internet (the Internet naive). In the research by Small et al. (2009) the two groups performed a variety of tasks from reading simple linear text through to conducting more in-depth Internet-based searching activities.

The findings were quite startling, and clearly demonstrate that the experience of using the Internet has an impact on brain activation. In terms of reading the standard linear based text, the two groups showed no significant differences. The two groups differed significantly in terms of brain activation patterns when engaged in the Internet-based searching activity. During this activity the Internet savvy participants demonstrated an increased pattern of activation in an area of the brain linked to decision-making and our ability to integrate aspects of complex information to synthesize goals and objectives. The Internet naive participants demonstrated no such activity in this area of the brain. Although the authors of the research do urge a degree of caution when interpreting the results, the suggestion is that the actual process of searching the Internet engages far more of the brain than the simple process of reading linear text. How such activity extends to the actual cognitive processes involved in the nature of Internet search is still an unknown, but in this research we have tenable evidence that an activity on the Internet is engaging more (or different parts?) of the brain than simply reading. Small et al. (2009) investigated this further to explore if this same re-wiring of neural pathways could be replicated in the Internet naive participants through a period of training. Remarkably, after just 5 hours of practice searching the Internet, naive participants demonstrated the same pattern of activation in the prefrontal cortex as the Internet savvy participants. As Small et al. point out, this change occurs after only a relatively short period of time engaged in activities many of us do on a daily basis for extended periods of time.

15.8 Attention and the Internet

The nature of attention in terms of cognition has been a topic that has garnered a great deal of research interest and is indeed seen as on the founding blocks of our information processing system alongside aspects such as memory and problem-solving. In this regard any attempt to summarize over a century's worth of research in this section would be an insurmountable task. Therefore, only the key aspects that have bearing on the discussion here will be introduced. Attention in the context of our online behaviour and activities has an important role to play, particularly where we are now bombarded with multiple pieces of information from a variety of sources at any one time. The role of attention in these situations would be to act as a filter and a focus, to be able to make sure that any of the irrelevant material we do not want stays out whilst ensuring that the things we do want come in. As you can guess, this process does not always go to plan and there are situations where elements of the external environment serve to attract attention away from what we should be doing, or to cause interference on tasks we are trying to complete.

15.9 The notion of multitasking and continuous partial attention

Carr (2010) recently identified a developing preference for material to be presented within a shorter timeframe, particularly where it relates to advertising and non-newsworthy information. This reflects an unwillingness to engage with material for lengthy periods of time. Some television channels now operate 60 second catch-up news sections that fall in-between programs that include a short, sharp shock mechanism for information dispersal. Many of these news-stabs also contain additional information in the form of text crawlers (usually highlighting the main headlines or information from social networking tools such as twitter). The net result of this is a lot of information in a very short space of time, with no metric for how much of this information is actually absorbed by the end user. Associated with this is the notion of **continuous partial attention** (CPA), a term that was originally used in a blog by Linda Stone (2009), a software executive, to describe a state of being engaged in numerous activities but never fully devoting our full focus to any of them (lindastone.net/qa/continuous-partial-attention). This process of distributed attention differs from the notion of multitasking as each task has a direct and relevant purpose related to our current goal objectives, and more importantly we can have a rest when we have finished. When we are engaging in CPA we do this for extended periods of time and scan for chances to engage with any type of material at any given time. This notion of 'we want it all and we want it now' aspect of our online lives is seen to be linked to a need to be connected, whether this is through email, instant messaging, social networking, news feeds, and so on (Stone, 2009). This constant state of heightened vigilance has associated cognitive costs, most of which are bad. It leads to increased levels of stress with individuals losing the ability to reflect on their actions, or to make key decisions related to planning.

Obviously all of this activity comes at a cost. Although initially there may be reciprocal benefits such as perceived increase in the amount of energy we can devote to specific tasks or the capacity to remember more information for longer, this does not last. The chemicals that govern our body in such situations can have a deteriorating effect on performance that in turn results in mistakes and errors. Stress has been demonstrated to have a significant impact on our ability to recall information, particularly where that information is emotionally arousing (Kuhlmann, Piel, & Wolf, 2005). Both acute and chronic forms of stress have also been demonstrated to compromise our ability to form memories (Koenig, Walker, Romeo, & Lupien, 2011) as well as having an impact on the ability to make judgements (Koenig et al., 2011). Increased levels of the stress hormones cortisol and adrenaline have also been linked to symptoms of depression and fatigue (Maddock & Pariante, 2001), thus demonstrating that although the benefits of an increased distributed level of attention may be good, the consequences could potentially be devastating. Small and Vorgan (2008) coined the term **'techno-brain burnout'** to describe this pattern of decay in cognitive capabilities as a result of prolonged and distributed attentional activity. Ophir, Nass, and Wagner (2009) investigated the possibility that there were distinct differences in the cognitive processes between those who frequently engaged in media multitasking and those who did not. This notion of media multitasking has been noted to be a more common activity in the age group that has been termed **'digital natives'**, usually between the ages of 8–18 (Rideout, Roberts, & Foehr, 2005). Of central interest to the discussion here is an unknown aspect that relates directly to how those who engage in chronic media multitasking process information in order to cope with different streams of information, and how such processes contrast with those individuals who infrequently engage in multitasking. As we have discussed throughout this chapter, research of this nature is particularly important given the notion that humans have limited processing capacities and are not the best at attending to multiple channels of information at any one time (Ophir et al., 2009). Ophir et al. (2009) suggested that those who are engaged in more intense and frequent media multitasking are more attentive to the irrelevant stimuli that appear within their immediate visual environment as well as the resulting memory representations.

The results from this study demonstrated some key points, showing that differences do exist in those who are engaged more heavily in online media multitasking compared with those who are not. Those individuals who were classified as frequently using media multitasking are seen to approach information processing in a different way to those who engage in this activity less frequently. Those who were termed heavy media multitaskers (**MMT**) appeared to have a greater difficulty filtering out the irrelevant stimuli presented to them and are less likely to ignore irrelevant information that enters memory as a result. Similarly frequent media multitaskers appear to be less effective in preventing a switch between relevant to irrelevant tasks. This was clearly demonstrated as heavy MMT were easily distracted by multiple streams of information versus those who were infrequent MMT. The infrequent MMT group demonstrated more effective allocation of attention to task-relevant information in the face of distraction. Lower MMT appeared to exhibit a stronger level of endogenous attention control allowing a clearer focus on a single task. Those defined as high MMT appeared to be driven to stimuli outside of the current task goals (Aston-Jones & Cohen, 2005).

15.10 Can we guarantee we are paying attention to everything online?

Varakin et al. (2004) highlight a key issue here that links directly into processing of information in an online environment. Web-based interactions are spatially limited visual experiences that are restricted by the parameters of the screen and the information contained within it. The erroneous assumption is that due to this restrictive environment we can pay attention to everything contained therein. The research literature related to attention has more recently highlighted two interesting aspects of our processing system, which suggest that our ability to 'see' things is not as good as we assume. Two phenomena have received a great deal of interest over the past several decades: **change blindness** and **inattentional blindness**. Each effect demonstrates that in certain situations we fail to see critical aspects of our visual environment, aspects that could have serious implications for our online security and in turn our general well-being.

15.10.1 **Change blindness**

The notion of *change blindness* was first introduced by Rensink, O'Regan, and Clark, (1997) to describe a quirk of our attentional system whereby we fail to see distinct changes in visual material presented to us. Research demonstrates that individuals often fail to notice fairly unique and obvious changes. Crucially, these changes are ones that are so large that they should have been fairly obvious for someone who is not directly involved in the task (e.g., a person's head in a visual display being swapped over). The general trend is for about 75% of participants to fail to notice such changes, even in the instance where the only actor in a short film changes from one person to another (Levin & Simons, 1997, Jensen, Yao, Street, & Simons, 2011). Research has also shown that individuals can still focus attention straight at the object that has changed or is changing but still fail to notice such a change happening (Jensen et al., 2011). Attempts to explain the existence of this phenomenon therefore have to address the finding that it is not due to a lack of attention (Jensen et al., 2011).

Varakin et al. (2004) highlight the impact of change blindness in the design of e-reading based software. Participants in this study were asked to trial software that allowed them to browse current news stories, with the key task to gather pieces of information located within target articles. Participants were then asked a series of questions based on the information that they had been presented, as well as a question related to any unexpected changes that had occurred during their navigation through the information. Despite large changes in the visual display only 50% of participants taking part in the study noticed these changes taking place. Here is evidence that even in the confined space of simple e-reading software users can still miss important and distinct changes in the visual display. As in the case of banner blindness, individuals are missing perceptually and semantically salient pieces of information and as such these are not reaching awareness.

Similar findings have also been observed for change blindness in a military context, with its inclusion here linked to the actual task itself. Durlach (2004) explored the susceptibility of individuals whilst using a military-based command and control system. The system provided a series of real-time updates related to current mission objects, details of enemy location, and that of friendly forces. Results demonstrated that participants were less likely to notice a change in a series of task-critical icons presented on-screen whilst another task window was closed and opened. Participants were 50% less likely to notice the change in the position of an onscreen icon when this occurred at the same time as a concurrent task window closing and reopening. Similar findings have also been reported by DiVita, Obermayer, Nugent, and Linville (2004).

We know that this type of research has some obvious implications in military settings but they can also fit into users' experiences of web-based activities. Anecdotally, web-users do not often use the Internet in isolation, with most running multiple tasks in the background or having multiple task windows open simultaneously. Research evidence suggests that if changes occur during the process of closing or opening such task windows, there is a greater chance of changes being missed (Durlach, 2004). Where these changes are linked to task-relevant information, or present key warnings/updates about the status of the current system, users are essentially missing material of critical importance. This could be something as simple as missing the fact that a meeting time has been changed in a shared calendar. However, there could be more serious implications for such incidences of lapses in attention, such as missing changes in bank balances or overlooking specific warning signs that might indicate malicious activity.

In an original study Steffner and Schenkman (2012) presented an exploration of change blindness in the context of viewing webpage information by exploring the impact individual aspects of the change and the complexity of the task environment had on the detection of change. The study included four distinct kinds of manipulation according to the size of the change, the complexity and location of the change, and whether the change occurred to a person or an inanimate object or aspect of the webpage. The researchers highlighted a series of hypotheses based on previous research in the change blindness literature, indicating that larger changes, changes in simple objects, changes on the left of the screen, and changes made directly to a person would all be easier to detect in the context of viewing a webpage. The results from the research by Steffner and Schenkman (2012) presented some interesting findings. In contrast to what had previously been assumed, changes occurring to a virtual person on a webpage were less easily noticed than those made to a non-person. Nonetheless, the research failed to highlight any significant difference in participants' abilities to detect change according to the manipulation of complexity. The research presented evidence that aspects of change blindness can impact on how we view information online but is obviously limited to one basic study. Crucially, this area warrants some further research with one of the key questions yet to be considered being the distinction between visual complexity and visual clutter. The authors presented no clear discussion on how these two processes impact directly upon levels of observed change blindness, aspects of which have been linked to notions of cognitive load as discussed earlier in this chapter. Participants also found objects located on the left-hand side of the screen more difficult to detect versus those located in the right. This could be related to work by Simola, Kuisma, Oörni, Uusitalo, and Hyönä (2011) who found that material placed on the right hand side of a webpage was more likely to interfere with text comprehension. This was seen as being indicative of this area benefiting from a more direct focus of attention versus that of the left. The following section reviews some conceptual aspects related to both phenomena that could begin to shape further research in this area, as well as beginning to suggest, in the absence of firm empirical data, the causes for such effects.

15.10.2 Inattentional blindness

The term *inattentional blindness* was first used by Mack and Rock, (1998) but the origin of the actual phenomenon has its foundations in earlier research on attention (Cherry, 1954, Broadbent, 1958). The concept of inattentional blindness is exhibited when we fail to miss novel and unexpected stimuli that appear in our visual environment whilst we are engaged in a concurrent task. Jensen et al. (2011) indicate that the typical tasks used to explore the notion of inattentional blindness shares a number of characteristics. Firstly, the observer is engaged in an attention-demanding concurrent task (usually termed the *primary task*). The primary task can fall under any number of specific types as long as it exerts sufficient demands on the individual's processing capabilities causing them to focus on key aspects of the visual display. Secondly, there is the inclusion of an unexpected event that occurs during the primary task. The unexpected event must be distinct enough to be visible to anyone not engaged in the primary task. Mack and Rock (1998) presented participants with a series of static visual displays in which a cross-type shape briefly appeared. Participants were asked to make a judgement according to which arm of the cross was longer (Jensen et al., 2011). On critical trials the unexpected event was presented within the visual display, usually another geometric shape presented somewhere in close proximity to the arms of the cross. Participants were asked to state if they had noticed anything that had not been presented in the earlier trials. As in most instances of research on inattentional blindness, 75% of participants failed to notice the inclusion of the unexpected event, even when the object was unexpected and novel (e.g., a bright red square: Jensen et al., 2011).

Exploring inattentional blindness in the context of online interactions has been very limited, and paves the way for future research in this area. Benway (1999) explored the failure of users to attend to an important aspect of the webpage containing critical pieces of task-relevant information. Employees were being encouraged to sign up to a training course via a brightly designed banner placed at the top of the screen. In follow-up interviews it appeared that the employees were successfully navigating to the webpage that contained the banner with the link to the relevant sign-up page for the training course, but were failing to actually read it. Benway (1999) later replicated this phenomenon in an empirical study, defining it as **banner blindness**. This is operationalized as the inattention to a prominent advert or banner containing task-relevant information. As discussed previously, such a trend is not isolated and has been documented in other research by Burke, Hornof, Nilsen, and Gorman (2005) and Simola et al. (2011).

15.11 Understanding the impact of attention in online tasks

Varakin et al. (2004) presented a series of theoretical 'hypotheses', which can be linked to why phenomena such as inattentional blindness and change blindness have a direct impact on the processing of information in online visual environments. These **illusions of visual bandwidth (IVB)** (see Varakin et al., 2004, for a fuller discussion of these) can help to define why such errors in the attentional system occur. The core suggestion is that we overestimate our capabilities when it comes to the processing of visual displays. Essentially the notion of an IVB states that there is a big mismatch between what we actually see and what we think we should be seeing. Aspects of inattentional blindness and change blindness relate directly to these aspects of overconfidence in our attentional system. The ramifications of the work by Varakin et al. (2004) in the context of cognitive processes online may not be directly obvious. IVBs are based upon individual experiences regardless of the specific visual environment. The use of anything online comes directly under such parameters. The factors that serve to influence susceptibility to inattentional and change blindness would almost certainly hinder a simple search-related task if information is located in areas not expected, or where there is a strong pull from material that is being presented in any given context for example, pop-up ads, email notifications, and so on. This may mean users could miss vital pieces of information that at first glance do not appear to be relevant to the current task objectives, but which upon closer inspection could yield critical information for the task in hand. There are multiple aspects of the computer-based visual environment that can all serve to create failures of attention in this regard. These include overlapping task windows, slowly loading webpages, cluttered screens, or poorly designed websites that have multiple icons with no link to task-relevance or functionality. Varakin et al. (2004) do note that many computer displays and webpages share a variety of distinct similarities to those types of visual environments used in both change blindness and inattentional blindness (Hudson, 2001). Research that explores these key facets of human attention in such environments is still very limited. What would be useful is a framework for exploring the susceptibility to such phenomena in the context of cyberspace. As eluded to previously in this chapter, there has to be some form of cost associated with missing very subtle changes in Internet pages we are using or completely ignoring things that are happening right in front of us. The goal for research in this area is to highlight these costs and explore the mechanisms through which such failures, if they do exist, could be mediated.

15.12 What about being interrupted?

In order to provide some context to the discussion in this section there is a quote attributed to Doctorow (2009, http://www.locusmag.com/Features/2009/01/cory-doctorow-writing-in-age-of.html) that describes the Internet as an 'ecosystem of interruptive technologies'.

The Internet offers us an expanse in which to carry out a variety of diverse activities. However, as a consequence to the very nature of this environment it also offers multiple distractions! For the most part discussion in the literature on disruptions focuses on times when aspects of the visual environment attract our attention not only away from a task in hand but to task-irrelevant material. There is another aspect to the research on interruptions that explores the effect of material that is not directly task relevant, but which may provide us with important pieces of information that could impact on that task (Roda, 2011). For example, receiving an email notification that alerts us to a change in a meeting time that could be related (but not relevant) to the notes we are currently typing up. Mark, Gudith, and Klocke (2008) noted that individuals who are interrupted often compensate in their concurrent workload by increasing the speed with which they do things. This has the residual effect of increasing stress levels, frustration, pressures of time and the overall perceived effort of doing the activity. Often, interruptions that contain information that is highly consistent with the current task being performed and can produce a clear facilitation effect (Cutrell, Czerwinski, & Horvitz, 2001, Li, Edwards, & Lee, 2002, Smith, 2010), helping us to work quicker or providing material we need to complete the task in hand. There are other situations, however, where the interruption is irrelevant or causes us to change the task we were currently working on, which can often have a significant impact on workflow and stress (Li et al., 2002).

Ou and Davison (2011) explored one aspect in the use of *Instant Messaging* (IM) in a work-based environment and although they noted that the use of IM was a significant predictor for interruption of work-based tasks, it failed to have a significant impact on the overall performance of the group. This pattern of results appears to be contrary to what we would have expected and has been explained in terms of the overwhelming benefits provided by communication within this environment, with the quick and efficient sharing of information. The use of IM was also seen to bolster aspects of team working, something that could perhaps be extended to aspects of wider social networking. Instant messaging use was noted to have a significant impact on perceived level of interactivity in the workplace and was also seen as a critical mediating factor in the development of mutual trust along with the quality of communication amongst individuals. In the context of this study, the use of IM only accounted for a very small percentage of the work-based interruptions (5%), which was considerably lower than interruptions from aspects such as telephone calls, emails, and meetings. What appears to be of critical importance here, particularly in terms of IM and computer-mediated communication, is the level of interactivity that it affords—two-way synchronous communication appears to be less disruptive as it focuses the point of interruption to a particular point in time, and also offers significant benefits in the form of social interaction.

Defining the notion of an interruption in the context of online interactions is quite broad, with Corragio (1990) defining the notion as 'an externally generated, randomly occurring, discrete event that breaks continuity of cognitive focus on a primary task' (Smith, 2010, p. 19). From this perspective the two key aspects to highlight are the notions of an external control and the unpredictability of the interruption-eliciting event. An exogenous shift by the user whilst navigating away from a current webpage to another one, and then the process of returning back to the original webpage is not identified as an interruption in this context. The crucial aspect here is the notion of interruption as a random and disruptive event that has a clear effect on the performance of the individual. In the context of online information processing users are subjected to a wide variety of interruptions to task performance. Where accessing information outside of the parameter of the website design may result in error messages, loss of content and context for the searching, and blocked access, these interruptions serve to disrupt the flow of information and can distract the user from completion of the primary task. There are also problems associated with the interruption from adverts that may appear to be task-relevant at first glance, system messages, warning messages, and news updates amongst just a few examples. The net result is a residual decrease in the amount of material that can be processed, particularly where the interruptions compete for resources already devoted to the primary task (Smith, 2010). The impact of interruptions on cognitive performance have been discussed in a variety of areas including time to complete task, number of errors, decision making, and general affective (emotional) state (Bailey & Iqbal, 2008).

15.13 Chapter summary

In this chapter there has been a very broad discussion of the ways in which we as active information processors can be hindered, improved, or misled by online material. The use of the Internet is still a relatively recent development in the overall history of humankind and it will take time to explore how it and associated technologies both impact upon and are impacted upon cognitive processes. A current generation of digital natives, individuals who have been subjected to the Internet from an early age, will be developing their cognitive capabilities alongside key technological advances. It is important that we understand how these processes are being affected further, particularly where being subjected to the online world could have a detrimental impact on our cognition.

The key aspects that have been discussed here are:

- The phenomenon of a transactive memory has been previously established as part of an offline social group. Research has now demonstrated that the Internet, particularly individual websites and search engines, is now becoming part of that social group. Individuals are now less likely to remember the factual information they have retrieved, but more so where they have retrieved that information from.

- Activities such as engaging in social networking can have a positive effect on certain aspects of cognition. This facilitation is assumed to come about as a result of 'training' in processes that link into underlying cognitive processes.

- Research has highlighted that two phenomena well documented in the offline world transfer well to the online world. Change blindness and inattentional blindness demonstrate that as individuals we are missing key aspects of our online environment.

- The use of hypertext as a medium for presenting information can have a residual impact on how much cognitive load we experience when reading material online.

- Attention in the online environment is directly affected by how much information we are being subjected to. A notion of continual partial attention means that individuals are now constantly being subjected to information without any downtime.

References

Alloway, T.P., Horton, J., Alloway, R.G., & Dawson, C. (2013). Social networking sites and cognitive abilities: Do they make you smarter? *Computers & Education*, 63, 10–16. doi:10.1016/j.compedu.2012.10.030.

Aston-Jones, G. & Cohen, J.D. (2005). An integrative theory of locus coeruleus-norepinephrine function: adaptive gain and optimal performance. *Annual Review of Neuroscience*, 28, 403–50. doi:10.1146/annurev.neuro.28.061604.135709.

Bailey, B. & Iqbal, S. (2008). Understanding changes in mental workload during execution of goal-directed tasks and its application for interruption management. *ACM Transactions on Computer-Human Interaction*, 14(4), 21–28.

Bartlett, F. (1932). *Remembering: A Study in Experimental and Social Psychology*. Cambridge: Cambridge University Press.

Benway, J.P. (1999). *Banner Blindness: What searching users notice and do not notice on the World Wide Web*. Unpublished Doctorial Thesis, Rice University, Houston.

Broadbent, D. (1958). *Perception and Communication*. London: Pergamon Press.

Burke, M., Hornof, A., Nilsen, E., & Gorman, N. (2005). High-cost banner blindness: Ads increase perceived workload, hinder visual search, and are forgotten. *ACM Transactions on Computer-Human Interaction*. Retrieved from http://dl.acm.org/citation.cfm?id=1121116 (accessed 10th September, 2014).

Carr, N. (2010). *The Shallows: How the Internet is Changing the Way We Think, Read and Remember*. London: Atlantic Books.

Cherry, E.C. (1954). Some experiments on the recognition of speech, with one and with two ears. *The Journal of the Acoustical Society of America*, 25(5), 975–79. doi:10.1121/1.1907229.

Conway, M.A. & Pleydell-Pearce, C.W. (2000). The construction of autobiographical memories in the self-memory system. *Psychological Review*, 107(2), 261–288. doi:10.1037//0033-295X.107.2.261.

Corragio, L. (1990). *Deleterious Effects of Intermittent Interruptions on the Task Performance of Knowledge Workers: A Laboratory Investigation*. University of Arizona.

Cutrell, E., Czerwinski, M., & Horvitz, E. (2001). Notification, disruption, and memory: Effects of messaging interruptions on memory and performance (1999). Retrieved from http://citeseerx.ist.psu.edu/viewdoc/summary?doi:10.1.1.26.418 (accessed 10th September, 2014).

Destefano, D. & Lefevre, J.-A. (2007). Cognitive load in hypertext reading: A review. *Computers in Human Behavior*, 23(3), 1616–1641. doi:10.1016/j.chb.2005.08.012.

DiVita, J., Obermayer, R., Nugent, W., &Linville, J.M. (2004). Verification of the change blindness phenomenon while managing critical events on a combat information display. *Human Factors: The Journal of the Human Factors and Ergonomics Society*, 46, 205–218.

Doctorow, C. (2009). Writing in the age of distraction. *Locus Magazine*. Retrieved from http://www.locusmag.com/Features/2009/01/cory-doctorow-writing-in-age-of.html (accessed 10th September, 2014).

Durlach, P.J. (2004). Army digital systems and vulnerability to change blindness. *US Army Research Institue for the Behavioural and Social Sciences* (available at: http://oai.dtic.mil/oai/oai?verb=getRecord&metadataPrefix=html&identifier=ADA433072).

Hudson, W. (2001). Designing for the grand illusion. *Association for Computing Machinery's SIGCHI Bulletin*, 8. Retrieved from http://www.acm.org/sigchi/bulletin/2001.6 (accessed 10th September, 2014).

Jensen, M.S., Yao, R., Street, W.N., & Simons, D.J. (2011). Change blindness and inattentional blindness. *Wiley Interdisciplinary Reviews: Cognitive Science*, 2(5), 529–546. doi:10.1002/wcs.130.

Johnson, G.M. (2006). Internet use and cognitive development: A theoretical framework. *E-Learning*, 4, 565–573.

Johnson, G.M. & Johnson, J.A. (2008). Internet use and complex cognitive processes. *IADIS International Conference e-Society*, 83–90.

Junco, R. (2012). Too much face not enough books: the relationship between multiple indices of Facebook use and academic performance. *Computers in Human Behavior*. doi:10.1016/j.chb.2011.08.026.

Kirschner, P.A. & Karpinski, A.C. (2010). Facebook® and academic performance. *Computers in Human Behavior*, 26(6), 1237–1245. doi:10.1016/j.chb.2010.03.024.

Koenig, J., Walker, C., Romeo, R., & Lupien, S. (2011). Effects of stress across the lifespan. *Stress*, 14 (September), 475–480. doi:10.3109/10253890.2 011.604879.

Kuhlmann, S., Piel, M., & Wolf, O.T. (2005). Impaired memory retrieval after psychosocial stress in healthy young men. *The Journal of Neuroscience: The Official Journal of the Society for Neuroscience*, 25(11), 2977–82. doi:10.1523/JNEUROSCI. 5139-04. 2005.

Levin, D.T. & Simons, D.J. (1997). Failure to detect changes to attended objects in motion pictures. *Psychonomic Bulletin & Review*, 4(4), 501–506. doi:10.3758/BF03214339.

Li, H., Edwards, S.M., & Lee, J.-H. (2002). Measuring the intrusiveness of advertisements: scale development and validation. *Journal of Advertising*, 31(2), 37–47. doi:10.1080/00913367. 2002.10673665.

Mack, A. & Rock, I. (1998). *Inattentional Blindness*. Cambridge, MA: The MIT Press.

Maddock, C. & Pariante, C. (2001). How does stress affect you? An overview of stress, immunity, depression and disease. *Epidemiologia E Psichiatria*, 10(3), 153–162. Retrieved from http://journals.cambridge.org/production/action/cjo GetFulltext?fulltextid=8265143 (accessed 10th September, 2014).

Mangen, A. (2008). Hypertext fiction reading: haptics and immersion. *Journal of Research in Reading*, 31(4), 404–419. doi:10.1111/j. 1467-9817. 2008.00380.x.

Mark, G., Gudith, D., & Klocke, U. (2008). The cost of interrupted work: more speed and stress. *Proceedings of the SIGCHI Conference on Human Factors in Computing Systems*, 8-11, 107–110. Retrieved from http://dl.acm.org/citation. cfm?id=1357072 (accessed 10th September, 2014).

Ophir, E., Nass, C., & Wagner, A.D. (2009). Cognitive control in media multitaskers. *Proceedings of the National Academy of Sciences of the United States of America*, 106(37), 15583–15587. doi:10.1073/pnas.0903620106.

Ou, C.X.J. & Davison, R.M. (2011). Interactive or interruptive? Instant messaging at work. *Decision Support Systems*, 52(1), 61–72. doi:10.1016/j. dss.2011.05.004.

Rensink, R., O'Regan, J., & Clark, J. (1997). To see or not to see: The need for attention to perceive changes in scenes. *Psychological Science*, 8(5), 1–6. Retrieved from http://pss.sagepub.com/content/8/5/368.short (accessed 4th December 2014).

Rideout, V., Roberts, D., & Foehr, U. (2005). *Generation M: Media in the Lives of 8-18 Year-Olds*. Menlo Park: Kaiser Family Foundation.

Roda, C. (2011). *Human Attention In Digital Environments*. Cambridge: Cambridge University Press.

Simola, J., Kuisma, J., Oörni, A., Uusitalo, L., & Hyönä, J. (2011). The impact of salient advertisements on reading and attention on web pages. *Journal of Experimental Psychology. Applied*, 17(2), 174–90. doi:10.1037/a0024042.

Small, G. & Vorgan, G. (2008). *iBrain: Surviving the Technological Alteration of the Modern Mind*. New York: HarperCollins.

Small, G.W., Moody, T.D., Siddarth, P., & Bookheimer, S.Y. (2009). Your brain on Google: patterns of cerebral activation during internet searching. *The American Journal of Geriatric Psychiatry: Official Journal of the American Association for Geriatric Psychiatry*, 17(2), 116–26. doi:10.1097/JGP.0b013e3181953a02.

Smart, P.R. (2010). Cognition and the Web. In *1st ITA Workshop on Network-Enabled Cognition: The Contribution of Social and Technological Networks to Human Cognition, Maryland, USA* (pp. 1–41).

Smith, J.E. (2010). *Examining the Effects of Interruptions on Processing of Online News*. PhD Thesis, The University Of North Carolina, Chapel Hill.

Sparrow, B., Liu, J., & Wegner, D.M. (2011). Google effects on memory: cognitive consequences of having information at our fingertips. *Science*, 333(6043), 776–778. doi:10.1126/science.1207745.

Steffner, D. & Schenkman, B. (2012). Change blindness when viewing web pages. *Work*, 41, 6098–6102.

Stone, L. (2009). *Continuous Partial Attention*. www.Lindastone.net. Retrieved December 12, 2013, from lindastone.net/qa/continuous-partial-attention (accessed 10th September, 2014).

Subrahmanyam, K., Greenfield, P., Kraut, R., & Gross, E. (2001). The impact of computer use on children's and adolescents' development. *Journal of Applied Developmental Psychology*, 22(1), 7–30. doi:10.1016/S0193-3973(00)00063-0.

Sweller, J. (1994). Cognitive load theory, learning difficulty and instructional design. *Learning and Instruction*, 4, 295–312.

Tarpley, T. (2001). Children, the Internet and other new technologies. In Singer, D. G. & Singer, J. L. (Eds), *Handbook of Children and the Media* (pp. 547–556). Thousand Oaks: Sage.

Varakin, D.A., Levin, D.T., & Fidler, R. (2004). Unseen and unaware: Implications of recent research on failures of visual awareness for human-computer interface design. *Human-Computer Interaction*, 19(4), 389–422. doi:10.1207/s15327051hci1904_9.

Wegner, D.M. (1987). Transactive Memory: A contemporary analysis of the group mind. In Mullen, B. & Goethais, G. R. (Eds), *Theories of Group Behavior* (pp. 185–208). New York: Springer-Verlag.

Wegner, D.M., Giuliano, T., & Hertel, P. (1985). Cognitive interdependence in close relationships. In Ickes, W. (Ed), *Compatible and Incompatible Relationships* (pp. 253–276). New York: Springer-Verlag.

Ybarra, O., Winkielman, P., Yeh, I., Burnstein, E., & Kavanagh, L. (2010). Friends (and sometimes enemies) with cognitive benefits: What types of social interactions boost executive functioning? *Social Psychological and Personality Science*, 2(3), 253–261. doi:10.1177/1948550610386808.

Further reading

The reader is directed to a selection of further readings that serve to expand key points in this chapter.

Carr, N. (2010). *The Shallows: How the Internet is Changing the Way We Think, Read and Remember*. London: Atlantic Books.
This book presents an excellent overview of how the Internet is shaping our cognition, and explores the key elements of how we learn and remember in the context of new technology.

Rosen, L. (2012). *iDisorder: Understanding Our Obsession with Technology and Overcoming Its Hold on Us*. London: Palgrave Macmillian.
If you are the sort of person that takes their mobile phone to bed with them this book presents an insightful (and scary) exploration of how technology is creating its own set of issues. Rosen also offers some key suggestions of how to overcome these issues.

Chabris, C.F. & Simons, D.J. (2011). *The Invisible Gorilla and Other Ways Our Intuition Decieves Us*. London: HarperCollins.
Funny, insightful and downright scary! Although not directly related to the impact of technology on our cognitive processes the book provides a clear exploration of how our attentional system is clearly not as great as we think.

Discussion questions

1. Critically consider the positive and negative impact of recent technological developments on cognition.
2. Outline typical distractions and interruptions that affect online performance. How can these be reduced?
3. What role do inattentional blindness and change blindness play in our attention to online material? Do you think these might be linked to Internet crime?
4. Describe and discuss the positive advantages that may arise from engaging in cognitive activity online.
5. Critically consider the role of age in terms of impact on cognitive performance online.

Glossary

419 scam – Nigerian scam a communication is received that asks you to move a large amount of money from a foreign bank, often by suggesting that you are the beneficiary of this large sum.

achievers (in gaming) people who want to accomplish tasks.

actual self one's own notion of who they are: your 'real' self. The person who you actually are right at this very moment.

anonymity when one's personal identity is unknown to others.

assertive self-presentation user's inclination to be proactive in how they yield desired impressions from others.

asynchronous communication communication that occurs with a time delay.

autonomy feeling in control of one's own actions and behaviours.

banner blindness inattention to a prominent advert or banner containing task-relevant information.

behavioural confirmation process through which one's interpretation or expectation of another person influences the way in which we interact with them.

behavioural residue cues that indirectly point to an individual's character or personality.

belongingness human need for social, cognitive and behavioural interaction with other people to fulfil a sense of belonging to a group or another person. Need for reciprocated feeling of love, being wanted, and cared for.

Big Five taxonomy for measuring personality that consists of **o**penness, **c**onscientiousness, **e**xtraversion, **a**greeableness and **n**euroticism (**OCEAN**).

bonding social capital achieved from strong ties which are shared with close, intimate others.

bridging social capital stems from weak ties or associations with others who may not be overly significant to our offline lives.

change blindness a failure to see distinct changes in presented visual material.

CMC computer-mediated communication.

cognitive behavioural therapy a client-centred psychotherapeutic therapy that uses both thought and behavioural patterns to address thought processes that underlie dysfunctional emotions and maladaptive behaviours.

cognitive load the amount of information that you can consciously hold at a given time.

collective intelligence collaborating in an online group can produce a shared intelligence.

collective self-esteem individual's self-identity that stems from their sense of belonging to one or more social groups.

Communication Privacy Management (CPM) theoretical aspects of online privacy and related principles.

competence need to feel able and capable to carry out activities.

computer crime online crime that occurs because a perpetrator has specialist knowledge about computer technology.

continuous partial attention (CPA) a state of being engaged in numerous activities but never fully devoting full focus to any of them.

crowd research collection of information from groups.

crowdfunding direct request for financial contributions from large groups of people.

crowdlabour a business sets a task that requires a certain skill or ability and large groups of online users work.

crowdsourcing outsourcing of work previously carried out by employees to large groups or networks within the online community.

cyberchondria unfounded concerns about one's health that arises from searching the Internet for health-related information.

cybercrime crime that is carried out in cyberspace.

cyberdeviance behaviours online that may not be illegal, but are considered to exist outside of socially accepted norms and beliefs of behaviour.

CyberMentors Young people aged 11–17 years take on a mentoring role to individuals experiencing online bullying.

cyber-porn sexually expressive content online.

cyberpsychology psychological processes, motivations, intentions, behavioural outcomes and effects on humans' online and offline worlds, associated with any form of technology.

cyber-trespass occurs when an individual crosses boundaries of ownership in online environments.

cyber-violence accessing and distributing of injurious, hurtful or dangerous materials online.

decay loss of information over time.

defensive self-presentation user's inclination to repair or restore a damaged impression.

deviance behaviour that may not be illegal, but is considered to exist outside of social norms and acceptable beliefs.

digital divide some people do and some people do not use the Internet. Can occur for diverse activities.

digital natives people born post-1980.

digital piracy illegal copying of digital media such as computer software, sound and/or video recordings without permission from the copyright holder.

disempowerment theory an employee's appraisal of a 'polluting' work event as a violation of his/her dignity results in a perception of subjective stress, leading to negative affect which in turn disrupts the employee's attitudes and behaviour at work.

distributed denial of service (DDoS) cyber attacks against governments, the recording industry, and private businesses by sending multiple repeated requests to servers that house online content in order to overload these servers and interrupt their performance.

downward social comparison occurs when we compare the self to people who we perceive to be worse at a given task, or have more negative traits and characteristics than the self. An evaluation of the self as being better than others.

electronic propinquity theory a relationship can also be formed entirely online, through a creation of psychological closeness that is created through computer mediated communication.

email overload arises from a number of factors that require increased levels of time in dealing with emails, including the number of emails received, the number of emails sent, and the time pressures of responding to emails.

emotional distance an emotional rift between two people that signifies a dysfunctional relationship and often contributes to relationship breakdowns.

ethnocentrism ethnicity becomes important and central to defining one's character.

experiential flow behaviours motivated by internal factors.

explorers (in gaming) people who investigate and experience new places.

familial relationships ties to blood relatives.

FAQ: Frequently Asked Questions a list of those questions and answers on a website that users are most likely to ask.

flash mob mass organization of people to carry out a certain task, organized via the use of online-media; often used to surprise other people without consent from local citizens or law enforcement.

Foldit online puzzle game where participants try to identify the structural configuration of proteins.

free riding individuals do not contribute to a group task but expect to gain the same reward from the group's performance.

functional distance the practical space between two locations. See also **physical distance**.

gamification use of video games or online games to improve a given ability.

generation gap differences between generations. In this context, these differences refer to the uses of mass media, especially the Internet.

generation next those who have grown up digitally, not knowing anything but a technical existence.

genuine self self that is less idealized or less managed.

goal-directed flow behaviours motivated by external factors.

gremes game-research hybrids that may allow the organization to use members of the crowd as research participants.

GST general strain theory.

halo effect people who are perceived to be physically attractive are considered to possess good traits or characteristics.

HFS – human flesh search online crowds are used as a search mechanism to locate or identify previously anonymous individuals.

homophily the liking of those who are similar to us.

human computer interaction interaction between humans and technology.

hyperlinks links that are embedded within a website or text that enable a user to move from one site or page to another.

hyperpersonal communication online communication that results in higher perceived levels of affection and emotion than similar offline communications.

hypertext mechanism for presenting electronic text.

ideal self who you would really like to be; the attributes and abilities that you would really like to possess.

identity your view of who you are; a constructed representation that integrates your experiences and goals.

identity claims explicit expressions of an individual's character or personality.

identity fraud using someone else's identity to carry out criminal activities.

identity theft stealing someone else's personal information in order to portray yourself as that person.

identity tourism a character is created that may be vastly different from other players within the same game world.

IGD Internet gaming disorder.

illness anxiety disorder a person experiences high health anxiety but no somatic symptoms.

illness cognitions a patient's own beliefs about their illness. See also **illness representations**.

illness representations a patient's own beliefs about their illness. See also **illness cognitions**.

illusion of visual bandwidth (IVB) overestimation of capabilities in terms of processing visual displays.

impression construction behaviours adopted to acquire particular impressions or to convey a particular impression.

impression formation the way that other people perceive us.

impression management the tactics and mannerisms used, often including various cues, to manage the way in which we want others to see us.

impression motivation one's desire to create specific impressions in other people dependent upon the situation in which one finds oneself.

inattentional blindness failure to attend to novel and unexpected stimuli that appear in our visual environment whilst engaged in a concurrent task.

individual differences characteristics and traits that can be unique to an individual or shared amongst a number of individuals, but that are not universally shared by all humans.

information overload perception of heightened processing requirements of information received.

informational influence group norms are adhered to because we believe that they have valuable or correct information, and/or the group members have a wealth of experience or knowledge.

in-group any group to which you belong.

interference When material interrupts access to information that we want to attend to, or retrieve. Term is used in relation to cognitive interference (i.e., accessing memories) and hardware interference (i.e., accessing online material).

Internet worldwide interconnected web.

internet localized and often restricted network accessed by a limited number of people

Internet self-efficacy belief in one's own ability to carry out the actions required to reach a goal on the Internet.

IP address Internet protocol number given to any digital device. Used for identification and location purposes.

irritators (in gaming) also known as *tanks*, players who attract the attention of opponents onto themselves.

killers (in gaming) people interested in eliminating any type of threat: role of creating damage and death within a game.

KIP model roles within an MMO are either kill, irritate, or preserve roles.

KiVa anti-bullying program in Finland.

knowing-doing gap discrepancy between one's knowledge of actions that need to be carried out and actually carrying out those behaviours.

lurker people who frequently visit a website but do not contribute to the content, discussions or communications on that site; they remain mere observers.

managed self the self that you construct to present to others.

millenials people born between 1982 and 1991.

MMORPGs massively multiplayer online role playing games.

MMOs massively multiplayer online games.

MMT media multitaskers.

moderator gatekeepers of content shared on diverse types of websites.

MOOCs massive online courses.

mood modification subjective experiences that people report as a consequence of engaging in their chosen technological behaviour and can be seen as a coping strategy.

narrative self collection of basic interactions and experiences that create your story of you.

need for cognition desire to employ cognitive efforts and the rewards of that effort.

need to belong motivation to maintain lasting, positive, and significant interpersonal relationships.

net-generation individuals born between 1977 and 1996

nocebo a substance that has no physical effect, but a perceived negative effect on an individual's condition.

normative influence group norms are adhered to in order to gain social approval from the group.

norms shared implicit or explicit standards of conduct and behaviour among group members.

objectivization the experience of being treated as an object.

online counselling (eTherapy, online therapy) delivery of therapeutic interventions by a trained professional to a client through the Internet.

online disinhibition effect people feel less restricted by social norms, rules and regulations when interacting online. Often leads to heightened levels of self-disclosure than in offline situations.

online identity the self that is constructed and portrayed online.

optimism bias when you believe that desirable events are more likely to happen to you than to other people.

organizational groups members are usually primarily interested in doing tasks for their work.

ought self attributes and abilities that we think we should possess based on others' views and opinions, e.g., the way you construct yourself to fulfil obligations, duties and responsibilities set by others.

out-group any group to which you do not belong.

phishing messages are sent to multiple email addresses claiming that the recipient's bank or financial institution has detected fraudulent charges on their account which need to be validated.

physical distance a geographical, tangible space between two or more people. See also **functional distance**.

placebo a substance that has no physical effect, but a perceived positive effect on an individual's condition.

preservers (in gaming) their role is to protect and heal others in a game.

privacy paradox although privacy is a concern for many when using the Internet, we need to share certain aspects of our information in order to carry out activities on the web.

private self-consciousness the extent to which we may consider the inner, subjective aspects of who we are, which are not directly observable by others.

pro-ana websites websites that promote pro-anorexia behaviours.

pro-mia websites websites that promote pro-bulimia behaviours.

propinquity relationships that are formed from current friendships, with people whom you are physically close to, or with whom you come into regular contact.

protection motivation (theory) user's perceptions of threat and potential preventative measures influence the likelihood to engage in risk management behaviours.

Proteus effect a being that can take on many different forms.

proxy services a server that is an intermediate between users.

public self-consciousness degree to which we consider how the observable aspects of the self are reacted to by other people.

quality circles approach employment of structured discussion techniques to discover solutions to a problem.

rape myths belief that rape is more the fault of the victim than the perpetrator; that the victim has behaved in a way to invite the act.

relatedness need for reciprocated feeling of love, being wanted, and cared for.

repeated exposure effect if you frequently experience the same person online, you might develop a closeness because you become familiar with that person.

rich get richer those who are more socially adept and better skilled at forming and maintaining friendships will forge more and stronger bonds online than those who are socially poor.

right to be forgotten a new law that makes online companies responsible for removing data if asked to do so.

salience technology becomes the most important activity in a person's life.

schemas stored categories of information.

SDST self-discrepancy theory.

SDT self (social) determination theory.

self-concept the way that you see your overall self, incorporating all aspects of you, including your intelligence, ability, appearance, links to other people and groups. How you view everything that makes you who you are. Overall collection of ideas we have about ourselves, our own perceptions of our identity.

self-esteem evaluation of oneself in a positive or negative manner.

self-presentation the way in which a person presents a version of themselves in any given situation.

shared interest groups members usually have a particular pastime and/or pursuit.

SIDE social identity model of deindividuation.

similarity attracts hypothesis people who are perceived to be of a similar level of attractiveness are more likely to become romantically linked to one another.

SIT: social identity theory when we identify with a group, we will categorise and compare ourselves to others based on that group membership.

SLT social learning theory.

SNS social networking site.

social capital the resources and benefits that can be derived from others.

social comparison the comparison of the self to others.

social compensation a person may choose to engage in online behaviours because they are lacking these or not finding fulfilment in their offline worlds.

social engineering a criminal manipulates the human element in a security chain to obtain information.

social enhancement occurs when a person feels that they are thriving through their online experiences.

social exchange theory relationships are built on a reciprocal give and take, cost and reward.

social facilitation performance on a task is better when carried out in the presence of others.

social identity the part of you that is characterized by the groups to which you belong.

social loafing group members reduce individual effort; they contribute just enough but not as much as they would do if carrying out a task on their own.

social overload perception of being overwhelmed by the diversity of interactions and social role demands.

social penetration theory the increasingly but gradual intimate exchange of personal information is the foundation of romantic relationships.

social spheres different social situations in which people exist.

socializers (in gaming) people who seek friendship and shared experiences.

somatic symptom disorder (SSD) somatic symptoms that are accompanied by significantly distressing symptoms or symptoms that are disrupting to daily life.

spam unwanted or unsolicited communications via the Internet.

SPT self-perception theory.

stigmatized identity groups members have a shared characteristic that is traditionally socially objectionable.

stimulation hypothesis time spent communicating with friends through CMC can enhance the quality of those friendships and have a positive effect on well-being.

stranger-on-the-train effect the divulging of personal information to someone whom we do not expect to see or meet again in the future.

SUDWG substance use disorder work group.

support groups members usually have medial, health or social difficulties.

synchronous communication communication that occurs without a time delay.

systematic volunteerism occurs when companies are required to submit information to government bodies.

techno-brain burnout pattern of decay in cognitive abilities as a result of prolonged and distributed attentional activity.

The Pirate Bay (TPB) an online media sharing service based on the exchange of indexed torrent files for music, software, video games, and movies.

thread a topic of discussion that invites replies from various people within a discussion group.

tolerance process whereby increasing amounts of time engaged in a technological behaviour is required to achieve the former mood-modifying effects.

toxic inhibition negative or destructive online interaction as a result of feeling less restricted by social norms, rules and regulations.

trait theories theories that attempt to explain individual personalities through a number of given characteristics.

transactive memory the way in which aspects of memory are offloaded to elements within the immediate environment.

upward social comparison occurs when we compare the self to people who we perceive to be better at a given task, or better in their traits or characteristics than the self. An evaluation of the self as being worse than others.

virtual identity suicide the complete deletion of all accounts one holds on social media websites.

visual intelligence non-verbal reasoning.

VR virtual reality.

web-based interventions programs that occur online to improve users' understanding, knowledge and awareness of health and mental health issues.

withdrawal symptoms unpleasant feeling states and/or physical effects that occur when a technological behaviour is discontinued or suddenly reduced.

work overload perception of unreasonable expectations regarding the ability to deal with messages within an available timeframe.

Index